The Nobel Prize and the Formation of Contemporary World Literature

The Nobel Prize and the Formation of Contemporary World Literature

Paul Tenngart

BLOOMSBURY ACADEMIC
NEW YORK • LONDON • OXFORD • NEW DELHI • SYDNEY

BLOOMSBURY ACADEMIC

Bloomsbury Publishing Inc, 1385 Broadway, New York, NY 10018, USA
Bloomsbury Publishing Plc, 50 Bedford Square, London, WC1B 3DP, UK
Bloomsbury Publishing Ireland, 29 Earlsfort Terrace, Dublin 2, D02 AY28, Ireland

BLOOMSBURY, BLOOMSBURY ACADEMIC and the Diana logo are
trademarks of Bloomsbury Publishing Plc

First published in the United States of America 2024
Paperback edition published 2025

Copyright © Paul Tenngart, 2024

For legal purposes the Acknowledgment on p. 214 constitute an
extension of this copyright page.

Cover design: Eleanor Rose
Cover photo: Nobel laureate Ernest Hemingway's Literary Nobel Prize diploma
from 1954 © Jeppe Gustafsson / Alamy

All rights reserved. No part of this publication may be: i) reproduced or
transmitted in any form, electronic or mechanical, including photocopying,
recording or by means of any information storage or retrieval system without
prior permission in writing from the publishers; or ii) used or reproduced in any
way for the training, development or operation of artificial intelligence (AI)
technologies, including generative AI technologies. The rights holders expressly
reserve this publication from the text and data mining exception as per
Article 4(3) of the Digital Single Market Directive (EU) 2019/790.

Bloomsbury Publishing Inc does not have any control over, or responsibility for,
any third-party websites referred to or in this book. All internet addresses given
in this book were correct at the time of going to press. The author and publisher
regret any inconvenience caused if addresses have changed or sites have ceased
to exist, but can accept no responsibility for any such changes.

Library of Congress Cataloging-in-Publication Data
Names: Tenngart, Paul, 1972- author.
Title: The Nobel prize and the formation of contemporary world literature / Paul Tenngart.
Description: New York, NY : Bloomsbury Academic, 2024. | Includes bibliographical
references and index. | Summary: "Explores the history, ambitions, and impact
of the Nobel Prize in literature as it gained a central position in 20th-century
global literary culture"– Provided by publisher.
Identifiers: LCCN 2023011575 | ISBN 9781501382123 (hardcover) | ISBN 9781501382161
(paperback) | ISBN 9781501382130 (epub) | ISBN 9781501382147 (pdf)
Subjects: LCSH: Nobel Prizes–History. | Literary prizes–History. |
Literature, Modern–20th century–History and criticism.
Classification: LCC PN171.P75 T46 2024 | DDC 807.9–dc23/eng/20230509
LC record available at https://lccn.loc.gov/2023011575

ISBN:	HB:	978-1-5013-8212-3
	PB:	978-1-5013-8216-1
	ePDF:	978-1-5013-8214-7
	eBook:	978-1-5013-8213-0

Typeset by Integra Software Services Pvt. Ltd.

For product safety related questions contact productsafety@bloomsbury.com.

To find out more about our authors and books visit www.bloomsbury.com
and sign up for our newsletters.

*In memory of
Rune Tenngart (1943–2021),
dad*

Contents

1	The Stockholm Consecration	1
2	Entering the Cosmopolitan Scene: The Rise of the Prize	19
3	Encompassing Everything: The Scope of the Prize	59
4	Making History: The Impact of the Prize	103
5	Defining Literature: The Poetics of the Prize	147
6	Looking Ahead: The Survival of the Prize	199

Acknowledgment	214
Appendix: Nobel Laureates in Literature 1901–2022	215
References	217
Index	239

1

The Stockholm Consecration

It all started with a childless millionaire. Swedish chemist, innovator, engineer, and businessman Alfred Nobel had made his money from inventing, manufacturing, and selling different kinds of explosives, including dynamite. A year before his death in December 1896, sixty-three-year-old Nobel changed his last will. The new document stated that his sons- and daughters-in-law together would inherit only 3 percent of his assets. Most of his considerable fortune would instead be used to fund an international prize for extraordinary achievements in Physics, Chemistry, Physiology or Medicine, Literature, and peace work (cf. Carlberg 2019: 492–515).

Nobel's keen interest in scientific progress was obvious, and his intense fascination for literature was a well-known fact. He was a big reader in many languages, and he wrote poetry in both Swedish and English. A couple of months before he died, he completed his first play, *Nemesis*, based on the same sixteenth-century events as *The Cenci* by Percy Bysshe Shelley, his favorite author. His engagement in world peace was guided by his close friendship with Austrian peace activist Bertha von Suttner. A more anecdotal and dramatic explanation of the inclusion of the peace category—and indeed of his very idea of financing an international prize in his memory—is the aftermath of Alfred Nobel's brother's death in April 1888. *Le Figaro*—the newspaper Parisian resident Alfred Nobel subscribed to and read every morning—mistook Ludvig for Alfred and published an obituary on the famous (and living) inventor. Nobel thus received a sudden insight into his own posthumous reputation, and it wasn't a comforting read. "A man who only with great difficulties can be seen as beneficial to humankind," he learned from the front page of *Le Figaro*, "died yesterday in Cannes. It was Mr. Nobel, the inventor of dynamite." (untitled article, 1888, my translation). The cosmopolitan Swede, who had built a very successful international business and earned a respected position in the world of science and engineering, would not go down in the history books as a good human being. Unless he did something radical to change his perceived impact on the world.

The idea of the individual human being's contribution to humankind was instructive in the way Alfred Nobel formulated his last will. The enormous capital he had earned from manufacturing and distributing explosives was to be used as a means to make the world a better and safer place. "All of my remaining realisable assets," his last will reads, "are to be disbursed as follows: the capital, converted to safe securities by my executors, is to constitute a fund, the interest on which is to be distributed annually as prizes to those who, during the preceding year, have conferred the greatest benefit to humankind" ("The Nobel Prize," 2022). It is from this idea of globally beneficial innovations, thoughts, textual compositions, and endeavors he identified the five distinct kinds of achievement to be rewarded:

> The interest is to be divided into five equal parts and distributed as follows: one part to the person who made the most important discovery or invention in the field of physics; one part to the person who made the most important chemical discovery or improvement; one part to the person who made the most important discovery within the domain of physiology or medicine; one part to the person who, in the field of literature, produced the most outstanding work in an idealistic direction; and one part to the person who has done the most or best to advance fellowship among nations, the abolition or reduction of standing armies, and the establishment and promotion of peace congresses.

The prizes in Physics and Chemistry were to be administered by the Royal Academy of Sciences in Stockholm, the prize in Physiology by Karolinska Institutet in Stockholm, and the Peace Prize by the Norwegian parliament Stortinget in Kristiania (now Oslo). The latter decision was made in order to even out the power balance between the two parts of the Swedish-Norwegian union, a gesture that illustrated the conflict-solving ambition of this particular prize.

For the prize in Literature, Alfred Nobel appointed the Swedish Academy—founded in 1786 by the Swedish king Gustav III—to be the executive institution. After Nobel's death, his attorney contacted the Permanent Secretary of the Swedish Academy, Carl David af Wirsén, who started to persuade his fellow academicians to accept the special assignment. This proved to be quite difficult, but eventually Wirsén had convinced a majority of the members. The Swedish Academy accepted to administrate the prize and formed a special Nobel Committee (consisting of Academy members) for preparing the annual decisions. A process was soon established in which the Committee received and assessed nominations from institutions and individuals within and outside Sweden, and then proposed a laureate to the Academy as a whole (cf. Rydén and Westerström 2018: 232).

In 1901, the first prize was awarded to French author Sully Prudhomme. Since then, 118 more authors have been awarded. The literary prize has been canceled seven times: in 1914, 1918, 1940, 1941, 1942, and 1943 due to the First World War and the Second World War, and in 1935 due to the lack of a worthy candidate. Four times a joint award has been given—Spanish author José Echegaray and Provençal poet Frédéric Mistral shared the honors in 1904, Danish authors Karl Gjellerup and Henrik Pontoppidan shared it in 1917, German-Swedish poet Nelly Sachs and Israeli author Shmuel Agnon received a joint prize in 1966, and so did Swedish authors Harry Martinson and Eyvind Johnson in 1974.

One of the first decisions made was to classify the discussions within the Nobel Committee and the Academy of the nominated authors and proposed laureates. Conflicts in the Academy were to be kept hidden, as well as comparisons between nominations from experts of different literatures and the reasons why some nominees were not considered worthy of the prize. For the purposes of future research, however, it was later decided that the restrictions were to be lifted after fifty years (Svensén 2001a: x–xi). In January each year, new protocols and written proposals are made available, shedding light upon yet another prize decision. These documents reveal which authors were nominated and which names were included on each year's short list. In January 2012, for example, it was revealed that Graham Greene was very close to being awarded in 1961, but that year's Nobel Committee decided in the end to recommend Yugoslavian novelist Ivo Andric instead of Greene (Neuman 2012). And in 2018, the public was informed that Greene had once again been thoroughly discussed in 1967. This time, Guatemalan author Miguel Ángel Asturias was eventually preferred at the expense of the well-known British writer (Schueler 2018). In the late 1930s, an unwritten law was agreed upon that said that a candidate cannot be selected as a laureate the first time he or she appears on the short list (Espmark 2021: 41).

It is striking how the Swedish Academy and, in particular, its Nobel Committee have written their own history. The accounts of Nobel Prize discussions, decisions, and implications have been produced by a range of members of these two institutions: Anders Österling (Österling 1967), Kjell Espmark (Espmark 1986; Espmark 2001; Allén and Espmark 2001; Espmark 2021), Sture Allén (Allén and Espmark 2001), Lars Gyllensten (Gyllensten 2000), Horace Engdahl (Engdahl 2013), and Anders Olsson (Olsson 2022). These accounts are very valuable as sources for our understanding of the prize's history, but they are not scholarly studies. Their writers haven't been able to avoid speaking for themselves and their own constellations of the Academy or the Committee, and many of their evaluations of former selections have been based upon documents inaccessible for neutral researchers and thereby unattainable for second opinions.

A disinterested analysis of the institution of the Nobel Prize in Literature and its role in the continually shifting arena of world literature has hitherto never been executed. In light of all the important conceptual and empirical work carried out by world literary scholars during the last twenty years, such a study is well overdue. In order to understand the logic of twentieth- and twenty-first-century world literature, the consecration mechanisms of the Nobel Prize—and its medial, cultural, geographical, and poetological conditions—need to be thoroughly and neutrally scrutinized.

The Nobel Prize selections contribute to a very central and expanse phenomenon in contemporary literary culture. Since the early twentieth century, James F. English concludes in his *The Economy of Prestige: Prizes, Awards, and the Circulation of Cultural Value*, cultural prizes have undergone a "simply tremendous growth." Awards to artistic and other cultural achievements "have been expanding in number and in economic value much faster than the cultural economy in general" (English 2005: 10). But the Nobel Prize in Literature is not like any other cultural award. It is, in several respects, a unique contribution to the field of cultural prizes and, as such, a very particular phenomenon in world literature.

First of all, the literary Nobel is a very early example of cultural awards. English describes it as a model prize that instigated the contemporary kind of award economy.

"The modern ascendancy," he writes, "of cultural prizes may conveniently be said to have started in 1901 with the Nobel Prize for Literature, perhaps the oldest prize that strikes us as fully contemporary, as being less a historical artifact than a part of our own moment" (28). The Swedish prize soon inspired other academies and cultural sponsors to establish their own awards: "Within just three years of the first Nobel ceremony in Stockholm, both the Goncourt and Femina literary prizes had been founded in France, and Joseph Pulitzer had declared his intention to launch, in emulation of Alfred Nobel, a series of annual literature and journalism prizes in America." English notices distinct "signs of Nobel envy" in many parts of the world: Japan's Praemium Imperial Prizes call themselves "Nobel Prizes for Art," the Peabody Awards see themselves as giving out a "Nobel Prize of Music," and the Neustadt International Prize for Literature is often referred to as the "American Nobel" (English 2005: 29).

But even as a model prize, the Nobel Prize in Literature has its very own structure, follows its own logic, and therefore has a specific kind of impact on the world. In the following pages, I will try to describe these particularities.

Relative Contemporaneity

Alfred Nobel's last will stated that the five prizes in his name should celebrate achievements made "during the preceding year." All the appointed executive institutions thought that this was an all too restricted time scope. The awards should have a certain actuality, they admitted, but scientific, diplomatic, and artistic work are often achieved during long periods of time—to be sure, more often than not such achievements are lifetime works (cf. Gyllensten 2000: 260). So, not more than a month after the donor's death, the Permanent Secretary of the Swedish Academy, Carl David af Wirsén, decided to change this particular instruction in the will. It would be much more reasonable, he argued, to award "a deserving œuvre" than a particular work (Rydén 2010: 530, my translation). When the formal statutes of the literary Nobel Prize were written a couple of years later, the instruction was indeed modified. In this document, the Nobel Foundation stressed that the prize-decisions should focus on "recent achievements," but that older works can be considered if their significance has not become apparent until recently (Espmark 2021: 11).

The history of the literary Nobel includes a couple of prize decisions based on a single title, but most of them are motivated by a set of texts, often sweepingly defined. Quite early on, a practice was developed that made many of the decisions guided by lifetime achievements rather than specific works. But the selected laureate had to be alive and still active. This way, the award was to look backward, in evaluating and acknowledging the laureate's past achievements, as well as forward, in expectation and encouragement of the laureate's future work. In the entire history of the literary Nobel, only one posthumous award has been given—to Swedish poet Erik Axel Karlfeldt in 1931.

With this modification of the donor's will, the Nobel Prize has kept a special identity in the midst of all the different literary awards it has helped to inspire. The French Prix

Goncourt, the American Pulitzer Prize, and the British Booker Prize are all awards to specific titles, and so was the first version of the Spanish Formentor Prize in the 1960s. After being reinstated in 2011, however, the Formentor was changed into an author's award instead of an award to a specific title. The International Booker Prize has been changed in the opposite direction: from 2005 to 2015 it was given to an author, but from 2016 onward it is awarding a single title. Another example of a lifetime achievement prize in line with the Nobel is the biennial Neustadt International Prize for Literature, funded and administered by the University of Oklahoma since 1970.

This balance between absolute contemporaneity and a longer temporal perspective has turned out to be a very good recipe in eschewing the worst risks of quickly becoming outdated. As a result, the Nobel Prize has had the chance to be received as a canon of "recent world literature," as it was phrased in a theme for a symposium on the award that was held in Paris in 2000 (Espmark 2021: 43). With this relative contemporaneity, the prize decisions are contemporary enough to be interventions into literary history in the making, while at the same time retaining enough temporal distance to the evaluated texts to be seen as grounded in substantial and thorough reflections. This way, the Nobel Prize has become "instrumental in enlarging our very understanding of what constitutes world literature today," as poet and scholar Ivar Ivask phrases it in the late 1980s (Ivask 1988: 199).

The Swedish Academy and its Nobel Committee have sometimes been criticized for lacking contemporaneity. This was a recurring argument in a survey on the prize conducted in 1951 by William F. Lamont for the American literary magazine *Books Abroad*. The Nobel, Lamont summed up, "being fundamentally intended by the donor for contemporary writers, should not have been given to writers whose major work had been done ten or more years earlier" (Lamont 1951: 12). One of the experts in the survey, Renée Lang of Wells College in Aurora, New York, stressed the conservative tendency in the Swedish prize decisions: the award has turned out to be "an honorary degree based on previous recognitions" (Lang 1951: 116).

Some critics have, on the other hand, pointed out the difficulties caused by the contemporary perspective. "It is, moreover," Lion Feuchtwanger reminded his readers in Lamont's survey, "a difficult, almost hopeless undertaking, to weigh and rank the literary merits of contemporaries. There is no doubt that the Elizabethan period was receptive toward literature and knew how to evaluate it; and there is no doubt that Ben Jonson would have received the prize over William Shakespeare" (Feuchtwanger 1951: 115). Indeed, several critics have criticized the Nobel Committee for being *too* contemporary in awarding writers who will become outdated all too soon, and in having a too narrow perspective to recognize true and durable literary quality. This is why, critics have argued, the Swedish intellectuals have missed the chance to award literary giants like Marcel Proust and James Joyce. Looking at the back list of laureates, Henri-René Lenormand concluded in 1951 that "it is disturbing to have witnessed the disregard for universal geniuses like Joseph Conrad of England, Ibsen and Strindberg for the Scandinavian countries" and "Chekhov, Tolstoy, Andreiev and Gorky of Russia" (Lenormand 1951: 117).

Culture, Capital, Crown—and Science

Every literary award involves a complex transaction between different kinds of capital, in Pierre Bourdieu's broad sense of the word. Cultural prizes, James F. English writes, are always instruments of cultural exchange between "artistic, social, political economic, and other forms of capital" (English 2005: 27). The Nobel Prize in Literature is no exception, but this specific award entails a more complex transaction than usual: appointing the literary Nobel laureate involves a different set of discourses of value than is usually the case.

Some of these particularities were summed up in two comments in the long reception history of the prize: in 1951, French literature scholar Henri Peyre wrote that the Nobel "has brought money and fame to literature" (Peyre 1951: 214); thirty years later English literature expert William Pratt used quite another set of connotations when he argued that every year a lucky writer is "being summoned to Stockholm" (Pratt 1988: 226). Whereas Peyre's idea connects the award to a contemporary culture of consumerism and celebrity, Pratt's links it to an old structure of court life and patronage.

Money is an essential issue in almost all literary awards, and the Nobel Prize comes with a larger sum than most prizes. The overall donation from Alfred Nobel was more than 30 million Swedish crowns (Carlberg 2019: 503; Gyllensten 2000: 280), which is the approximate equivalent of 2.5 billion Swedish crowns and 245 million US dollars in today's currencies. This money was placed in funds, but it was also used to administrate the prize, and, a couple of years later, to cover five even sums of prize money to the different Nobel Prizes. Each of the first awards in 1901 came with the sum of 150,000 Swedish crowns (Gyllensten 2000: 280), which is the equivalent of approximately 950,000 USD in today's currency. Since then, the sums have been fluctuating due to both capital gains and decisions from the Nobel Foundation. In 2020, the Foundation decided to raise the prize money from 9 to 10 million Swedish crowns per award (Beslic 2020), which is the approximate equivalent of 1 million USD.

The large sum of prize money was a big talking point when the will was revealed in January 1897. It was also a central part of Alfred Nobel's fundamental idea. The prizes shouldn't only be restrospective rewards for achievements already made, but they were also, and more importantly, intended to help scholars, peace activists, and authors in their future endeavors. The Nobel Prizes were intended to indirectly fund new discoveries, diplomatic actions, and literary pursuits. That's why the sum of prize money had to be as hefty as possible.

Having money makes you earn more money, not only through interests and other capital gains, but also through the social and cultural attraction of economic success. Alfred Nobel's generous donation inspired many resourceful Swedes, and led to many more donations that quickly made the Swedish Academy a very wealthy organization, much richer, for example, than its model, the French Academy (Gyllensten 2000: 205). All this money strengthened the Academy's position in the Swedish cultural landscape, and made it possible for the members to fulfill their traditional, domestic obligations as well as administrate the new international prize.

Along with the cultural status and the money, the Nobel Prize in Literature also comes with a very different kind of capital: a time-honored, European royal glamour. The Swedish Academy is a royal academy. It was founded by king Gustav III in 1786 and still today enjoys the official protection of the Swedish monarch. So does the administrating body of the prizes in Chemistry and Physics, the Royal Academy of Sciences. Therefore, it was decided early on that the four Nobel Prizes decided in Stockholm should be handed over by the Swedish king at a special ceremony on the day of Alfred Nobel's death, December 10.

The intimate connection between, on the one hand, the cultural capital of high-brow literature, industrial, dynamite money from the donor and, on the other, the feudally rooted status of the old Swedish monarchy, has been the target of a recurring criticism of the Nobel Prize. Indeed, the ceremonious role of the Swedish king adds an old-fashioned and conservative, not to say reactionary and undemocratic, dimension to the award. But repeated criticism is, as James F. English has shown, an integral part of modern cultural prizes. Prizes for artistic and creative work simply "cannot fulfill their social functions unless authoritative people—people whose cultural authority is secured in part through these very prizes—are thundering against them" (English 2005: 25).

More importantly, the royal patronage gives the Nobels a dimension of glamorous festivity that all other internationally renowned literary prizes lack. English points out that the combination of dry, systematic administration and festive celebration is a very important factor in the way cultural prizes work, a custom that goes all the way back to the festivals of music, poetry, and drama in classical Greece. The connection between artistic competition and "culture parties on a grand scale" is essential in the history of prizes (English 2005: 31–32). The prize-giving ceremony at the Stockholm Concert Hall on the afternoon of December 10, and the subsequent banquet at the City Hall with many prominent guests—including former laureates, the royal family, and members of the Swedish parliament—add a very special kind of glory to the prize. This royal glory was, as we shall see later on, very important in establishing an intense and recurring recognition of the prize in international media. And it's a kind of glory that lingers on: when the American magazine *World Literature Today* dedicated a special issue to the Nobel Prize in 1988, the cover showed the latest literary laureate, Joseph Brodsky, receiving the medal and the check from king Carl XVI Gustaf of Sweden.

The problematic aspect of the royal protection has generally been a low-key issue in the history of the prize, with a few brief spurs now and again of public criticism, especially from the political left. But the inherent conservative—or reactionary— connections to the royal power of the king became an acute and fundamental problem in the worst crisis so far in the history of the prize: the #MeToo scandal in 2018 and 2019, when the husband of an Academy member was first accused of sexual assaults and rape, and then sentenced to prison. The Swedish Academy's inability to deal with this scandal in a direct and distinct way revealed a lack of transparency and democratic ideals in the very fabric of the institution. The Academy came forth as an outdated and elitist closed circle of cultural power. In this crisis of trust, the royal connection was far from glorious. It rather added fuel to the protests against a reactionary body of power still rooted in the eighteenth century.

The results were disastrous: the 2018 Nobel Prize was postponed, several members left the Academy in protest, and the very institution of the Nobel Prize in Literature was thoroughly tainted in the eye of the public—domestically as well as internationally. The prize hasn't as yet totally recovered from these events, and it is not certain that it ever will.

The fourth kind of capital immanently involved in the complex transaction of the Nobel Prize is the prestige of science. In the second half of the nineteenth century, science rose to a new level of recognition, respect, and importance. Scientific methods were applied to the human mind (Psychology) and human behavior (Sociology), and also influenced the discipline of Philosophy in a fundamental way, for example through August Comte's positivism. Indeed, the Nobel Prizes in Chemistry, Physics, and Medicine, and the acknowledgment they received in the early history of the prize, were in themselves distinct signs of this new status of science in Europe and North America.

With the Nobel Prize in Literature, the classic literary values of elegant and poignant expressions, original textual composition, and thorough reflections of life were linked to the modern and pragmatic values of science. Being placed side by side with innovative and important achievements in Chemistry, Physics, and Medicine, literary endeavors gained relevance and actuality in a modern world. Apart from the Nobel Prize, there is no widely known modern prize that in this way transgresses and bridges the borders between what C.P. Snow in the late 1950s famously called "the two cultures" of science and the humanities (Snow 2001). Like no other important cross-cultural phenomenon, the Nobel Prize lets the two domains of knowledge reciprocally increase each other's symbolic capital.

This traffic of values was strongly manifested when the Nobel Library was presented in 1901. Its first head librarian, Karl Warburg, proudly described this brand-new institution as a *"laboratory"* for all the people involved in the literary prize:

> It will supply all the instruments they need. First of all, every literary, biographical, encyclopedic, and bibliographical reference book available, so that nobody will have to go outside the walls of the Nobel Institute to look for relevant information. It should further include a collection as complete as possible of all countries' works of literary history, literary criticism, literary essays, and literary monographs; an expansive collection of all countries' literary journals, current issues as well as from many years back in time; a rich library in History, Philosophy, Art History, and other disciplines in the humanities; and Classic and Swedish literature; as well as, finally, that which will be the presigeous core of the library: *the largest possible selection of contemporary foreign literature.*
>
> (Warburg 1901, my translation, italics in the original)

Warburg's conception of the library as a laboratory and its collection of literary books as instruments bore all the marks of the scientifically optimist Zeitgeist at the turn of the century. And this connection between literary evaluation and scientific investigation has lingered on in the discourse surrounding the Nobel Prize.

The French literary scholar Pascale Casanova uses it, for example, when she calls the Swedish prize a "unique laboratory" for "what is universal in world literature" (Casanova 2005: 73).

The Nobel Prize thus makes four very different pillars of power and prestige—high-brow literature, economic capital, the royal crown, and science—endorse and confirm each other's values and positions in the modern world. Industrial money is gilded with royal glamour, scientific benefits, and cultural sophistication. The monarchy earns a more modern aura in connection with industrial success and scientific achievements, as well as an intellectual image in supporting the forefront of international literature. Scientific laboratory work is lifted up to the heights of industrial efficiency, royal luster, and philosophical reflection when supported by the Nobel Foundation and the king, and positioned side by side with the most celebrated contemporary thinkers and authors. And literature, finally, is imbued with the pragmatism, vigor, and force of capitalism, the ceremonial, refined dignity of the crown, as well as the systematic rational thinking and usefulness of modern science. The Nobel Prize is a complex transaction in which very different sets of values are exchanged—sometimes logically, often quite irrationally, and in certain cases even paradoxically.

This complex set of exchanges makes the Nobel Prize a very strong international institution, but it also includes potential threats. A drop of prestige for one of these pillars may have a demeaning effect on the others.

Cosmopolitan Dreams

The fifth Nobel Prize is no less important for the identity and status of the literary award. If the proximity of the three scientific awards renders the literature prize an aura of utility, then the connection to the Peace Prize reinforces the international perspective and the air of cosmopolitanism. The Peace Prize awards diplomatic solutions between conflicting nations, urges people to seek intercultural understanding, and encourages respect for different interests and points of view. These ambitions have also been instructive in many literary prize decisions.

The intercultural perspective is fundamental for the literary prize. Many other important literary awards are restricted in scope to a single market, a single literary language, or a limited designated cultural or political sphere—the French Goncourt, the American Pulitzer, and the Booker, which was enlarged in scope in 2014 from being restricted to books written by Commonwealth, Irish, South African, and Zimbabwean writers to having any Anglophone literary title as a potential winner. Well-known prizes with a fundamentally international perspective on literature are much younger than the Nobel, and they are, it's fair to say, established with the Nobel Prize in Literature as a model—the Formentor, the Neustadt Prize, and the International Booker Prize, a spin-off of the Booker that from 2005 onward has awarded literature originally written in any language but available in English translation.

The connection between the Peace Prize and the Nobel Prize in Literature has sometimes fueled the notion that the literary prize decisions are politically motivated. This criticism has often ignored the fact that these two prizes are administered by two totally different institutions, institutions that, moreover, are active in two completely separate and independent nations since the dissolution of the Swedish-Norwegian Union in 1905. It must be noted, however, that the Swedish Academy historically has not only included scholars and authors, but also politicians, for example Hjalmar Hammarskjöld, who was the Swedish Prime Minister between 1914 and 1917, a member of the Academy from 1918 to his death in 1953, and a member of the Nobel Committee between 1932 and 1946 (Svegfors 2010). The connections between the literary prize and international diplomacy have never been closer than between 1954 and 1961, when Hjalmar Hammarskjöld's son Dag was an active member of the Swedish Academy and at the same time Secretary-General of the United Nations. Despite the fact that the UN leader often was, for obvious reasons, absent from Academy meetings, he took "an important, in some cases crucial part" in many of the Nobel Prize decisions (Rydén and Westerström 2018: 512, my translation).

Alfred Nobel lived a genuinely international life. He was born in Stockholm in 1833, but the family moved to Saint Petersburg in Russia when he was nine, where he went to school and trained to become a chemist. Soon after his return to Stockholm in 1859, Nobel realized the value of international legal rights for his inventions and went abroad to secure patents in different countries. This way, he successively established a very successful international business with factories and offices in most European countries as well as in North America. He spent many years in Paris, and died in San Remo, Italy, in 1896, but he was known as a vagabond, always on the move, and he was fluent in five languages: Swedish, Russian, German, French, and English.

The idea of the Nobel Prize was formed when these international experiences merged with Alfred Nobel's anxious thoughts on his own posthumous reputation and with the pacifist activism of his dear friend Bertha von Suttner. When she sent him her 1889 novel *Die Waffen nieder!* (*Lay Down Your Arms*), he answered: "How do you think I would be able to sell my gunpowder in a world of universal peace?" Eventually, she managed to win him over for her cause, partly by currently sending him the issues of the pacifist magazine she was the editor of, also called *Die Waffen nieder!* (Carlberg 2019: 492–504, my translation). The Nobel Peace Prize was quite a grand result of von Suttner's endeavors, especially since she became a laureate herself in 1905.

Grounded in a genuine belief in the possibilities of understanding across cultural borders and languages, the literary award reflects Alfred Nobel's cosmopolitan attitude to the world, its differences and its common, universal interests. It is not a coincidence that a literary magazine including articles by both Germaine de Staël and Johann Wolfgang von Goethe was found on Alfred Nobel's desk when he died. In the early decades of the nineteenth century, these two writers initiated the idea of world literature, a concept that would gain traction by later thinkers and critics like Karl Marx and Georg Brandes. The Swedish engineer's taste in literature was very much in line with this internationalist current in nineteenth-century European criticism. His literary interest was genuinely cosmopolitan, and he believed in global progress and man's ability to improve the quality of human life all over the world. His favorite author was, after all, Percy Bysshe Shelley. Nobel intensely appreciated the Romantic poet's radical idealism and passionate love of humankind (Schück 1939: 512). Creating a firm canon of world literature was a central part of this plan to ennoble humanity.

But Alfred Nobel was by no means a literary expert. Besides being a skilled chemist and engineer and an experienced and shrewd businessman, he was a big reader with a keen and persistent interest in improving his own literary writing skills. But he was not a trained literary scholar or a professional critic. Exactly how he envisioned the shape and scope of an international canon of literary texts is nowhere to be found in his documents. He probably had quite vague ideas of how to define the concept of world literature. To be sure, more than 120 years after his death, scholars of Literary Studies still haven't found any kind of consensus as to what these two words mean.

Does world literature consist of the best texts written? Are these texts, then, beneficial to humankind because they are stylistic, compositional, and thematic models, perfect examples for everybody to learn from? Or does the concept of world literature rather signify literary texts that are relevant to all humanity? Are these texts beneficial to humankind because they actually concern each and every one of us? Or is world literature rather a name for a body of literary texts that collectively represent all of humanity, and whose benefit to humankind lies in the way they give the readers a multifaceted collection of insights into fundamentally different human positions, perspectives, and conditions? These are complex questions that the donor probably did not dig very deep into.

More important than Alfred Nobel's own notion of what world literature is and how it is beneficial to humankind, is, of course, the approach with which the different constellations of the Swedish Academy and its Nobel Committee have executed the task of selecting laureates. What fundamental idea of world literature and its values have dominated the history of the Nobel Prize? Does this history include separate periods in which the prize decisions have been instructed by distinctly different ideas of international literature? And how do the Swedish Academy's and the Nobel Committee's ideas of and attitudes toward literature and different literary phenomena relate to other positions within the enormous field of domestic and international literatures? This kind of questions have been central in the structuring of this study.

Canon Formation from the Side

In order to understand what impact and what gestures the Swedish Academy and its Nobel Committee have made since the first prize in 1901, we need to position these institutions on some kind of geo-cultural map. It is of crucial importance, I think, to consider what part of the world the prize selections come from. The fact that it is a Swedish prize has strongly contributed to constructing its unique image and maintaining its importance. It's difficult to deny the fact that the Stockholm perspective makes the Nobel Prize in Literature a very special kind of cultural consecration.

One of the nominated authors for the 1901 prize was Hungarian scholar Franz Kemény, who was proposed to earn the Nobel honors because of a substantial work suggesting the establishment of a World Academy, a "Welt-Akademie" (Kemény 1901; Richter 2023). Such a transnational academy, the Hungarian writer argued, could bypass nationally restricted interests and support common, transnational scientific and cultural aims. Kemény stressed that this World Academy couldn't possibly be placed in a central and powerful city like Paris or London. But Budapest would be a good location. Kemény was not selected for the Nobel Prize in Literature, and his book on a World Academy was unceremoniously dismissed as "lacking value" (Svensén 2001a: 8, my translation), but his ideas closely reflected what Alfred Nobel had managed to establish in Stockholm. And just like Kemény suggested in relation to his potential academy, it was crucial that the assemblies of intellectuals and scientists administrating the Nobel Prize were not located in one of the big European centers, but outside the most prestigious and influential cultures, as well as beyond the imperial rivalry between France, Germany, and Great Britain.

Still today, it is very important, I think, that the performative act of giving out the world's most significant literary prize does not take place in one of the cultural or economic centers of the world—not in New York City, Los Angeles, London, or Paris, and not in Tokyo, Beijing, or Rio de Janeiro. One of the distinct characteristics of the award is that the venue for this consecration into the uppermost stratum of international literary importance is Stockholm.

Despite her recurring identification of Paris as the world's literary center, Pascale Casanova sees the Nobel Prize in literature as "a prime, objective indicator of the existence of a world literary space" (Casanova 2005: 73). This "annual canonization," realized through a decision made by the Swedish Academy and executed by the Scandinavian monarch, is, Casanova insists, continually confirming the centrality of world literary dominance and the unequal relations between literary languages, cultures, and traditions. But Stockholm is not Paris. In terms of cultural centrality, Stockholm is rather very far from the capital of France. The Swedish city sits quite remotely on the northern fringes of Europe, and its language is spoken by only 0.1 percent of the world's population. Stockholm and Sweden do not enjoy a central position in the world, either politically, economically, or culturally.

What kind of literary power, then, does the Swedish Academy exert, and how can this small and remote institution maintain its importance year after year, decade after decade? Well, one thing is certain: this power is neither identical with the central literary position of Paris, nor with the international cultural dominance of London and New York. Clearly, the Nobel Prize's huge bearing on world literature follows its own rules and conditions. Despite being firmly dependent on general mechanisms of twentieth- and twenty-first-century intercultural exchange, the story of the prize's rise to global importance and its staying power at the zenith of international literary discourse designate a unique trajectory of international cultural influence.

According to a world systems approach to literary intercultural traffic (cf. Edfeldt et al. 2022), the Swedish literary culture belongs to the semi-periphery. Sweden is not a central space for international literary discussions, nor does it belong to the periphery.

Alongside a couple of other geo-cultural spaces—e.g., Spanish, Italian, and Danish—it occupies a middle ground between, on the one hand, the hyper-central Anglophone and the central French, German, and Russian literary cultures, and, on the other, literary peripheries like Hindi, Bulgarian, and Finnish. The Nobel Prize is, thus, a consecration made from the side, a literary canonization decided and executed in a cultural space distinctly positioned outside the center. Instead of confirming the strictly hierarchical structure of world literature, as Casanova has it, the global significance of the Nobel Prize rather disrupts the general dominance of French, English, and North-American literary cultures. The Swedish prize clearly disturbs Casanova's idea that a literary text written outside the center needs to be consecrated by the center in order to reach global recognition. On the contrary, through the Nobel Prize a semi-peripheral space exerts a highly significant influence on the distribution of world-literary prestige.

Apparently, the world republic of letters is not only governed from Paris, London, and New York. The importance of the Nobel Prize seems to show that there is not only one literary center in the world, not even only two or three. It's not a coincidence, I think, that this distinct influence from the literary semi-periphery mirrors Sweden's particular role in twentieth-century international politics. The Scandinavian country was neutral in the Second World War, and it maintained its neutrality—at least officially—in the polarized post-war world. Unlike its neighbors Norway and Denmark, Sweden is still not a member of NATO, nor was it ever a part of the Soviet-controlled Eastern Europe.

This political neutrality has created a fertile ground for diplomacy. From the 1940s and onward, Sweden produced several important negotiators: Raoul Wallenberg, who managed to save tens of thousands of Hungarian Jews from Nazi Germany; Dag Hammarskjöld, the second General-Secretary of the United Nations from 1953 to his premature death in a plane crash in 1961; and Olof Palme, Swedish Prime Minister for two spells, 1969–76 and 1982–6, who continually criticized both US and Soviet foreign policies and took a very firm stand against the US war in Vietnam, the Soviet intervention in Czechoslovakia, and the South African Apartheid system. Sweden's role as a Western country being a constant thorn in the side of NATO made it an ideal place for Bertrand Russell's and Jean-Paul Sartre's 1967 public trial against US war crimes in South-East Asia, intermittently called the International War Crimes Tribunal, the Russell Tribunal, the Russell-Sartre Tribunal, or the Stockholm Tribunal. It is worth noticing that the two main organizers had both been selected for the Nobel Prize in Literature: Russell was awarded in 1950, whereas Sartre refused to receive the honors in 1964.

When it comes to economic ideology and distribution policy, the Swedish welfare state—systematically initiated, executed, and adjusted by the governing Social Democratic Party from the 1930s onward—has been poignantly described as a third way, combining capitalism and socialism. In line with this ideological compromise, the Swedish Academy's neither-nor position between the world literary centers and the numerous cultural peripheries of the world renders the consecrating power of the Nobel Prize an opportunity to adopt a third way of exerting world literary influences—negotiating between the imperialistic urges of the centers and the resistance of the peripheries. Paradoxically, then, it is exactly this semi-peripheral position that enables the Nobel Prize to enforce a central world literary importance. In managing to appear as a neutral arbiter not affiliated with any of the contenders, the Swedish Academy and its Nobel Committee enjoy the power of the third party, with a warrant to make compromises between the center and the periphery as well as between different literary centers and different peripheries.

From several international perspectives, the Nobel Prize represents a Scandinavian rather than a specifically Swedish perspective. But the perceived values of these perspectives are more or less identical. Receiving the Nobel Prize in Literature on her husband's behalf, Lady Clementine Churchill read the absent Prime Minister's speech to the Nobel Foundation. Amidst his intense pride, Winston Churchill took the opportunity to praise the geo-political context that had honored him:

> The world looks with admiration and indeed comfort to Scandinavia, where three countries, without sacrificing their sovereignty, live united in their thought, in their economic practice, and in their healthy way of life. From such fountains new and brighter opportunities may come to all mankind. These are, I believe, the sentiments which may animate those whom the Nobel Foundation elects to honour, in the sure knowledge that they will thus be respecting the ideals and wishes of its illustrious founder.
> ("Award to Sir W. Churchill," 1953)

Thirty-two years later, French laureate Claude Simon expressed similar thoughts. This is how the novelist praised Scandinavia:

> It is no mere chance, namely, or so it seems to me, that this institution has its seat and deliberates its choices here in Sweden, more precisely in Stockholm, at more or less the geographical centre or, if you prefer it, the crossroads of four nations whose populations, though small, by virtue of their culture, their traditions, their civility and their laws, have made Scandinavia so great that it is a kind of privileged and exemplary islet on the fringe of the iron world of violence we today inhabit.
> (Simon 1985)

We must, of course, read these accounts with a pinch of salt: flattering the institution that has honored you is an integral part of the acceptance speech genre. However, these grateful speeches still express a widely spread idea—a cultural cliché—of Scandinavia that has been beneficial in establishing and maintaining the status and identity of the Nobel Prize.

But the ostensibly neutral position of the Swedish Academy not only leads to compromises between opinions, agendas, and ideologies. It also offers a way out of the struggle for dominance and recognition. The Nobel Prize has continually had the function of reminding us that cultural expressions are more than tools to impose our own perspective on others, even when these expressions are internationally transmitted. There is more to literature than politics and ideology. The announcements of the winners, the prize motivations, the Concert Hall ceremony, and the acceptance speeches at the City Hall banquet later that evening, all create a potential refuge from conflicts, a temporal sanctuary in which aesthetic values and qualities may thrive. This independence from politics is perhaps illusory, but the organizers and participants are often given the benefit of the doubt. The royal glamour and the time-honored traditions making their distinct marks on the events may put off some people, but they certainly make others watch and listen.

The importance of the Nobel Prize in Literature thus also calls into question Pascale Casanova's total focus on power. She is not wrong in assuming that the relations between literary cultures and languages are hierarchical. Her focus on cultural power struggle, inherited from Immanuel Wallerstein's theory of global economy and Pierre Bourdieu's sociological approach on culture, has produced many important results. What the Nobel shows, however, is that power isn't everything: there are not only fighters in the world literary arena. Amongst languages, cultures, and nations struggling for recognition and dominance, there is also room for diplomacy. In awarding the Nobel Prize in Literature, the semi-peripheral Stockholm is the middle sibling of world literature, a space of compromises between self-sufficient firstborns and defiant lastborns.

We must not forget, however, that the semi-peripheral position of Stockholm has also had a degrading effect of the prize's prestige. Over the years, several international critics have raised their concerns about the fact that eighteen more or less randomly chosen persons in the remote town of Stockholm have such an influence on the literary world. The depth of knowledge and the width of perspectives in the Academy and the Committee have repeatedly been questioned—especially in connection with certain surprising selections of laureates. International experts have lamented the naïvité of the Swedish judges, and been annoyed by a tendency amongst them to display an arrogant unawareness of their own limitations. But the irrationality and randomness of the Nobel Prize power are integral parts of the specific Stockholm kind of literary consecration: although not logical, well-earned, or motivated, it has time and again proven strong and stable.

In contemporary world literary theory there are two opposite ways, I would argue, to describe the relations between literary cultures and languages: the literatures of the world are either seen as *concentrically* or *eccentrically* structured. The concentric view is based on Wallenstein's world systems theory and most influentially expressed in Casanova's work. For Casanova, there is an absolute literary center in the world—a "Greenwich Meridian of literature"—in which the "set of interconnected positions" that she calls a "world literary space" is created and maintained (Casanova 2005: 277–8). To enter this space from a peripheral position, you need to be consecrated by the center. The center thus continually upholds its power in exporting its own literature to various parts of the world, as well as in deciding what texts are worthy of international recognition. Like rings around a stone dropped in water, languages and cultures can be closer to or farther away from the center, but they are all dependent on it. A similar view is offered by Johan Heilbron's studies of translation patterns, described as "uneven flows" in a system based on a "core-periphery structure" (Heilbron 1999: 431–2). Indeed, I have myself adopted this concentric view in this chapter when referring to the Swedish literary position as semi-peripheral.

The eccentric view on world literature, on the other hand, proposes a flat structure in which the patterns of intercultural literary relations are much more complex and multifaceted. One example is Shu-mei Shih's adaptation of world historian Joseph Fletcher's theory of an intricate web of international relations. For Shih, world literature is a field of "relationalities across time and space" characterized by "multiple nodes" and "relations of all kinds" (Shih 2015: 431, 434, and 437). A literary culture is not restricted to one particular space in one single world system, it rather simultaneously exists in various networks. "If Vietnamese literature," she exemplifies, "should be considered in terms of a world Francophone literary network, it must also be considered alongside Anglophone and, especially, Sinophone literary networks" (435). Other flat descriptions of world literary connections include Alexander Beecroft's idea of "literary biomes" and "literary ecologies" that exist side by side and may thrive in different ways (Beecroft 2015: 25–7), and David Damrosch's notion that "the system of world literature" always resolves "into a *variety* of worlds" (Damrosch 2003: 12, italics in the original).

I would argue that concentricity and eccentricity are much more than two opposing theoretical constructs. For one thing, I do not think that they exclude each other. They rather designate two different but equally valid perspectives on literary interrelations. Second, I do think that these two kinds of theories mirror how literature actually exists in the world. Just like both cosmopolitanizing and vernacularizing processes take place simultaneously in all kinds of literature and sometimes even in one and the same particular text (cf. Edfeldt et al 2022; Ekelund et al 2022; Helgesson et al 2022; Kullberg and Watson 2022), the relations between literatures are perpetually subjected to simultaneous concentric and eccentric movements. The disappointed words by Erich Auerbach from the early 1950s of a "process of imposed uniformity, which originally derived from Europe, continues its work, and hence serves to undermine all individual traditions" (Auerbach 2013: 66), still serve as a valid description of concentric tendencies in contemporary world literature. But Édouard Glissant's idea of how poetry exists in the world is equally accurate: "The poet's word leads from periphery to periphery, and, yes, it reproduces the track of circular nomadism; that is, it makes every periphery into a center; furthermore, it abolishes the very notion of center and periphery" (Glissant and Wing 1997: 29). These eccentric movements take place right under the nose of the increasingly centralized uniformity of other kinds of literary expression, distribution, and reception. Concentric and eccentric processes are active anywhere, sometimes in and around different kinds of literature, and sometimes in different ways of dealing with the same texts. Together they shape what we call world literature.

Most consecrations of world literature are concentric. Dominant parts of the international book market and systems of literary value are, as Heilbron, Casanova, and many others have convincingly shown, forms of concentric consecration in that they both originate in and continuously confirm the cultural power of Paris, New York, and London. Another good example is the International Booker Prize. With this prize, literary texts from other parts of the world are lifted up into an international domain of prestige by the center—first by being translated into English, then by being awarded by the London prize-institution. After being consecrated, the title is marketed all over the world as an award-winning book of world literature.

The Nobel Prize is, on the other hand, an eccentric kind of literary consecration. Just like an eccentrically mounted sheave in mechanic engineering (a disc that is fixed offset from the center of the axle), the members of the Swedish Academy make their canon selections from the side: not from the center, nor from the absolute periphery, but from a position between center and periphery. The Nobel is not unique in this capacity. It is, for example, challenged by Formentor, a prize institution eccentrically positioned on the Spanish Mediterranean island of Mallorca. But it is difficult to compete with such an old and established prize as the Nobel, which remains the most important eccentric consecration in world literature today. Whatever author is selected by the Nobel Committee, I would argue, the prize decision disturbs the existing hierarchies of power and status between literary traditions, markets, and languages. This factor of disturbance strongly contributes to maintaining the importance of the prize. The eccentric consecration is not easily brushed off, because the power structures involved are quite complicated. The Swedish position is still a European position, with all the benefits that come with this. But the Swedish Academy works from the very periphery of that privileged, European cultural domain.

The simple fact that French citizens have the highest representation amongst the laureates, closely followed by British and US authors, definitely confirms Casanova's notion of Paris as the center of world literature. That English is the most awarded literary language also confirms Heilbron's notion of Anglophone hyper-centrality in literary traffic across markets and languages, and so does the fact that Rabindranath Tagore explicitly received the prize in 1913 because of the English translations of his Bengali poetry. But these confirmations as such do not originate in the center. The power of confirming the hierarchy is executed from outside its most powerful position.

The centrality of Paris, New York, and London is, however, more explicitly challenged when the Nobel Committee selects authors from other places. The overall power structure is disturbed, for example, by the overrepresentation of Swedish laureates. The eight awards to domestic Swedish authors (Selma Lagerlöf in 1909, Verner von Heidenstam in 1916, Erik Axel Karlfeldt in 1931, Pär Lagerkvist in 1951, Nelly Sachs in 1966, Harry Martinson and Eyvind Johnson in 1974, and Tomas Tranströmer in 2011) are competitive gestures indirectly manifesting the confident (and in the eyes of most international critics, thoroughly absurd) idea that twentieth- and twenty-first-century Swedish literature is almost as rich as its French and British counterparts, as important as German literature, and more significant than contemporary Spanish or Italian theatre, prose, and poetry.

A less national but perhaps equally self-centered tendency is the overrepresentation of Scandinavian authors among the laureates. Together with the eight Swedish awards, the three Danish (Karl Gjellerup and Henrik Pontoppidan in 1917, and Johannes V. Jensen in 1944) and three Norwegian (Bjørnstjerne Bjørnson in 1903, Knut Hamsun in 1920, and Sigrid Undset in 1928) awards construct a poignant idea of a regional, North European hub of literary gravity, and if we add the Finnish (Frans Eemil Sillanpää in 1939) and the Icelandic (Kiljan Halldór Laxness in 1955) awards, the Nordic countries even seem to equal France as the most important geo-cultural space in world literature.

Awarding Danish authors is also a gesture of recognition between two semi-peripheral spaces. Semi-peripheral Stockholm executes a global consecration of the equally semi-peripheral Copenhagen, without seeking approval from the center. The same eccentric gesture is at work when Italian and Spanish authors are awarded and invited to Stockholm. There is no need for them to make a stopover in Paris. Members of the Swedish Academy and their external experts have had, and still do have, genuine and direct knowledge of these semi-peripheral literatures. The Swedish judges may, of course, have been influenced by Parisian recognitions of, say, Giosuè Carducci (1906), Salvatore Quasimodo (1959), Vicente Aleixandre (1977), and Dario Fo (1997), but such a world stage acknowledgment has by no means been necessary. The Nobel consecrating act does not directly involve the French, American, and British publishers, critics, and intellectuals, but its announcement will inevitably be recognized and made publicly known by media in these centers.

An eccentric widening of the international literary canon also happens, of course, whenever the Swedish Academy awards writers from the literary peripheries of the world. When writers from Belarus (Svetlana Alexievich in 2015), Peru (Mario Vargas Llosa in 2010), Saint Lucia (Derek Walcott in 1992), Egypt (Naguib Mahfouz in 1988), Nigeria (Wole Soyinka in 1986), Guatemala (Miguel Ángel Asturias in 1967), and Yugoslavia (Ivo Andric in 1961) are awarded, peripheral literary cultures or languages are globally recognized through the lens of one particular semi-peripheral space. A special kind of consecration occurs when a particular literary culture within the realms of a central language is awarded. The significant representation of Irish authors (William Butler Yeats in 1923, George Bernard Shaw in 1925, Samuel Beckett in 1969, and Seamus Heaney in 1995) amongst the many awards to literature written in English is an illustrative example of this.

The international gravity of the Nobel Prize in Literature is based, then, on a very special kind of consecration with its own mechanisms. This book will explore these mechanisms from a wide range of angles: the award's history and ambitions, its strategies and aesthetics, and its different levels and kinds of impact will be scrutinized, discussed, and positioned in a world literary context. When did the Nobel Prize become a fulcrum for world literary canonization, and what strategies did the Swedish Academy use to make this happen? To what extent have the Academy and its Nobel Committee managed to create a balance between different languages, literary cultures, traditions, and ideologies in their continual distribution of literary significance? What kind of aesthetics do the decisions rely on and spread, and how has the prize contributed to definitions of what literature is and should do? What has been the prize's impact on different cultures, literatures, and languages—locally, regionally, nationally, and internationally? And what does the future of the prize look like? What must the Swedish Academy do to retain the status of the prize for future generations of readers, critics, publishers, and writers?

How has, in sum, the Nobel Prize in Literature contributed to the formation of twentieth- and twenty-first-century world literature?

2

Entering the Cosmopolitan Scene: The Rise of the Prize

When the Permanent Secretary of the Swedish Academy exits his office at Börshuset in central Stockholm after that year's final Nobel Prize meeting, he is met with a large number of journalists from all over the world. And at the very moment he reveals the name of the honored author, the prize decision becomes top news almost everywhere. With its literary prize, the Academy in Stockholm has managed to find a direct channel from its semi-peripheral Scandinavian position to the center of world literary discourse. Indeed, this Swedish institution has in itself become one of the centers of world literature. When did the Nobel Prize earn this centrality in the ongoing formation of contemporary world literature? And how did it happen?

My survey of international press reactions to the prize decisions from 1901 to 2022 gives a clear idea as to when the annual reception reached the strong, broad, and direct level of recognition it enjoys today. The decisive change happened in the 1950s. It was in this decade that the Stockholm decision became front-page, breaking news in Western Europe and North America, regardless of the cultural background of the newly appointed laureate. Since then, the prize announcement has remained a news priority in mid-October every year. The question of how this came about has a more complicated answer. On a general level, the road to the 1950s is a step-by-step development toward higher recognition, but it includes several speed bumps and rocky passages. Several disparate factors have instructed this winding trajectory, including different media strategies from Stockholm, a whole lot of lucky timing successively overcoming a couple of instances of bad timing, and, of course, larger changes in the infrastructure of international news coverage.

The process started well before the first prize was given. After Alfred Nobel's death in December 1896, it wasn't certain that his last will would be accepted. Parts of the Nobel family were strongly opposed to the idea of giving the money away to a prize-giving foundation, and the executor of the will, Alfred Nobel's attorney Ragnar Sohlman, had to use all the tricks in the book to realize the final wish of his client, including secretly posting packages of highly valuable securities from Paris to London and Stockholm (Gyllensten 2000: 260–1). On New Year's Eve, the Swedish press revealed that the millionaire had donated most of his fortune to a prize foundation ("Alfred Nobels testamente" 1896), and the following days several domestic newspapers quoted large passages from the will (cf. "Alfred Nobels testamente," 1897a and 1897b).

Alfred Nobel's intentions were strongly praised. His will was received as a gift to humanity, and the late engineer was posthumously portrayed as a modern hero—not only for supporting endeavors in science, peace work, and literature across cultures and nations, but also for placing his native country on the map. In deciding to place the prize foundation in Sweden and selecting Swedish institutions to administer the prizes (except the Peace Prize), Alfred Nobel came forth as a real patriot. One of the leading Swedish newspapers, *Svenska Dagbladet*, wrote that Nobel's generous will was the most noble gesture that any Swede had done since king Gustav II Adolf donated a large sum from his private assets to Uppsala University in 1624 ("Alfred Nobels testamente," 1897c).

The official opening of Alfred Nobel's last will did also stir quite an international interest. On January 7, Parisian *Le Figaro* wrote that his will was a glorious memorial of Nobel's love for humanity, before quoting—in French translation—the central passage in the will where the donor describes the five prize categories (Ovize 1897). In the important and broadly read Austrian paper *Neue Freie Presse*, Bertha von Suttner a couple of days later summed up her personal memories of the late engineer in an article that dominated the front page (Suttner 1897).

When it comes to the literary prize, the attorneys had to interpret an ambiguity in Nobel's will. The donor had written that he wanted the "academy in Stockholm" to be responsible for the prize, without specifying which of the different academies in the Swedish capital he was thinking of. Having reached the conclusion that Alfred Nobel must have meant the Swedish Academy, Ragnar Sohlman paid his friend Carl David af Wirsén a visit in order to persuade the Permanent Secretary to try to convince the Academy to accept administrating the literary award. It didn't take Sohlman long to get Wirsén on board. The literary critic of international literature immediately understood that this grand and ambitious international prize was exactly what he needed in order to restore his bruised position within the Academy, and exactly what the Swedish Academy needed in order to reclaim the position as the most central institution in Swedish culture (Rydén 2010: 526–7).

It took a lot more for Wirsén to convince the other members of the Swedish Academy to accept the new task. Administrating an international prize was not, many members argued, what they were supposed to do. It simply wasn't part of their assignment. The Swedish Academy was founded to serve Swedish culture and the Swedish language, not foreign cultures and languages. After a long and heated discussion, however, Wirsén managed to win a sufficient number of Academy members over to his side, and his suggestion to accept Nobel's assignment was finally approved. In this decision, the Academy not only overruled the arguments from many of its own members, but also went against the expressed will of its highest protector, the Swedish king Oscar II, who was distinctly opposed to the idea that Alfred Nobel's money would be given to foreigners. When the basic statutes of the prize were eventually agreed upon and written, including important adjustments of Alfred Nobel's instructions, the first prizes were finally awarded on December 10, 1901, five years after the donor's death. As a silent protest, Oscar II refrained from attending the ceremony at the Musical Academy in Stockholm (Rydén 2010: 573–6).

But what happened then? How did the rest of the world react to the actual prize decisions of the Swedish Academy? I will not, of course, be able to cover the whole world in this chapter. I will instead restrict my scope to what has been identified as the threefold center of the twentieth- and twenty-first-century Western literature: Paris, London, and New York. On the following pages, the Nobel Prize's path toward the center of world literary attention will be traced through the prize-decision reactions in one central newspaper from each of these centers: the Parisian *Le Figaro*, the London-based *Times*, and the *New York Times*.

Early Breakthroughs and Setbacks (1901–13)

On a general level, the five Nobel Prizes were an immediate media success. Reports on the first awards in Physics, Chemistry, Physiology, Peace, and Literature were published in more than a hundred newspapers all over the world in December 1901 (Quinn 1995: 197). But if we focus on the literary prize and its recognition in Paris, London, and New York, we get a more diverse picture. The international media coverage during the first decade was uneven and generally quite low. Before the outbreak of the First World War, however, the recognition in Paris, London, and New York of the literary prize became significant and stable.

All the 1901 prizes were intensely recognized in *Le Figaro*, and it is very clear that it was the literary prize that was seen as the most interesting and important of the five Nobels. The same day they were handed out in Stockholm and Kristiania, *Le Figaro* dedicates two front-page articles to the literary laureate Sully Prudhomme—one report on the actual award (G.D. 1901), and one interview with the poet (Sorel 1901). In next day's issue of *Le Figaro*, all the laureates were presented in a long front-page article taking up a whole column ("Les lauréats du Prix Nobel," 1901), and a second article described the very idea of the Nobel Prize in a substantial and sympathetic way (Sjoestedt 1901).

This intense media coverage had to do with the fact that prizes in both Literature and Peace were awarded to Frenchmen. The economist Frédéric Passy, who shared the Peace Prize with Swiss social activist Henri Dunant, was indeed called "our venerable compatriot" by *Le Figaro* ("Les lauréats du Prix Nobel," 1901, my translation). But the substantial attention was also a result of the prize-giving institutes having informed the French newspaper beforehand about their decisions. The articles on Sully Prudhomme were published before the laureates were announced at the Musical Academy in Stockholm. In next day's paper, the French public was told how that came about: "Before everybody else, *Le Figaro* was yesterday the first newspaper to know the names of the laureates who later in the day were announced by the Swedish Academy and the Norwegian Storting" ("Les lauréats du Prix Nobel," 1901, my translation). Leaking information to particularly important international newspapers was part of a media strategy, and informing *Le Figaro* in advance about the two prizes to French citizens indeed turned out to be a successful way to gain attention.

The new literary prize was also acknowledged in London and New York, but the British and American reactions were significantly less intense than the French. On the day after the ceremony in Stockholm, the *Times* published a short report on page six on all the five prizes. Prudhomme was briefly mentioned. That's all. The American response was almost as restricted. A couple of weeks after the announcement, the *New York Times* published an interview with the Peace Prize winner Frédéric Passy ("Frederic Passy Interviewed," 1901), and Sully Prudhomme was briefly mentioned in a general article on current events ("The Magazines," 1901).

For obvious reasons, the focus of the British recognition of the first Nobel Prizes was quite different from the French. A month after the prize ceremony in Stockholm—on January 7 and January 11, 1902—two letters to the editor urged British intellectuals to work actively to convince the Swedish Academy to select a British author for the next award (letters to the editor, 1902). A couple of days later, the editor reported that a "Nobel Committee of the Society of Authors" had indeed been founded in London, "for the purpose of recommending candidates for the prize for the most distinguished name in pure literature" ("The Nobel Prize for literature," 1902). The founding of this committee must be seen as the breakthrough of the prize's recognition in the UK. In their first committee meeting, British critics and scholars agreed that they had been slow in acknowledging what was going on outside the UK borders: "It was a subject of legitimate regret that," the *Times* reported from the inauguring meeting on January 14, "while all the other countries of Europe competed for the prize last year, England entirely abstained from so doing" ("The Nobel Prize for literature," 1902). This discussion got a US equivalent a year later when the *New York Times* speculated on potential prizes to Americans ("Nobel Prizes for Only Few," 1902), but the American speculation had a more general perspective on the Nobel Prize institution as such; it was not restricted to the literary prize.

The domestic Swedish reaction to the first-ever Nobel Prize in Literature was a bit of a scandal. With an open letter (in Swedish) to Russian novelist Leo Tolstoy, published in a national Swedish newspaper, forty-two well-known Swedish intellectuals, scholars, painters, composers, and authors criticized the fact that the Nobel Prize had been awarded to Prudhomme and not to the famous Russian author (cf. Rydén 2010: 581–6). The list of protesters included authors August Strindberg, Selma Lagerlöf, Verner von Heidenstam, Per Hallström, and Hjalmar Söderberg; painters Carl Larsson, Anders Zorn, and Bruno Liljefors; educational thinker Ellen Key; and composers Wilhelm Stenhammar and Wilhelm Peterson Berger. Many of the protesters would later become members of the Swedish Academy, and two of them would indeed receive the Nobel Prize in Literature.

The early Nobel Committees' unwillingness to award Tolstoy has remained a common critical issue when the Nobel history is discussed. At the time, Carl David af Wirsén argued that Tolstoy's best works were written a long time ago and that his more recent religious and political writings were strange and lacked clarity and reason. Wirsén also expressed his reluctance to give a significant amount of prize money to a person who explicitly despised the whole monetary system (Rydén 2010: 592 and 602).

This early scandal was, however, almost exclusively a Swedish media storm. The first award did not lead to any equivalent reactions in Paris, London, or New York. The loudly critical domestic recognition of the new literary prize left no trace whatsoever in *Le Figaro*, the *Times*, or the *New York Times*.

Next year, the intense French media recognition continued, despite the fact that the 1902 award was given to a German author, historian Theodor Mommsen. The announcement was not as recognized and discussed as the preceding award to Prudhomme, but it wasn't far behind. On the day after the festivities in Stockholm, the distribution of Nobel Prizes was given two whole columns in *Le Figaro*, albeit on pages three and four. Under the signature "Knud.", the paper's correspondent reported directly from the ceremony. The French readers were told who attended the event, what music was performed, and, of course, the names of the laureates. Mommsen was given more attention than the others, which confirms the fact that the literary prize was regarded as more important than the other four awards in the French public sphere. A substantial introduction of Mommsen's works was accompanied with a lengthy quote from Carl David af Wirsén's presentation of the German historian at the prize ceremony (Knud. 1902).

The *Times* did not publish any report at all from the announcements and the ceremony in Stockholm in December 1902. Theodor Mommsen was not mentioned in the London paper until his death in November 1903. The *New York Times* was equally indifferent to this second literary prize. In the autumn and early winter of 1902, the American paper presented the Peace Prize winner and the Medicine Prize winner in two separate articles, and on December 8, the *New York Times* published a report on the upcoming Nobel festivities. But there was no mention of Mommsen. In early January 1903, the New York paper had a short article on the German author and his support of the German Social Democratic Party, but, strangely enough, this article did not mention the fact that he was the latest Nobel laureate in Literature ("Prof. Mommsen Writes on German Political Aspect," 1903). Already in its second year, then, the Nobel Prize in Literature experienced a distinct setback in British and American recognition, at odds with its continuously strong position in Paris.

The recognition of Bjørnstjerne Bjørnson's 1903 award was just as restricted in London and New York. The *Times* did not mention the Norwegian author at all. The *New York Times* was only slightly more interested. Bjørnson was mentioned in a brief report on all five Nobel Prizes on December 11 ("Nobel prizes awarded," 1903), and again in a similar short article two days later ("Topics of the Times," 1903). This year the reports in *Le Figaro* were also very sparse. The Parisian paper only published a single sentence on the Bjørnson Prize on December 11, briefly informing the French public about the honors given the night before ("Dernières nouvelles," 1903). We can conclude that the decision to award a Scandinavian author this early in the history of the prize was not a success when it comes to establishing an interest in the new award in France, Great Britain, and the United States.

In December 1904, the *Times* had a short report from the ceremony in Stockholm, but the literary laureates "M. Mistral" and "Don José Echegaray" were only mentioned in passing ("The Nobel Prizes," 1904). A year later, there was no mention at all of the Henryk Sienkiewicz prize, and in 1906 only two sentences in a report from the ceremony mentioned that year's Italian laureate, Giosuè Carducci. This does not mean, however, that the Nobel Prize in Literature was seen as unimportant by the editors of the *Times*. Even if the prize to Sienkiewicz was totally ignored, there was a substantial report in November 1905 from the latest meeting of the English Nobel lobbyists in the "Nobel Prize Committee of the Society of Authors." The article shows how important a Nobel Prize to a British author would be:

> The CHAIRMAN expressed the hope that the English Nobel Committee would not be discouraged if the prize of £8,230 should this year be awarded to a foreign poet or poets, since we have the assurance for the Director of the Swedish Academy that any "idealistic" writer, strongly supported by the authors of England, "has every prospect of gaining the Nobel Prize for Literature at some future time." Mr. AUSTIN DOBSON suggested that unanimity and persistence were of the greatest importance, and that the committee should not be impatient if the prize were not immediately given to the English candidate.
> ("The Nobel Prize for Literature," 1905)

The English national pride in connection to the prize decisions in Sweden was also strongly evident in the report from the 1906 ceremony, where it was pointed out that the "Italian Press gratefully acknowledges the gracious act of King Oscar and the compliment paid to Italian literature" (untitled article, 1906).

The awards to Mistral, Echegaray, and Sienkiewicz were neither very recognized in *Le Figaro*. Given the fact that one of the laureates was a French citizen, it is quite remarkable that the shared 1904 award did not result in more than this single sentence: "It is the great Provençal poet Frédéric Mistral and M. Echegaray who receive the prize for literature" ("Hors Paris," 1904, my translation). Perhaps the headline of this tiny article holds a clue as to why the news of the awards was seen as insignificant—"Hors Paris" means "Outside Paris." Mistral was neither a Parisian poet, nor a poet of the French language. He was presented as "grand" (great), but he was not given very much more attention than his fellow Spanish laureate. The news from the 1905 ceremony was placed, just like the 1903 report, under the summing-up headline "Dernières Nouvelles." Sienkiewicz was very briefly mentioned alongside the names of the other four laureates ("Dernières nouvelles," 1904).

This early in the history of the Nobel Prize, the interest in the Swedish prize institution as such—including the awards for Chemistry, Physics, Medicine, and Peace—was generally a bit stronger in the *New York Times* than in the two European newspapers. And after the silence in 1902 and the quite humble recognition of Bjørnson's prize in 1903, Frédéric Mistral and Henryk Sienkiewicz were both quite acknowledged. In Mistral's case, it was the poet's initiative to donate his prize money to an ethological museum that stole the headlines ("Poet's Ethological Museum," 1904; "Mistral and the Nobel Prize," 1905). And in December 1905, the *New York Times* published three different articles on the literary prize: one text anticipating the ceremony, one report directly from the ceremony, and one comment on Sienkiewicz' take on Poland's role in the aftermath of the Russian-Japanese war ("To Get Nobel Prizes," 1905; "Nobel Prizes," 1905; "Sienkiewicz Fears Kaiser," 1905). Oddly enough, José Echegaray was not mentioned at all in the *New York Times*.

The 1906 Nobel Prizes marked a distinctly increased French recognition. The five new laureates were substantially presented in a long article on the third page of *Le Figaro*, and the ceremony itself got a detailed and somewhat dramatic description: "It's tonight, at half past six, that the solemn distribution of the Nobel Prizes is taking place," the newspaper's man in Stockholm reported ("Les prix Nobel," 1906, my translation). The other four laureates, however, were given more attention than the Italian poet Giosuè Carducci, which reveals that the rise in recognition in 1906 marked an increased interest in the Nobel Prize generally, not particularly in the literary prize. But this new general interest probably paved the way for the following year's very intense recognition of the Rudyard Kipling award. In December 1907, *Le Figaro* dedicated almost three whole front-page columns specifically focused on the literary Nobel Prize. The article was signed by E.M. de Vogüé, who was very sympathetic with the Swedish Academy's choice of laureate. "Well judged, Scandinavians!" he exclaimed in rejoice (de Vogüé 1907, my translation).

In fact, the French recognition of the Kipling award even surpassed its British equivalent, despite the fact that 1907 was the year when the English intellectuals were finally rewarded for their systematic endeavors. The year before, the Carducci prize had only resulted in a two-sentence mention in the *Times* (untitled article, 1906), but some weeks later, in February 1906, the Italian poet was substantially introduced in the *Times Literary Supplement* ("Giosuè Carducci," 1907), followed by a couple of short reports on his failing health and death (untitled articles, 1907a). The Kipling award later that year was mentioned in three articles, and the author's name did appear in a headline, but all of these articles were very short, and one of them did not report on Kipling's work and his award as such, but on the intense French reactions to the Swedish prize decision ("The Nobel Prizes. Award to Mr. Rudyard Kipling," 1907; untitled article, 1907b; "The Nobel Prizes," 1907). And when the year 1907 was summarized in the *Times* on December 31, the Nobel Prize was left out. Kipling was indeed mentioned in this summarizing chronicle, but only in relation to his Canadian reading tour earlier that fall. Nothing was said about the award he received in December. The first Nobel Prize given to an English author, then, was definitely recognized in London, but not at all as distinctly as in France.

In the *New York Times*, the Carducci prize was just as acknowledged as in *Le Figaro* ("Nobel Prize for Carducci," 1906), and the Kipling award was almost as acknowledged ("Nobel Prize for Kipling," 1907; "Kipling to Get the Prize," 1907; untitled article, 1907c). The announcement of the first Anglophone literary laureate was thus much more recognized in New York than in London. In the American newspaper, Kipling's name appeared in two headlines and also in a third article around the time of the prize announcement. An important detail further illustrates the Nobel Prize's quite high newsworthiness in the United States: the *New York Times* wrote about both the Carducci and the Kipling awards already in November, when the Swedish Academy had made a public announcement in advance, whereas *Le Figaro* and the *Times* waited for the actual ceremony before mentioning the prize decisions of 1906 and 1907.

During the period 1908–11, the three papers significantly differed from each other when it comes to recognizing the literary laureates. In all of them, the 1908 award to Rudolph Eucken got less attention than the Kipling prize the year before. Next year, the first woman literary laureate was awarded, Swedish author Selma Lagerlöf. In the *Times*, this event was even less acknowledged than the Eucken prize. In the *New York Times*, the award to Lagerlöf was not mentioned at all—which was clearly a setback in the American newspaper's quite high level of Nobel recognition since 1904—but a translation of a short story by the Swedish author was published in the paper a couple of weeks later on January 2, 1910. In *Le Figaro*, by contrast, the Lagerlöf award was loudly and enthusiastically received. Here, the announcement of the five Nobels was front-page news in a long article that continued on the second page. Selma Lagerlöf was the first laureate to be presented, and her work was given a whole column. The reporter, Marc Hélys, was excited about the decision: "All her work," he wrote, "bears the mark of her noble soul; all of it, all the way to the shortest of her stories, all the way to the delicious volume composed for children: *The Wonderful Adventures of Nils*" (Hélys 1909, my translation). This positive recognition of the Swedish author was strongly confirmed by the fact that a short story by Lagerlöf was published in the paper's *Supplément Littéraire* that same day. Next day, a second front-page article included a substantial discussion on the significance of the first female literary laureate.

In 1910, the award to German poet Paul Heyse was only very briefly mentioned in *Le Figaro* and the *Times*. His name was included in short reports from the Nobel ceremonies, but his work was not presented at all (untitled article, 1910; "Les prix Nobel," 1910). The laureate was much more recognized in the *New York Times*, where his work was substantially introduced in a separate article ("Nobel Prize for Heyse," 1910). Just like in 1906 and 1907, the American paper reacted directly upon the prize announcement in November rather than waited for the December ceremony in Stockholm.

The following year, this procedure was also adapted by the *Times*, which helped to give Belgian author Maurice Maeterlinck much more attention in the London paper than Heyse, Lagerlöf, and Eucken ever did. On November 10, the *Times* had a short article on the announcement which was followed by a report from the ceremony a month later ("Nobel Prize Awarded to M. Maeterlinck," 1911; untitled article, 1911). This increased interest in the literary prize was even stronger in the United States. Already in mid-October, the *New York Times* speculated on who would win that year's Nobel Prize, and the editor's qualified guess was Maeterlinck ("Nobel Prize to Maeterlinck," 1911; "The Nobel Literary Prize," 1911). A month later, the paper reported from the announcement in Stockholm that the Belgian author would indeed be honored ("Award to Maeterlinck," 1911), and in December the *New York Times* published a report from the ceremony ("Nobel Prize Winners Receive Awards," 1911). And that was not the end of it. On January 12, the paper reported from Maeterlinck's plans for the prize money ("Maeterlinck Founds Prize," 1912). In addition to all this specific attention to Maeterlinck, the *New York Times* also published a general article on all the five prizes and the prize institution as such on December 3 ("What Nobel Intended by the Prizes Awarded in His Name," 1911). The attention given to Maurice

Maeterlinck in the *New York Times* was the most intense recognition that any of the literary laureates had experienced so far.

Despite the fact that Maeterlinck's work was in French, *Le Figaro* only mentioned his name very briefly in a short report about all the five prize decisions ("Les prix Nobel," 1911). Whereas the first Nobel Prize to Prudhomme led to a kick stark of medial recognition in Paris, the following two Francophone literary awards to Mistral and Maeterlinck did nothing to increase the Prize's recognition and position on the Parisian literary scene.

For the announcement of the 1912 award, the Swedish Academy did a little media stunt that proved quite successful: they announced the prize to the German poet and playwright Gerhart Hauptmann on his fiftieth birthday on November 15. This made *Le Figaro* publish a report from Berlin, where Hauptmann celebrated his jubilee and his Nobel Prize in one go, plus a substantial presentation of his literary works (untitled articles, 1912a). The *Times* also reported from the double celebration in Berlin (untitled article, 1912b). Two days earlier, the London paper had had a larger piece on Hauptmann's œuvre ("Gerhart Hauptmann," 1912). In New York, the newspaper reported on the Hauptmann award on December 16 ("Nobel Prize to Hauptmann," 1912), and published a longer piece on the author's thoughts on religion. The very long headline of the latter confirms the success of the Swedish Academy's timing: "Gerhart Hauptmann Writes on the New Religion. The Keynote of It Is Tolerance, According to the Famous Poet-Dramatist Who Has Just Won the Nobel Prize for Literature and Celebrated His Fiftieth Birthday" ("Gerhart Hauptmann Writes on the New Religion," 1912). The significant American interest in the Nobel Prize is confirmed by the fact that the *New York Times* had published not one but two articles before the announcement, with speculations on who would be that year's literary laureate. The first one proved to be correct. On October 6, the literary editor guessed that "Hauptmann, Fifty Years Old, to Get Special Honors. Perhaps the Nobel Prize Will Be Added to the World-Wide Celebration of the Playwright's Birthday Anniversary" ("Hauptmann," 1912). But two weeks later he had changed his mind and instead thought that French novelist Anatole France would be awarded ("Nobel Prize to M. France," 1912). These speculations, as well as the fact that the *New York Times* also published an editorial criticizing the Swedish Academy's actual decision ("Hauptmann's Prize," 1912), clearly illustrate that the Nobel Prize in Literature was seen as a very important event in the literary circles of New York.

The first era of Nobel attention ended on a high note in Paris, London, and New York alike. The decision to award Rabindranath Tagore with the 1913 prize made big news in all three newspapers. In *Le Figaro*, the report from Stockholm was placed in the top-right corner of the front page. Under the very visible headline "Rabindranath Tagore / PRIX NOBEL," Maurice Leudet described the award as a surprising Nobel Prize to an author without—until now—any significant world reputation but with a central position in his Bengali home country (Leudet 1913). In the same issue, *Le Figaro* also had a short, untitled article with a quote from the British *Daily Mail* that expressed a delighted reaction on the Swedish decision (untitled article, 1913a). And this year, even the report from the prize-giving ceremony in December was recognized on the front page of the Parisian paper ("Les Prix Nobel," 1913).

The Tagore award was the most recognized Nobel Prize decision thus far in the *Times*. The announcement in November resulted in one article with a text from Reuter ("The Nobel Literature Prize," 1913), plus a report directly from the newspaper's correspondent in Stockholm, who talked about a general reaction of both surprise and joy: "The newspapers this morning express some surprise at the unexpected decision of the Swedish Academy to confer the Nobel Prize for Literature on the Indian poet Rabindranath Tagore. The choice, however, is hailed as a very happy one, and extracts are quoted from the English translation of the poet's work *Gitanjali*" ("Swedish Tribute to Mr. Tagore," 1913). Just like *Le Figaro*, the *Times* also published a report from the Stockholm ceremony a month later, in which the Bengali poet and novelist is mentioned alongside the other four laureates (untitled article, 1913b).

Substantial as they were, the reactions in *Le Figaro* and *The Times* to the Tagore prize were still significantly surpassed by the reports and reflections on this award in the *New York Times*. The first article about the announcement ("Nobel Prize Given to a Hindu Poet," 1913) was followed a week later by an introduction of the poet, who was said to have been "Entirely Unknown Outside His Own Country," but so central at home that "the Bengalis Call this 'the Epoch of Rabindranath'" ("The Hindu Poet," 1913). A week later, the *New York Times* published a third article on the prize decision in which the laureate was compared with Walt Whitman ("Tagore," 1913). From a twenty-first-century world literary perspective, this comparison strikes an interesting chord in juxtaposing two postcolonial literary positions through the gaze of the European center. A fourth article published in early December described Rabindranath Tagore's quick rise to international fame thanks to the Swedish prize ("Rabindranath Tagore's Fame," 1913). It was followed by an article with speculations about next year's laureate ("Nobel Prize for Hardy," 1913) and a report from the ceremony ("The Nobel Prizes," 1913). And in January 1914, two more articles discussed the Bengali author from new perspectives ("India's Poet," 1914; Ruger 1914). These eight articles in the *New York Times* collectively formed, by far, the most intense reactions to any single Nobel Prize until the outbreak of the First World War.

How, then, can we summarize the international recognition of the first twelve years of the Nobel Prize? Well, we can, first of all, conclude that the new literary prize *was* substantially acknowledged in Paris and London as well as in New York, and this recognition was supported by the other four Nobel Prizes. The prize-giving ceremonies were newsworthy in themselves, and the variety of the awards gave the literary laureates a general position in the newspapers rather than a particular, less central place alongside other literary or cultural news. Furthermore, it is evident that the decision to chronologically separate the announcement of the prize from the prize-giving festivities was a productive strategy that increased the level of attention.

The recognition given to the prize decisions was not, however, evenly distributed over the years and across the three newspapers. This uneven attention was only partly an effect of what kind of author was awarded. Several of these early laureates—for example, Paul Heyse, Selma Lagerlöf, and Maurice Materlinck—were quite recognized in one or two of the central papers, but not very much in the others. The nationality of the laureate was not totally and constantly a deciding factor. The first award was definitely very acknowledged in France due to the fact that Sully Prudhomme was French, but the award to Rudyard Kipling was more acknowledged in the *New York Times* and *Le Figaro* than in the *Times*. Some of the decisions, however, appear to have been quite important for the level of media attention. The 1908 prize to Rudolf Eucken got almost no recognition in any of the three papers. At the other end of the spectrum, we find the last of these early awards. The surprising decision to award a non-European author in 1913 led to the most intense media recognition so far. The idea to honor Rabindranath Tagore thus turned out to be the first media success in the history of the prize.

Position Re-Established (1914–29)

The first real crisis in the Nobel Prize's path to top international attention was the First World War, not only because the international awards were overshadowed by the news from the front, but also due to the fact that several prizes were canceled or postponed. The international recognition of the Nobel Prize institution thus dropped significantly after the Tagore prize in 1913. In the following decade, however, the media attention returned to the prize decisions. During the course of the 1920s, the recognition of the literary Nobel even took a significant step forward.

In the *Times*, there was no mention at all of the literary prize between January 1914 and November 1917. Nothing was written about the fact that the 1914 prize was canceled, or about the Swedish Academy's decision to postpone the 1915 prize to 1916. And the British paper did not report from the announcement in November 1916 that French novelist Romain Rolland was given the 1915 award and that Swedish poet Verner von Heidenstam was awarded the 1916 prize. *Le Figaro* was slightly more interested during these years of crisis. The French newspaper did not report anything in 1914 and 1915, but it did briefly mention the awards to Rolland and Heidenstam in November 1916 ("Le prix Nobel," 1916). In the *New York Times*, there was nothing about the canceled 1914 prize, but a year later the American paper shortly mentioned that the 1915 prize was postponed ("No Nobel Prize This Year," 1915). In December that year, the *New York Times* even published a very substantial article speculating on next year's prize: it looked, reporter A.E.B. Fries wrote, like Verner von Heidenstam would be awarded in 1916 (Fries 1915). This whole-page presentation of the Swedish poet, who only "may" get next year's prize, stands out as an anomaly in the three newspapers' reports from Stockholm during this period of intense international conflict. When Fries' prediction actually came true a year later, the *New York Times* did not acknowledge it.

The Danish prize in 1917, shared by Karl Gjellerup and Henrik Pontoppidan, was briefly mentioned in all three papers (untitled article, 1917a; untitled article, 1917b; "Danes Get Nobel Prize," 1917). In London, these awards also resulted in a separate article in the *Times Literary Supplement* ("Danes and the Nobel Prize," 1917). But none of the three newspapers mentioned that the 1918 prize was canceled or that the 1919 prize was postponed. The *New York Times* did have a very brief article on the canceled

1918 and 1919 Peace Prizes, but nothing was said about their literary equivalents ("No Nobel Prizes for 1918 and 1919," 1919).

When the international crisis had settled down and the Nobel Prize decisions seemed to return to normal in 1920, it was the *Times* that reacted most intensely. The 1917 prize to Gjellerup and Pontoppidan had been the first announcement since the start in 1901 that was given most attention in the *Times* compared to *Le Figaro* and the *New York Times*. In 1920, this happened again. On November 13, the London paper had a long article on the double announcement of the 1919 and the 1920 awards. The works of both Carl Spitteler and Knut Hamsun were introduced, but the 1919 Swiss laureate was more substantially presented than the Norwegian, and Spitteler was the only one mentioned in the headline: "Nobel Prize Surprise / Literature Awarded to a Swiss Poet." The article confirms that it is the surprise of the choice that stirred the great interest: "The Swedish Academy has awarded the Nobel Prize for Literature in 1919 to the Swiss poet Carl Spitteler, of Lucerne, and for 1920 to the Norwegian writer Knut Hamsun. The latter choice has been fully expected and is generally approved, but much astonishment is felt as to the former" ("Nobel Prize Surprise," 1920). The surprise had to do with that fact that many critics had expected an award to the English novelist and poet Thomas Hardy. The *Times'* correspondent in Stockholm quoted two Swedish newspapers criticizing the Swedish Academy for ignoring Hardy.

Spitteler was also the most interesting name for *Le Figaro* and the *New York Times*. In the Parisian paper, both laureates were mentioned in relation to the announcement in November, but it was only the Swiss poet's work that was presented ("Les Prix Nobel," 1920). The *New York Times* expressed exactly the same uneven interest. The Spitteler choice prompted a headline and a substantial presentation of his work, whereas Hamsun was only briefly mentioned ("Nobel Prize Winner Beloved By Swiss," 1920). Both literary prizes were, however, distinctly overshadowed by that year's Peace Prize awarded to the sitting president of the United States, Woodrow Wilson. This decision led to a long series of articles in the *New York Times* in November and December 1920.

With the Spitteler award, the Nobel Prize definitely returned to the center of attention in the *Times*. This comeback occurred a year later in the *New York Times* and *Le Figaro*. The award to French novelist Anatole France was substantially recognized in all three papers. In the Parisian paper, both the announcement as such and the ceremony in Stockholm a month later made it to the front page ("Anatole France," 1921; "Prix Nobel," 1921), and the London paper published both a brief news article from Reuter, a report from positive reactions in Sweden and quite a substantial presentation of France's novels ("The Nobel Prize for Anatole France," 1921; untitled article, 1921; "M. Anatole France's Nobel Prize," 1921). Alongside a report on the very announcement, the *New York Times* published substantial presentations of France's work in the regular paper as well as in its appendix "Book Review and Magazine" ("Nobel Prize Awarded to Anatole France"; Gorman 1921; Ybarra 1921).

During the following two years, different kinds of temporary setbacks in attention occurred. The 1922 prize to Spanish playwright Jacinto Benavente did not stir a great fuss at all in the two Anglophone papers, but it was duly acknowledged in Paris (untitled article, 1922; "Nobel Prize for Einstein," 1922; "Le prix Nobel de Littérature," 1921).

The opposite is true for the 1923 award to Irish poet William Butler Yeats: whereas *Le Figaro* didn't write anything at all about this particular prize, both the *Times* and the *New York Times* gave this decision a substantial attention ("Mr. W.B. Yeats," 1923; "Presentation of Nobel Prizes," 1923; "Nobel Prize Awarded to William B. Yeats," 1923; "£7,500 Nobel Prize Surprises Yeats," 1923). With the 1924 award to Polish novelist Wladyslaw Reymont, the prize decision was yet again distinctly recognized in all three papers. The *Times* published a short article on the announcement as well as a report from the paper's correspondent in Warsaw with a presentation of Reymont's work (untitled articles, 1924). In the *New York Times*, the announcement led to three different articles with thorough presentations of the Polish novelist's œuvre ("Gives Nobel Prize to Polish Author," 1924; "Poland's Nobel Prize," 1924; Le Clerc Phillips 1924), and in Paris, the Swedish prize decision was front-page news ("Le Prix Nobel de Littérature est décerné à un Polonais," 1924).

The award to George Bernard Shaw is a special case. In November 1925, the Swedish Academy announced that that year's award was postponed, a decision that was acknowledged in New York but not in Paris or London. In the Parisian paper, the belated prize announcement of the 1925 award in November 1926 led to quite a thorough presentation of the Irish playwright's œuvre on the front page (Alguazils 1926), whereas the *Times* only reported on the fact that the Irish author accepted the honors but not the prize money ("Mr. Shaw and the Nobel Prize," 1926; untitled article, 1926). This story stirred a very limited interest in London compared to the reactions in New York. The *New York Times* published as many as eight articles in November and December 1926 on Shaw's refusal to accept the money, alongside one substantial article on the playwright's literary work ("Approve Award to Shaw," 1926; "Lost in Leaking Dory," 1926; "Shaw Takes Honor, but Not Nobel Cash," 1926; "Shaw Wants Subject Thrashed Out," 1926; "Shaw Prize Ruling to Be Made Today," 1926; "Shaw Will 'Hold' Nobel Prize Money," 1926; Atkinson 1926; "Shaw's Refusal of Prize Money May Be 'Transient', He Says," 1926; Morgan 1926). This was the most intense attention given to any single Nobel Prize in the American newspaper thus far.

The four remaining awards of the 1920s were highly and evenly recognized in the *Times*, *Le Figaro*, and the *New York Times*. On Grazia Deledda's prize—which was the 1926 award, but announced and given belatedly in November and December 1927—the *Times* reported directly from the correspondent in Stockholm on the announcement and published a presentation of Deledda's work from the paper's correspondent in Milan ("1926 Nobel Prize for Literature," 1927). A month later, the reporter in Sweden described the ceremony in Stockholm, where "Signora Grazia Deledda" was present ("Stockholm Ceremony," 1927). In *Le Figaro*, the announcement was front-page news, but instead of a substantial presentation of her work, the paper referred to last week's "supplément littéraire," which included a short story by Deledda ("Les prix Nobel," 1927a). A couple of weeks later her name was mentioned in a report from the prize ceremony ("Les prix Nobel," 1927b). The *New York Times* did not report from the ceremony this year. Instead, the paper devoted almost a whole page to Deledda's literary achievement, including a rich introduction to her work by their expert in Italian literature, Renzo Rendirome (Rendirome 1927).

A year later, two literary awards were given: the 1927 prize to French philosopher Henri Bergson, and the 1928 prize to Norwegian novelist Sigrid Undset. In the *Times* and in *Le Figaro*, both laureates were given substantial presentations in direct relation to the double announcement—Bergson's philosophy was slightly more recognized than Undset's novels in the *Times*, and *Le Figaro* mentioned his name but not hers in the front-page headline ("Nobel Prize Awards," 1928; Alguazils 1928). Both these papers also reported from the December ceremony ("Distribution of Nobel Prizes," 1928; "Une allocution de M. Henry [sic.] Bergson," 1928). In the *New York Times*, by contrast, Undset was initially the most interesting name. Under the headline "Mme. Sigrid Undset Wins Nobel Prize," Bergson was mentioned and presented, but it was the Norwegian novelist who was the focus of attention ("Mme. Sigrid Undset Wins Nobel Prize," 1928). A couple of weeks later, however, Bergson is thoroughly acknowledged in two long articles, one in the ordinary paper and one in its magazine ("Bergson Surprised to Get Nobel Prize," 1928; Recouly 1928).

Nothing was written in any of the three newspapers on the fact that Undset's award was the second prize to a woman writer announced during a span of two years, or that these two prizes were only the second and third awards given to female authors. A related detail is the fact that the first woman laureate, Selma Lagerlöf, is mentioned in the *New York Times* on November 21 on the occasion of her seventieth birthday ("Selma Lagerloef is 70," 1928). But no connection was made between Lagerlöf, Deledda, and Undset.

The decade ended on a high note with the award to German author Thomas Mann. On November 13, 1929, the *Times* reported on the announcement from its correspondent in Berlin, along with a presentation of earlier German Nobel laureates in Literature and an introduction to Mann's work ("Nobel Prize Awards," 1929). The great interest in the award is illustrated by an advertisement on November 22 from Mann's British publishing house Secker, offering four titles written by the latest Nobel laureate: the novellas *Early Sorrow* (*Unordnung und frühes Leid*) and *Death in Venice* (*Der Tot in Venedig*), his latest novel *The Magic Mountain* (*Der Zauberberg*), and the novel that the Swedish Academy especially mentioned as earning him the prize: the family chronicle *Buddenbrooks* (*Buddenbrooks: Verfall einer Familie*) (advertisement, 1929). In *Le Figaro*, the report on Mann's award was the centerpiece in the paper's newly established section on literature, theatre, and art. The German writer and his work were given detailed and initiated introductions by the signature J.P., who wrote that Thomas Mann's most important titles were little known in France. By way of characterizing his œuvre, *Buddenbrooks* was called "the Rougon-Macquart of Lübeck" in a reference to French author Émile Zola's well-known cycle of novels (J.P. 1929, my translation).

The attention given to Thomas Mann in London and Paris was, however, significantly exceeded by the recognition this award got in the *New York Times*. And whereas the George Bernard Shaw prize announced in 1926 had stirred a great interest due to the laureate's refusal to accept the prize money, this time most of the attention was, on the contrary, directly connected to Thomas Mann's literary works. Two articles described the author's reaction to the award and what he intended to do with the money ("Mann Deeply Moved on Hearing of Award," 1929; "Thomas Mann to Build Home," 1929), but three long articles were devoted to thorough discussions of his books ("Thomas Mann Wins Nobel Prize for 1929," 1929; Frank 1929; Reuter 1929). The reception in the *New York Times* of the Thomas Mann award was the most substantial media response so far to a single Nobel Prize since the start in 1901.

When summing up this period of Nobel Prize history, we can conclude that the prize institution was quickly re-established after the crisis in attention and acknowledgment caused by the First World War. Two factors were important for the prize to avoid being completely overshadowed by news from the violent international conflict. First of all, the Swedish Academy did not completely stop selecting laureates during the years of crisis, but managed to award two authors in 1916 and two in 1917. Thereby, the world was reminded of the Swedish prize throughout the period. And secondly, the different Nobel Prizes were not canceled or postponed at the same time. The unevenly distributed pauses in giving out prizes in Chemistry, Physics, Medicine, Peace, and Literature helped to secure that the Nobel Prize institution as such didn't really take a break, despite the state of Europe. After having survived the 1910s, the literary prize came out stronger in the following decade. Through the course of the 1920s, the Nobel Prize in Literature did not only regain the media position established before the war, but indeed strengthened its status as a significant world event that the three leading newspapers in Paris, London, and New York had to report on and react to in November each year.

This strengthened position was connected to another, just as important development. In the 1920s, the very literary aspect of the award was successively moved into the center of attention. Throughout the decade, substantial descriptions of the literary works themselves—rather than the authors, their cultural backgrounds, and the prize-giving institution as such—increasingly dominated the media reports, a tendency that culminated in Thomas Mann's award in 1929. A telling detail is the fact that none of the three papers had any report from the 1929 prize ceremony. The literary works awarded had entered the center stage at the expense of the royal glory surrounding the ritual in Stockholm. In temporal terms, this means that the focus of attention had been moved from the actual prize-giving event in December to the November announcements.

One last observation needs to be pointed out. Despite the fact that the literary prize gained recognition from its proximity to the other four Nobel prizes, a closer look at the 1920s media attention makes it quite clear that the literary award was the leading star. There are exceptions to this rule—for example, the coverage of Woodrow Wilson's Peace Prize, and Albert Einstein's prize in Physics in 1920 and 1922—but the tendency is very distinct. Unlike most of the other laureates, the literary prize recipients were often presented in separate articles. When this was not the case, it was still the literary prize that most often was presented first and was given most column space. The reception in London, Paris, and New York of the Nobel Prizes in Literature between 1914 and 1929 reflected a time and a world when literature was regarded as a very important transnational phenomenon. When Lars Gyllensten—by then former Nobel Committee Chair—argued in 2000 that the literary award was the Nobel Prize that had been given most recognition through the years, he was absolutely correct

(Gyllensten 2000: 256). This hierarchy of attention between the categories was in place right from the start in 1901, but it was strengthened through the course of the first three decades in the history of the prize.

A Broader Significance (1930–39)

The tendency in the 1920s toward an increased media attention continued in the next decade. Throughout the 1930s, the media recognition of the prize decisions was generally higher than in the preceding decade, but it included some ups and downs—especially a couple of very significant ups.

The 1930s started with an explosion of attention, at least in the United States. The reason for this bombshell was the fact that this year the Swedish Academy selected an American author for the Nobel Prize in Literature—novelist Sinclair Lewis. In November and December 1930, the *New York Times* published at least thirty-five separate articles on Lewis. That was a record media recognition of a single prize decision so far, and it would stand for many years. The American articles on the award showed a great variety. On the day after the announcement in Stockholm—November 6—the *New York Times* published two texts: one shorter editorial reaction ("Mr. Lewis's Nobel Prize," 1930) and one long article on the prize decision, illustrated with a photograph of the author—the first inclusion of a photographic portrait of a laureate in these three papers ("Nobel Prize Goes to Sinclair Lewis," 1930). Next day, there was a shorter text on the reactions in France and Sweden ("France and Sweden Laud Award to Lewis," 1930). Later that month, two substantial essays by S.J. Woolf on Lewis' novels were published in the *New York Times Magazine* (Woolf 1930a; Woolf 1930b).

Several articles were published that applauded the Stockholm decision and praised the laureate's prose ("Newman Praises Lewis as Crusader," 1930; "Shaw Agrees with Lewis about Us," 1930), and one separate text discussed Lewis' appearances on newsreels ("Sinclair Lewis in Films," 1930). But everything wasn't rosy and perfect. Over a two-month span, as many as eight articles in the *New York Times* criticized the prize decision and Lewis' novels ("Nobel Prize Award to Lewis Is an 'Insult' to America," 1930; "Van Dyke Explains Nobel Prize Attack," 1930; "Assails Award to Lewis," 1930; "Dimnet Deplores Honoring of Lewis," 1930; "Finds 'Main Street' Unfair," 1930; "Lewis Would Exile All Our Reformers," 1930; "Lewis Finds Irony in 'Serious' America," 1930; "Critical of Award to Sinclair Lewis," 1930). These texts led to one article criticizing these critics ("Potter Assails van Dyke," 1930), and three other texts in which Lewis' own responses to the criticism were quoted ("Lewis Indifferent to Coolidge Criticism," 1930; "Sinclair Lewis Off," 1930; "Sinclair Lewis Hits Old School Writers," 1930).

The *New York Times* also published an article on Sinclair Lewis' ambition to learn Swedish in preparation for the upcoming receptions, visits, and tasks in Stockholm ("Lewis Takes Swedish Courses," 1930). Then there were reports on the author's travels to Sweden via a short stop in Germany ("Nobel Prize Winner Sails for Germany," 1930; "Sinclair Lewis off for Sweden Today," 1930), and an article on the fact that the prize money—an amount of $46,350—would soon be handed over to the American writer

("Nobel Prize Checks to Be Paid Today," 1930). On December 10, the *New York Times* reported from the ceremony in Stockholm ("King Gustaf Fetes Nobel Prize Men," 1930), and then five different articles described what Sinclair Lewis was doing and who he was meeting on his stay in Sweden ("Mr. Lewis at Stockholm," 1930; "Lewis Is Lionized by All Stockholm," 1930; "Festivities Tire Lewis," 1930; "Crowd Hears Lewis Talk at Gothenburg," 1930; "Mr. Lewis Mentions the Drama," 1930). In addition to these reports, the laureate's Nobel lecture was published in its entirety, almost filling up a whole page ("Text of Sinclair Lewis' Nobel Prize Address at Stockholm," 1930), which led to further acclaim: two articles were devoted to positive reactions to his speech in Stockholm ("Dr. Phelps Praises Lewis' Prize Speech," 1930). We can safely conclude that the first American Nobel Prize in Literature was received as a historical occasion in the US public sphere.

One of the most recognized aspects of the Lewis prize was the fact that the writer had declined the domestic Pulitzer Prize just four years earlier. In 1926, Lewis refused to accept the American award for his novel *Arrowsmith* due to the Pulitzer's outspoken endorsement of literature that presented "the highest standard of American manners and manhood." The Nobel Prize, Lewis declared in his first interview in November 1930, was a different matter. There was, he said, "an enormous difference between the two prizes": whereas the Pulitzer wanted to strengthen a normative national code of conduct, the Nobel was "an international prize with no strings tied." He would receive the Swedish award without any reservations: "I feel the highest honor and gratification at being the first American to be awarded the Nobel Prize in literature, and I am accepting it with pleasure" ("Nobel Prize Goes to Sinclair Lewis," 1930).

The *New York Times*' reactions to the Lewis prize did not only include national pride and discussions on how the satirical novelist portrays the American people. They also stressed that the 1930 Nobel Prize was an award to a widely read popular writer. In the first article announcing the prize, the paper pointed out that Lewis' novels had sold in almost 2 million copies in the United States, that they were popular with Swedish readers, who read them in the many Swedish translations available, and that more than 100,000 copies of German translations had been sold in the last ten years ("Nobel Prize Goes to Sinclair Lewis," 1930). The Nobel Prize to Sinclair Lewis, the American paper stressed, was an award to a best-selling writer; it was an acknowledgment of the idea that the highest level of literary quality may be found in commercially successful and broadly accessible literature.

The Lewis prize was also distinctly recognized in *Le Figaro* and the *Times*. In the Parisian paper, the award was the leading event in the section "Lettres, Théatre, Sciences et Arts," and the laureate was given almost a whole column with a substantial presentation of his novels and his position in the US literary landscape ("M. Sinclair Lewis lauréat du Prix Nobel," 1930). The *Times* published reports from the announcement in Stockholm, from reactions to the prize in the United States, as well as from the ceremony in Stockholm ("The Nobel Prize for Literature," 1930; untitled article, 1930), and just like the Thomas Mann prize the year before, the laureate's British publisher—in Lewis' case Jonathan Cape—paid for big advertisements solely based on the prize decision (advertisements, 1930). Furthermore, on December 13, a photographic exposé from different events in different parts of the world included a photo from the writer's visit to Stockholm. The caption read: "The king of Sweden presenting the Nobel Prize for Literature to Mr. Sinclair Lewis, the American writer, at Stockholm" (photograph, 1930). After the first article on the prize announcement in the *New York Times* in November, this was the second photograph of literary Nobel laureates published in these three newspapers.

This high level of recognition had partly to do with the fact that Lewis was the first ever American laureate. The award led to national pride in the *New York Times* and gave the *Times* and *Le Figaro* a reason to introduce a new literary culture in their discussion of internationally significant literature. But the intense interest in Lewis was not only prompted by his nationality and the subject matters of his novels, with their satirical explorations of the specificities of American society and culture. It had also to do with its address and its accessibility. Lewis' novels *Main Street* (1920), *Babbitt* (1922), *Arrowsmith* (1925), and *Elmer Gantry* (1926) were translatable, available, and accessible novels with a mainstream appeal for a broad range of different readers interested in modern life and the development of twentieth-century Capitalism and Liberalism.

The notion that the outreach of the awarded works helped to increase media recognition of the prize itself is confirmed by the reactions to Nobel awards later in the 1930s. It is not a surprise that *Le Figaro* thoroughly acknowledged the 1937 prize to French realist novelist Roger Martin du Gard, who was very known in France for his *roman-fleuve*—or cycle of novels—*Les Thibaults*, a series in many volumes following the lives of two brothers from 1904 to the end of the First World War. By the time Martin du Gard received the Nobel Prize, the eighth and last volume of this cycle was yet to be published. Martin du Gard's award was announced on the front page of *Le Figaro* on November 12, 1937, with a large, graphically advanced headline and a painted portrait of the author ("Le Prix Nobel de Littérature," 1937). In the same issue, *Le Figaro* published one long, substantial article on the laureate and his literary achievements (Rousseaux 1937), one shorter article on the voting process in the Swedish Academy that had resulted in the selection of the French writer ("Le vote de l'Académie Suédoise," 1937), and one more text on how the newspaper managed to get hold of the front-page portrait of the author, who was known for his aversion to being photographed ("Les Echos," 1937).

The Martin du Gard prize was announced on the front page of the *New York Times* as well. The article included a report from Paris, where the reporter had tried to meet the laureate in person but was informed that he was on his way to the Mediterranean. However, the *New York Times* correspondent did find his sister-in-law, "Mme. Marcel Martin du Gard," with whom he could have a chat. The series *Les Thibaults* was described alongside a recommendation of another work by Martin du Gard: the novel *La Vielle France* (available in English as *The Postman*), presented as one of the writer's "outstanding works" and "a 1933 best-seller." The last comment clearly confirms the significance of a wide readership for these reports ("New Yorker Shares Nobel Prize," 1937).

In the *Times*, the news of Martin du Gard's prize was announced alongside the news of two other Nobel Prizes—to George P. Thomson in Physics and to W.N. Haworth in

Chemistry. Despite the fact that both Thomson and Haworth were English and worked at the Imperial College of Science and the University of Birmingham, it was the French literary laureate who dominated the report. The article began as well as ended with the news of Martin du Gard's award. The two British scientists were squeezed in between the two-fold presentation of the novelist ("Nobel Prizes," 1937). Just like in 1929 and 1930, the news of the 1937 Nobel Prize was followed up by advertisements of available British books by the laureate. This time it was the publisher Bodley Head who, under the headline "Nobel Prize for Literature, 1937," advertised the two volumes of *The Thibaults* available in English translations (advertisement, 1937).

Next year's prize-decision also got a substantial reaction in all three papers. The award to novelist Pearl Buck was the third American prize, and the decision was front-page news in New York. On the day after the announcement, the *New York Times* published two texts on the decision: one news article on the front page and one editorial comment ("Pearl Buck Wins Nobel Literature Prize," 1930; "Nobel Prize Winner," 1930). After that, the paper published sex articles on the author up until the end of December, including a long, whole-page essay by S.J. Woolf (Woolf 1938), one reporting on reactions to the decision in Sweden and Finland ("Award Perturbs Swedes," 1938), and two on Pearl Buck's stay in Stockholm while receiving the award ("Swedish King Gives Mrs. Buck Nobel Prize," 1938; "Mrs. Buck Guest at King's Dinner," 1938). In the *Times*' article on the announcements of the prizes for Literature and Physics, the literary award was definitely prioritized, a focus made very clear in the headline ("Nobel Prizes. Award for Literature to Pearl Buck," 1938). A couple of weeks later, the London paper also reported on the American laureate boarding the Normandie in New York, with her husband and stepdaughter, in order to "attend the annual Nobel Prize celebration in STOCKHOLM" (untitled article, 1938). And in *Le Figaro*, a photo of the laureate and a presentation of her work illustrated the front-page news of the prize decision ("Le Prix Nobel de Littérature," 1930).

In retrospect, the award to Buck has been one of the most criticized in the history of the Nobel Prize. For later commentators, the Buck decision has become a symbol of the 1930s Nobel Committees' lack of interest in Modernism and their outdated focus on accessible prose writers whom posterity has deemed less important. Reading the first reactions to the Pearl Buck prize in the late fall and early winter of 1938, however, it seems like the direct, contemporary critical voices toward this award were restricted to Swedish literary circles. Unlike the reception of the Sinclair Lewis prize, there was no domestically American critique of the 1938 prize decision reported in the *New York Times*, and neither *Times* nor *Le Figaro* mentioned any negative reactions. On the contrary, the *Times* described Buck's 1931 novel *The Good Earth* as "a remarkable study of Chinese life" ("Nobel Prizes. Award for Literature to Pearl Buck," 1938). The only critique reported in the three papers was to be found in a report in the *New York Times* from the Scandinavian reception. The correspondent in Helsinki mentioned "several caustic criticisms by Swedish authors and critics," and wrote that some of them "pour scorn on the Swedish Academy." In Finland, on the other hand, the decision was received "with greater equanimity." The American novelist was "extensively read in Finland": 20,000 copies of the Finnish translation of *The Good*

Earth had been sold so far, the correspondent informed his American readers, which was "an extraordinary record for a book in this country" ("Award Perturbs Swedes," 1938). Just like in the three papers' direct reactions to the Sinclair Lewis and Roger Martin du Gard awards, the wide popularity of Pearl Buck was stressed as a sign of quality, not a diminishing factor.

The rest of the 1930s awards did not enjoy such a generally high recognition in the three papers. The prize to British novelist John Galsworthy was given an intense attention in the *Times* and the *New York Times* in November and December 1932. In the former, the award was discussed in four articles and referred to in one separate portrait of Galsworthy in a photo gallery ("Nobel Prize for Literature," 1932; untitled articles, 1932; photo gallery, 1932). In the American paper, eight articles presented and discussed the award, the laureate and his work ("Nobel Science Prize Won by Dr. Langmur," 1932; "Book Notes" November 11, 1932; "Topic of the Times," 1932"; "Book Notes," November 21, 1932; "Galsworthy Will Not Go to Sweden," 1932; "Galsworthy Ill with Chill," 1932 ; "Four Nobel Prizes Presented by King," 1932), including an almost page-long review of his latest novel *Flowering Wilderness* (Hutchison 1932). The attention given to Galsworthy in *Le Figaro*, however, was much more limited—only one short article announced the prize decision of 1932 ("Le Prix Nobel de Littérature," 1932).

The responses to the awards to playwrights Luigi Pirandello and Eugene O'Neill formed a different pattern. Both of these prizes were very recognized in the *New York Times* and *Le Figaro*. In November 1934, the Pirandello award was the first to make it to the front page of *Le Figaro* since the shared prize to Henri Bergson and Sigrid Undset in 1928. Two years later, Eugene O'Neill was acknowledged with a front-page article and a separate photo a couple of pages into the paper ("Le Prix Nobel de Littérature est décerné à l'écrivain américain O'Neill," 1936; "Le Prix Nobel de Littérature," 1936). And the next day—just two days after the announcement—*Le Figaro* published a long article with an in-depth discussion of the American's plays (Morand 1936).

In the *New York Times*, Luigi Pirandello and his work were presented and discussed in as many as eleven articles in November and December 1934, including a very substantial first reaction with a photograph of the laureate ("Luigi Pirandello Wins Nobel Prize," 1934; "Topics of the Times," 1934; "Wit and Wisdom In Pirandello," 1934; "The Critics' View of the American Theatre," 1934; "Pirandello's Play Welcomed in Dublin," 1934; "How to Write a Play," 1934; "King Gustav Gives Prizes," 1934; "Topics of the Times," 1934; "Books and Authors," 1934; "Pirandello to Visit U.S.," 1934; "Pirandello Play Opens," 1934). It almost goes without saying that the second American Nobel Prize in Literature was given an even more intense attention in the late fall of 1936. The Eugene O'Neill award resulted in thirteen articles from November 11 to the prize ceremony reports a month later, including a (quite accurate) speculation before the announcement ("Eugene O'Neill mentioned For Nobel Literary Prize," 1936), a long first-page response to the prize-decision news ("Nobel Prize Awarded to O'Neill," 1936), a substantial essay in the magazine (Neuberger 1936), and several articles on delighted reactions from Europe ("Yeats Is 'Delighted' at Award to O'Neill," 1936; "American Week in London," 1936; "Reinhardt Praises American Theatre," 1936).

In the *Times*, however, there was no article announcing the prize to Luigi Pirandello—only a single photo of the Italian playwright with a brief caption, in a collage of pictures from different world events (photograph, 1934). The only other mention of the Italian playwright in the late fall and early winter of 1934 was to be found in an advertisement for his play *As Your Desire Me*, which was staged at the Royalty theatre in London (advertisement, 1934). Eugene O'Neill was more recognized, but the single article announcing the prizes in Literature, Chemistry, and Physics ("Nobel Prizes," 1936), plus a telegram a month later on the ceremony in Stockholm (untitled article, 1936), was a very limited response compared to the reactions in New York and Paris.

Whereas the responses to the Ivan Bunin prize in 1933 were also quite diverse—intense in the *New York Times*, with five articles, including a page-long essay ("Nobel Prize Goes to Bunin," 1933; "Topic of the Times," 1933; Nazaroff 1933; "Books and Authors," 1933; "Bunin Is Acclaimed in Nobel Ceremony," 1933); limited in *Le Figaro*, with just one, short article ("Le Prix Nobel de Littérature," 1933); and sparse in the *Times*, with just a brief mention in a general article on the Nobel Prizes, plus a short telegram from the ceremony (telegram, 1933)—the reactions to the Erik Axel Karlfeldt award in 1931 were very restricted in all three papers. Karlfeldt was a unique laureate in several ways. He was the only author to win the prize posthumously. He was also the only former Permanent Secretary of the Swedish Academy to be awarded, and he was the first laureate who had explicitly refused to be honored when nominated several years earlier. Despite these particularities, Karlfeldt's prize was least recognized by the contemporary international press of all the awards in the 1930s. In the *Times*, Karlfeldt's prize was only mentioned in a single, very brief report, in which the laureate's name was misspelt three times—he was called "M. Erik Axel Karlseldt" ("Posthumous Award of Nobel Prize," 1931). In *Le Figaro*, the Swedish poet was briefly mentioned in a short article at the bottom of the section "La Vie Littéraire" ("Le Prix Nobel de Littératture," 1931), and in the *New York Times* there was also just a short article on the prize announcement in October, a brief report that included two different spellings of the laureate's first name—"Erik" and "Eric" ("Nobel Prize Awarded to Dead Swedish Poet," 1931). The idea to award their own (in a double sense) turned out to be quite a bad strategy for the Swedish Academy's ambition to maintain international interest and respect for the Nobel Prize institution. The meagre response to the 1931 award in *Le Figaro*, the *Times*, and *New York Times* distinctly confirms Lars Gyllensten's notion that the many early Scandinavian awards were damaging to the international status of the Nobel Prize (Gyllensten 2000: 262).

The prize to Finnish novelist Frans Eemil Sillanpää in 1939 is a special case. In *Le Figaro*, the announcement in Stockholm was completely overshadowed by news from the Second World War. The Parisian paper didn't mention the laureate and the prize decision at all. Two days after the Swedish Academy's announcement, there was a report from Helsinki, but this was solely concerned with the military conflict between Finland and the Soviet Union ("L'U.R.S.S. réclamerait à la Finlande," 1939). In the *New York Times*, however, the Sillanpää award was quite big news. The American paper had a substantial report the day after the announcement ("Nobel Prize Given to Finnish Writer," 1939), followed by two shorter mentions ("Topics of the Times," 1939; "Books and Authors," 1939), one photo of Sillanpää with the caption "F.E. Sillanpaa, the Finnish Novelist, Who Receives This Year's Nobel Prize for Literature" (photograph, 1939), and a short note—amidst dismal reports from the "European Conflict"—on the writer's journey from Finland to the ceremony in Sweden with his seven children ("Incidents in European Conflict," 1939).

In stark contrast to the complete silence in Le Figaro, the award to Frans Eemil Sillanpää also led to a fervent reaction in the Times. On the day after the announcement, the London paper published two articles: one on the prize decision itself and one on the reactions in Finland ("Nobel Literature Prize. Honour for Finnish Author," 1939; "A Great Patriot and Liberal," 1939). The Times' correspondent in Helsinki saw the prize as an important political gesture from Sweden in support of their neighbors: "The whole of Finland rejoices at the selection of M. Sillanpää for the award of the Nobel Prize for Literature. The award is doubly valued, because it comes at a time of serious political crisis." A month later, the prize was brought up again, not in relation to the prize ceremony but in a report on the Soviet bombing of Helsinki on December 21 ("Two Raids on Helsinki," 1939).

Apart from this last prize, which was decided upon and reacted to in a very special period in history, the recognition in Paris, London, and New York of Nobel awards from the 1930s shows two distinct tendencies. One is the intense American interest in the prize. Considering the fact that this was the decade when not only the first but the three first literary laureates from the United States were selected, this strong interest is not surprising. But the New York Times' coverage of Nobel Prizes was already high in the three first decades of the award's history. The 1930s was not the decade when the American interest in the Nobel Prize in Literature awakened, but the decade when it was greatly expanded.

The second tendency has to do with what kind of literature was awarded. In the 1930s, the Swedish Academy decided to award more widely read authors than before, and this change in priorities toward accessible and broadly appreciated literature increased the international media attention devoted to the prize. Furthermore, this new focus was distinctly connected to the appreciation of a new literary continent, since both Sinclair Lewis and Pearl Buck were perfect examples of writers with a wide address. The tendency to award more widely distributed and read literature has been strongly criticized in retrospect, not least by later members of the Swedish Academy (cf. Espmark 1986: 70–83; Gyllensten 2000: 260). But as long as newspaper recognition goes, the Swedish Academy's strengthened interest in American literature and accessibility turned out to be quite successful.

World Consecration (1944–53)

Because of the war, no Nobel awards were given between 1940 and 1943. Naturally, then, the attention on the prize dropped significantly during these years. When the prize decisions were resumed in 1944 onward, however, the media recognition quickly caught up and was soon as high as it had been in the 1930s. At the end of the 1940s, a new platform of international media coverage was reached. By then, it is fair to say that the strong and immediate responses in *Le Figaro*, the *Times*, and the *New York Times* endorsed the Nobel institution's power to exert world literary consecration.

The cancellation of the prize decisions and ceremonies resulted in a total silence in the *Times* and *Le Figaro* on the Nobel Prize issue. No reports were published in any of these years on the Swedish Academy's decisions to cancel the prizes. The war demanded almost all of the attention in Great Britain and France. The *New York Times*, by contrast, never let the war disrupt their interest in the Nobel. Each and every fall, the American paper reported from Stockholm and the Academy's decisions not to select any laureate that year ("Nobel Prizes Reported Suspended," 1940; "1940 Nobel Prizes Canceled," 1941; "The Nobel Prizes," 1941; "No Nobel Prize This Year," 1942; "Nobel Prizes Suspended," 1943). In October 1942, the *New York Times* even published an article in anticipation of that year's prize decision, but the speculations proved futile ("To Select Nobel Prize Winners," 1942). And in both 1942 and 1943, the New York paper published reports on substitute dinners in honor of Alfred Nobel, held in New York on the donor's birthday December 10. To these events, a range of Nobel laureates, "most of them refugees," were invited, and they attended the festivities in order to celebrate the democratic values that the Nobel institution had represented and distributed in pre-war times. The events were called "liberty dinners" ("The Nobel Dinner," 1942; "Nobel Anniversary Celebrated Here," 1943). New York readers were not allowed to forget about the Swedish and Norwegian awards that were temporarily put on hold.

When the Nobel awards returned in 1944, things got back to normal in the *New York Times*. The prize to Danish novelist and poet Johannes V. Jensen prompted three substantial articles: one report on the announcement, illustrated with a photo of the writer ("2 U.S. Scientists Win Nobel Prizes," 1944), a separate article on Jensen's work published a couple of weeks later (Hackett 1944), and one whole-page essay in the "Book Review" section when December 10 was getting closer (Toksvig 1944). The 1945 award to Gabriela Mistral was paid slightly more attention: four articles were published, including a whole-page essay in "Book Review" (Adams 1945), and a report from the Stockholm ceremony, illustrated with one photo of the Swedish king handing over the Medicine prize to the discoverer of penicillin, Alexander Fleming, and one of him handing over the Literature medal and diploma to Mistral ("King Gustaf of Sweden Presenting 1945 Nobel Prizes," 1945). The paper presented Gabriela Mistral as "one of the best-known Spanish-language poets and also one of the first South American women to hold public office" ("Expert on Atoms Win Nobel Prize," 1945).

Apart from these texts on the actual laureates, the *New York Times* also published two articles in anticipation of the prize decisions. In November 1944, the paper could inform the readers that American authors John Steinbeck, Willa Cather, and Ernest Hemingway were close to being awarded, but that Jensen was the favorite ("Nobel Board Studies Literature Nominees," 1944). A year later, the *New York Times* reported that the shortlist included Mistral, Steinbeck, French poet Jules Romains, and Swiss writer Charles-Ferdinand Ramuz ("Steinbeck Candidate for Nobel Award," 1945). This extra attention was the result of the Swedish Academy's strategy to announce the shortlist of nominated authors shortly before the actual decision was made, a media strategy that they later dropped in favor of the surprise dramaturgy of announcing the name of the actual laureate without any pre-information whatsoever. For the American recognition of the mid-1940s awards, the two-step announcement strategy proved quite successful as a media strategy.

In the *Times*, things were almost back to normal with the 1944 award, although the recognition of Jensen was more restricted than the reports on the last laureates before the war ("The Nobel Prize for Literature," 1944). In the responses to the following year's award, the level of attention was completely restored, with a substantial presentation of "Señorita Mistral" and her poetry ("Nobel Awards. Literature Prize for Chilean Authoress," 1945), as well as a report from the ceremony in which the writer made a point of the fact that the solemn Nobel tradition was thankfully restored (untitled article, 1945). In Paris, the silence surrounding the Nobel Prize in Literature lingered on a bit longer, since no reaction to the Johannes V. Jensen prize was published in *Le Figaro*. The Swedish Academy's announcement of Gabriela Mistral's award, however, ended up—just like the prize news before the war—on the front page, and this restored recognition included quite a substantial presentation of the laureate's work ("Le Prix Nobel de Littérature à la poétesse chilienne Gabriela Mistral," 1945).

An important detail in these first post-war news of Nobel decisions is the fact that the literary prize was by default treated as the most important of the five awards. The literary laureates were most likely to be acknowledged with separate articles, and when several prizes were presented together it was most often the literary laureate who was introduced first and referred to in the headline. An overall look at the post-war reports in the three papers confirms what the *New York Times* expressed in relation to the André Gide award in 1947: the literature prize was "considered the plum of the Nobel awards" ("Gide Gets Nobel Literature Prize," 1947).

In the *Times* and *Le Figaro*, quite a big leap forward was taken in the responses to the Gide prize. It does not come as a surprise that the Parisian paper substantially and joyfully recognized this decision on the front page with a big photograph of the laureate: Gide was not only a French writer, but he had also contributed with several texts to *Le Figaro*. With both national and collegial pride, the laureate was presented as "our best contemporary prose writer" and "our eminent collaborator" ("ANDRÉ GIDE obtient le Prix Nobel de Littérature," 1947, my translations). This first reaction was followed up two days later with a second front-page article, this time an interview with André Gide by *Le Figaro*'s "special reporter" René Mossu (Mossu 1947, my translation). A month later, the report from the ceremony in Stockholm, where the prize was received by the French ambassador to Sweden, was also given a front-page position ("Les Prix Nobel 1947," 1947).

The big attention paid to the Gide prize in the *Times* is perhaps a bit more surprising. Despite the fact that there were two English laureates this year—Edward Appleton in Physics and Robert Robinson in Chemistry—it was Gide who stole the show. A photo of the French writer was published as well as a separate article on his work (photographs, 1947; "M. André Gide Awarded Literature Prize," 1947). An important aspect of this extended recognition is the fact that the Swedish Academy's prize motivation was quoted in both *Le Figaro* and the *Times*. The focus of these responses was, then, not only on the awarded author and what kind of literature has been consecrated, but also on what the members of the Nobel Committee were thinking when they placed this particular literary œuvre above all the others. The 1947 award was the first prize that prompted (in the three newspapers studied) this kind of focus on the Committees' own aesthetic discussions.

This increased attention was confirmed and firmly established in the following years with the responses to the T.S. Eliot prize in 1948 and to the announcement of the awards to William Faulkner (who was given the 1949 prize a year later) and Bertrand Russell in 1950. The reactions to the Eliot award in *Le Figaro* were almost as strong as those to the Gide prize a year before, with a photo of the US-born British laureate and a presentation of his work in a front-page article that continued on page two. The reporter was delighted by the choice of laureate, since his work was among the "peaks of 20th century world literature." Eliot was "one of the great poets in search of the Eternal in a world that has lost it" (A.R. 1948, my translation).

In the *Times*, T.S. Eliot had to share the moment with British laureate in Physics, P.M.S. Blackett, but as many as three articles were devoted to the two prize winners the day after the announcement. And the London journalists made no attempt of hiding their feelings of national pride: "Once more, in the naming of Mr. T.S. ELIOT for literature and PROFESSOR P.M.S. BLACKETT for physics, this country has a double cause for pride in this year's award—which is not diminished by the fact that MR. ELIOT was born American" ("Nobel Prizes," 1948; untitled article, 1948; "The Nobel Awards," 1948). The 1949 prize was postponed one year, but this disruption had no negative effect on the recognition of the two literary awards announced in 1950. In the *Times* as well as in *Le Figaro*, William Faulkner and Bertrand Russell were substantially introduced the day after the announcement. In Paris, the announcements were front-page news, and in London both prize motivations were quoted ("Nobel Prizes for Literature," 1950; "Le romancier américain FAULKNER et le philosophe anglaise RUSSELL reçoivent le prix Nobel de littérature," 1950).

The responses in the *New York Times* followed a slightly different pattern. In 1946, the recognition of the Hermann Hesse award was more restricted in the *New York Times* than in the *Times* and *Le Figaro*, which is a rare state of affairs so far in the history of Nobel Prize reception. The limited response to Hesse followed the same logic as the intense and expanded responses to the Lewis, Martin du Gard, and Buck awards had done in the 1930s: the New York paper appreciated popular writers rather than narrowly distributed high-brow authors. "The novels, poems and essays of the literature winner, Hermann Hesse," one American commentator concluded with disappointment, "are not widely known" ("Six Americans Win Nobel Prizes," 1946). In another article, the journalist wrote that he could only understand the 1946 prize decision as a political statement: "If, as Secretary Anders Oesterling [*sic*.] of the Swedish Academy suggests, this honor recognizes an early revolt against German anti-humanism, we can understand it" ("For Service to Mankind," 1946). This was perhaps also why André Gide was not paid as much attention in the New York paper as in London and Paris.

The award to T.S. Eliot, however, was substantially recognized in the *New York Times*, with a front-page headline, a photograph of the laureate, and a quoted prize motivation the day after the announcement ("T.S. Eliot Receives 1948 Nobel Award," 1948). A couple of weeks later, this report was followed up with an in-depth essay in the "Book Review" (Muir 1948). This response was, however, distinctly surpassed by next year's reactions. In November and December 1950, the awards to William Faulkner and Bertrand Russell were presented and discussed in fifteen articles, of which several were substantial discussions of their respective work (see for example "Faulkner and Bertrand Russel Get Nobel Awards for Writings," 1950; "What French Readers Find in William Faulkner's Fiction," 1950; "Russell Envisions a World at Peace," 1950). It's not fair to say that Russell was overshadowed by Faulkner, but the American novelist was definitely the focus of attention. In a long article, Charles Poore expressed his support for the decision to award Faulkner, and his main argument was that the novelist was—contrary to popular belief—widely read by the American people. Using information of sold copies and pointing to frequent appearances in anthologies, Poore argued that Faulkner was—up until now—much more appreciated by the ordinary reader than he was discussed by critics: "You might say that no one in America reads Faulkner—but the people" (Poore 1950).

A distinct confirmation of the fact that the Nobel Prize in Literature quickly had not only restored its former position after the Second World War, but in fact had reinforced it, is the initiative in 1950 by the American literary quarterly *Books Abroad* to ask 350 "experts in belles-lettres" of what they thought of the Nobel Prize decisions so far. This big inquiry resulted in one summarizing article by William F. Lamont (Lamont 1951), and eighteen individual texts responding to the question "What's Wrong with the Nobel Prize?," published in two volumes of the periodical.

As the question suggests, all of the experts were not totally happy with the choices made by the Swedish Academy in the first fifty years in the history of the prize, but the very idea to conduct this kind of grand inquiry and give it so much space, time, and attention says very much about how important the Nobel Prize in Literature as an institution for international literary consecration had become in the early fifties—especially in the United States. In these issues of the journal, the award was definitely treated as one of the most important powers in the collective and multilayered process that formed a transcultural world literary canon. The existence and scope of the American survey confirmed *Le Figaro*'s definition of the prize in relation to the T.S. Eliot award: to receive the Nobel Prize was to gain "world consecration" (A.R. 1948, my translation).

This central importance was further confirmed in the summer of 1953, when the members of the National Arts Foundation of New York presented a plan to establish a new international prize to people whose work has been of "service to humanity." The idea was to decide upon five categories "in such special fields as architecture, sculpture, music, dancing, painting, and drama, including films and television," but the "five fields covered by the Nobel prize—peace, physics, chemistry, literature, and medicine—would be excluded." Prize money would be "roughly in the lines of the Nobel Prize" ("Prizes for 'Service to Humanity,'" 1953). The Swedish award was undoubtedly the model, and the new prize was not thought to be a competing award but a complementary one, covering the fields not mentioned in Alfred Nobel's will. The focus on art and communication made it quite evident that it was the Nobel Prize in Literature rather than the scientific Nobel awards that was the most direct inspiration for this American initiative.

Breaking News (the 1950s and Onward)

A final step of increased recognition of the annual prize decisions occurred in the 1950s. This step was made through a generally higher immediate acknowledgment of the prize announcements, but also—and perhaps more importantly—through a couple of particularly medial awards: the ones to François Mauriac, Ernest Hemingway, Winston Churchill, Albert Camus, and Boris Pasternak. With the announcements of these awards, the Nobel Prize in Literature became what it still is today: a cultural phenomenon that by default steals a large part of the international media show at one designated moment each year.

In Paris, this leap toward a more intense and acute recognition of the prize happened in 1952. The announcement on Thursday, November 6, that that year's Nobel Prize in Literature would be awarded to François Mauriac resulted in two photographs of the laureate on the Friday front page of *Le Figaro*: one portrait of Mauriac himself and one photo of him being congratulated by the Swedish ambassador in Paris. This front page also included a long article on the prize decision ("Le prix Nobel de littérature," 1952), which was followed up on the last page with a signed article discussing the laureate's work (Prasteau 1952), an unsigned text presenting Mauriac's biography ("Biographie de François Mauriac," 1952), and a box of facts listing all the eight French Nobel laureates in Literature ("François Mauriac," 1952).

This intense recognition is not totally surprising, considering that Mauriac was a very visible intellectual in the French public sphere at the time—especially for readers of *Le Figaro*. In the month leading up to the announcement of his award, the writer and journalist contributed with several long, personally written chronicles on current affairs placed in the top-left corner of the front pages. Some of these articles were even announced the day before with a little front-page box broadcasting "TOMORROW: François Mauriac" (Mauriac 1952a, 1952b and 1952c; "DEMAIN: François Mauriac," 1952, my translation). The 1952 laureate was one of *Le Figaro*'s own, and the paper took a tiny slice of credit for his award:

> This Nobel Prize honors French letters and journalism. Everybody knows, in this house, how much he is one of ours. Everybody is familiar with the swiftness and the vehemence of his reactions when he is typing, when a text, a show, a circumstance interests, amuses or irritates him. In a couple of moments, the article is conceived, written, and delivered in full frenzy.
> ("Le prix Nobel de littérature," 1958 my translation)

Every editor and journalist at *Le Figaro* seemed extremely proud of their newly appointed Nobel Prize winner.

In London, the leap in media recognition came a year later. After the quite limited attention given to Pär Lagerkvist in 1951 (a fact that once again confirms the strategic losses of selecting Swedish laureates) and Mauriac in 1952, the *Times* totally exploded with reports on and reactions to the decision to award the Nobel Prize in Literature to the sitting Prime Minister of Great Britain, Winston Churchill, in November 1953. The media frenzy started with an informed speculation published a day before the actual decision was made in Stockholm. On October 14, the *Times* reported directly from the Swedish capital:

> The Swedish Academy, the body that every year awards the Nobel Prize for Literature, is to meet on Thursday to decide who is to have it this year. There is, in fact, very little doubt that when the short official announcement is issued after the meeting the winner will prove to be Sir Winston Churchill.
>
> ("Nobel Prize for Literature," 1953)

This is yet another example of the successful strategy of the Swedish Academy to inform the public of the most discussed contenders before making the final decision. The speculation in the *Times* was based on the Nobel Committee's decision to suggest Churchill's name to the Academy. The Committee suggestion was made public on Tuesday, October 13, and the final prize decision was to be made at the Academy assembly two days later.

The Committee's strategy to make their indefinite decision public created anticipation and expectation, but without making any promises and without releasing all the tension. There was, perhaps, "very little doubt" about the outcome of the meeting, but a small room for the tiniest of doubt still remained. The British public couldn't be totally sure. This first article on the expected announcement was quite substantial. It contained a description of the "extremely lively" discussion on possible candidates that had taken place "not only in Sweden but all over the world" this year. The Stockholm correspondent also speculated on the possibility that the Prime Minister had already been approached and "indicated his acceptance" of the honor. The article also argued that an award to Churchill—not for his political and strategic achievements as a leader during the Second World War, but for his skills and impact as a writer and speaker—would be a very special case in the history of the Nobel Prize. Never before had a world leader, let alone a sitting Prime Minister, been awarded with the literary award. The favorite candidate had a tighter schedule than most authors, which was why, the reporter wrote, this year's final decision would be made and announced earlier than usual.

One wonders what would have happened if the Swedish Academy had changed their minds at the last moment and decided on someone else, for example Ernest Hemingway, who was also mentioned in the speculations. Well, we will never find out, because on October 15 the Swedish Academy announced Churchill's name. Next day, the *Times* was filled with national pride. Two articles reported on the award, and the Swedish Academy's prize motivation was quoted in both of them.

Apart from the fact that the laureate was a current political leader, the reports pointed to two other unique points: this award was the first Nobel Prize in Literature to honor oratory brilliance ("The Nobel Prize Winner," 1953), and it was the first in which "the public [had] been wholeheartedly engaged in the discussion" ("Swedish Academy's Tribute," 1953). Everybody seemed happy with the selection, and the laureate was receiving greetings from many foreign leaders who wanted to congratulate him on his triumph ("Many Congratulations," 1953). Judging from the tone of triumph and rejoice in the *Times*, it is not far-fetched to suspect that this Swedish prize decision was received as yet another—but a very special and important one—confirmation of the recent military victory. Great Britain had won the war, these triumphant reports seem to underline, and its biggest war hero was duly celebrated—this time not only by Britons but by the whole world!

The intense and multi-angled response to the announcement of the final decision showed another constructive effect of the Nobel Committee's strategy to communicate an almost certain decision: newspapers were given time to prepare for their reactions to the proper announcement, to gather angles on the prize winner, and to distribute writing assignments to suitable journalists.

After the immediate reactions to the announcement, the *Times* published several texts on Churchill being congratulated and celebrated for the award. There was one report from a banquet in London where the laureate was congratulated in an elegant speech ("Master of English Prose," 1953), and the day after the Prime Minister's seventy-ninth birthday on November 30, the British public was informed of a large birthday cake "adorned with representations of the Garter Ribbon, the Nobel Prize, and the Prime Minister's many books" (untitled article, 1953a). In November and early December, the *Times* published several updates on the upcoming trip to Stockholm.

Early on, the readers were informed that the laureate himself would be unable to attend the ceremony, since he was needed at the Bermuda Conference with US President Dwight Eisenhower and French Prime Minister René Mayer. It was his wife, Lady Churchill, who boarded the "aircraft of Scandinavian Airlines" on December 8, accompanied by their daughter, Mrs. Soames (untitled article, 1953b). Then the London paper devoted a couple of articles on Lady Churchill's different activities in Stockholm. In the long report from the prize ceremony, we note that the national pride of having your political leader honored by a foreign institution resulted in tender words returning the love. The *Times* wrote that the world "looks with admiration and indeed comfort to Scandinavia," which made the honor bestowed upon Churchill even grander ("Award to Sir W. Churchill," 1953). In these reports, the whole event came forth as a reciprocal diplomatic gesture bringing the two countries tightly together.

All in all, the *Times* published almost twenty articles on the Churchill prize in October, November, and December 1953, which is quite another level of media response than ever before. In terms of attention and recognition, selecting the British Prime Minister was a genial move by the Swedish Academy. The reporters in the *Times* were flattered, and this sentiment strengthened the acknowledgment of the prize's importance.

In relation to the two following awards—to Ernest Hemingway in 1954 and Icelandic novelist Halldór Kiljan Laxness in 1955—the recognition of the prize in the London paper dropped a bit, but the decisions were treated with respect and the works of both authors were duly presented alongside quoted prize motivations ("Mr. E. Hemingway's Nobel Award," 1954; "Nobel Prize for Icelander," 1955). In 1956, the Spanish laureate Juan Ramón Jiménez was given a more substantial recognition—"Señor Jiménez" was actually the first literary Nobel laureate to be presented with a photo in the *Times*' initial reports on prize announcements ("Nobel Prize for Literature," 1956).

Next year, 44-year-old French writer Albert Camus became the second-youngest literary laureate (after Rudyard Kipling, who was only forty-one when receiving the award in 1907), and this decision was intensively acknowledged in the *Times*, with a substantial presentation of Camus' work—complete with a photo of the laureate and a full citation of the prize motivation—in direct relation to the announcement ("French Author Honoured," 1957), a long essay in the *Times Literary Supplement* (Thody 1957), and an article on political effects of the prize ("Appeal for Hungarian Writers," 1957). A couple of days after the announcement, publisher Hamish Hamilton had a big advertisement with this offer:

> ALBERT CAMUS
> Winner of the Nobel Prize
> for Literature, 1957
> His latest novel
> The Fall
> (advertisement, 1953)

The Stockholm prize decisions were definitely big news in mid-1950s London—culturally, politically, and commercially.

And then it exploded again. The award to Russian poet and novelist Boris Pasternak in 1958 led to just as many articles in the *Times* as the Churchill prize had done five years earlier. Pasternak was a controversial writer whose latest novel, *Doctor Zhivago*, published in Italy in 1957, had been refused publication in the U.S.S.R. due to its critical description of the Soviet system. The interest of this award was huge in London, not least because of the strong reactions from Soviet officials to the Swedish Academy's gesture. In several articles, Pasternak's urge and ability to come to Stockholm for the prize ceremony were described and discussed. At first, he said that he would definitely attend the festivities, but when authorities informed him that he would not be allowed to return to the Soviet Union after receiving the award, he changed his mind. The affair went back and forth, and the *Times* followed every twist and turn, with several reports from reactions in different parts of the world.

Whereas the Churchill prize had been more or less directly related to the Second World War, the Pasternak prize was discussed in London as a Cold War award (see for example "Nobel Prize for Mr. Pasternak," 1958). In their strong connections to international politics, these prizes were quite close to the Nobel Peace Prize, at least from an international and medial point of view. The enormous attention given to both of them shows that politically charged prizes were much more acknowledged than other prizes, but this new level of recognition also affected more neutral awards. The 1953 and the 1958 awards helped to lift up the general level of attention in the *Times* devoted to the Nobel Prize in Literature. From the Pasternak prize onward, each announcement has been given a very substantial recognition in the London paper.

This platform of very high recognition was reached a bit earlier in the *New York Times*. Throughout the 1950s, the attention given to the prize announcements was generally higher in the American paper than in the *Times*—and there were a few more peaks of media response. Just like in the *Times*, Winston Churchill's name dominated the *New York Times* in October, November, and December 1953. Alongside the reports from the conference with Eisenhower and Mayer in Bermuda, the American paper published speculations on the upcoming prize decision ("Churchill Reported Nobel Prize Winner," 1953), articles on the prize announcement ("Churchill Wins Nobel Prize," 1953), on different reactions to the prize ("Triumph and Tragedy," 1953; "Award to Churchill Assailed in Sweden," 1953), on Clementine Churchill's visit in Stockholm ("Lady Churchill to Accept Prize," 1953), on Winston Churchill's achievements as a leader and as a writer (Breit 1953; "The Pen Is Mightier," 1953; "Churchill Creed: 'Old Words Best'," 1953), and on his future writing plans ("Churchill's Wife Reveals He Is Writing a New Book," 1953). In addition to all this, the *New York Times* also published the laureate's memoir *The Second World War* in thirty parts between October 23 and November 26 (Churchill 1953).

Whereas the response to the Churchill prize was just as strong in New York as it was in London, the very intense reactions in the *Times* to all the implications of Boris Pasternak's award were significantly exceeded by the enormous attention given to this prize in the *New York Times*. In October, November, and December 1958, the New York newspaper published no less than seventy-two articles on Boris Pasternak, his works, and the consequences of his award. Apart from numerous articles on all the political twists also covered by the *Times*, the *New York Times* also published a whole-page article in the "Book Review" on *Doctor Zhivago* ("A Letter of Rejection," 1958), and a detailed report on how the Swedish Academy and the Nobel Foundation dealt with Pasternak's forced absence at the ceremony in Stockholm ("Pasternak Cited at Nobel Session," 1958).

Not surprisingly, the reactions to the prizes to Ernest Hemingway formed another peak in the 1950s Nobel reports in the *New York Times*. The announcement of the 1954 award was received with as many as four articles in next day's paper: the news report itself, which was placed on the front page and illustrated with a big photo of the laureate and his wife Mary Hemingway ("Hemingway Is the Winner of Nobel Literature Prize," 1954), one editorial reaction ("Mr. Hemingway's Prize," 1954), one article on the novelist's inability to travel to Stockholm in December ("Winner Rules Out Trip to Stockholm," 1954), and one substantial discussion on the fifth American and sixth US-born literary laureate's strengths as a writer ("Hemingway's Quality Built on a Stern Apprenticeship," 1954).

The Churchill prize was not as acknowledged in *Le Figaro* as it was in the *Times* and in the *New York Times*, but it was still quite a big issue in the Paris paper. Just like in the British and American papers, the Nobel Committee's suggestion to the Swedish Academy earned a place on the front page of *Le Figaro*. Since the Committee had decided to recommend Churchill, the article said, the British Prime Minister was the "great favorite" to win the prize. The decision was not "definite" as yet, but "the choice made by the committee is traditionally confirmed by the Academy." Once again, the not-quite-definite signals from the Swedish capital created interest and a little bit of tension ("Sir Winston Churchill," 1953, my translations).

Next day, the Paris paper announced that its literary supplement would serialize A. Duff Cooper's documentary book on the relations between Churchill and Charles de Gaulle, starting the following weekend. And when the final decision had been made by the Swedish Academy, *Le Figaro* published a front-page photo of the British laureate, followed up by two substantial articles on page eleven, one of them with an in-depth presentation of Churchill's works ("Le prix Nobel de literature à Sir Winston Churchill," 1953; Ogliastro 1953).

The reaction in *Le Figaro* to the Ernest Hemingway prize in 1954 was almost as strong. On Friday October 29, a photo of a smiling American writer adorned the front page, and the accompanying article presented the prize decision and quoted the Swedish Academy's motivation ("Ernest Hemingway reçoit le Prix Nobel," 1954). In addition to this, the front page also included a long, substantial chronicle by Jean Dutourd describing the characteristics of Hemingway's prose (Dutourd 1954).

The Albert Camus award in 1957 got significantly more recognition in Paris than the prizes to Churchill and Hemingway. This year, the beforehand speculations were a bit less secure, but *Le Figaro* still published a very visible front-page article on Thursday October 17, the same day the final decision would be made in Stockholm. It seemed like a safe bet to expect a French laureate this year: "Approaching the attribution of the 1957 Nobel Prize for Literature," the article observed, "more and more persistent rumors are heard in Swedish literary circles according to which the distinction will this year be given to a French writer. The name Albert Camus is the most frequently mentioned" ("Attribution aujourd'hui du prix Nobel de literature," 1957, my translation). Next day, the front page was dominated by the news of the final decision: the announcement article on top of the page was illustrated with a photo of the laureate, and a second article below was signed by the critic Jacques Lemarchand, who gave Camus' work a substantial presentation ("Albert Camus prix Nobel de littérature," 1957; Lemarchand 1957). Inside the paper, page fourteen was almost completely devoted to the Camus award, with an article by Jean Prasteau and two unsigned texts presenting different angles on the laureate, including a reaction from the 1952 laureate François Mauriac (Prasteau 1957; "Albert Camus prix Nobel de littérature 1957," 1957; "Un français d'Afrique du Nord," 1957).

In the paper's first reaction to the expected 1958 prize to Pasternak, *Le Figaro* described an announcement strategy that had become a tradition: "Following a well-established tradition, the secrecy of the Swedish Academy members' vote will no doubt be jealously kept until this morning. But Stockholm already knows that Boris Pasternak is the Nobel laureate of 1958" ("Boris Pasternak prix Nobel de littérature," 1958). Both the secrecy of the final decision and the information on the Nobel

Committee's suggestion—sometimes described by *Le Figaro* as a leak, sometimes as a public announcement—followed the customs. The combination of these two traditions made up quite an efficient media strategy that created two different kinds of breaking news annually announced on two consecutive front pages.

The initial response to the Pasternak award was not as strong in *Le Figaro* as the reactions to the Camus prize, but just like in the *Times* and the *New York Times*, the recognition of the 1958 award was a prolonged affair in the Parisian paper. All in all, the acknowledgment in *Le Figaro* of the twists and turns surrounding Pasternak's prize and his attempts to travel to Stockholm was just as intense as in the other two papers (e.g., "Prix Nobel de littérature," 1958; Chatelain, 1958; "Boris Pasternak n'ira sans doute pas à Stockholm," 1958; "Pasternak exclu de l'Union des écrivains soviétiques," 1958).

By 1958, every announced award also had a retrospective effect. The new prize decision was an opportunity to market books by old laureates. The prestigious literary magazine *La Nouvelle Revue Française*, published by the leading French publisher Gallimard, for example, followed up the announcement of the Pasternak prize by marketing its publisher's editions of the laureate's works: "Please note that the essential works by Pasternak in French translation are the *Essai d'Autobiographie* and the famous novel *Le Docteur Jivago*, both of which are found in the series 'Du Monde Entier'" (*La Nouvelle Revue Française* 1958: 6, my translation). Then the magazine seized the opportunity to advertise some of Gallimard's other available translations:

> Please also note the names of authors in our catalogue who have received the Nobel Prize: in 1913, Rabindranath Tagore (Bengali literature),—in 1928, Sigrid Undset (Norwegian literature),—in 1929, Thomas Mann (German literature),—in 1930, Sinclair Lewis (American literature),—in 1933, Ivan Bunin (Russian literature),—in 1934, Luigi Pirandello (Italian literature),—in 1936, Eugene O'Neill (American literature),—in 1937, Roger Martin du Gard (French literature),—in 1945, Gabriela Mistral (Spanish-Chilean literature),—in 1947, André Gide (French literature),—in 1949, Bertrand Russell (English literature),—in 1950, William Faulkner (American literature),—in 1954, Ernest Hemingway (American literature),—in 1955, Halldor Laxness (Icelandic literature),—in 1957, Albert Camus (French literature).

At the end of the 1950s, then, every prize announcement was front-page news with a strong commercial potential. It was also an opportunity to gain cultural capital by boasting a broad backlist of highest-quality international literature.

After 1958, reports from the prize-decision announcements in Stockholm have remained at this breaking-news level of recognition. There is, then, no point to go through them in detail here. But even though the media attention in general has been quite stable up until 2022, there have been interesting exceptions as well as some important tendencies worth noticing in the reception of announcements from the 1960s onward. On the following pages, I will point out some of these observations.

In 1964, information on the Nobel Committee suggestion led to quite a problem when it was reported that Jean-Paul Sartre had refused the award before the final decision had been made. The laureate announcement was planned for Thursday, October 22, but already on Tuesday the Swedish newspaper *Dagens Nyheter* reported that Sartre had written a letter to the Swedish Academy in which he politely expressed his wish not to be selected ("Sartre tackar nej till Nobelpriset," 1964). In face of these news, *Le Figaro* pointed out that the members of the Swedish Academy had four options: (1) they could go ahead and appoint Sartre as the laureate despite his alleged refusal to accept the award; (2) they could resist the Nobel Committee's suggestion and give the prize to someone else (the article mentions Nelly Sachs, Miguel Ángel Asturias, and Norwegian writer Tarjei Vesaas as potential alternatives to the French writer and philosopher); (3) they could postpone the prize decision; and (4) they could cancel the 1964 prize altogether ("L'affaire Sartre," 1964). A couple of days later, *Le Figaro* informed the French public that the Swedish Academy had decided to go with the first option.

Even though the Sartre award thus revealed a problem with the leaking information on the Nobel Committee suggestion, it was also a good example of how the well-advised expectations created a media stir. In October 1964, the Sartre affair broke through the many reports in *Le Figaro* from the ongoing Olympic Games in Tokyo. Two speculative articles were published on Wednesday 21 and Thursday 22 on the potential award to the French writer. On Friday 23, an illustrated front-page article announced the final decision, and inside the paper the breaking news was followed up by a whole page with five different articles discussing the award ("Jean-Paul Sartre," 1964; "L'affaire Sartre," 1964; "Jean-Paul Sartre prix Nobel de littérature," 1964; Stromberg 1964; "L'écrivain le refuse et s'en explique," 1964; Maulnier 1964; "Des académiciens nous disent …," 1964; "L'homme et son œuvre," 1964). With Jean-Paul Sartre's refusal, the institution of the Nobel Prize probably lost some of its prestige, but in terms of media coverage the decision was a success.

Five years later, the *Times*' response to the prize announcement showed a distinct resemblance with later-day paparazzi journalism. The paper's desire to get a direct reaction from the newly appointed laureate turned into an exciting story when it was revealed that Samuel Beckett was on a trip in southern Tunisia at the time of the announcement and couldn't be reached directly ("Samuel Beckett Wins Nobel Prize," 1969). The following day, the *Times* reported that Beckett had gone "into hiding" to avoid the media circus around the award ("Beckett Goes into Hiding," 1969). But then, a couple of days after the announcement, he suddenly appeared in the lobby of his hotel in Tunis. He officially declared that he accepted the prize and posed in front of the photographers with a triumphant cigar in his mouth ("Beckett to Accept Prize," 1969). The London paper was pleased with the Swedish Academy's selection of Beckett, and expressed its joy through a pun: "Godot Has Arrived" one of the headlines on October 24 said, playfully referring to the laureate's famous play *En attendant Godot* (*Waiting for Godot*), first staged in 1953. After the Beckett award, the race between journalists to find the new prize winner and arrange an interview with him or her has been important parts of the Nobel media coverage. Most years, the laureled writers have duly accepted the sudden fuss, and politely answered all the questions from literary laymen. On other occasions, laureates have been less placable, which in itself has created news.

But when it comes to media attention, it is very difficult to beat the political controversy surrounding the 1970 award to Russian novelist Aleksandr Solzhenitsyn. The *Times* reported extensively on all the heated discussions of this particular prize decision, including diplomatic reactions from the Soviet Union, responding statements from Sweden, and the Soviet officials' refusal to grant the laureate permission to travel to Stockholm (see for example Bonavia 1970a; Bonavia 1970b; Bonavia 1970c; Bonavia 1970d; "Solzhenitsyn will go to Stockholm," 1970; "Russian rush," 1970; "Rostropovich is silent on letter," 1970; "Lukacs solo," 1970; "Solzhenitsyn has no passport," 1970; "Solzhenitsyn is not going to Stockholm," 1970; "Scooped," 1970; "Nobel ceremony attack on Solzhenitsyn," 1970). The attention given to this prize even surpassed the *Times*' coverage of Churchill's and Pasternak's awards. And the issue wasn't resolved by the end of 1970. Four years later, Solzhenitsyn was finally allowed to go to Stockholm and receive his prize. In the international media reports from this event, the Russian writer totally stole the center stage from that year's two laureates, Swedish authors Eyvind Johnson and Harry Martinson ("1970 Nobel prize presented to Solzhenitsyn," 1974).

In 1970, *Le Figaro* did not have any substantial beforehand information on the upcoming prize decision. There had been a campaign for Solzhenitsyn, but the paper also mentioned Jorge Luis Borges, Pablo Neruda, and Patrick White as potential winners. On Wednesday October 7, the Swedish Academy suddenly announced— earlier than usual—that the name of the laureate would be revealed the following day. This "rushed decision" took *Le Figaro* by surprise and created tension. The reporter speculated whether the Swedish Academy wanted to speed up the announcement in order to avoid a new Pasternak affair ("Aujourd'hui prix Nobel de Littérature," 1970, my translation). Next day, the final decision was on the front page of *Le Figaro* ("Soljenitsyne a accepté le prix Nobel de littérature," 1970). The acknowledgment of the controversial award continued on the last page, where three signed and two unsigned articles discussed the Academy's choice and Solzhenitsyn's work (K.S. 1970; Simon 1970; Lacontre 1970; "Quatre livres traduits en français," 1970; "Les commentaires," 1970). In the following weeks, the editors and reporters of *Le Figaro* kept their readers updated on the Russian author's attempts to travel to Stockholm (e.g., "Soljenitsyne revouvelle son intention de se render à Stockholm," 1970).

A look on later prizes reveals that national pride is still an issue in relation to the laureate selections. The 1985 award to Claude Simon led to a significant front-page reaction with a photo of the writer. Inside the paper—in the section "La vie culturelle"— Simon's prose was thoroughly presented with a long article by Michel Nuridsany and two boxes of facts (Nuridsany 1985), but the front-page article was more focused on the fact that the laureate was French: "The French writer Claude Simon," the article started, "yesterday saw himself selected by the Swedish Academy for the 1985 Nobel Prize for Literature. France, who received the first Nobel Prize in Literature in 1901 and also holds the total record with eleven titles, has not obtained the prize since 1964—the year when Sartre refused it" ("Claude Simon prix Nobel de littérature," 1985). Three years later, the award to Naguib Mahfouz led to a just as intense reaction inside the paper, with a photo of the laureate, two boxes of facts (one of which once again pointed out that French authors had dominated the Nobel selections), and three articles that discussed Mahfouz as the first Egyptian and the first Arabic Nobel Prize laureate ("L'Egyptien Naguib Mahfouz prix Nobel de littérature," 1988; Le Clec'h 1988; Khoury-Gatha 1988). This information did not, however, make it to the front page. The 1988 award got a much more limited attention on the front page than the Simon award, with only a very short mention and a reference to the articles on page 35 in the section "Lettres" ("Nobel," 1988). As far as breaking news goes, the eleventh French award was a far better story than the first Arabic one.

Another expression of national focus is shown in the considerable recognition in the *New York Times* of the Toni Morrison award in 1993. The previous year, Derek Walcott from the Caribbean island of St. Lucia had been awarded, a decision that was met with both respect and joy in the New York paper. The US writer Morrison was given exactly the same front-page coverage as Walcott: the day after the two announcements, photos of both authors appeared in the top-left corner of the front pages, and these portraits illustrated substantial introductory articles on their respective literary achievements (Rule 1992; Grimes 1993). The difference between the two responses is to be found in the number of follow-up articles. Unlike Walcott's, Morrison's prize was further acknowledged on the day after the announcement with two separate articles on her work and a collection of excerpts from five of her novels (Kakutani 1993; "The Essence of Toni Morrison," 1993; "Poetry in Prose: A Morrison Sampler"). And two days later, two more articles found new angles on the prize decision ("A Nobelist Delves into the Language," 1993; "Toni Morrison Casts Spell for Students at Princeton," 1993).

Another kind of huge attention was given the 2012 prize to Chinese novelist Mo Yan. The laureate's complex relation to the Chinese government and his depiction of China made this prize newsworthy from several points of view. The award was discussed in two long articles in the *New York Times* the day after the announcement (Jacobs and Lyall 2012; Bernstein 2012). Next day, two more articles were published as well as excerpts from Mo Yan's novels (Jacobs 2012; Tatlow 2012a; Mo Yan 2012), and a week after that there were three more (Lovell 2012; Tatlow 2012b; Siems and Yang 2012). In relation to the prize ceremony in Stockholm on December 10, this substantial attention was followed up by two more articles on Mo Yan's position in China and his relation to the cosmopolitan literary community (McDonald 2012; Lagerkvist 2012).

The reactions to the Morrison and Mo Yan prizes were, however, greatly surpassed by the enormous publicity stirred by the award to Bob Dylan in 2016. In terms of prompting media attention, this prize had it all. The laureate was well known everywhere, and many people around the world had a strong relation to his work, but the prize itself came as a big surprise to most experts when it was announced on October 13. The decision did not leave many commentators indifferent: they were either excited when receiving the news or strongly critical to what the Swedish Academy was trying to achieve. The media situation was of course much more diverse and complex in 2016 than ever before, with different kinds of digital platforms and podcasts to spread the news of and react to Dylan's prize. But in terms of traditional print media coverage, more than ten articles were published in the *New York Times* the day after the announcement (e.g., "Nobel Prize in Literature Awarded," 2016; Garner 2016; Marcus 2016; Osipova and Pareles 2016), followed by at least six articles the next day. And this was just the start of an enduring explosion of publicity in the following months—on the prize decision itself, on the characteristics and importance of Dylan's work (in the United States and in the rest of the world; for poetry, music, and cultural history, as well as for social movements and politics), and on Patti Smith's performance as the laureate's delegate at the Stockholm ceremony. The award to Bob Dylan broke several patterns in the history of the Nobel Prize in Literature. And one of them was the pattern of media recognition.

The reactions to the Dylan prize were not as expansive in *Le Figaro* as in the *New York Times*, but the French response was both immediate and intense. On Friday 14, a large portrait of the laureate illustrated the front page, and the headline focused on the surprise of the decision ("Prix Nobel de littérature: la surprise Bob Dylan," 2016). Inside the paper, a complete page was devoted to the award, with another big photo of Dylan and four signed articles presenting and discussing his songs (Nuc 2016; Neuhoff 2016; Delerm 2016; V.S. 2016). The common theme in these articles was the prize decision's fusion of popular culture and the highest form of cultural consecration. The writers stressed that the members of the Swedish Academy had made a brave choice, but they also pointed out potential problems with the surprising award.

But even if the Bob Dylan decision, as Éric Neuhoff wrote in his contribution in *Le Figaro*, may, in the long run, create problematic ambiguities and erase constructive distinctions between different kinds of cultural expressions, the short-term media effect was intensely positive. The Nobel Prize institution had suddenly made itself known far beyond highbrow literary circles. News of the Swedish Academy's selection had risen above the general noise of a chaotically new, digitized, and diversified media landscape. This weekend in October 2016, the Nobel Prize in Literature was on everybody's lips.

Concluding Remarks

When the first prize decision was reported in more than a hundred newspapers in many parts of the world, the Nobel Prize in Literature immediately entered the center of world attention. That didn't mean, however, that the award was established from the start as a stable presence on the cosmopolitan cultural stage. Far from it. The first years of the prize's history were quite rocky. The international responses to the second, third, fourth, fifth, and sixth prizes varied, but the awards to Rudyard Kipling in 1907, Gerhart Hauptmann in 1908, and, especially, Rabindranath Tagore in 1913 made the Nobel Prize a central cosmopolitan phenomenon, almost impossible to ignore by critics discussing international literature. The centrality of the Nobel Prize was threatened by the outbreak of the First World War, but after the war its position was quickly restored.

In the 1920s and 1930s, the award's importance was reinforced and expanded, and after the Second World War the Nobel successively earned a new, more intense kind of media position that included dramatic news reports as well as in-depth comments.

If Pascale Casanova is right when she writes that "the Nobel Prize is a prime, objective indicator of the existence of a world literary space" (Casanova 2005: 73), the trajectory of the award's increasing importance mirrors the modern formation of the World Republic of Letters. Through the first five decades of the twentieth century, the Nobel Prize in Literature did not only enter and became firmly rooted in the world literary space, but it also strongly contributed to establish, shape, and maintain this space.

This was achieved with the help of very different kinds of gestures. In line with the donor's will, the Swedish Academy had stressed literature's benevolent contribution to the quality of human life, but the prizes had also made particular literary cultures take pride in their own traditions and acknowledge the strengths and specificities of foreign literatures. The award to Kipling is a good example of a prize that both fulfilled domestic desires to finally be rewarded and opened up channels for cross-cultural appreciation.

Through the decades, the prize decisions have also helped to invite new kinds of literary value into the world literary space, like the values of availability and wide attraction in the works by John Galsworthy, Roger Martin du Gard, and Pearl Buck, or the value of formal experimentation in T.S. Eliot and William Faulkner. The institution of the Nobel Prize has also invited new literatures and languages into the World Republic of Letters, for example Rabindranath Tagore's Bengali, Sinclair Lewis' American, Gabriela Mistral's Chilean, and Yasunari Kawabata's Japanese, but it has also indirectly stressed and reinforced the fact that this Republic is built on a Western Liberal ideology, not least by selecting politically entrenched writers like Winston Churchill, Boris Pasternak, Aleksandr Solzhenitsyn, and Gao Xingjian.

From a medial point of view, the Nobel Committee and the Swedish Academy have used different strategies in order to keep the prize relevant and interesting. The solemn and royal ceremony in Stockholm was an important talking point in the prize's early history. A bit later, the idea to separate this old-world dramaturgy from the prize announcement helped to produce front-page attention. For long periods, the recurring procedure of dropping the names of possible candidates before the final decision was made by the Swedish Academy created excitement, expectations, and tension—and helped newspapers to be prepared for the proper prize announcement. A crucial aspect of keeping the world interested in the prize has, of course, been the very selection of laureates. Surprising choices have helped the Nobel to stay at the center of attention, and so have politically controversial decisions and selections of very popular writers and public figures.

But the ability to create a great stir in the moment is just one aspect of what has been required by the Swedish Academy in order for the Nobel Prize to maintain its position in the world literary space. If the majority of the chosen laureates had not been respected for their aesthetic achievements, the prize would be nothing but a media stunt. In the long run, surprises and controversial selections are only supporting effects. The Swedish Academy must continuously convince the international public that their choices first and foremost have to do with literary quality. But the institution of the Nobel Prize needs both the media strategies and the notion of literary quality to stay relevant. And these two aspects don't have to go together all the time.

The award to Pearl Buck was a medially important prize in 1938, but it didn't take very long until critics questioned the literary quality of her works. Later Academy members have lamented the fact that Buck was awarded, but the immediate effect of the decision was productive and her prize has remained a talking point ever since, underscoring the difficulties of contemporary canonization. Between the two literary prizes announced in 1920, the award to Carl Spitteler definitely overshadowed the one given to Knut Hamsun—not least because the choice of the Swiss laureate came as a big surprise, whereas the selection of the Norwegian novelist was expected. In the long run, however, Hamsun's name has been more beneficial to the prestige of the Nobel than Spitteler's, despite the fact that the Norwegian's reputation has been seriously bruised due to his sympathetic attitude toward Nazi-Germany. Hamsun is today one of the very few Scandinavian writers who most international critics think deserved the prize.

James F. English characterizes our age as a period of "prize frenzy" in which "the cultural universe has become supersaturated with prizes." We give out much more awards, he concludes, than "our collective cultural achievements can possibly justify" (English 2005: 17). How is it, then, that the Nobel Prize stands out in this prize-filled cultural landscape? Why has this particular literary award, and not any of all the others, been blessed with a special aura? Well, one reason is timing. The Nobel is an old prize. English calls it "perhaps the oldest prize that strikes us as fully contemporary," and sees it as a model for both the Goncourt and the Pulitzer (28-9). In Casanova's terminology, we find that the Nobel Prize in Literature entered the world literary space very early on, which is the decisive reason why it played a foundational role in forming the twentieth-century World Republic of Letters. Decade by decade, the Swedish Academy has managed to maintain this position, making the Nobel Prize a permanent central presence in the consecration of contemporary world literature.

3

Encompassing Everything: The Scope of the Prize

Alfred Nobel had a vision. With his economically significant, international literary prize he wanted to create a united, cross-cultural space in which literary achievements from all over the world could be acknowledged, compared, and distributed. In positioning the literary prize alongside three different awards in Physics, Chemistry, and Medicine, the donor let the scientific virtues of objectivity and utility spill over to the field of literature. These imported virtues strengthened the idea that literary achievements written in different languages and disparate cultural contexts *could* be compared and evaluated side by side, and that the most valuable text published anywhere in the past year *could* be identified.

This steady belief in universal values is distinctly confirmed by the inclusion of a fifth category of praise and reward, the Peace Prize. Scientific achievements, aesthetic contributions, and diplomatic efforts were all seen as possible to assess, compare, and stratify. It's this steady universalism that made Nobel emphasize in his will that he wanted the most deserving candidates to be awarded, regardless of their nationality and their sex (Rydén and Westerström 2018: 531f).

But despite his fundamentally cosmopolitan outlook on science, literature, and international relations, Alfred Nobel still thought about his home country. It was important to him that the prize decisions were to be made by Swedish experts and that the awards were to be handed out in Stockholm, apart from the Peace Prize, which was given to the other half of the Swedish-Norwegian union. Nobel had spent most of his career abroad, but he wanted to place his fortune in his native country. This way, his great individual achievements would give Sweden and Norway a golden opportunity to earn a respectable position on the international stage.

Alfred Nobel's life coincided with the era of world expositions, to which nations from all over the world were invited to show their best achievements in a number of different fields. In London (1851 and 1862), Paris (1855, 1867, 1878, 1889), Vienna (1873), Philadelphia (1876), Melbourne (1880–81), Barcelona (1888), and Chicago (1893), international stages were established in which particular nations could boast their contributions to the world. Another expression of this general mixture of nationalist and internationalist sentiments was Pierre de Coubertin's revival of the Olympic Games. The first modern, international Olympic Games were held in Athens in April 1896, seven months before Alfred Nobel died. Science, literature, and peace cannot perhaps be placed under the Olympic motto of "citius, altius, fortius" (faster, higher, stronger), but Nobel's idea of five international prizes shares Coubertin's celebration of achievements, improvement, and resourcefulness. These two spectacular international manifestations both originate from the conviction that various kinds of efforts can be compared and ranked—across national and cultural borders. Cultural prizes, James F. English writes, involve a "strange practice" of equating "the artist with the boxer or discus-thrower, by a conception of art as a content or competition" (English 2005: 2).

To a large extent, then, the idea of the Nobel Prize is typical of its time. The Swedish prize institution poignantly illustrates the Zeitgeist of "world projects," as media archaeologist Markus Krajewski calls the many large-scale endeavors to bring order to the world launched at the beginning of the twentieth century (Krajewski 2014). A clear sign that Alfred Nobel's vision was far from unique is the fact that among the nominees for the first Nobel Prize in Literature we find Hungarian intellectual Franz Kemény and his recently published book *Entwurf einer internationalen Gesamt-Akademie, Welt-Akademie* (Draft of an international world academy), an ambitious work arguing that the modern age needs a transnational academy with the whole world as its scope of practice (Svensén 2001a: 7 and 8; cf. Richter 2023).

World Ambitions

Luckily for Nobel's vision, the Swedish Academy was led at the time by the literary critic Carl David af Wirsén. Ever since he was appointed Permanent Secretary of the Academy in 1884, he had fought against Swedish provinciality and promoted an international, transcultural perspective on literary history and contemporary literature. His interests lay mainly in the big European tradition, with which he was convinced that domestic Swedish authors were unable to compete. This attitude gave him long-standing enemies. The leading Swedish critic Oscar Levertin was one of them. The most celebrated poet of the 1890s, Verner von Heidenstam, was another. Wirsén's worst enemy, however, was a fellow cosmopolitan, Sweden's most notorious writer at the time, August Strindberg.

Wirsén's posthumous reputation has been harsh. He is almost always seen as an old-fashioned moralist, a stern defender of outdated literary values and a sworn enemy of the new, modern, and innovative generation of authors, who have since then enjoyed a firmly canonized position in the written history of Swedish literature (cf. Espmark 1986; Rydén 2010; Rydén and Westerström 2018). From a twenty-first-century world literary perspective, however, this negative assessment of Wirsén's must be at least partly challenged. He was, after all, "the internationalist in an era of nationalism," as his biographer Per Rydén phrases it (Rydén 2010: 577, my translation). Wirsén's stubborn internationalism has had quite a strong and beneficial influence on Swedish culture—it was exactly this attitude that made the Nobel Prize in Literature come to life.

Wirsén's international approach can be compared with that of the leading literary scholar at the time, Henrik Schück, professor of Literary Studies at Uppsala University.

In managing to establish an international literary perspective on the academic study of literary history, Schück has been, in retrospect, celebrated for saving Swedish literary education from provincialism and nationalism. Ever since Schück's reformation of the discipline, students haven't been able to study Swedish literature separately at Swedish universities. Domestic literary history has always been read in relation to foreign literature, a tradition that aligns well with recent developments in international literary studies. Schück and Wirsén disagreed on many things, but they did share an inclusive interest in foreign literatures at the expense of nationalist literary sentiments and limitations. What Schück fought for at Swedish universities, Wirsén promoted in newspaper coverage and in the Swedish Academy. "An Academy whose task it is to assess the literature of its own country," he wrote in 1897, "cannot do without deep knowledge of the most excellent achievements of foreign literature" (Rydén 2010: 534, my translation). According to both Wirsén and Schück, Swedish literary matters were too limited and too insignificant to be interpreted and discussed in isolation.

When the executor of Nobel's will, Ragnar Sohlman, paid a visit to the Permanent Secretary in January 1897 to explain what the deceased engineer posthumously offered the Swedish Academy, Carl David af Wirsén saw a unique chance to establish a link from the peripheral, small, and insignificant Swedish literary culture to continental Europe and its big tradition of classics and masterpieces. The donor's predilection for world literature was exactly in line with Wirsén's tastes and ambitions. But the timing was also strategically perfect for the Swedish Academy and its Permanent Secretary. Wirsén had been in trouble, and his power was beginning to fade, and so was the reputation of the royal institution he was leading. The large donation from Alfred Nobel's estate was a golden opportunity for Wirsén to retain his esteem and reinforce his position at the center of Swedish literary culture.

In Wirsén's view, Alfred Nobel's money placed a great responsibility in the lap of the Swedish Academy. If the eighteen Swedish intellectuals were to fail to deal with Nobel's will in a constructive and professional way, they would deprive the most important contemporary authors of a unique chance to earn an exceptional but well-deserved recognition. In a poem he publicly read at the first prize ceremony in 1901, Wirsén reminded the present Academy members and other dignitaries that this new responsibility, as it was stated in the donor's will, concerned humankind. In executing the task to annually select a laureate, the members had accepted to look beyond their own interests and work for the "generally good" (Rydén 2010: 578, my translation). But Wirsén also admitted that the donation gave the Academy a great opportunity to, all of a sudden, occupy a powerful position "within world literature" (Schück 1939: 521). Nobel's last will gave the sitting members the chance of a lifetime to make a lasting international impression, and to pass this influence on to future generations of Swedish intellectuals.

Wirsén's enthusiastic willingness to let the eighteen members of the Swedish Academy realize Nobel's idea of a world literary prize was not at all commonly shared. On the contrary, his eagerness to accept the task of distributing Nobel's money according to the conditions stated in the will met a strong opposition. Literary critic Oscar Levertin thought that Wirsén's criticism generally treated dead authors better than living ones, and foreigners more honestly than Swedes. (cp. Rydén 2010: 583) If they accepted to administer the prize, the members risked letting Wirsén's preference of foreign literature take its hold on the collected work of the Academy. The pivotal poet of the new generation, Verner von Heidenstam, painted a gloomy picture of the future, in which mediocre foreign writers were awarded while worthy Swedish authors were excluded from the Academy's attention (Rydén 2010: 544f). Another opposition, sharper and much more painful for the deeply conservative Wirsén, came from the Swedish king. Oscar II was strongly opposed to the idea that Swedish money should leave the country: it would be "unpatriotic" by the Academy to award foreign authors (Rydén 2010: 526, my translation). He even called on the donor's nephew Emanuel Nobel, urging him to stop the prize. Later on, when Wirsén had won this battle and Nobel's last will eventually was executed by the Academy, Oscar II refused to attend the first prize ceremony in 1901, where he was supposed to hand out the prize to Sully Prudhomme.

Other protests came from within the Swedish Academy. Several of the members thought that the prize was at odds with the institution's task to support Swedish culture, Swedish literature, and the Swedish language. The new mission ordered by the wealthy engineer went beyond the original commitment designed in the late eighteenth century by Gustav III. Historian Carl Gustaf Malmström, for example, feared that all the work necessary in administrating the international prize would make the Academy neglect the important domestic issues that its "royal founder entrusted her consideration and care." The new, enormous task would "transform the institution from a Swedish academy to a cosmopolitan literary tribunal" (Schück 1939: 517f).

Despite Carl David af Wirsén's negative aftermath, not least among later Academy members, the result of his energetic persistence and successful struggle to realize Nobel's vision has been far from lamented. It was not, of course, an easy task to launch and establish—from scratch—a widely respected international prize in literature. In Le Figaro, E.M. de Vogüé acknowledged this huge challenge in 1907 when commenting on the selection of the first British laureate, Rudyard Kipling: "Their choices require a bit of diplomacy, of the kind that harms no-one. As distributers of a worldwide prize, they need the fair elegance to successively salute the genius of each people" (de Vogüé 1907, my translation). Most later members of the Academy have agreed that the Nobel Prize has been constructive in giving Sweden a prominent position on the international literary field, and in rendering the Swedish Academy a unique international influence. In essence, they are quite happy that Wirsén took up the fight for a cosmopolitan outlook on literature.

And Wirsén's internationalism quickly became an axiomatic attitude through which a confident belief in a very wide outreach grew strong. His successor as the Academy's Permanent Secretary, historian Harald Hjärne, argued in 1914 that the Nobel Committee's task was to acknowledge an overriding, common culture beyond particular conditions and expressions. The Nobel Prize in Literature should reward "generally human objectives and conditions" rather than nationally anchored achievements (Espmark 1986: 41, my translation). The universal ambition was underlined in 1922 by the next secretary, writer Per Hallström, who reminded the Academy that the prize was "intended for the whole world's diverse literature" (Svensén 2001b: 30, my translation). Despite the fact that Hallström nursed a deeply rooted skepticism toward all things French, and a distinctly dismissive attitude toward American culture and literature, he confidently took on the role of being an expert of all the world's literature. Apart from his numerous reports on a wide range of very different authors in relation to prize decisions, this self-appointed overall expertise was put to use in his gigantic project *Världslitteraturen— de stora mästerverken* (World literature: the great masterpieces), an anthology in fifty volumes published between 1925 and 1929, edited by Hallström and two fellow Academy members.

Before Anders Österling became an Academy member in 1919, its Permanent Secretary in 1941, and Nobel Committee Chair in 1947, he had a long experience of introducing foreign poetry and prose to the Swedish public. After long journeys in Germany, France, and Italy, he called himself a cosmopolitan. He translated, amongst many others, Charles Baudelaire from French, Thomas Mann from German, Eugene O'Neill from English, Eugenio Montale from Italian, and Johannes V. Jensen from Danish. He also wrote an academic dissertation on Stendhal and planned to write a doctoral thesis on William Wordsworth—all while he considered Italy to be his second homeland (Westerström 2013: 370). From the early 1920s onward, Österling was enrolled by the Stockholm publisher Bonniers to select and edit foreign novels in Swedish translation for the two series "Moderna romaner" (Modern novels) and "Gula serien" (The yellow series), and in 1943 he edited the extensive anthology *All världens lyrik* (Poetry from all over the world) for the same publishing house. During the First World War, he was worried about the state of contemporary literature: a "world literature in Goethe's sense," he wrote in 1916, "is unthinkable as long as the literatures from the different countries adore the idea of the nation and carry it in front of themselves as a sharpened sword" (Westerström 2013: 334, my translation). For Österling, administrating the Nobel Prize in Literature was a means to rebuild and maintain a cosmopolitan literary space beyond the specific interests of different countries and cultures.

The Academy's cosmopolitan ambitions under Anders Österling are neatly illustrated by the fact that the sitting Secretary-General of the United Nations, Dag Hammarskjöld, was appointed as a member of the Swedish Academy in 1954. Until his untimely death in an airplane crash in 1961, Hammarskjöld played a substantial part in discussing and selecting literary laureates.

The European Template

All through the history of the prize, the ambition has been to continually award the best contributions to world literature. But what literary texts qualify to be part of that category? Well, Academy and Committee members have seldom expressed any direct definitions of what they classify as world literary texts and œuvres, but between the lines their arguments, motivations, and presentations reveal quite distinct premises and perspectives. These premises have gone through substantial changes since the early stages of the prize.

Trying to convince the rest of the Academy to accept Alfred Nobel's will to administer the prize, Carl David af Wirsén stressed the golden opportunity to award "the great men of continental literature" with a distinguished honor and a significant amount of money (Schück 1939: 521, my translation). For Wirsén, the laureates he had in mind were obviously male, and they came, just as obviously, from the European continent. In Wirsén's reasoning, the word "continental" was synonymous with "cosmopolitan," and cosmopolitan literature meant world literature. As the first Nobel Committee Chair, Wirsén did not really consider literature beyond Europe as relevant for the world literary prize he was trying to establish. In fact, such a thought didn't even strike him. In line with Pascale Casanova's description of the world literary space, Wirsén's literary interests were predominantly French, a fact that is apparent in the way he handled the first prize.

If we compare this early establishing of what kind of authors are suited for the Nobel Prize with David Damrosch's three categories of world literature—classics, masterpieces, and "windows on the world"—Wirsén's ideal is easily defined (Damrosch 2003: 15). He was not interested in experiencing new cultural perspectives through poetry, narratives, and dramatic texts. Literature should contribute to universal and existential reflections, not to insights into cultural relativity. Literature should build upon what you already knew as a cultivated and well-read European, not give you radically new ideas on life, society, and the world. Wirsén would have loved to acknowledge classics. Quite often, he lamented the state of contemporary literature and argued that the best literary texts were written a long time ago. But he could not, of course, award the Stendhals, Shakespeares, and Goethes. All he could hope for was to be able to identify one or two future classics. All he could do was to search for the contemporary masterpieces written in the great European literary tradition.

Carl David af Wirsén was of course far from unique in his inclination to equal world literature with the canonical European tradition. On the contrary, his Eurocentric perspective on literature was very much the norm in his cultural context. When one of his most fierce enemies, Oscar Levertin, criticized the Academy for not giving the first Nobel Prize to Henrik Ibsen, his argument was that the Norwegian playwright was "known from the North Cape to Messina—he is played everywhere" (Rydén 2010: 594, my translation). The definition of "everywhere" is clear: it means all over Europe.

Even though Wirsén was criticized for being conservative, limited, and stubborn in his literary tastes, his fundamental view on cosmopolitan literature lingered on in the Academy long after his death. In reviewing the proposal to give Rabindranath Tagore the prize in 1913, Per Hallström pointed out that the Bengali poet wrote in a classic style, despite the fact that he came from "a more primitive culture than ours" (Rydén and Westerström 2018: 229–30, my translation). Hallström was oriented toward German rather than French literature, but just like Wirsén's, his literary interest was focused on European masterpieces. When discussing Luigi Pirandello's *Sei personaggi in cerca d'autore* (*Six Characters in Search of an Author*) in 1934, for instance,

Hallström was not totally convinced of its merits: "The play is not a firm and complete masterpiece," he concluded (Rydén and Westerström 2018: 333, my translation). It is Hallström's strong tendency to equate the canonical European literary tradition with world literature that explains his negative attitude to North American literature. For him, the "youthfully abortive" US culture suffered from "spiritual unoriginality" and "flatness" (Svensén 2001b: 154, my translation), and it is not until he reads Sinclair Lewis's satirical portrayal of these national characteristics in his novel *Babbitt* that Hallström finds a worthy North American candidate.

In order to construct a canon of contemporary world literature with a wide credibility, the members of the Swedish Academy have continually been faced with the issue of balance. A mechanical system of even distribution of honors between countries, cultures, and languages would of course ruin the Academy's desirable role as neutral, qualified, and independent, but a too evident pattern of preferences would give the impression of cultural bias toward certain literary traditions. Such an impression would be very destructive for the status of the prize.

In the first decade of the prize's history, a kind of rotation principle was established: "as far as it is possible," the Committee writes in 1904, "the Nobel prizes should gradually circulate between different countries" (Espmark 1986: 149, my translation). This aim toward geographical and cultural balance is evident in several of the records from early discussions in the Nobel Committee. In 1902, for example, Carl David af Wirsén would promote Frédéric Mistral if it weren't for the fact that the first prize went to Sully Prudhomme the year before (Rydén 2010: 603). Even though Mistral wrote in Provençal and not French, the history of the prize couldn't start off with two awards to French citizens. A year later, the Prudhomme prize was still too recent. Mistral was now placed as a back-up name, ready to be quickly brought in should the Norwegian Bjørnstjerne Bjørnson decline to accept the prize. The Provençal poet and writer eventually received the honors in 1904, sharing the award with Spanish author José Echegaray.

In awarding Polish novelist Henryk Sienkiewicz in 1905, the Academy partly wanted to compensate for a negligence of the Slavic languages (Espmark 1986: 29), and in 1907, the Committee's general notion was that the world was ready for an English award. Wirsén promoted Algernon Charles Swinburne, but the members instead agreed on Rudyard Kipling. In their proposal to the Academy, the Nobel Committee stressed that an award to Kipling would not only acknowledge the writer himself and his narrative talent. It would also be "a tribute to England" (Svensén 2001a: 145, my translation).

One of Harald Hjärne's central ideas as Committee Chair was that the Academy shouldn't neglect the smaller languages (Rydén and Westerström 2018: 145), an ambition that resulted in the Swedish and Danish prizes to Verner von Heidenstam, Karl Gjellerup, and Henrik Pontoppidan in 1916 and 1917. But this policy gave his successor, Per Hallström, a bit of trouble. In 1922, Hallström was worried about the distribution gaps in recent decisions. It had been, after all, sixteen years since any of the "south-Romance countries" were rewarded, and eighteen years since the so far solitary Spanish prize (Svensén 2001b: 33). This is why he suggested Jacinto Benavente rather than William Butler Yeats for the 1922 award. And when the Committee in 1930 found five American names among the proposed writers, the argument of allocation was difficult to ignore. No American author had been rewarded in the first three decades of the prize's history. Time had come to expand the geocultural scope of the prize. The Committee eventually decided upon Sinclair Lewis, in a close race with fellow American novelist Theodore Dreiser (Svensén 2001b: 146ff). Two years later, when the first Russian writer was awarded, no geographical argument was written down, but the decision to give the 1933 prize to Ivan Bunin, Per Rydén and Jenny Westerström write, must have been at least partly motivated by an ambition to widen the scope of honors—geographically, culturally, and language-wise (Rydén and Westerström 2018: 331).

The Academy's ambition in the 1950s to distribute the prizes as widely as possible is evident in Dag Hammarskjöld's opposition to this non-aesthetic principle. "I can't avoid getting the impression," he wrote in a letter to Anders Österling, "that the Academy in its ambition to reach national variation, and variation also in the rewarded kinds of literature, is limiting its own license" (Rydén and Westerström 2018: 513, my translation). This critical approach did not, however, stop Hammarskjöld from using the argument of balanced distribution when he supported Boris Pasternak. In another letter to the Permanent Secretary he agreed that since a French writer, Albert Camus, was awarded the preceding year, it would be adequate to give the 1958 prize to a Russian poet. But then, Hammarskjöld added, he really hoped that "the Academy next year, before it's too late, will create balance by rendering an equivalent recognition to the parallel case of Perse and Amers" (Rydén and Westerström 2018: 517–18, my translation). The Secretary-General of the UN had tried to convince his fellow Academy members for some time to award the French poet Saint-John Perse for his book *Amers*. He had to wait yet another year, but in 1960 his wish was fulfilled. By then, the prizes to Pasternak and Italian poet Salvatore Quasimodo had created enough temporal distance to the latest French award.

The problem of balance between European countries, languages, and literary traditions returned in 1964, when the Committee's work boiled down to a choice between the French philosopher and writer Jean-Paul Sartre and the British poet W.H. Auden. The central argument against Sartre was that "only extremely pressing reasons could justify a fifth award to the same country after such a short time" (Espmark 1986: 91, my translation). But eventually—despite the fact that as many as four French writers had already been awarded since the end of the Second World War (Gide in 1947, Mauriac in 1952, Camus in 1957, and Perse in 1960), and despite the fact that only three years had passed since the Perse prize—Auden's advocates were voted down. This time, the ambition to distribute the graces was overruled by other arguments.

But a couple of years before that, one of Anders Österling's central arguments for awarding the Yugoslavian novelist Ivo Andric was to add a new language and a new part of Europe to the list of laureates (Rydén and Westerström 2018: 257–9). In 1961, these arguments were successful and Andric received the prize.

Between Universalism and Pluralism

The early Academy and Nobel Committee constellations generally defined literary value from a traditional cosmopolitan perspective—a normative transnational position that is an option, not a necessity, for certain privileged people but inaccessible for others (cf. Hollinger 2001). This idea of world literature, firmly based on a European outlook on the world, stems from a belief in universal aesthetic values according to which literary quality is a stable phenomenon that exists beyond cultural, linguistic, and political differences. And as James F. English has shown, the rise of cultural prizes in the twentieth century is intimately connected to this universalist idea of art as autonomous and transcendent: "the ideas of timelessness and immortality, in particular," he concludes, "are invoked constantly in the discourse of and about them" (English 2005: 49).

The idea of cosmopolitan universalism remained strongly dominant in the prize discussions and decisions up until the mid-1960s, but when Anders Österling was succeeded by Karl Ragnar Gierow as Permanent Secretary, a change toward a less normative and more inclusive definition of literature was successively established. This development followed the observations made by Henri Peyre in the collective American assessment of the first fifty years of the Nobel Prizes in 1951. "It is meaningless to say," the expert in French literature wrote, "that the Academy should grant the prizes only 'for distinguished literary achievement', for not five men will agree on the definition of those words." Instead of pretending to award absolute and universal aesthetic values, the Swedish Academy should nurse the ambition to widely distribute the prizes geographically and culturally: "I would like the emphasis to be shifted away from France, England and America, whose writers are abundantly recognized, to smaller countries whose writers are in danger of remaining long unnoticed" (Peyre 1951: 213).

Gierow, who was appointed Permanent Secretary in 1964 and became Nobel Committee Chair in 1970, was the leading force behind the culturally inclusive symposia in English arranged by the Swedish Academy in the late 1960s. One of these ambitious conferences with intellectuals, scholars, and writers from different parts of the world was devoted to the "problems of international literary understanding," another focused on literary translation, and a third symposium discussed the "place of value in a world of facts" (Rydén and Westerström 2018: 648; Gyllensten 2000: 208). These international conferences were no doubt a great asset for Gierow in his annual challenge to lead the Committee's selection process.

During his time as Chair, Karl Ragnar Gierow initiated a thorough re-evaluation of the Eurocentric history of the prize decisions (Gyllensten 2000: 262). A world literary prize, he argued, cannot restrict its selections to authors from one or two continents, but must acknowledge literary achievements made in all of them. As a result, external experts were engaged to write reports on literatures that Nobel Committee members were not very familiar with. In 1973, future member and Chair Per Wästberg filed his report on African literature, focusing on the Nobel candidates Léopold Sédar Senghor, Wole Soyinka, and Chinua Achebe (Wästberg 2020: 314). The culturally pluralist attitude was perhaps most concretely manifested in the prize motivations from the early 1970s. Chilean poet Pablo Neruda is given the honors in 1971 for a poetry that "brings alive a continent's destiny and dreams," and Australian novelist and playwright Patrick White is awarded in 1973 for introducing "a new continent into literature" ("The Nobel Prize," 2022). These motivations are not based on universalist ideas of essential literary qualities, but on the notion of a common human need for cultural multiplicity. The writings of Neruda and White are not primarily honored because they are classics or masterpieces, but because they give voice to new perspectives and offer new windows on the world. Writing from South American and Australian perspectives is in itself a literary value.

Gierow was not the first Academy member to view the Nobel task as an expansion of the circle of attention toward unnoticed literatures and (for Western readers) hidden treasures in different corners of the world. His take on world literature had its precursors. An early example of a pluralist decision is the Rabindranath Tagore prize in 1913. Even though the Bengali author was specifically rewarded for his English translations, the honors were first and foremost intended to bestow an œuvre firmly rooted in a South Asian literary tradition and culture (cf. Rydén and Westerström 2018: 230). This is also how the international press interpreted the award. Reporting on the award in *Le Figaro* the day after it was announced, critic Maurice Leudet pointed out that Tagore hadn't, until now, enjoyed a "worldwide reputation," but "in Bengal he is considered eminent" (Leudet 1913, my translations). After the death of Carl David af Wirsén in 1912, the 1913 prize was a break away from the great continental European tradition that the first Committee Chair promoted. Together with the Scandinavian awards to Heidenstam, Gjellerup, Pontoppidan, and Hamsun in 1916, 1917, and 1920, the first non-European Nobel Prize in Literature was part of a slightly adjusted focus toward less traditionally central literatures.

The most important Academy member behind the 1913 prize was Per Hallström. It was Hallström who wrote, two decades before he was appointed Permanent Secretary, the expert review of British author T. Sturge Moore's proposal to give Rabindranath Tagore the award, and his evaluation of the Bengali poet made fellow Academy member Verner von Heidenstam reply in a letter: "What you say about the Indian sounds good. It is necessary to break the routine in one way or another" (Espmark 2001: 137, my translation). With the help of Hallström's review, Heidenstam then phrased a strong argument for Rabindranath Tagore in the Nobel Committee during the fall of 1913 (cf. Rydén and Westerström 2018: 225), and after these successful negotiations Hallström contently concluded in a letter to another Academy member: "I think this is the most festive moment in the history of the Nobel institution" (Rydén and Westerström 2018: 226, my translation). In his public introduction to Rabindranath Tagore's œuvre in 1914, Hallström stressed the fact that the newly awarded author wrote in quite another tradition than the general European reader was used to. Unlike his narrative prose, the Swedish intellectual argued, the laureate's poetic and dramatic works were not influenced by the Western literary tradition (Hallström 1914: 327). Awarding Tagore for his poetry collection *Gitanjali* was clearly intended to widen the scope of the prize.

As shown in Chapter 2 (pp. 27–8), the award to Tagore did stir a great interest and, at least temporarily, expanded the focus of international literary discourse in Europe,

North America, and East Asia. When Kjell Espmark calls the 1913 prize "a half-hearted attempt to include Asian linguistic areas" (Espmark 2021: 43), he is, I think, a bit ungenerous to the pioneering ideas of Hallström and von Heidenstam. But it is difficult to deny that the 1913 prize decision has been used as an "alibi" against accusations of Eurocentrism, as Swedish scholar Stefan Jonsson expresses it (Jonsson 2013). The Tagore award indeed remained the only non-European and non-North American award for thirty-two years, and the only Asian literary Nobel for another twenty-three.

As Committee Chair, a position he started in 1922, Per Hallström continued to work toward a more inclusive view of world literature. In his first Committee address to the Academy, he warned his fellow members that "the Nobel prize, which is intended for the whole world's varied literature, decided by Nobel's compatriots, successively could be restricted to a more limited general circle." He added:

> We must be careful when evaluating those literary works that are more foreign to us. They cannot only be read from our own demands, but must also be evaluated from their own particular conditions and from what we suspect they mean in the contexts in which they were written, where literary traditions and common cultural perspectives make their content and form accessible.
>
> (Svensén 2001b: 30, my translation)

This attitude was supported by literary historian Henrik Schück, who argued in 1933 that it was wrong to "strictly apply our Swedish literary taste" on literary works from other cultures and traditions. As far as possible, the Nobel Committee should "try to understand and appreciate their view on literature" (Espmark 1986: 74).

Another precursor of a pluralist view of literature was Hjalmar Hammarskjöld, a very special member of the Academy and the Nobel Committee. Hammarskjöld was Prime Minister of Sweden during the turbulent years 1914–17. A year after he was forced to resign in March 1917, he was appointed to the Swedish Academy, and from 1932 he was a member of the Nobel Committee. Despite his aristocratic background and his political power, Hammarskjöld described himself as representing the people in the work and negotiations of the Academy and the Committee. In relation to the cultural elite of intellectuals, professors, and writers, he wanted to represent the ordinary reader in the literary discussions and decisions. Even though this publicly displayed self-image probably was a case of false humility (cf. Svegfors 2010: 93–4), Hammarskjöld's contributions to the Academy's work did indeed stand out, especially when it comes to suggesting Nobel laureates from different parts of the world.

More than a decade before the first South American prize (Gabriela Mistral in 1945), Hammarskjöld made two propositions to the Committee in 1933: first, that that year's award should go to the Brazilian novelist and playwright Henrique Maximiano Coelho Neto, and second, that Coelho Neto should share the prize with his Argentine colleague, novelist and essayist Manuel Gálvez (Svensén 2001b: 192). Even today, in 2022, the Nobel Prize in Literature has never been awarded to any Brazilian or Argentine author. Hammarskjöld wanted to correct this imbalance very early on. That same year, the former Prime Minister also suggested a laureate from quite another part of the world and with a completely different literary profile: Indian philosopher Sarvepalli Radhakrishnan, who was to become India's second president in 1962. Hammarskjöld did not continue to pursue Coelho Neto and Gálvez, but he was very persistent with Radhakrishnan, following up his 1933 proposal to award the Calcutta professor of philosophy with new formal nominations in 1934, 1935, 1936, and 1937 (Svensén 2001b: 192, 209, 223, 241, and 264).

Hjalmar Hammarskjöld was also Gabriela Mistral's loudest advocate. The poet was first nominated by Chilean historian Luis Galdames in 1940. Next year, Hammarskjöld was caught by Galdames's enthusiasm and filed his own nomination of Mistral. In 1942, 1943, and 1944 Hammarskjöld kept suggesting Mistral—in 1942, he was supported by a nomination from Brazilian writer Afonso Costa—but it was not until she was suggested for the sixth year in a row by a second Academy member, newly appointed Elin Wägner, that the Committee was finally convinced (Svensén 2001b: 307, 318, 326, 334, 344 and 352). Hjalmar Hammarskjöld's continual interest in non-European literature, it seems, did not have the ear of the rest of the Committee, but the former politician had a companion in the Committee Chair, Per Hallström. In his 1940 review of the proposed authors, Hallström stressed Mistral's non-European qualities as a poet:

> In the past, one has solely been acquainted with [South American] authors who have more or less been imitators of different European masters and fashions, but this poetess has undoubtedly an original gift and a strong and distinctive personality. She may be welcomed as a worthy literary representative of her vast continent.
>
> (Svensén 2001b: 311 my translation)

In many ways, the 1945 prize was an equivalent to the Rabindranath Tagore prize in 1913. With thirty-two years apart, these two selections were solitary expressions of a literary interest beyond Europe and the United States. Per Hallström was central for both these exceptional decisions, Hjalmar Hammarskjöld worked hard for the second one.

Both Kjell Espmark and Per Rydén and Jenny Westerström criticize Per Hallström and Hjalmar Hammarskjöld for adhering conservative poetics and therefore being impeding factors in the modernization of the literary Nobel Prize in the 1920s and the 1930s. The two members rejected what Rydén and Westerström call "innovators" (Rydén and Westerström 2010: 292 and 331) and Espmark calls "pioneers" (Espmark 1986: 84). Hallström's and Hammarskjöld's posthumous reputations are good examples of the fact that you can define what is modern in very different ways. No, these two central members of the Nobel Committee did not fight for the acknowledgment and inclusion of the—in retrospect—very important European modernist authors from the decades leading up to the Second World War, but they *did* try to expand the scope of the prize to South American and Asian authors. From a twenty-first-century world literary perspective, this culturally and geographically inclusive view on literary quality and values comes forth as just as modern—in some ways perhaps even *more* modern—than the arguments for awarding Paul Valéry, Hermann Hesse, and Robert Musil.

Just like many other reviewers of former prizes, Rydén, Westerström, and Espmark are aesthetically very close to the Western European modernist poetics that has dominated large parts of twentieth-century literary criticism, confirming Pascale Casanova's strong connection between Modernism and the culturally imbalanced world-literary space centered in Paris, London, and New York. This connection also instructs the much more positive posthumous reputation of Hallström's successor as Permanent Secretary and Committee Chair, Anders Österling. Hallström was not impressed by what he called "the modern monumental novel" of the 1920s and 1930s, and he hesitated in acknowledging the broadly relevant value of the abstract poetic constructions of modernist poetry (Rydén and Westerström 2010). Whereas Hallström found these compositions inaccessible and elitist, Österling was a strong promoter of the Modernist works of Paul Valéry, T.S. Eliot, and William Faulkner.

A more delicate matter is the position of Academy member Sven Hedin, who was an immensely popular explorer and travel writer—a real hero for many Swedish boys with his bold adventures in Asian deserts and mountains—when he was appointed in 1913. In 1902, Hedin had been the last Swedish citizen to be knighted, and in 1914 he strongly contributed to strengthening the Swedish monarchy by ghost writing king Gustaf V's famous "borggårdstal," a public speech for a stronger Swedish military defense held in front of thousands of supporting farmers. Hedin saw Germany as his second home, and he sided with the Germans in both World Wars, which made him very problematic for the Swedish Academy after 1945. Attempts were made to expel him, but he remained a member until his death in 1952 (Rydén and Westerström 2010: 485).

Despite these explicit tendencies toward nationalism and fascism, Sven Hedin was genuinely interested in literature beyond the European horizon. In connection with Rabindranath Tagore's prize in 1913, Hedin became good friends with the Bengali laureate, so good, in fact, that Tagore dedicated his 1928 collection of poems *Fireflies* to the Swedish adventurer and Academy member. In 1938, Sven Hedin was the driving force behind awarding American author Pearl Buck. The formal nomination was filed by Hedin and fellow Academy members Bo Bergman and Torsten Fogelqvist, but it was Hedin's description of the writer's achievement that instructed Committee Chair Per Hallström's words in the review leading up to the affirmative decision. In Hallström's address to the Swedish Academy, Buck was praised for her "biographies of her parents, the missionary couple in China" and her "novels on Chinese farmers," which were "distinctly remarkable" in their "authenticity and richness in depicting a world that is little known and very inaccessible for Western readers." Hallström continued with an argument that distinctly connects his suggestion to Hedin's field of expertise and claim to fame: "These novels are already significant as exploits of exploration, and they include passages of high literary value" (Svensén 2001b: 284). The award to Pearl Buck was clearly a window-on-the-world prize much more than a prize to a literary masterpiece, and this pluralist literary quality was definitely based on accessibility rather than formal skill and mastery.

In his Buck nomination, Hedin was representing the ordinary reader and the literary text's ability to open the door to another culture and society, whereas Anders Österling, who was opposed to the idea of awarding Buck, first and foremost defined literary quality as the ability to master and develop formal literary qualities. Sven Hedin thus both promoted an inclusive literary taste in accessible literature and, in other contexts and situations, a right wing, at times pro-fascist politics. This combination helps the advocates of Modernism—especially in hindsight—to confirm the connection between progress, Western literary experimentalism, and the idea of universal modernity.

After the Second World War, literary Modernism became a dominating poetics behind the prize decisions, which resulted in a distinct focus on the strongest European and North American literatures. In 1963, the *Washington Post* criticized the Academy for neglecting authors from Latin America, Asia, and Africa (Espmark 1986: 170), but the Academy and its Nobel Committee did not have a united opinion on the matter. Academy member Sigfrid Siwertz thought that they should "look beyond the usual big cultural contexts and award someone outside the literary highway" (Espmark 1986: 107, my translation), but Hjalmar Hammarskjöld's son Dag, who had replaced his father in 1954, defended the idea of absolute literary qualities and saw a limited value in the principle of a wide distribution. "Unfortunately," he wrote in a letter to Anders Österling in 1957, "there aren't enough great authors for us to execute the desirable variation and still be fair" (Rydén and Westerström 2010: 513, my translation).

With Karl Ragnar Gierow at the wheel, the pluralist attitude to literature and literary value became a fundamental principle. This is distinctly noticeable in the prize motivations and presentations of laureates such as Asturias, Kawabata, Neruda, and White. The years between 1966 and 1973 stand out as a particularly pluralist period, and the tendency was recognized by the international press. Political controversy was definitely a news trigger in relation to the prize announcements in the 1960s, but the expansion of the prize's scope to new countries and cultures did not go unnoticed. The 1967 decision to award Miguel Ángel Asturias resulted in bigger headlines in the *Times* than the controversial prize to Jean-Paul Sartre had three years earlier. The Guatemalan novelist and diplomat was substantially quoted the day after the announcement. "This Nobel prize," he proudly stated from his home in Paris, "can be an important step for the Guatemalan people towards a more precise consciousness of itself, a great confidence in itself" ("Nobel Prize for Guatemalan," 1967).

A second wave of expanding ambition occurred in the 1980s, with the first Nigerian prize to Wole Soyinka and the first Arabic prize to Naguib Mahfouz. Soyinka's reaction to being selected was clearly in line with the idea of a broader geographical and cultural distribution of world literary recognition. "I accept it," the newly appointed laureate said about the award in December 1986, "as a tribute to the heritage of African literature, which is very little known in the West. I regard it as a statement of respect and acknowledgement of the long years of denigration and ignorance of the heritage on which all of us have been trying to build" ("Selected Soyinka," 1986). Commenting on the Anglophone prizes between 1968 and 1988, expert in British and American poetry William Pratt admitted in the late 1980s that the "geographic and ethnic scope of the Nobel Committee's choices" was "wider than mine would have been," pointing to the facts that Beckett was born in Ireland and lived most of his life in Paris, White was Australian, Saul Bellow was born in Canada to Jewish parents, and William Golding was born in London (Pratt 1988: 226). Pratt could have added that a fifth Anglophone laureate during these years, Wole Soyinka, was born and raised in Nigeria.

One of the risks of awarding authors from neglected literary cultures in an attempt to acknowledge a multitude of cultural perspectives on the world, has been the potential exotification inherent in such an interest in foreign traditions and aesthetics. When the Swedish Academy took one of its first big leaps of expansion in 1968 in awarding the first Japanese laureate, Yasunari Kawabata, Japanese critics were "perplexed," critic Yoshio Iwamoto writes. On the one hand, the Swedish decision stirred a jubilant national pride, on the other, many critics wondered why Kawabata was chosen and not one of all the other domestically renowned writers, for example, the more cosmopolitan Yukio Mishima:

> Why Kawabata, without doubt the most "Japanese" in his artistry, when there were in their estimation other writers more international in their appeal? Could it have been the "exoticism" the Nobel Committee perhaps perceived in Kawabata's work—not the soundest criterion for a literary award—that was the decisive factor?
> (Iwamoto 1988: 218)

This suspicion was fueled by the prize motivation, which stressed the laureate's ability to express "the essence of the Japanese mind" ("The Nobel Prize," 2022), as well as by Permanent Secretary Anders Österling's presentation address, which further described this "Japaneseness" and characterized Kawabata's literary achievements as a "spiritual bridge-building between East and West" (*Nobel Prize Library* 1971: 5).

Less risky was the tendency in Gierow's pluralistic ambitions to acknowledge and appreciate culturally and linguistically transcendent literature. In presenting the 1969 laureate Samuel Beckett, for example, he wrote: "one and the same prize is awarded to one man, two languages and a third nation, in itself divided" (Gierow 1970: 46, my translation). Since the Beckett prize, experiences and depictions of cultural transcendence have been stressed as literary merits several times, most notably in relation to Isaac Bashevis Singer (1978), Czeslaw Milosz (1980), Elias Canetti (1981), and Joseph Brodsky (1987) (see also Pratt 1988: 227).

Gierow was not alone. An important person at his side was Lars Gyllensten, appointed to the Academy in 1966 and to the Nobel Committee two years later. Between 1977 and 1986, Gyllensten was Permanent Secretary of the Swedish Academy, and between 1983 and 1987 he chaired the Committee (Gyllensten 2000: 243). In a policy declaration in the early 1970s, Gyllensten stressed the fact that the Committee's task was to decide between "independent and original achievements, each with its own particular vision, aim and ambition," in short accomplishments that were "eo ipso incommensurable" (Espmark 1986: 101, my translation). Gyllensten wanted to change the prize decisions in what he called a "pragmatic" direction. The Nobel institution should be used to recognize neglected genres and insufficiently acknowledged literary cultures as much as original and innovative authors. After taking over from Gierow as Permanent Secretary in 1983, Gyllensten continued to work toward a pluralist inclusion. To decide upon a Nobel laureate, he wrote in 1984, was not to give a prize to the best author in the world, because "such a person does not exist." For Gyllensten's Committee, the Nobel Prize was not a competition between comparable accomplishments, but a reward to one out of a great number of just as worthy laureates. In the name of universalism, he argued, a "great injustice has been committed" by former constellations of the Nobel Committee. "Europe has been favored," he concluded, and it's high time to gradually correct this bias (Gyllensten 1984, my translations).

Lars Gyllensten's pluralist view gained traction throughout the 1970s and was a dominating principle in the next decade. When he dramatically left his assignments in the Academy in 1989 (the rules prohibited him from formally resigning), as a protest against the institution's non-reaction in the Salman Rushdie affair, his influence on the prize decisions and discussions had been enormous. Gierow's and Gyllensten's pluralist poetics led to a long-standing expansion of the Nobel task, at work long after they left the Academy themselves. In 1986, Kjell Espmark talked about the Nobel Committee's widened area of surveillance. The members were faced, he wrote, with an increasingly more distinct "global responsibility" in their prize decisions (Espmark 1986: 140, 144, and 146, my translation). In his memoirs *Minnen, bara minnen* (Memories, just memories) from 2000, Gyllensten acknowledged this permanent change. It was Karl Ragnar Gierow who initiated the process toward a wider distribution in the 1960s, Gyllensten wrote at the turn of the century, but his ambitions had only recently been fully realized (Gyllensten 2000: 262, my translation).

But an acknowledgment of a geographically and culturally widened responsibility does not necessarily entail a pluralist view on literature. The realization of Gierow's and Gyllensten's vision from the 1980s onward did in fact take place alongside a gradual return to a universalist poetics. It already started in the late 1970s. Artur Lundkvist, who had become an Academy member in 1968 and a member of the Nobel Committee a year later, acknowledged, in an article from 1977 in the leading Swedish newspaper *Dagens Nyheter*, that the "linguistically and nationally smaller literatures" had been underrepresented in the Nobel prize history (Lundkvist 1979, my translation). But this was a pattern, Lundkvist argued, that the Swedish Academy couldn't and shouldn't counteract, for several reasons:

> The Academy is often criticized for ignoring Asian, African, and other remote literatures. But I doubt that there is, as yet, very much to be found there. Those are literatures that (with some exceptions, chiefly Japan) do not seem to have reached the stage of development (artistically, psychologically, linguistically) that would make them genuinely important outside their own contexts.
>
> The Nobel Prize is once and for all Occidental, and it stands to reason that it cannot be guided by other than Occidental values.

In this rationale to keep working within traditionally Western literary standards and focusing on European and North American authors, Lundkvist merged three different statements: (1) that separate literatures by default undergo historical processes of progress from primitive to advanced stages; (2) that literatures that are remote from

Lundkvist's own North-European standards are not as advanced and evolved as Occidental literature; and (3) that the Nobel Prize is culturally entrenched and therefore must build on Occidental principles. Taken together, these statements formed quite a different standpoint than Karl Ragnar Gierow's and Lars Gyllensten's.

Artur Lundkvist's first two statements were built on an idea of universal literary progress. Since Lundkvist's article, such a belief in a universally valid standard of literary quality gradually replaced the pluralist view. In his historical assessment from 1986 of earlier laureates, *Det litterära Nobelpriset. Principer och värderingar bakom besluten* (The literary Nobel Prize: principles and values behind the decisions), Kjell Espmark displayed a strong confidence in distinguishing between good and bad prize decisions. Espmark, who became an Academy member in 1981, Nobel Committee member in 1988, and was Committee Chair between 1988 and 2005, leaned against a universal aesthetic when he un-hesitantly identified "insignificant" laureates, pointed out former Nobel Committees' "inadequacy," and criticized the "absurd discussion" in the 1938 Committee that took the proposal to award Margaret Mitchell for her best-selling novel *Gone with the Wind* seriously (Espmark 1986: 45, 64, and 77–8, my translations). From his historical distance, Espmark dismissed whole decades of prize decisions (81), and praised other Academy constellations for being aesthetically "sensitive" (97). The Committees who awarded the accessible and widely read authors Sinclair Lewis, John Galsworthy, Roger Martin Du Gard, and Pearl Buck were criticized for being "tragically handicapped in facing the rich literary supply" (165).

Espmark's assessment of earlier prize decisions was clearly written from a position within the very institution whose history he was discussing. He was a spokesperson for the Academy, and his strong opinions came forth as expressing the poetics of the sitting assembly. These opinions were based on an aesthetics that placed literature above and beyond historical situatedness on a level of universal literary qualities.

In his memoirs, Lars Gyllensten described Kjell Espmark as one of his opponents during his last years before leaving his Academy work in 1989. The tension between a pluralist and a universalist view on the Nobel Prize was part of this conflict. When working on the Wole Soyinka prize motivation, Gyllensten wanted to include a reference to the vernacular cultural and literary Yoruba tradition, but his successor as Permanent Secretary, Sture Allén, was opposed to such a reference. And since Espmark supported Allén, the motivation ended up being much less specific, with a general formulation of Soyinka's "wide cultural perspective." Even if Gyllensten, according to Per Wästberg, had been strongly against the decision to award Wole Soyinka in the first place (Wästberg 2020: 322), he described, in retrospect, his role in the 1986 prize motivation discussion as that of a supporter of the culturally specific at the expense of the sweepingly universal. For Gyllensten, this discussion illustrated the new power structure in the Nobel Committee and the Academy, with Allén and Espmark in central positions. With this change, focus was shifted toward the generally human (Gyllensten 2000: 242–3).

A couple of years after the Soyinka conflict, Kjell Espmark was appointed Committee Chair, and his aesthetics was evident in the prize motivations from the last two decades of the twentieth century, where universal aesthetic qualities were identified in many of the laureates' works, especially the non-European and non-North American laureates. Kenzaburo Oe's work, for example, was said to create "a disconcerting picture of the human predicament today," and Gao Xingjian was awarded for "an œuvre of universal validity." In some of these prize motivations, however, the universalist and the pluralist views overlapped when a laureate's work was honored for successfully combining cosmopolitan and vernacular stances. One example of this is the Naguib Mahfouz motivation. The Egyptian writer was awarded for forming "an Arabic narrative art that applies to all mankind."

Permanent Secretary Horace Engdahl's famous dismissal of US literature as insular and isolated in an interview with Associated Press in October 2008, was also based on a universalist poetics firmly rooted in a European literary template. At that time, no American writer had been awarded since the Toni Morrison prize in 1993, and before Morrison there had been a twenty-nine-year gap back to John Steinbeck, if we don't count American laureates born outside the United States—Joseph Brodsky, Czeslaw Milosz, Isaac Bashevis Singer, and Saul Bellow.

Engdahl's statement should partly be understood as a political standpoint expressed at the end of the George W. Bush era. Also, his negative assessment of contemporary North American letters was to some extent a critique of the US literary market rather than a dismissal of the domestic aesthetic tradition from Poe, Melville, and Dickinson onward. Engdahl pointed out that the US market was self-contained and nationally closed in an argument that resonated quite distinctly with the revitalization of world literary criticism that had rapidly gained traction in the first decade of the new century, with pivotal works by Pascale Casanova, David Damrosch, and Franco Moretti. When Engdahl criticized American publishers for publishing too few literary translations, he echoed, for example, sociologist Johan Heilbron's observation from 1999 of a very hierarchical international pattern of literary exchange, in which Anglophone literary cultures are much less open for foreign influences than any other market (Heilbron 1999). But Horace Engdahl's critical points were nevertheless guided by a firm belief in universal literary values most likely to be found in Europe. It is not a coincidence, he said, that most Nobel laureates have been European: "It is obvious that strong literature exists in all larger cultures, but Europe is still the centre of the literary world, not the USA" ("Engdahl i AP-intervju," 2008).

Kjell Espmark's universalist approach was further expressed in his and Sture Allén's short introduction to the Nobel Prize from 2001, *Nobelpriset i litteratur. En introduktion* (*The Nobel Prize in Literature: An Introduction*), and its slightly expanded new editions from 2006 and 2014. All three versions were published by the Swedish Academy, who also made them available for an English audience through Erik Frykman's translations (Allén and Espmark 2001b, 2006, and 2014). In these historical overviews, Allén and Espmark repeated Espmark's criticism from 1986 of the 1930s, and they frequently used the quite normative word "masters" for recipients they thought deserved the award (Allén and Espmark 2014: 33, 37, 38, 41, and 48).

Such a prescriptive view on literature is also evident in the Nobel Prize Museum in central Stockholm, where the Swedish Academy has had the chance to present its most significant task. On a series of digital posts, the museum visitors are informed that from 1921 to 1930 "a number of highly successful selections" were made. Between 1901 and 1910, however, the prize was "most often awarded to less significant and now forgotten authors such as Sully Prudhomme, Giosuè Carducci, and Henryk Sienkiewicz." Only two selections from this first decade "are now considered to have been truly merited—Rudyard Kipling and the first female Literature Laureate, Selma Lagerlöf." The sign summing up the 1930s prize discussions echoes Espmark's critical assessment of the decade in *Det litterära Nobelpriset*: "The fact that Margaret Mitchell's Gone With the Wind was seriously discussed as possible grounds to award the prize is often cited as evidence of the Academy's populist approach at the time."

In his overview of the last two decades, *Nobelpriset i litteratur—ett nytt sekel* (*The Nobel Prize in Literature—a New Century* in Robin Fulton Macpherson's translation) from 2021, Kjell Espmark played down this universalist approach to literary values. The 1930s was still described as a dark period in the history of the prize, responsible for several cases of "irreparable neglect," but Espmark was more cautious than in earlier accounts when he called this decade a "somewhat populist phase." The use of the words "master" and "masterpiece" was also considerably more restricted than before (Espmark 2021: 9, 22, 24, 31, and 45). In fact, in this last overview Espmark seemed to adhere to a more pluralist ideal in Gyllensten's tradition when he proudly concluded that the prize decisions in the 2000s and 2010s had "fulfilled the function which the 'pragmatic' policy promised" (26). This pride had to do with what Espmark identified as the two strongest tendencies since the turn of the century in the prize decisions: (1) to acknowledge literature's function as giving testimonies, and (2) to "give justice to more and more aspects" and widen the scope of the award—geographically and generically as well as gender-wise (21).

But Espmark's was just one voice of many Academy members—and all prizes since 2000 have not stressed testimonial aspects or been widening the world literary circle of attention. Explaining the Nobel Committee's work in 2015, its Chair Per Wästberg denied any geographical consideration: for him, the best literature was the best literature, no matter who wrote it and where it was written. "Nation, sex, religion mean nothing. Geography is not our subject," he summarized the Committee's task to find the best-suited laureate among all the writers of the world (Wästberg 2015, my translation). When author and critic Kristian Leandoer resigned from his position as an external member of the Nobel Committee in December 2019, he pointed out a lingering conservatism in the decision process. He had thought that his task was to "restore the Nobel prize by making it relevant in a world which does not accept gender differences of the order of 100 to 14, and does not accept that literature can be written and read only in the language of the colonial powers" (Espmark 2021b: 41). Instead, Leandoer saw a prize institution firmly rooted in an unperturbed male and Western normativity. And he didn't notice any real inclination to change this state of affairs.

In a presentation at a Nobel symposium in Stockholm in August 2022, Committee Chair Anders Olsson argued that "the Nobel Prize is and has always been considered a universal prize." Olsson's discussion was built on a broad definition of universality—including the range of distribution, representation, and acclaim—and he saw the pragmatic view of Gierow and Gyllensten as being "less universal in the sense of accessibility," but "more universal in including writings that were not, yet, widely spread and acknowledged." In interpreting all former attitudes of the Nobel Committees as variants—either successful or problematic—of universality, Olsson downplayed earlier attempts to pluralize and particularize Nobel literature. His argument that earlier attempts to pluralize literary values threatened "both the autonomy of literary judgment and, arguably, the reputation and prestige of the prize" confirms a dominating universalist aesthetics in recent Nobel Committees (Olsson 2022).

It may seem odd that the pluralist view of literary value has lost traction within the Academy and the Nobel Committee since the 1980s. From this very decade onward, postcolonial and other critical approaches to literary studies have, after all, been continually promoting a non-normative acknowledgment of the historical and ideological situatedness of every literary act and text. The recent tendency to replace the singular noun "literature" with "literatures" to stress the disparate particularities of literary production, distribution, understanding, and evaluation is a tangible result of this development. How can we explain the Swedish Academy's overall inclination to go against this grain?

Well, I think an explanation is most clearly manifested in the way the 1980s prize motivations stressed the *balance* between the vernacular and the universal, and in Anders Olsson's notion of an inclusive universality. In general, academy members from the 1980s up until today have not, I think, been opposed to literary pluralism as such. On the contrary, most of them have seen it as their task as Nobel Prize judges to guard the multiplicity of world literature by selecting and recognizing what they have found to be the most universally valuable cases in the enormous pool of specifically important texts. Consecrating a series of texts and œuvres written in incommensurably different situations has been, among other things, to point out the universal value of the particular.

The Problem of Access

A central argument against Carl David af Wirsén's willingness to accept Alfred Nobel's challenge had to do with the Academy members' ability to execute the task. Did the eighteen members really have the necessary skills and knowledge to evaluate literature from all over the world and annually decide upon the most valuable achievements made in contemporary literature? Did they have the required access to world literature? Many thought that they certainly did not, and these skeptics were found outside as well as within the Academy. At an Academy meeting in May 1897, historian Carl Gustaf Malmström argued that the Nobel task was so vast that "hardly any existing institution in the world had the required expertise to execute it with the required expertise" (Schück 1939: 523, my translation).

The limited access to all the world's literatures has, of course, first and foremost to do with language skills. In retrospect, Henrik Schück wrote that Wirsén was being very naïve in taking for granted that the institution he led collectively had enough skills to cover "at least all European languages" (Schück 1939: 511). The issue of an alleged combination of naïvité and megalomania in the Swedish Academy has been raised many times in the history of the prize. One criticism has been, for example, that the failure to award any Russian author during the first three decades of the prize had to do with the fact that none of the early twentieth-century members knew Russian (Rydén and Westerström 2018: 515). And if there have been various significant blanks in language skills from a European perspective, one wonders of course about the ability to assess literature written in all the other languages of the world. These very obvious limitations have resulted in condensed powers and responsibilities for particular members with wide language skills—for example, Permanent Secretary and Nobel Committee Chair Per Hallström (Rydén and Westerström 2018: 218), who read a significant range of (European) languages.

But the question of access is not only a matter of language. Many Committee members have also struggled with the lack of knowledge of and insights into the proposed authors' cultural contexts. The interpretative gaps between the potential laureates and the Swedish reading perspective have been a constant challenge. The annual literary evaluation, Anders Österling wrote in 1950, includes being constantly "on guard when assessing that which is foreign to us, and to value it not only according to our own qualifications, but also in relation to its own prerequisites and to what we suspect it means in its original cultural context" (Österling 1950: 92, my translation).

This classic hermeneutic problem has not only to do with understanding in a rational sense. The big challenge has been to acknowledge and deal with the great variation in emotional access. Deciding between William Butler Yeats and Jacinto Benavente for the 1922 prize, Per Hallström reflected, required a comparison and a choice between the Irish and the Spanish literary and cultural traditions:

> It is easier for the Irishman, with his background in the very intense English poetic culture, to capture our emotions and enchant the lyrical sense that we Swedes have in common with Germanic people in general, than for the Spaniard, who represents quite a different kind of poetry.
>
> (Svensén 2001b: 30, my translation)

The Irish Yeats was emotionally closer to the evaluating Swedish intellectuals than the Spanish Benavente. The Committee Chair urged his fellow Academy members to bear this bias in mind when discussing his suggestion to award the latter. Eighteen years later, Hallström returned to this argument in discussing Gabriela Mistral. The Chilean poet was admired all over her own "southern continent," but her poetry was a challenge for Scandinavians, not only formally but also because it stemmed from a "different emotional life than ours." In comparing her contributions to world literature with European authors like Paul Valéry and Johannes V. Jensen, the Academy members "must get used to finding authenticity in unfamiliar qualities" (Svensén 2001b: 311, my translations).

But the question of access and required abilities is wider still. Many of the members in Wirsén's time argued that discussing foreign literature was very far from their intended assignments (Rydén 2010: 528–9). To be sure, the Swedish Academy didn't and doesn't only consist of literary experts like critics, writers, and professors of Literary Studies. To a large extent, the learned assembly has included linguists and historians whose task within the institution has been to preserve and support the Swedish language and the Swedish cultural heritage. The eighteen members who appointed the first Nobel laureate in 1901 also included three theologians and one scientist. This left quite a limited number of Academy members with required skills to evaluate specifically literary qualities and achievements.

In trying to convince the Academy to accept the task offered to them by Alfred Nobel, Wirsén flattered the members: they were eighteen well-read and highly skilled intellectuals, whose responsibility, by a fortunate turn of events, was about to become significantly widened (Rydén and Westerström 2018: 25). Wirsén himself was sufficiently qualified, at least in his own mind. He had, after all, diligently covered international literature for the Academy's own newspaper *Post- och Inrikes Tidningar* for almost twenty years when the Nobel assignment was dropped on his doorstep (Rydén 2010: 539). This experience earned him respect and authority within the Academy. He seemed to know what kind of work the international prize would require, and he appeared to be absolutely sure that the Academy members would be able to execute the new task without neglecting their ordinary assignments—and without making fools of themselves. Wirsén's provenly wide literary knowledge helped him to win over most of the skeptics, and thereby secure the majority vote for taking up Alfred Nobel's challenge (Rydén 2010: 600).

One of Wirsén's central arguments was that the Swedish Academy would not be alone in the decision process. The members were going to get help, from domestic experts as well as from institutions and individuals abroad. It was settled that no author was to be discussed by the Committee as a potential laureate unless he or she had been formally proposed. The invitation to nominate laureates was sent out widely: a range of academies, university institutions, and literature professors were directly encouraged to send their suggestions to Stockholm. Apart from academic specialists in literature, it was decided that all former laureates were also allowed and encouraged to send nominations. During the first years of the prize, Wirsén discouraged his Academy colleagues to file their own proposals (Rydén 2010: 563), but this remained a possibility.

It was decided that the Nobel Committee was obliged to evaluate every single proposed author. They had to be prepared for surprises. Wirsén arranged a network of handpicked experts of different particular literatures who could be put to work when needed (Rydén 2010: 544f). The external experts' task was to produce written statements of the proposed authors within their fields of expertise, all in order to help the Committee reach its own evaluation of the candidate. Most of these experts have worked from outside Academy and Committee, but it has not been uncommon that a scholar has started as an external expert and ended up as a member of the Academy and the Committee. Often, these former external experts have continued to function as experts from within (cf. Rydén and Westerström 2018: 42).

These practices have, at times, distinctly restricted the range of perspectives, opinions, and tastes in the decision process. During quite a long period of time, for example, Per Hallström was not only Permanent Secretary of the Academy and

Committee Chair, but also by far the most consulted expert in English, German, Italian, and Scandinavian literature. Hallström was an Academy member from 1908 to 1960, Committee member between 1913 and 1946, Committee Chair between 1922 and 1946, Permanent Secretary between 1931 and 1941—and from 1913 up until his death in 1960 he wrote more than 350 expert statements on very different authors writing in more than four languages (Rydén and Westerström 2018: 216, 227, and 236). The system that was intended to secure a wide distribution of workload and influence has thus occasionally evolved into gigantic individual tasks for single individuals, and a very centralized power.

After the Hallström era, the number of statements from external experts increased (Rydén and Westerström 2018: 707). This change also involved a wider range of experts from different parts of the world. When Chinese scholar Tsu-Yü Hwang criticized the Academy in 1984 for being all too Eurocentric, he suggested that they would "take their time to consult experts from all over the world" (Hwang 1984, my translation). The Permanent Secretary at the time, Lars Gyllensten, answered that the process was arranged "exactly like that" (Gyllensten 1984, my translation). But, he added, one of the problems with the consultation system was the fact that the Swedish Academy members also had to be able to evaluate the foreign experts. It was difficult to "choose the right one and to know for certain if the experts are reliable, impartial etc in their statements."

This discussion mirrors a central problem of twenty-first-century world literature education and research. When Franco Moretti, in his highly influential article "Conjectures of World Literature" from 2000, urged literature scholars to pursue a "second hand" kind of literary studies constructing "a patchwork of other's people's research," he prompted a very productive inspiration to seek and use expert help from colleagues all over the world (Moretti 2013: 48). But he left one important question unanswered: how, exactly, are we to know whose research to consult and whom to avoid? What experts in (to us) inaccessible literatures are available (to us), and how do we know if these experts are reliable if we cannot compare them with all the experts that, for different reasons, are not available? It is difficult—if not immanently impossible—to apply the academically required critical evaluation of such sources. From 1901 onward, then, the Swedish Academy's continual use of external experts illustrates a substantial epistemological issue that has been around all through the twentieth century, but that has become central for literary studies in general since the revitalization and increased importance of world literary perspectives in our own century. The Swedish Academy's attempt to take literature from all over the world into account in its annual award decisions thus mirrors René Étiemble's idea that doing culturally and geographically inclusive literary research is to do "the impossible." But this impossible task, he adds, is something that we are obliged to pursue (Étiemble 2013: 102).

But it is not the proposers or the external experts who select the Nobel laureate. Their suggestions and statements are only helpful documents used in the process toward a sharp proposition from the Nobel Committee, and a final decision by the Academy. At the end of the day it is the eighteen Academy members' own evaluation of the suggested authors' written work that determines the result. The Swedish intellectuals must themselves be able to acknowledge, assess, and compare thematic, compositional, and stylistic qualities. In this assignment, they rely heavily on translations (see Edfeldt et al 2022: 81–121, for a wider discussion of translators in relation to the Nobel Prize).

The fact that Henryk Sienkiewicz's work already existed in Swedish translations in the 1880s and had been frequently published in Sweden since then, helped to win him the 1905 prize (Rydén 2010: 567). The famous and widely read poet Hjalmar Gullberg's interpretations of Gabriela Mistral in the early 1940s, Juan Ramón Jiménez in the 1950s, and Giorgos Seferis in the early 1960s, were crucial for the 1945, 1956, and 1963 prizes (Rydén and Westerström 2018: 435, and 512), to give three other significant examples of the crucial role of translations. In the 1956 discussion, Jiménez was not Committee Chair Anders Österling's first choice, but his reading of Gullberg's "beautiful translations" decided the matter (Rydén and Westerström 2018: 512, my translation). A more recent example is the award to Claude Simon in 1985. In a reaction to this prize, John L. Brown wondered if the French novelist would have been awarded if it weren't for Paris-based Swedish critic C.J. Bjurström's translations. Simon's novels are quite difficult, Brown argued, and probably not accessible enough for the Swedish Academy's members in the original (Brown 1988: 208). And the controversial decision to award Italian playwright Dario Fo in 1997 should be seen in light of Fo's reception history in Sweden. The Swedish tradition of staging Fo's plays dated back to the 1950s, and it included a couple of famous theatrical productions in the 1970s. Since the 1960s, several of his plays had been available in Swedish translations when he was selected in the late 1990s (Espmark 2021b: 27).

There have also been cases, of course, when the Committee has hesitated due to the lack of reliable translations. When they discussed Greek poet Kostís Palamás in the 1920s, for example, the Committee members could only conclude that the available translations were insufficient in order to identify the "musical and associative magic" that his original poems were known for (Svensén 2001b: 79). Palamás was proposed fourteen times (every year between 1926 and 1938, and then again in 1940), and in 1930 new Swedish translations were available. Unfortunately for Palamás, these translations didn't display that lyrical magic the members had hoped for (Svensén 2001b: 151–2).

At least in one case, an existing translation has been a distinct disadvantage for the proposed author. Frédéric Mistral had been proposed every year since 1901, and in 1904 Carl David af Wirsén had almost decided to suggest the Provençal poet. The fact that a Swedish translation of Mistral's epic poem *Mirèio* was about to be published that fall would make the decision very timely. But when Carl Rupert Nyblom's translation came out, Wirsén was very disappointed. In fact, he found the book so substandard that he was convinced that a prize to Mistral would be strongly criticized by those who only knew the poet from Nyblom's interpretation. He sadly concluded that his "dear friend" Nyblom had "spoiled Mistral's chances" of being awarded (Rydén 2010: 604, my translation). In the end, Mistral actually did get the prize that year, but he had to share it with José Echegaray.

Swedish translations do not only establish linguistic access to potential laureates, but they also help to acknowledge and arouse interest in their work. An illustrative example of this is the Elias Canetti prize in 1981. Canetti had published books since the 1930s, and he wrote in German, a language most of the Academy members were very familiar with. But he wasn't available in Swedish until 1975, when the early novel *Die Blendung* (*Auto-da-Fé*) was translated by Eva Liljegren. That same year, the author was introduced to the Swedish reading public by a presentation of his œuvre in *Artes*, a literary magazine sponsored by the Swedish Academy (Edfelt 1975). Four years later, this first appearance in Swedish was followed up by two books: Johannes Edfelt's Swedish rendition of Canetti's collection of essayistic notes, *Die Provinz des Menschen. Aufzeichnungen 1942—1972* (*The Human Province*), originally published in 1973, and Hans Levander's translation of his memoir *Die gerettete Zunge: Geschichte einer Jugend* (*The Tongue Set Free*), originally published in 1977. When the Academy decided on Canetti in the fall of 1981, the cosmopolitan European author had thus enjoyed a couple of years of late but significant recognition in Sweden, and the Nobel acknowledgment was totally in line with the author's presence in the Swedish literary public sphere at the time.

It is not uncommon that Swedish translators of future laureates have also been members of the Swedish Academy. Many of the most influential Committee members have been professional translators of prose, poetry, and dramatic works. Three of the mentioned translators above—Hjalmar Gullberg, Carl Rupert Nyblom, and Johannes Edfelt—were, for example, active Academy members when introducing Gabriela Mistral, Giorgos Seferis, Frédéric Mistral, and Elias Canetti to a Swedish audience. An obvious guess is, of course, that these members supported the candidates whose literary works they had worked so intimately with. Some cases are more obvious than others.

The list of authors translated into Swedish by Anders Österling before they were awarded the Nobel Prize is very long. Österling's translations of Thomas Mann, John Galsworthy, Eugene O'Neill, Hermann Hesse, Johannes V. Jensen, T.S. Eliot, Salvatore Quasimodo, and Eugenio Montale were probably essential for most of the decisions made in 1929, 1932, 1936, 1946, 1944, 1948, 1959, and 1975 (Rydén and Westerström 2018: 427, 429, 465; Espmark 1986: 153–4). In the 1950s, Dag Hammarskjöld fought a long battle for Saint-John Perse. He helped fellow Academy member Erik Lindegren to translate the French poet into Swedish, and in August 1960 he translated the poem "Chronique" himself in order to convince Österling of Perse's qualities. Later that autumn, Perse was awarded thanks to these translations and to Hammarskjöld's written expert review from 1955 (Rydén and Westerström 2018: 527; Espmark 1986: 92). In more recent times, sinologist and Academy member Göran Malmqvist was not only the Committee's expert on Chinese literature when Gao Xingjian was awarded in 2000. Malmqvist had also translated several plays, many short stories, and two novels by Gao into Swedish. The most recent one, a Swedish rendition of the novel *One Man's Bible*, had been published earlier that same year.

In some of these cases, connections between particular Academy and Committee members and awarded œuvres are so intimate that you wonder if they don't qualify as conflicts of interest. Taking an active part in giving the most important literary prize to an author you have translated and introduced yourself, is partly to market your own work. Without doubt, such a decision will be very beneficial for your own career—financially as well as in gaining cultural capital.

The importance of translations in the Nobel prize decision process makes Swedish a special literary language in the global network of literary distribution (cf. Edfeldt et al 2022: 81–121). Œuvres perceived as Nobel contenders seem to be more readily translated into Swedish than into author languages. It is, for example, interesting to observe how much more available Syrian poet Adonis (pen name for Ali Ahmad Said Esber) is in Swedish than in English. The most ambitious single work by this long-standing favorite to win the prize, the massive *Al-Kîtab* (The book), has not been translated into English but is available in three expansive Swedish volumes. Adonis has still not received the prize and maybe he never will, but the very chance of him being awarded in the near future might be worth the effort of making his works available in Swedish.

Committee and Academy members have not, however, been totally dependent on translations into Swedish. Other translations have also been helpful. Carl David af Wirsén read Henryk Sienkiewicz in French. He even published reviews of French Sienkiewicz translations in Swedish newspapers (Rydén 2010: 568). And Anders Österling based his positive interest in Boris Pasternak on an Italian translation of the novel *Doctor Zhivago* (Rydén and Westerström 2018: 516). This recurring state of affairs has led to a strong disadvantage for authors writing in languages very far from Swedish. In his critical 1984 article in the Swedish daily *Göteborgs-Posten*, Tsu-Yü Hwang described the special criteria non-Western authors must fulfill in order to be awarded:

1. He or she must have produced the very best literary works in an ideal direction.
2. He or she must get hold of another author, preferably of the same outstanding quality, who can translate these works into a Western language.

(Hwang 1984, my translation)

A couple of years later, Hwang's arguments were repeated by Bernth Lindfors of University of Texas from the perspective of African literatures. It makes sense, Lindfors wrote, "for a small academy based in Europe to limit its awards to writers working in international languages that at least a few of its members can read without the intervention of translators." Beyond these languages, "the jurors would have to rely entirely on secondhand contact with the texts and on secondhand opinions regarding their literary value." Given these limitations, he concluded, "it appears unlikely that anyone writing only in an African language will ever be considered seriously for the Nobel Prize in Literature" (Lindfors 1988: 222). This way, the Nobel Prize not only confirms but also expands and intensifies the hierarchical pattern of intercultural and interlingual literary traffic.

As Johan Heilbron and many others have shown (Heilbron 1999), English is a hyper-central language when it comes to international literary distribution, with a very high literary export and a very low import. French, German, and Russian enjoy central positions, and a couple of other European languages (including Swedish) have a semi-peripheral position. Almost all languages originating in Africa and Asia are very peripheral. They simply remain inaccessible for most readers of the world. In her *The World Republic of Letters*, Pascale Casanova argues that cultures remote from the European and North-American literary centers need to adjust their literary traditions in order to be internationally acknowledged (Casanova 2004: 183). Several case studies support this general observation. Takashi Inoue has shown that Yasunari Kawabata's novels were made much more vague in European translations in the 1960s and thereby gained accessibility for Western readers (Cheuk and Inoue 2022), Julia Lovell points out that Chinese officials started a project in 1979 in order to produce the first Chinese Nobel laureate in Literature through adapting to Western literary norms (Lovell 2006), and Hülyn Yildiz has traced Orhan Pamuk's path to the Nobel Prize via his work at US institutions Columbia University and the Iowa International Writing Program (Yildiz 2022). Already in 1992, Pamuk's world literary ambitions were obvious for some critics. Yildiz quotes an American review of *The White Castle* in which the critic, Güneli Gün, argued that the novel was "a book made for export":

> Pamuk, who has deliberately set out to become a world-class writer, has borrowed the attitudes and strategies of Third World authors writing for the consumption of the First World. Not only does he know all the tricks, he never misses one. His work translates like a charm precisely for the same reason Isabel Allende's work travelse easily into English.
>
> (Gün 1992: 62)

There is, of course, a definite risk that these geocultural adjustments lead to a more or less systematic standardization of internationally distributed literature, a normative process that not only produces a watered-down aesthetics, but also reinforces Western cultural hegemony. The potential glory of a Nobel Prize thus contributes to what Erich Auerbach in 1952 famously described as the "process of imposed uniformity" that "serves to undermine all individual traditions" (Auerbach 2013: 66). The Nobel Prize in Literature is one of the central international institutions maintaining such a process.

When it comes to translations and the Nobel Prize, the first non-European award to Rabindranath Tagore in 1913 is a special case. The Bengali author was available in Swedish through a translated collection by Andrea Butenschön, published with an introduction by William Butler Yeats in the fall of 1913. Butenschön's translation and the Irish poet's foreword probably helped his case, but Tagore was not awarded for this book, nor for his original Bengali texts. Instead, he earned the prize thanks to his own translation into English of the poetry collection *Gitanjali*. The Bengali author's very act of giving access—to his own œuvre, of course, but also through this œuvre to the literary tradition of the Indian Peninsula—was put forward as a central merit. The prize motivation praised the way he had "made his poetic thought [...] a part of the literature of the West" ("The Nobel Prize," 2022). At the time, there was only one Academy member who could read Bengali, linguistics professor Esaias Tegnér (Rydén and Westerström 2018: 81), but the decision to award Tagore was not informed by his expertise (Svensén 2001a: 291–306). The Committee members simply didn't think they needed to consult him. The poet's own translations were sufficient.

Very early on in the history of the prize, a special librarian was appointed by the Nobel Foundation to build a Nobel Library. Since then, his successors have administered and perpetually enlarged the collection, all in order to help assigned experts and Committee members gain access to as much literature as possible from as many parts of the world as possible. Presenting the newly founded institution in the spring of 1901, the first Nobel Librarian, Karl Warburg, proudly called his library "a Swedish world institution" (Warburg 1901, my translation). This collection of books from everywhere is certainly another example of what Markus Krajewski calls "world projects" from the first decade of the new century, closely linked to but not identical with the Nobel Prize project. Wirsén shared Warburg's pride, and stressed the necessity of such a world library for the Academy members and the Committee's expert reviewers in their grand task of evaluating literature from all over the world (Wirsén 1901). But Warburg's grand ambitions were also criticized. Swedish writer Axel Lundegård questioned his idea of completeness. If the Nobel Library really managed to collect "all published literary texts of the world" under one roof, the writer asked, how on earth would the Academy members find the time to read them all? (Lundegård 1901, my translation) For Lundegård, the very idea of an all-encompassing collection of the literatures of the world was both unrealistic and hubristic.

In his response to Tsu-Yü Hwang's critique in 1984, Lars Gyllensten poignantly summed up the problem of access: "We do consult experts," he explained, "but eventually we have to make an independent decision and must then rely on translations. And it is not always the most original and best authors who are translated" (Gyllensten 1984). The Nobel Committee has had very different kinds of relations to the diverse literary languages and literary traditions of the world. There is no way around this fundamental condition instructing the biased prize-decision process.

The Nominations

In order to expand the influence on the award beyond the small circle of the eighteen Academy members, it was decided from the start that the Nobel Committee would only discuss names that had been formally nominated. The necessary qualifications for sending in a valid proposal have been fairly stable throughout the history of the prize. To be considered, nominations must be signed by members of established academies, professors of literature, aesthetics, or history, or by former laureates. This process is, of course, built on nineteenth-century conditions, hardly with any thought given to literary cultures beyond Europe and North America, a fact that has affected the prize-giving process up until this day. As Berndt Lindfors wrote in 1988:

> There is no Tanzanian Academy to counsel the Swedish Academy on the merits of authors who have contributed masterworks to Swahili literature. The rare

individuals and groups who study the literatures written in Yoruba, Hausa, Sesuto, Xhosa, Zulu, Shona, and three dozen other African languages lack a proper vehicle for transmitting nominations to Stockholm each year.

(Lindfors 1988: 222)

The nomination process thus relies heavily on traditional European academies and university disciplines, on cultural structures that simply do not exist everywhere in the world.

The nomination procedures also allow members of the Swedish Academy and the Nobel Committee to suggest laureates, which of course limits the distribution of influence. Quite a few of the laureates have indeed been internally nominated. Between 1901 and 1919, as many as six out of nineteen laureates were proposed by members of the Swedish Academy—Henryk Sienkiewicz, Rudolf Eucken, Maurice Maeterlinck, Romain Rolland, and Carl Spitteler. Additionally, Giosuè Carducci was nominated by Academy member Carl Bildt and three external proposers, and Selma Lagerlöf by seven Academy members alongside thirteen external proposers. But this early in-house tendency is nothing compared to the following twenty-year period. From 1920 to 1939, eleven out of nineteen awards were given to authors proposed by Academy members—Knut Hamsun, William Butler Yeats, Wladyslaw Reymont, George Bernard Shaw, Grazia Deledda, Thomas Mann, Sinclair Lewis, John Galsworthy, Eugene O'Neill, Roger Martin du Gard, and Pearl Buck. This does not mean, however, that the processes leading up to these seventeen prize decisions were altogether internal affairs. Many of these authors were originally nominated by external proposers and then re-nominated by Academy members. Internal proposals are often the results of reflection, research, and reading in the Committee and the Academy triggered from the outside. After the prize to Pearl Buck in 1938, a rule was added that prohibited the Academy to award an author the first year he or she was nominated (Espmark 1986: 41).

For the first prize decision in 1901, thirty-seven nominations were sent to the Academy.[1] Most nominations came from French intellectuals, and one of these French suggestions was a joint proposal signed by seventeen persons. Many suggestions had also been sent from Germany. This French and German dominance reflects Carl David af Wirsén's strong orientation toward the big European literary cultures, especially France, and probably also shows how the Academy arranged its initial invitations to foreign institutions and intellectuals to send in suggestions. The remaining nominations came from eleven other European countries, but none of them was posted in the UK. This was corrected in the second year of the prize, when British nominations surpassed both French and German suggestions.

---

[1] This number and the following numbers of proposals and proposers remain approximations, since it is not always clear in the Nobel Committee documents when an author is suggested by a joint proposal or when he or she is suggested by several separate ones. Also, on some occasions no proposer is stated. Every joint proposal has been counted as one.

The first non-European proposers appeared in 1904, when two professors at the University of Adelaide, South Australia, nominated British art historian R. Langton Douglas. The following years, quite a few nominations were received from the United States—and one each from New Zealand and Chile. Between 1901 and 1909, there are seventeen non-European out of a total of roughly 280 proposals. In the following two decades, the ratio of non-European proposals decreased to 9 out of 265 and 10 out of 270, but the distribution of nominations was still successively widened in the sense that they included suggestions from Canada and India in the 1910s, and from Brazil, Uruguay, Peru, and Panama in the 1920s.

During the 1930s, the Academy experienced an explosion of nominations. This acute increase of proposals included a couple of very large numbers of suggestions gathered together in collective letters, which makes it difficult to assess the total amount of proposals and the balance between European and non-European proposers. In 1931, Spanish literary scholar Ramón Menéndez Pidal was nominated by twenty-seven members of the Real Academia Española, twenty-one members of the Real Academia de la Historia, six members of the Real Academia de Bellas Artes de Toledo, fourteen members of the Portuguese Academy, seven members of the Faculté de Philosophie et Lettres in Brussels, fifty-two professors of roman languages from Germany, Austria, and Switzerland, plus a large number of individual proposers from France, Germany, the UK, Denmark, Belgium, the Netherlands, Italy, Spain, Portugal, Ireland, Canada, the United States, Mexico, Costa Rica, Uruguay, Argentina, and Algeria. The following year, the Academy received about 800 proposals from "countries all over the world," according to the Committee protocol, suggesting US writer Upton Sinclair as that year's Nobel laureate. These proposals had been gathered by a special committee and sent to Stockholm by its secretary Ernest S. Greene from New York. Apart from the nationalities mentioned above, we also find Cuban, Venezuelan, Colombian, Brazilian, Chilean, Bolivian, Peruvian, Egyptian, Lebanese, Palestinian, Indian, and Tasmanian proposers between 1930 and 1939.

In the 1940s, the nominations were fewer than in the preceding decade but more than in the 1920s. In this ten-year period, proposals were sent from Mexico, Chile, Brazil, Argentina, Australia, New Zealand, Egypt, Palestine, and Iran, besides all the nominations signed in Europe and the United States.

In the 1950s, the number of nominations was more than doubled compared to the 1940s. Part of this increase was the explosion of suggestions for selecting Ramón Menéndez Pidal in 1956 ("Nomination Archive," 2022). Ninety-five separate proposals nominated Pidal this particular year—and one of these nominations was signed by nine proposers, one by thirteen, three by fourteen, and two by sixteen. The nominations of Pidal aside, there was still a distinct increase in this decade, a rise in interest that did not correspond with a geocultural widening of the nominators. There were proposals from Venezuela, Israel, Egypt, Bengal, and Japan—and many from Argentinian scholars and critics—but these were a small minority compared to all the European and North American suggestions. Amongst the latter, we notice that fantasy writer and Oxford scholar J.R.R. Tolkien nominated British novelist E.M. Forster, and that newly appointed laureate Winston Churchill proposed British historian George Macauley Trevelyan, famous for his trilogy on Italian general Giuseppe Garibaldi.

Next decade, there was another considerable increase in the number of nominations. Almost 1,100 laureate suggestions were sent to the Swedish Academy between 1960 and 1969. Proportionally, there was still a clear European bias, but there were also nominations from Bengal, Brazil, Venezuela, Peru, Bolivia, and a significant number of suggestions—nine throughout the decade—came from Japanese scholars or institutions, including the Japanese Academy, the Japanese PEN Club, and the Japanese Authors' Club. One suggestion was sent by Dong-Ho, scholar of Vietnamese Literature at the University of Saigon. Toward the end of the 1960s, we also notice several nominations from Persian and Arabic intellectuals: three from Iran, three from Egypt, one from Kuwait University, and one from the University of Jordan.

How, then, does the geographical and cultural distribution of the proposed authors look like? Well, there is definitely a connection between the cultural and geographical backgrounds of proposers and the background of nominated authors, but we find no absolute correlation between them.

For the first prize in 1901, twenty-five authors from nine different cultural backgrounds were nominated: twelve French, three German, three Swiss, two Italian authors, and one each from Spain, Portugal, Poland, Hungary, and Finland.[2] For the 1902 prize, the nominated authors had increased to thirty-four: seven German, seven British, six French, three from Spain and three from Norway, two Russian and two Italian, and one author each from Ireland, Finland, Hungary, and Poland. It is not surprising that the proposed French authors were surpassed by German and British ones, but it is, I think, somewhat remarkable that as many as six different authors from France were suggested to follow up the Sully Prudhomme prize.

If we sum up the whole period between 1901 and 1909, we note that French authors were the most frequently suggested during the prize's first decade, despite the fact that this dominance swiftly decreased after a couple of years. In the first nine years of the prize, thirty-seven French authors were nominated, thirty-six British, twenty-four German, sixteen Spanish, fifteen Italian, eight US authors, seven Belgian, seven Swedish, six Norwegian, six Russian, six Czech, six Polish, five Danish, five Greek, three Swiss, two Irish, two Portuguese, two Hungarian, two Finnish, and one author each from Canada, New Zealand, and Chile. There is an obvious European dominance in this list of 198 proposals, but we also note that the scope of the prize did reach— slightly but distinctly—beyond Europe. Just a couple of years into the history of the prize, the annual award discussions were no longer an altogether European affair.

The first suggested non-European author was the Canadian poet William Chapman, proposed in 1904 by a French professor for his newly published collection *Les Aspirations: poésies canadiennes* (The aspirations: Canadian poems). The second non-European suggestion was a special case. For the 1905 award, New Zealand writer Godfrey Sweven was proposed for his utopian science-fiction novel *Limanora: The Island of Progress* from 1903. The nomination was signed by John Macmillan Brown,

---

[2] Taken together, these numbers—and the following numbers of proposed authors—do not really show the amount of authors suggested, but rather the amount of proposals suggesting authors from different geographical and cultural backgrounds. When the same author is proposed more than one year, each single nomination is counted.

professor of Classics and English at the University of New Zealand in Christchurch—and science-fiction writer with the pen name Godfrey Sweven. Brown managed to manipulate the Academy and bypass the strict rule that disqualified self-proposals. Sweven's work was considered and thoroughly discussed by the Nobel Committee, who found its thematic contents interesting but its narrative style too didactic and monotonous. The first proposed US authors were philosopher Borden Parker Bowne, aesthetics scholar George Lansing Raymond, and poet William J. Neidig—all suggested in 1906 by different scholars from different universities in the United States. That same year, Chilean prose writer Pedro Pablo Figueroa was the first South American author to be proposed as a Nobel laureate.

It is not surprising that these early nominations are hugely dominated by male authors. Only ten of the suggestions nominated women writers, and six of them proposed the same name, Selma Lagerlöf, who was suggested in 1904, 1905, 1906, 1907, 1908, and 1909. The first woman to be nominated was German prose writer Malwida von Meysenbug, proposed as a laureate in 1901 by French historian Gabriel Monod, followed by French novelist Émilie Lerou in 1904, Polish writer Eliza Orzeszkowa in 1905, and Friedrich Nietzsche's sister Elisabeth Förster-Nietzsche in 1908.

In the 1910s, French authors were still the most frequently suggested laureates, but the Danes were not far behind. This is connected to the fact that the Norwegian Bjørnstjerne Bjørnson and the Swedish Selma Lagerlöf had already been awarded in the 1900s, while the southern Scandinavian neighbors still waited for their turn. The thirty Danish suggestions eventually resulted in the joint award to Karl Gjellerup and Henrik Pontoppidan in 1917. The same tendency can be noted with Swiss suggestions: as many as eighteen proposals to award Swiss authors were sent to the Academy up until Carl Spitteler's 1919 award, which was decided and assigned belatedly in 1920.

In 1913, Rabindranath Tagore became the third proposed author from outside Europe and North America after Sweven and Figueroa, and three years later a second author from the Indian subcontinent was nominated, when a member of the Royal Asiatic Society of London and the secretary of the Bengal Academy of Literature jointly suggested the Bengali poet Roby Datta. Within Europe, the distribution of proposed laureates was spread to Bulgaria (Penco Slavejkov in 1912 and Ivan Vazov in 1917), Ukraine (Ivan Franko in 1916), and Iceland (Gunnar Gunnarsson in 1918). A special proposal during this second decade was the 1916 suggestion that the prize should be given to the Pali Text Society, "for the publication of the standard literature of the early Buddhist literature and of the Pali literature" (Svensén 2001a: 351). This proposal was signed by the society's founder, Thomas William Rhys Davids, who was also a member of the British Academy. The members of the Nobel Committee took Rhys Davids' suggestion seriously, and they did not see it as a self-proposal.

The gender distribution was more or less stable during the first twenty years of the prize. From 1910 to 1919, four women were nominated eleven times in total: US historian and writer Molly Elliot Seawell in 1910 and 1911, Austrian novelist Marie von Ebner-Eschenbach in 1910 and 1911, Italian writer Grazia Deledda in 1913, 1914, 1915, 1917, and 1918, and Elisabeth Förster-Nietzsche in 1916 and 1917.

In the 1920s, the French proposals were no longer dominant. The seventeen French suggestions were as many as the Norwegian ones, fewer than the twenty British and the twenty-five Italian, and distinctly overshadowed by German authors, who were proposed forty-five times during the decade. After the war-ridden 1910s—during which Swedish sympathies oscillated between the Entente and the Alliance—German culture made a grand comeback in the proposals, leading up to the Thomas Mann prize in 1929, the first German award since Gerhart Hauptmann's in 1912.

During the first half of the 1920s, US historian Wilbur Cortez Abbott (suggested in 1920) was the only non-European author proposed, but in 1926 the scope of the proposals were widened, with suggestions to award Chilean writer and poet Vicente Huidobro and Uruguayan poet Juan Zorrilla de San Martín. A year later, US novelist Edith Wharton was proposed, and in 1928 children's literature writer Edith Howes from New Zealand and Venezuelan poet, novelist, and historian Rufino Blanco-Fombona were suggested. Also, this year Juan Zorrilla was suggested a second time. There were just two Swedish nominations in the 1920s, but quite a few other Nordic proposals: seventeen Norwegian, twelve Danish, six Finnish, and four Icelandic. Within Europe, the distribution was wide, including a proposal from a Parisian scholar to award Armenian author Avetis Aharonian.

In the period between 1920 and 1929, there was a significant rise in proposals to award women writers: twenty-eight proposals with thirteen different names. Elisabeth Förster-Nietzsche was nominated once again in 1923, and Grazia Deledda, who was suggested five times in the preceding decade, returned continually to the nomination list in 1920, 1921, 1922, 1923, 1924, 1925, and 1927 (when she belatedly received the 1926 prize). Edith Wharton was proposed in 1927 and 1928, and Edith Howes in 1928. Italian writer and journalist Matilde Serao was suggested four years in a row between 1922 and 1925, and Norwegian novelist Sigrid Undset was proposed in 1922, 1925, 1926, and 1928. Swiss author Dora Melegari, who wrote in both Italian and French, was suggested for the 1923 prize, and Spanish poet and novelist Sofía Casanova was suggested in 1926. Italian poet Ada Negri was proposed in 1927, and French poet Mathieu de Nouilles, German philosopher and historian Ricarda Huch, and Spanish writer and painter Blanca de los Ríos were all proposed for the 1928 award. Finally, Spanish novelist and playwright Concha Espina was proposed three years in a row at the end of the decade.

1928 was the year with most women on the nominations list, with seven female names out of thirty-six in total. And one of these seven proposals turned out to be successful when that year's decision process ended with Sigrid Undset becoming the third woman to receive the Nobel Prize in Literature.

In the 1930s, German authors were still very frequent in the list of nominations, but they shared the top position with Finnish suggestions. The thirty-three Finnish nominations in this decade reflect the fact no Finnish author had been awarded as yet. And the surge of proposals throughout the 1930s would finally result in Frans Eemil Sillanpää receiving the 1939 prize. Apart from Germans and Finns, the decade saw many French, Austrian, Norwegian, British, Russian, Danish, and US suggestions—and as many as twelve proposed authors from Portugal.

But the 1930s proposals also included a distinct widening of the geographical scope. Indian authors were proposed ten times: Sarvepalli Radhakrishnan five times, Bensadhar Majumdar twice, Sanjib Chaudhuri twice, and H. M. Benerjee once. Argentinian (Carlos María Ocantos once and Manuel Gálvez three times), Venezuelan (Clotilde de Arvelo once and Rufino Blanco-Fombona three times), and Hebrew (Chajim Nachman Bialik twice and Saul Tchernichowsky twice) writers were nominated four times each. Brazilian (Coelho Neto and Flávio de Carvalho) and Peruvian (Francisco García Calderón and Ventura García Calderón) authors had two nominations each, and one author each from Chile (Egidio Poblete), Ecuador (Víctor Manuel Rendón), Australia (Henry Handel Richardson, pen name for Ethel Florence Lindesay Richardson), Cuba (Laura Mestre), Egypt (Asis Domet), Georgia (Grigol Robakidse), Afghanistan (Mohammad Hosein Khan), and China (Hu Shih) were suggested during these ten years. This cultural expansion is to be compared with the low number of Swedes—only five domestic authors were proposed between 1930 and 1939.

In the 1930s, the rise in female nominations continued, but not, however, in proportion to all the male authors proposed. Throughout the decade, thirty-two suggestions were sent to the Academy proposing female literary laureates. Portuguese poet and writer Maria Madalena de Martel Patrício was nominated five times, while Croatian writer of children's books Ivana Brlic-Mazuranic was suggested four times. Among the nominated authors we also find US writers Edith Wharton and Margaret Mitchell, Venezuelan poet and novelist Clotilde de Arvelo, and Cuban translator and writer Laura Mestre. Three Finnish female writers were suggested: Sally Salminen, Maria Jotuni, and Maila Talvio. Among the nominated women we also note Austrian philologist Elise Richter, Dutch poet and radical political writer Henriëtte Roland Holst, and British non-fiction writer Violet Clifton, known for her biography of her husband Talbot Clifton, *The Book of Talbot* from 1933.

As a result of the Second World War, there was a distinct decrease in nominations between 1940 and 1946—and quite a few suggestions from this period were signed by Academy members. The international political crisis strongly affected the nomination process, but the procedure did not cease. All through the difficult years of disrupted international infrastructure and communication, literary Nobel Prize suggestions kept coming in, and they were all discussed by the Nobel Committee. No awards were given between 1940 and 1943, but the firm belief in the importance of world literature was stubbornly kept alive.

The decrease in nominations in the early 1940s went hand in hand with a slightly narrower geographical scope. During the first four years of the decade, there were only five authors nominated from literary cultures beyond Europe and North America: Chilean poet Gabriela Mistral, who was suggested three years in a row between 1940 and 1942; Argentinian novelist Enrique Laretta, who was nominated in 1942 by a large group of Argentinian, Spanish, and Brazilian intellectuals; Chinese philosopher and writer Lin Yutang, who was proposed by Academy member Sven Hedin as well as laureate Pearl Buck in 1940; Buenos Aires-born Carlos María Ocantos, who was suggested in 1943 by a member of the Spanish Academy in Madrid; and Indian poet, philosopher, and politician Sri Aurobindo, who was nominated by the London-based Royal Society of Literature, also in 1943. The high number of internal proposals did not lead to a rise in nominated Swedish authors. Domestic names were only suggested five times throughout the 1940s.

A more radical, although not surprising, change in this decade was the steep decrease of German suggestions. If we exclude Hermann Hesse, who resigned his German citizenship in 1923 in favor of a Swiss passport, only three German authors were nominated throughout the 1940s: poet and writer Hans Carossa in 1942 and 1949, Ricarda Huch in 1946, and Thomas Mann, who was suggested to be awarded a second time in 1948 by two members of the Swedish Academy.

French authors dominated the 1940s proposals, but British and US authors were not very far behind. Finnish nominations dropped significantly after the Sillanpää prize in 1939, whereas Portuguese suggestions were still many: fifteen proposals between 1940 and 1949, all of them in vain, of course, since the first award to an author from Portugal wasn't realized until 1998. In 1944, the first Iranian author was proposed when poet Abolghassem Etessam Zadeh was suggested by a scholar of French literature at the University of Teheran. In 1947, Christian thinker and social reformer Toyohiko Kagawa became the first nominated Japanese writer.

Proportionally, women writers were more represented in the 1940s nominations than ever before: 14 percent of the suggestions proposed female laureates, compared to 10 percent in the previous decade and 13 percent in the 1920s. Many of these names lingered on from the 1930s—Gabriela Mistral, Maria Madalena de Martel Patricío, Marie Under, Maila Taivo, Ricarda Huch, and French Catholic writer Henriette Charasson. New names were Bulgarian poet Elisabeta Bagryana, US social activist and reformer Dorothy Canfield Fisher, and French novelist Sidonie Gabrielle Colette. The proportion of nominated women dropped significantly in the 1950s to less than 7 percent ("Nominaton Archive," 2022). Amongst the proposed female writers, we find Polish novelist Maria Dabrowska, who was nominated seven times in just one year, 1959, and Romanian exile-princess Marthe Bibesco, famous for her 1923 French novel *Isvor, pays des saules* (*Isvor: The Country of Willows*) but also widely read as Lucile Décaux, the pseudonym she used for writing popular romances.

Besides the ninety-five nominations of Ramón Menéndez Pidal in the 1950s, we notice suggestions to award Egyptian writer Taha Hussein in 1950, 1951, and 1952, and eight suggestions between 1951 and 1957 to award Hebrew and Yiddish poet Zalman Shneur. In 1954, Jaroslav Seifert was proposed for the first time. But he had to wait another thirty years to be awarded. Taha Hussein was frequently nominated throughout the 1960s—in 1960, 1963, 1967, twice in 1962, 1964, and 1969, and four times in 1968. His fellow Egyptian writer Tawfik El-Hakim was nominated in 1969. In this decade, four Persian authors were also proposed for the Nobel Prize: Hossein Ghods-Nakhai, Z. Rahnema, Basilj Khalkhali, and Mohammad-Ali Jamalzadeh Esfani—the latter in 1965, 1967, as well as in 1969—and for the 1969 prize, Vietnamese writer and journalist Ho Huu Tuong was nominated. Four different Japanese authors were frequently nominated in the 1960s: Junzaburo Nishiwaki was suggested every year between 1960 and 1968, Jun'ichiro Tanizaki was proposed every year between

1960 and 1965, Yasunari Kawabata every year between 1961 and 1968, and Yukio Mishima was suggested in 1963, 1964, 1965, 1967, and 1968. All these nominations culminated with the 1968 prize to Kawabata. Perhaps on a more anecdotal note, we notice that J.R.R. Tolkien was nominated three times by three different external proposers. The proportion of nominated women was significantly lower in the 1960s than in the preceding decade: of all the proposed names only 4 percent were female.

Because of the Swedish Academy's practice of strict secrecy, we don't know very much about the nominations after 1973. One thing we do know, however, is that a huge number of suggestions have been sent to the Academy each year from many parts of the world. According to Lars Gyllensten's memoirs, the number of nominations was between 120 and 140 each year in the 1980s (Gyllensten 2000: 267). Today, the Swedish Academy receives about 200 nominations every year (Olsson 2022). Administrating all these suggestions from most corners of the world is indeed one of the central challenges for the Nobel institution. This worldwide network of annual proposals creates a world-literary infrastructure of its own.

The Actual Distribution of Awards

The ambition to distribute the prize honors widely across nations, cultures, and languages has been there from the start. The title of a German comprehensive account of Nobel Prize history from 1983 accurately illustrates this aspiration: *Die Literatur-Nobelpreisträger: ein Panorama der Weltliteratur im 20. Jahrhundert* (The literary Nobel laureates: a panorama of 20th century world literature) (Wilhelm 1983). The ambition has indeed been to successively construct a panorama of the most valuable contributions to contemporary world literature. But how have the actual prize decisions been distributed across the globe? What kind of canon has been constructed by the awards?

Well, an overall assessment of all the prizes from 1901 to 2022 reveals a massive European dominance. Of the 119 laureates, more than 80 have been born in or have been long-standing residents in European countries. Thirteen of the awarded authors have been US citizens, and nine of them have been born in Africa or have lived in African countries. Seven of them have had Asian origins, and four have been Latin American. When it comes to specific nationalities, France has still most laureates, followed by Great Britain and the United States, and then Germany. The fifth most awarded nationality is Sweden, with eight awarded authors. Six authors have been Spanish, and six have been Italian. Poland can boast five laureates, and so can Russia if we include the Soviet Union and émigré writers Ivan Bunin and Joseph Brodsky. Four laureates have had Irish nationalities, and Switzerland, Denmark, and Norway have three authors each. The rest of a total of forty-four nations can only boast one or two awarded authors each. Taken together, there are as many as twenty-five different nationalities among the European laureates.

Literary œuvres in twenty-four different languages have been awarded with Nobel Prizes. English is by far the most awarded language: approximately a fourth of the laureates are at least partly awarded for texts in English. The second, third, and fourth most awarded literary languages are French, German, and Spanish. Then we find Swedish, Italian, Russian, Polish, Danish, and Norwegian. If we exclude Turkish, there are only five non-European languages among the awarded œuvres: Japanese, Chinese, Arabic, Hebrew, and Bengali.

The European dominance is at its strongest during the first three decades of the prize. From 1901 to 1929, twenty-nine awards were given. Except for Rabindranath Tagore in 1913, all of these early prizes honored European authors. Within Europe, on the other hand, the awards were widely distributed. German authors were selected six times during the first three decades, and French authors were awarded five times. Italian, Spanish, Polish, Irish, Swedish, Danish, Norwegian, and British (if we count George Bernard Shaw as both Irish and British) authors were awarded two times each. Outside these nationalities, we find Belgian poet Maurice Maeterlinck and Swiss author Carl Spitteler.

In the 1930s, the world of the Nobel Prize in Literature widened. In 1933, the first prize to a Russian author was given, albeit Ivan Bunin had lived in France since 1920. There seems to have been, Rydén and Westerström write, a bit of a curse when it comes to Russia and the Nobel Prize (Rydén and Westerström 2018: 514f.). Leo Tolstoy never received the prize, to the angry surprise of many critics, and when the Russian literary tradition was finally awarded, the award went to an exiled poet who had left his home country because of the Bolshevik rule. But the Bunin prize was still an expansion to the east. More significant, perhaps, is the fact that Sinclair Lewis received the first US prize in 1930. Just a couple of years later, this award was followed up by the prizes to Eugene O'Neill and Pearl Buck. With these three US awards, the total European dominance of the Nobel Prize in Literature was finally broken.

After the Second World War, the widening to the west continued. With the 1945 award to Chilean Gabriela Mistral, the distribution of prizes reached a fourth continent. Mistral had been a serious contender already in 1940, and when the intended French laureate Paul Valéry died in July 1945, the Nobel Committee saw a chance to give "a gesture to Latin America," as Anders Österling phrased it in a letter to Committee Chair Per Hallström (Espmark 1986: 150, my translation). In 1948, 1949, and 1954, the North American representation was emphatically confirmed with prizes to T.S. Eliot, William Faulkner, and Ernest Hemingway. These awards aside, there was a distinct European bias in the awards given from 1946 to 1965, even though Albert Camus was born in Algeria and Saint-John Perse in Guadeloupe. In this period, there was quite a strong French bias, with prizes to André Gide, François Mauriac, Camus, Perse, and Jean-Paul Sartre, but the most striking tendency was the many Anglophone awards in the ten-year period after the Nobel was resumed in 1944: Eliot (1948), Faulkner (1949), Bertrand Russell (1950), Winston Churchill (1953), and Hemingway (1954). To put it crudely, in the distribution pattern of the late 1940s and the early 1950s, it is easy to see who won the war.

Arguing for the Yugoslavian candidate Ivo Andric in the early 1960s, Committee Chair Anders Österling referred to "the more or less legitimate critique" against the geographically narrow distribution of the prize (Rydén and Westerström 2018: 529, my translation). Andric was indeed awarded in 1963, but the most distinct geographical and cultural expansion in the history of the prize occurred a couple of years later, from 1966 onward. The second half of the 1960s saw prizes to an Israeli author (Agnon in 1966), a Guatemalan (Miguel Ángel Asturias in 1967), and a Japanese writer (Kawabata in 1968). In the early 1970s, the second Chilean poet was awarded (Pablo Neruda in 1971), and then a fifth continent was introduced in 1973 with Australian writer Patrick White. After this expansion, an eight-year all European and North American period passed until the widening continued with prizes to Colombian Gabriel García Márquez (1982), Nigerian Wole Soyinka (1986), Egyptian Naguib Mahfouz (1988), South African Nadine Gordimer (1991), and St. Lucian Derek Walcott (1992).

In Paris, the 1957 prize to Albert Camus was received as at least partly an African award. The responses in *Le Figaro* to this prize announcement stressed the fact that Camus was a North African author born and raised in Algeria. At the same time, the laureate was still regarded as a French writer: he is "un français d'Algérie" (a Frenchman from Algeria) and "[u]n français d'Afrique du nord" (a Frenchman from North Africa). (Prasteau 1957; "Un français d'Afrique du nord," 1957) In light of the ongoing violent conflict between Paris and Algeria—which started in 1954 and wasn't resolved until the Algerians earned their independence from France in 1962—it was certainly a politically charged issue how to describe the cultural belongings of the 1957 laureate. If we put the Albert Camus prize in brackets, African literature was introduced with a sudden bang in the second half of the 1980s, with three prizes in the course of five years.

Language-wise there was still, however, a distinct Anglophone bias in the last two decades of the twentieth century, with the awards to William Golding in 1983, Soyinka in 1986, Joseph Brodsky (who wrote partly in English, partly in Russian) in 1987, Gordimer in 1991, Walcott in 1992, Toni Morrison in 1993, and Seamus Heaney in 1995.

In the first decade of the new millennium, four laureates had cultural belongings beyond Europe and the United States: Gao Xingjian (China), V. S. Naipaul (Trinidad and Tobago), Doris Lessing (Southern Rhodesia), and Jean-Marie Gustave Le Clézio (Mauritius), even though the latter three also had distinct European domiciles and backgrounds. Among the laureates from the 2010s, Chinese writer Mo Yan is the only author with a distinct cultural background outside Europe and North America.

Nordic authors—from Sweden, Denmark, Norway, Iceland, and Finland—have been strongly favored by the Swedish Academy, especially if we consider the number of speakers in the Nordic languages and the Nordic cultures' general international presence outside the Nobel Prize context. Several international commentators have criticized this "provincial pro-Scandinavian bias," as Oskar Seidlin of Ohio State University called it in the American survey from 1951 (Seidlin 1951: 217). This bias was most significant in the first three decades of the prize. From 1901 to 1939, as many as nine awards were given to Nordic authors: two in the first decade (Bjørnstjerne Bjørnson and Selma Lagerlöf), three in the 1910s (Verner von Heidenstam, Karl Gjellerup, and Henrik Pontoppidan), two in the 1920s (Knut Hamsun and Sigrid Undset), and two in the 1930s (Erik Axel Karlfeldt and Frans Eemil Sillanpää). The great concentration of Scandinavian prizes from 1916 to 1920—four out of five prizes!—is partly explained by the Swedish ambition to stay neutral in the First World War (cf. Espmark 1986: 44).

The first prize after the Second World War was Danish (Johannes V. Jensen in 1944). In the 1950s, two Nordic prizes were given (to Swedish Pär Lagerkvist and Icelandic Halldór Kiljan Laxness), and the following two decades saw three Swedish awards. In 1966, Nelly Sachs shared the prize with Israeli author Shmuel Agnon. Sachs was born in Germany and wrote in German, but she had lived in Sweden since 1940 and had become a Swedish citizen in 1952. In 1974, the two Swedish authors Harry Martinson and Eyvind Johnson shared the prize. After that, only one Nordic prize has been given: to Swedish poet Tomas Tranströmer in 2011.

Prizes to non-Swedish Nordic authors ceased in the middle of the twentieth century. Jensen is the last non-Swedish Scandinavian laureate, and Laxness is the last non-Swedish Nordic author to be given the honor by the Swedish Academy. But the Swedish bias has continued. As shown above, Sweden is the fifth most awarded country when it comes to the laureates' cultural backgrounds, and Swedish is the fifth most awarded literary language. In this light, it is quite ironic that it was Eyvind Johnson who prevented a prize to Karen Blixen in 1959, despite the fact that the Danish author of *Out of Africa* was suggested by the Nobel Committee. Johnson thought that a new Scandinavian prize after Jensen and Laxness would be too much, and his successful argument probably made it possible for himself to be awarded fifteen years later (cf. Espmark 2021b: 30–1). From an outside perspective, it is difficult to avoid the impression that the Swedish Academy is first and foremost awarding their own, especially since five of the eight Swedish laureates were or had been members of the Academy when awarded (Heidenstam, Karlfeldt, Lagerkvist, Martinson, and Johnson), and a sixth (Lagerlöf) were to become a member five years after receiving the prize.

In the early years, there was a heated discussion within the Swedish Academy on whether the Nobel Prize in Literature should be given to Swedish authors or not. The first Nobel Committee Chair, Carl David af Wirsén, was strongly opposed to awarding Swedes. In order for a Swedish author to receive the prize, he thought, the decision must be free from every single glimmer of doubt (cf. Rydén 2010: 617). The Swedish Academy already did, after all, give out several domestic literary awards. The advocates for Nordic prizes were supported by the way Alfred Nobel phrased his will: the prize should go to "the worthies person, whether or not they are Scandinavian" ("Alfred Nobel's will," 2022). The early award to Norwegian poet Bjørnson confirmed this binary idea of Scandinavia on the one hand, and the rest of the world on the other, and in 1909 there was a strong opinion against Wirsén to "remind the world that Nobel's homeland also has a literature" (Espmark 1986: 33, my translation), as Academy member Alfred Melin described it. That year—with seven members as signing proposers—the Academy ignored Wirsén's protests and decided upon Selma Lagerlöf (cf. Rydén 2010: 619).

The second Swedish prize, to Verner von Heidenstam in 1916, can partly be explained by the difficulties of deciding between different European cultures in time of war, but by this time there was a strong opinion in the Academy in favor of Swedish prizes. Wirsén had died three years after his defeat in 1909 and could not protest any more. The first Swedish laureate had herself become an Academy member in 1914, and she was keen on awarding more Swedish laureates. "Alas,"

Lagerlöf wrote in 1916, "if we only could keep the Prize in Sweden for many years to come" (Edström 2002: 428, my translation).

Well, Selma Lagerlöf did not totally convince the other members. The third Swedish prize was not given until 1931, but that award was, on the other hand, quite remarkable. When the Academy decided to give the Nobel Prize to poet Erik Axel Karlfeldt, they did not only pause the westward expansion of the distribution in yet again settling on a Swede. This particular Swedish author did not even have an international reputation to speak of—unlike Lagerlöf, and unlike the widely famous August Strindberg, who was never awarded. More importantly, Karlfeldt had died seven months before the Academy decided to award him in November 1931. That year's prize was the first posthumous Nobel Prize in Literature—and so far the only one that has ever been given. In fact, in 1974 the Academy ruled out the possibilities of awarding authors posthumously (cf. Rydén and Westerström 2018: 193). Furthermore, Karlfeldt had not only been an Academy member, but indeed its Permanent Secretary from 1913 to his death. Another bias was the fact that with the Karlfeldt prize, the Academy honored a third Swedish author from the same generation of authors, "nittitalisterna" (writers of the nineties), who had made a dramatic collective breakthrough in the 1890s. And another thing: the Nobel Committee had already considered awarding Karlfeldt in 1919, but he had gracefully refused to be suggested to the Academy. His colleagues thus waited until he could no longer protest before they awarded him. The Karlfeldt prize in 1931 is an anomaly in so many ways, and it is quite odd that scholars and later Academy members have not discussed the decision more substantially and critically.

Unlike the Karlfeldt prize, the joint award to Eyvind Johnson and Harry Martinson in 1974 stirred up quite a storm. The critique of the Academy's decision to award two of their own was so stern that it led to a real crisis, for the Swedish Academy as such as well as for the two laureates. According to Per Rydén and Jenny Westerström, the fierce critique of the 1974 shared award eventually became an unhealed wound for the Swedish people (Rydén and Westerström 2018: 651).

Beyond the imbalanced distribution across continents, cultures, and languages, there has been a clear gender bias in the history of the Nobel. This was noted in the assessment of the first fifty years of the prize made by the American journal *Books Abroad* in 1951. In summarizing the 350 experts' opinions, William F. Lamont concluded that women writers had not "been given their fair share of the prizes" (Lamont 1951: 11). By that time, only five women had been selected by the Swedish Academy. From our historical point of view in 2022, the numbers are only slightly better. All in all, only 17 of the 119 laureates have been women. One would, perhaps, guess that this imbalance was greater in the beginning of the prize's history, but that is not entirely true.

The ninth award was given to the first female laureate Selma Lagerlöf in 1909. The decision was met with jubilant joy and excitement by the Swedish women's rights movement. In central Stockholm, a big party was arranged on December 13 to celebrate the laureate and the symbolic step taken by the Swedish Academy toward an equal society ("Selma Lagerlöf och vår fest," 1909). After the Lagerlöf prize, there was a seventeen-year break, but in the 1920s two women received the prize with just one year apart: Grazia Deledda in 1926 and Sigrid Undset in 1928. Ten years later, Pearl Buck received the fourth female prize, and seven years after that (but only two prizes, since no awards were given from 1940 to 1943) Gabriela Mistral was awarded. Considering the gender structure in Western societies and cultures at the time, five awards to woman writers in the first five decades of the prize were perhaps not too bad. The strongest male dominance occurred after that. During the forty-five-year period from 1946 to 1991, only one female author was awarded: Nelly Sachs, who shared the 1966 prize with Shmuel Agnon. There was an all-male period of twenty years between Mistral and Sachs, and a twenty-five all-male period between Sachs and Gordimer, which is all the more remarkable considering the rise and spread of Feminist ideas in both Europe and North America in the 1960s, 1970s, and 1980s.

From 1991 onward, the gender gap has decreased significantly. In the 1990s, 2000s, and 2010s, there have been three women laureates each decade. And the 2020s have started with two female laureates and only one male.

Concluding Remarks

In accepting to execute the literary part of Alfred Nobel's will, the Swedish Academy took on a huge and difficult task. Throughout its history, the limitations of the Nobel Committee have been raised and discussed by its own members as well as by external critics. The literatures of the whole world are, of course, far from equally accessible for the Committee. Some literary traditions are very close to the Swedish judges' cultural perspectives and knowledge, whereas others are totally out of reach—linguistically as well as culturally, philosophically, and emotionally. And between these extreme positions, there is a thick and complex continuum of accessibility levels. But the numerous constellations of the Nobel Committee have continued to select laureates. This gesture is built on a bold claim: in annually selecting Nobel laureates, the Committee and Academy members display the belief that their own tastes, frames of references, and experiences have a general, cosmopolitan validity, without which they couldn't make reasonably fair comparisons between very different kinds of literary achievements.

Some of the members of the Nobel Committee have, however, been the first ones to admit the significant gap between these claims and the actual distribution of awards. Up until the 1930s, the Nobel Prize was a European affair—and the only exception of Bengali author Rabindranath Tagore did little more than confirm this Eurocentral template. In the 1930s, the scope of the prize widened both eastward and westward. Ivan Bunin was the first author writing in Russian to be awarded, and the prize motivation stressed his position within the tradition of Russian narrative fiction. More distinctly, the prizes to Sinclair Lewis, Eugene O'Neill, and Pearl Buck welcomed North American literature into the privileged clique of Nobel laureates. With the prize to Chilean poet Gabriela Mistral in 1945, Latin America was also included. The Latin American presence in the Nobel world literary space was confirmed twenty-two years later by the prize to Guatemalan novelist Miguel Ángel Asturias, and in 1968 Japanese literature was admitted into the list of laureates with the award to Yasunari Kawabata. From the 1980s onward, the strong bias toward European and North American literature has been less obvious, but it is fair to say that European traditions, aesthetics, subject matters, and experiences still dominate in the awarded literary œuvres.

The mechanisms of the nomination process have contributed to the eventual enlargement of the Nobel Prize's cultural scope. Changes in the patterns of nominations have forced the Nobel Committee to re-evaluate their definitions of world literature and their ideas of world literary values. In several cases, we note that increasing nomination activities of a certain kind tend to eventually result in an affirmative prize decision. In the 1930s, the substantial amounts of proposals suggesting Finnish writers led to the Frans Eemil Sillanpää award in 1939, and in the 1960s, the decision to award Kawabata was preceded by a large number of nominations proposing Kawabata or one of his fellow Japanese writers Junzaburo Nishiwaki, Jun'ichiro Tanizaki, and Yukio Mishima. Being nominated by many proposers has not been, however, a guarantee for winning the prize. The huge number of intellectuals, for example, who nominated Spanish scholar Ramón Menéndez Pidal in the first half of the 1960s, were not successful.

The system of external reviewers was intended to help the Nobel Committee and the Academy to reach beyond their own fields of expertise. For long periods in the history of the prize, however, the actual use of external reviews did not produce a broad distribution of the responsibilities. A couple of particularly active Committee members have taken on very wide assignments, and thereby been very powerful in the decision process.

Several of the most influential members of the Nobel Committee have been advocating universalist ideas of literary values. To a certain extent, perhaps, a belief in constant and non-situated aesthetic values beyond cultural, historical, and ideological contexts, is an integral part of the basic logic of an international literary prize. The Academy members are not alone in their conviction that their decisions have—or should have—some kind of global validity. One of Pascale Casanova's central arguments for the existence of a world literary space is the "(almost) unanimous belief in the universality of the Nobel Prize" (Casanova 2013: 278). Casanova's parenthesis opens up for the possibility of minor exceptions, but the idea of the Nobel Prize's universality, she writes, is almost in itself a universal notion. To be sure, Alfred Nobel couldn't possibly have imagined a more successful realization of his grand vision of distinguishing what contemporary literary works are and will be most beneficial for humankind.

But literary universalism is nonetheless clearly at odds with a strong tendency in twenty-first-century literary theory to criticize a naïve celebration of privileged cosmopolitan perspectives. Influenced by historian David Hollinger (cf. Hollinger 2001), and with central arguments from postcolonialist literary theory, many world-literary scholars have pointed out the privileged blind spot of European cosmopolitanism and developed alternative theoretical perspectives on transnational positions (cf. Robbins and Lemos Horta 2017; and Stevic and Tsang 2019). Emily Apter's sharp argument "against world literature" is such a critique of a Western universalist inclination to ignore fundamental differences between cultures and languages (Apter 2013). Likewise, the Warwick Research Collective (WReC) warns against the optimistic embrace of globalization and proposes a new theory of world literature based on the fundamental reality of inequality (WReC 2015), and Jennifer Wenzel criticizes the main stream of world-literary theory for endorsing the idea of a hegemonized world (Wenzel 2019).

There have been central and powerful Committee members, however, with a pluralist view on literary values and functions, more in line with twenty-first-century ideas of cultural incommensurability and literary untranslatability. For a distinct period of time, such an aesthetics was the rule rather than the exception in the prize-decision process. Just like the universalist aesthetics, the pluralist principle has, of course, its problems and pitfalls. When you evaluate and promote literary works written in traditions very remote from your own, you always run the risk of exoticizing the cultural space you're interested in but not very familiar with. And the aesthetics of representation has a clear disadvantage in its normative effects, especially when the selection is made from a position close to the center. The particular author selected to represent a specific literary tradition, language, or culture tends to make invisible all the non-selected literary phenomena of that tradition, language, or culture.

Despite all its problems and risks, the broad geocultural ambition of the Nobel Prize in Literature has at least one very productive dimension: it makes apparent the fundamental challenges that every reader of world literature is confronted with. The annual selection of laureates raises questions of the possibilities and impossibilities of intercultural understanding through literature, a central issue in David Damrosch's field-defining monograph *What Is World Literature?* (Damrosch 2003). And if we dig just a little bit into the conditions of awarding different kinds of Nobel laureates, we will soon find ourselves discussing the mechanisms of "bibliomigrancy," as B. Venkat Mani calls the "accessibility or inaccessibility to imaginative texts from elsewhere" (Mani 2011: 293), or other kinds of distributional and translational conditions instructing literary traffic between markets, cultures, and languages (cf. also Hofmeyr 2004; Tenngart 2016; Tenngart 2020). And when we look into the processes of nominating and externally reviewing potential Nobel laureates, we find interesting attempts to create spaces of intercultural collaboration—spaces that are, I dare say, absolutely necessary if we want to understand literature in a geoculturally inclusive way.

4

Making History:
The Impact of the Prize

The short-term effect of the Nobel Prize in Literature is significant. The annual prize announcement is one of the few truly worldwide literary news events. And every year, all the newly appointed laureates are subjected to a great number of portraits and introductory articles in literary journals and magazines all over the world. For a long time, the American literary quarterly *World Literature Today*, for example, published a special issue each year dedicated to the latest Nobel laureate (see Ivask 1988: 197). This acute recognition varies a great deal from laureate to laureate, but every single one of them receives a substantial media attention, without exception, a simple fact that in itself strongly illustrates the Nobel Prize's significant international impact.

But what about the more durable effects of the prize? Does the Nobel institution make literary history? Well, a specific kind of Nobel status does tend to stick to the selected authors with a very sustainable glue: the fact that they are laureates is absolutely central in most presentations of them and their work, in the years directly after the prize ceremony as well as long after the event. The prize is, T.S. Eliot said in his Nobel speech, "the highest international honor that can be bestowed upon a man of letters." (Eliot 1969: 435) Every author who receives this award, Spanish critic Manuel Durán wrote in 1988, enters "a magic circle, a sacred space which he inhabits in the company of the happy few, the handful of writers selected over the years as representing the highest embodiment of modern literary art" (Durán 1988: 214). And the absence of Nobel status tends to nurse durable annoyance and feelings of neglect, in connection with specific authors as well as in relation to whole literary traditions and cultures. The Nobel Prize in Literature is an effective label of aesthetic quality. Even if its substance is continually questioned, this label tells us that sometime during the last 120 years a group of more or less neutral intellectuals has thought that this author belongs to the uppermost level of international literature.

One reason why the Nobel consecration is so stable and robust is the fact that it is reciprocal. The collective study *Northern Crossings: Translation, Circulation and the Literary Semi-periphery* shows that while authors, translators, and publishers are canonized by the Nobel Prize, the prize itself relies on the laureates' nimbuses in order to continually retain its status. This process follows a "dialectic of consecration," in which an already canonized laureate lends his or her prestige to the Nobel institution, which, in its turn, lends its retained prestige to a formerly not so canonized author when making him or her a laureate (Edfeldt et al 2022: 120). This way, the award process manages to maintain a reciprocal support between prize-giving institution and literary accomplishments.

This dialectic relies upon variation. The Swedish Academy must hand out different kinds of Nobel Prizes—sometimes expected and sometimes surprising, sometimes totally uncontroversial and sometimes more daring—in order to sustain the effects of this reciprocal consecration. For some laureates, the Nobel Prize is just another confirmation of their generally recognized importance, for others the award is their most important consecration factor. For a third category of laureates, the Nobel honors will turn out to be their only claim to fame. There is, in short, a great variation between different prize decisions and their impact on literary history.

Impactful Awards

Nobel Prize laureates' presence and centrality in different contexts can be explored in many quantitative ways. Danish collective research project Fabula-NET has, for example, examined their presence on the digital reader platform goodreads.com—how often they are read within this community, and how their works are rated. These analyses have resulted in three categories: *popular*, *solid*, and *forgotten* prize-winners (Rosendahl Thomsen 2022). Another test of Nobel writers' long-term importance is their presence on university reading lists. In his blog on the digital "Open Syllabus Explorer," Joe Karaganis reports on his 2020 investigation of the last forty winners. The most taught laureate by far, he concludes, is Toni Morrison. J.M. Coetzee, Gabriel García Márquez, and Kazuo Ishiguro also appear frequently on courses in literature, whereas Jaroslav Seifert, Tomas Tranströmer, and Claude Simon are almost never taught (Karaganis 2020). These are all very interesting and important numbers that empirically support general ideas about the writers' different cultural positions after being appointed Nobel laureates. They do not, however, separate the effect made by the award itself from other kinds of consecration. To be sure, Toni Morrison is frequently taught at universities for many other reasons than her being a Nobel Prize laureate.

To sum up the first fifty years of the Nobel Prize in Literature, US literary journal *Books Abroad*, issued by the University of Oklahoma, made a grand assessment in 1951 of the awards thus far. The discussion was spread out over three issues, starting with a survey conducted and reported by William F. Lamont. Lamont had sent out a questionnaire to 350 critics, authors, and academics, who, in the article writer's own words, collectively formed an "international jury of experts in belles-lettres" (Lamont 1951: 11). These experts were asked two questions:

> (1) If outstanding literary achievement were the sole criterion for the selection for the Nobel prize winners, which of those authors who have already won the prize would you consider unworthy of it? (2) Which other authors, living or dead, overlooked by the Nobel committee, would you consider worthy of the prize?

Lamont's report was published in early 1951, but the survey itself was conducted in 1950 before it was announced that Bertrand Russell won that year's award, and that William Faulkner was belatedly selected as the 1949 laureate. In the two succeeding issues of the journal, Lamont's report was supported by eighteen individual responses: four German critics, three French, one Belgian, and ten scholars or writers from the United States contributed with short texts.

Sixteen years later, *Books Abroad* followed up this survey with a symposium on the choices and omissions of the Nobel Prize Committee. The result of this new inquiry was published in a special issue of the journal, in which the prize history up until 1966 was scrutinized from eighteen different perspectives: French and Belgian, German, Nordic, Spanish and Spanish South-American, Slavic, Italian, English and Irish and American, Bengali, Greek, Hebrew, African, Arabic, Brazilian, Chinese, Indonesian, Japanese, Persian, and Urdu literature. The responding experts were fewer this time around, but the quarterly's readers received substantial responses from a much wider scope of different literary cultures and traditions. This second survey was less quantitative and much more qualitative than the first one. As such, it was also slightly more subjective and opinionated than the 1951 survey.

In 1988, a second symposium on the Nobel Prize was arranged by the journal, which by then had changed its name to *World Literature Today*. This time, twelve scholars and critics were asked to comment upon the prizes between 1967 and 1987 from the points of view of Arabic, South East Asian, Francophone, Hispanic, Japanese, African, Anglophone, Jewish, Brazilian, Nordic, German, and nationless literature.

In addition to these three broad inquiries, several separate articles have distributed subjective views of hits and misses in the Nobel prize history, of which George Steiner's "The Scandal of the Nobel Prize" in the September 1984 issue of the *New York Times Book Review* is probably the best known (Steiner 1984). Read together, these assessments from different periods and different cultural and geographical angles give quite a substantial impression of more or less general ideas on the diverse long-term values of the different awards.

The 350 experts in William F. Lamont's survey were of the collective opinion that the Swedish Academy so far had "generally made good selections" (Lamont 1951: 11). Of the thirty-nine laureates honored between 1901 and 1948, twenty-two were seen as worthy recipients, and eleven of these were viewed as especially good choices: Selma Lagerlöf, Gerhart Hauptmann, Anatole France, George Bernard Shaw, William Butler Yeats, Sigrid Undset, Thomas Mann, Luigi Pirandello, Eugene O'Neill, André Gide, and T.S. Eliot. In his individual response, Renée Lang from Wells College, New York, presented a slightly different list of favorites that included Theodor Mommsen, Giosuè Carducci, Henri Bergson, John Galsworthy, and Hermann Hesse (Lang 1951: 116). German-American author and art historian Alfred Neumeyer reported that in his opinion the selection committee had "not done so badly": around 50 per cent of the choices had been good and constructive, a ratio he rated as "fair enough" (Neumeyer 1951: 119). French scholar Henri Perruchot argued that the Nobel Prize had been "more satisfactory than many of the decisions of certain national academies."

(Perruchot 1951: 120) His case in point was the Swedish Academy's decision to honor André Gide, a writer avoided by the committees of the Goncourt Prize and the Académie Française. In his 1967 review of the Francophone prizes, Gene J. Barberet from the University of Connecticut was also positive to the Bergson and Gide awards. Barberet admitted that it was more difficult to discuss the later awards than the earlier ones, but he thought that the prizes to François Mauriac, Albert Camus, and Jean-Paul Sartre all reflected both importance and quality (Barberet 1967).

American scholar Robert E. Spiller pointed out in 1967 that the prize to William Faulkner in 1949 was an especially constructive decision, since this recognition revitalized the reception of the novelist and resulted in a new, more substantial understanding of his work (Spiller 1967: 35). This argument was confirmed by the fact that Faulkner received two Pulitzer Prizes after his Nobel award—for the novels *A Fable* and *The Reivers* in 1955 and 1963. Spiller was quite generous in his evaluation of the Swedish Academy's American selections. For him, not only the Faulkner prize but also the awards to O'Neill, Eliot, and Ernest Hemingway were all "bull's-eye hits on the part of the Committee" (Spiller 1967: 34).

In the 1967 inquiry, critics sometimes took a step back and commented on prizes given before the Second World War. Two early prizes that stood out as significantly important from this late 1960s perspective were the ones to Gerhart Hauptmann and Rabindranath Tagore. In selecting the German playwright, Theodore Ziolkowski argued, the Swedish Academy showed a fair amount of integrity and independence toward Hauptmann's domestic reputation in Germany, where he was still a controversial figure in 1912. Hauptmann's importance for the development of German twentieth-century drama had proven the Nobel Committee right (Ziolkowski 1967: 14). And if the invited expert from Florida Presbyterian College, Albert Howard Carter, were forced to choose only one prize-worthy author from twentieth-century Asian and African literature, it would be Tagore (Carter 1967).

The significant impact of the Tagore prize is distinctly confirmed by the reception history of the Bengali writer. The surprising 1913 award was enthusiastically received in many parts of the world. It instantly made Tagore famous, and invitations poured in from everywhere. The outbreak of the First World War restricted his travels, but he managed to visit both Japan and the United States in 1916 and 1917. After the war, his European tour was met with excitement and interest in many countries, and in 1921 he was finally able to start his "triumphant procession through Germany," as Martin Kämpchen puts it (Kämpchen 2011: 6, my translation). Ever since, Rabindranath Tagore has been one of the most central authors in the context of world literature.

Just like the 1967 inquiry, the 1988 symposium arranged by *World Literature Today* did not result in any quantifications and ratios of constructive prize decisions. The special issue only included reports from discussions and individual reactions to the overall question of good and bad choices made by the Swedish Academy between 1967 and 1987. In his introduction to the individual contributions, Ivar Ivask mentioned one successful choice: the Czeslaw Milosz prize in 1980, which he contrasted to the much less impactful Jaroslav Seifert award in 1984. What made the decision to honor

Milosz much better than the decision four years later, Ivask argued, was the fact that the 1980 prize was "both a coronation *and* a discovery of a major poet" (Ivask 1988: 198). According to this line of thinking, the best prizes have simply not been the awards to the most qualified laureates; no, the best prize decisions have been those that created world recognition of a worthy but formerly not widely known laureate.

The actual consequences of the Swedish Academy's decisions were also central for George Steiner's critical assessments in 1984. According to Steiner, the best Nobel awards were those with which the Swedish Academy had made "discoveries"—decisions that showed the world a new name worthy of literary attention (Steiner 1984). He mentioned two recent laureates as good examples: Czeslaw Milosz and Elias Canetti. In selecting these writers, the Swedish Academy surprised the world and gave critics, scholars, and readers access to qualitative, substantial, and important literary texts that they wouldn't have found without the Nobel. Older cases of discoveries, Steiner argued, were Salvatore Quasimodo and Carl Spitteler. Some of the selections praised by the American critic exemplify another long-standing effect of the Nobel: the possibility of re-evaluation. Along with France, Shaw, and Mann, Steiner argued that Rudyard Kipling was a good choice by the early Nobel Committees. In the 1951 survey, Kipling was not seen as a worthy laureate. In the follow-up inquiry sixteen years later, his value was distinctly improved, and in 1984 Steiner appointed him one of the best choices ever. One of the important discoveries in Steiner's article, Carl Spitteler, was seen as an unworthy laureate in both 1951 and 1967. Unsurprisingly, there is no consensus to be found in the retrospective assessments of prize decisions.

The issue of impact was also decisive for Comparative Literature professor John L. Brown when he assessed the recent French Nobel Prizes in 1988. Brown agreed with George Steiner that the Swedish Academy generally had made "very few genuine discoveries," but he added that this observation was not confirmed by the Francophone prizes in the 1960s, 1970s, and 1980s. Yes, Jean-Paul Sartre was already "universally acclaimed" when he refused to receive the prize in 1964, but with the other three French prizes from this period—Saint-John Perse in 1960, Samuel Beckett in 1969, and Claude Simon in 1985—the Swedish Academy did "testify to a desire to recognize the new and the innovative" (Brown 1988: 210).

What is then, according to these critics from the 1950s, 1960s, and the 1980s, the recipe for a successful Nobel Prize decision? Well, the selected author and his or her work should, for one thing, prove worthy in the long run. It is, of course, impossible to know how a literary œuvre will be read and assessed by posterity. To succeed in appointing future classics, the Nobel Committee does not only need a very sophisticated nose for sustainable aesthetic qualities, but also a significant level of pure luck. Secondly, to create a real impact the Swedish Academy also need to be able to identify the new and the innovative among contemporary literary achievements. It takes a lot of courage and confidence to fulfill this requirement, and the boldest decisions always run the risk of being complete failures in the unforgiving eyes of future critics executing their power to be wise long after the event.

Summing up the most substantial evaluations of the prizes, a couple of names stand out as generally applauded decisions. From the early history of the prize, Gerhart

Hauptmann and Rabindranath Tagore are repeatedly mentioned as important laureates. Of the decisions from the 1920s and 1930s, critics have tended to agree that the awards to Yeats, Mann, Pirandello, and O'Neill were significantly constructive prizes, not least because of the fact that all of these authors were still productive at the time of their awards. The Nobel Prize helped to put their later works in the absolute limelight of cosmopolitan literary discussions. From the post-Second World War era, the William Faulkner prize has been especially applauded for its impact on the American novelist's reception. Kjell Espmark pointed out in 2021 that Faulkner's work was a fundamental inspiration for a whole range of younger authors, including Toni Morrison, and that this wide inspiration was to a significant extent made possible by the Academy's decision to honor the novelist. "Perhaps no other prize," Espmark concluded, "has meant more than that of 1949" (Espmark 2021: 48). Generally celebrated decisions from the 1950s onward include the awards to Juan Ramón Jiménez, Salvatore Quasimodo, Saint-John Perse, Giorgos Seferis, and Czesław Miłosz, all of whom are considered to be domestically big names made internationally acknowledged by the Swedish Academy.

From the late twentieth century and the decades after 2000, there are no big inquiries available on the impact of different awards. It is, however, easy to see that the prizes to Derek Walcott, Toni Morrison, V.S. Naipaul, and J.M. Coetzee helped to put postcolonial literature in focus, thereby urging the international literary discourse and many national cultural discussions to acknowledge the importance of colonial histories throughout the world. The award to Abdulrazak Gurnah had a special kind of impact on this discussion, at least from a Scandinavian point of view. Before the announcement of the 2021 prize, many critics speculated that the time had come to reward another author addressing postcolonial issues. This discussion was quite centered around two names—Kenyan writer Ngugi wa Thiong'o and Antiguan-American novelist Jamaica Kincaid. When the Swedish Academy did confirm the general speculations, but instead of one the most expected names decided on the much lesser-known Gurnah, they indirectly stressed the fact that postcolonial literature was much more vast and much more varied than reports in newspapers and other public media acknowledged. Postcolonial issues, the selection indirectly pointed out, could not be restricted to a couple of names and a few bilateral relations.

In her keynote address "World Literature and Minorisation" at a conference in Leuven in May 2021, Francesca Orsini said: "If you're a non-English author, you need to be a Nobel Prize winner or a global bestseller to be acknowledged in UK book reviews, including the *Guardian*, who boasts the ambition of having a world-wide news coverage" (Orsini 2021). If Orsini is right, the Nobel Prize is still a hugely important factor instructing what literary works are discussed, distributed, and read around the world, but the prize decisions are much more important for non-English and non-European literature than for English and European authors. According to Orsini's observation, the members of the Nobel Committee have a recurring opportunity to make a real impact on contemporary world literature. And this impact could, in its turn, affect people far beyond literary matters.

The Unawarded

When asked in 1988 to assess the Swedish Academy's decisions from his point of view, Yugoslav critic Jovan Hristic generously answered: "Ivo Andric received the Nobel Prize in 1961. I cannot think of anyone else who deserved it" (Czerwinski 1988: 212). Most international experts have been much less sympathetic toward the selection of laureates. Indeed, when critics have discussed the limited impact of the Nobel Prize, they have often pointed to a range of important authors who should have been but never were awarded by the Swedish Academy. And it is obvious that many of the works and œuvres that have—in retrospect—earned central positions in the written history of twentieth-century literature did not receive any Nobel honors. Only two of the ten twentieth-century authors in Harold Bloom's *The Western Canon* are, for example, Nobel laureates: Samuel Beckett and Pablo Neruda (Bloom 1994).

This criticism is sometimes unreasonable and anachronistic, as Kjell Espmark has convincingly shown (Espmark 1986: 164). Franz Kafka had not published any of his important novels *Das Schloss* (*The Castle*), *Der Prozess* (*The Trial*), and *Amerika* when he died in 1925; Marcel Proust had only published two of the seven volumes of *À la recherche du temps perdu* (*In Search of Lost Time*), having earned his breakthrough with the Goncourt Prize in December 1919 for the second book in the series, *À l'ombre des jeunes filles en fleurs* (*In the Shadow of Young Girls in Flower*), when he died in 1922; and Rainer Maria Rilke's most influential work *Duineser Elegien* (*Duino Elegies*) came out as late as 1923, only three years before the German poet passed away. To argue that the Swedish Academy should have been able to recognize these future classics in time—without any of them having been nominated by external proposers—is simply not fair. When George Steiner wondered in 1984 if we possibly can take seriously an institution that has passed over Joyce, Proust, and Kafka, it's easy to argue that the American critic ignored the basic historical conditions of the prize (Steiner 1984). Ivar Ivask, who conducted the 1988 collective assessment of Nobel Prize history for *World Literature Today*, called this recurring lamentation of omitted modernist giants a "largely irrelevant cliché" that he wanted to avoid in his survey. "It is hard to understand," he explained, "why the Swedish Academy should be blamed for overlooking the artistic achievement of authors whose reputations in their lifetime were of an esoteric, limited nature and who gained worldwide fame essentially only posthumously" (Ivask 1988: 197–8).

Other instances of neglect could be explained by bad timing. Throughout the 1930s, Committee Chair Per Hallström ruled out Paul Valéry for being too exclusive, and when new aesthetic values broke through in the following decade, and the Swedish Academy finally leaned toward honoring Valéry in 1945, the French modernist poet died before the decision was finalized (Rydén and Westerström 2018: 436). The Academy had to quickly find an alternative and decided upon Gabriela Mistral. Another example of unfortunate timing is the case of prose writer Shen Congwen, who was about to earn the first-ever Chinese Nobel award when he died in 1988 (Espmark 2021: 44).

From his historical perspective in the late 1980s, Ivar Ivask pointed out some obvious omissions in the prize history regarding literary languages and cultures. The

Swedish Academy, he concluded, had been "predominantly Eurocentric in its choices" in not being able to award any author whatsoever writing in Arabic, Persian, or Turkish. But it was even more remarkable, he argued, that three of the richest literary cultures from Latin America had never been awarded: "It is absolutely astonishing that no Argentinian, Brazilian, or Mexican author has yet been deemed worthy of the highest literary accolade, although every lover of literature knows that it is precisely these three literatures that have produced such widely read modern classics as Borges and Cortázar, Guimarães Rosa and Drummond de Andrade, Paz and Fuentes!" (Ivask 1988: 198) Soon after Ivask's article was published, the prizes to Naguib Mahfouz in 1988 (who was, by the way, strongly recommended as a future laureate by the expert in Arabic literature Roger Allen in the *World Literature Today* survey (Allen 1988: 203)) and Octavio Paz in 1990 would correct two of these omissions—and in 2006, Orhan Pamuk finally became the first Turkish laureate. But Persian, Argentinian, and Brazilian writers are still waiting for their turn.

The written result of Herbert Howarth's 1967 symposium included separate articles devoted to the then unawarded traditions of Arabic, Persian, Chinese, Japanese, Indonesian, Urdu, and Brazilian literature, and all the experts of these literary traditions mentioned worthy Nobel candidates (Wormhoudt 1967; Ramsaran 1967; Foster 1967; Birch 1967; Goodman 1967; Wickens 1967; Raffel 1967; Coppola 1967). From all of these potential literatures, only Japanese and Chinese laureates have been selected since the survey was conducted.

In the 1988 survey, Syed Amanuddin pointed to the multitude of literary languages and cultures in South Asia, and mentioned a range of writers from the Indian subcontinent that would have been worthy laureates, for example Urdu poets Mohammed Iqbal and Faiz Ahmed Faiz, Gujarati writer Umashankar Joshi, Hindi writers Suryakant Tripathi Nirala and Sachidananda Vatsyayan Ajneya, Punjabi poet and novelist Amrita Pritam, and political activist and thinker Mahatma Gandhi, who wrote in both Gujarati and English. Among the emerging contemporary writers, Amanuddin mentioned Anita Desai and Salman Rushdie as worthy future laureates (Amanuddin 1988: 204–7).

When it comes to Japanese literature, the 1988 survey exemplified the risk inherent in awarding authors from non-European and non-North American literary traditions. When a specific literary language has to wait a long time before getting awarded, it becomes more important than ever which author is selected when the time comes. Yoshio Iwamoto pointed out that the first Japanese Nobel Prize in 1968 was a choice between the three authors Yasunari Kawabata, Yuko Mishima, and Jun'ichiro Tanizaki, all of whom were available in English and French translations. While Kawabata received the prize and many European critics wondered why the Swedish Academy didn't choose Mishima instead, most scholars of Japanese literature agreed that "Tanizaki was by far the most deserving of Nobel recognition among Japanese writers of this period." But even if the Japanese were "somewhat perplexed" by this selection, Iwamoto adds, the Kawabata prize did lead to "[n]ational jubilation." Although not the most expected one, the decision to award Kawabata was "a felicitous choice" (Iwamoto 1988: 218).

Of all the African writers suggested as worthy laureates in the 1967 and the 1988 survey, very few have been awarded. In the earlier review, John Ramsaran mentioned Léopold Sédar Senghor, Mongo Beti, Chinua Achebe, Wole Soyinka, J.P. Clark, Birage Diop, Camara Laye, Tschicaya U Tam'si, Ezekiel Mphahlele, Ngugi wa Thiong'o (in 1967 still called James Ngugi), and Ferdinand Oyono (Ramsaran 1967). In the latter survey, Bernth Lindfors repeated Rasmaran's suggestion of awarding "Africa's premier novelist" Chinua Achebe, and also mentioned Nadine Gordimer, Alan Paton, André Brink, Athol Fugard, and J.M. Coetzee as worthy and potentially constructive laureates (Lindfors 1988: 223-4). Soyinka, Gordimer, and Coetzee have indeed been awarded since their names were suggested in these surveys, whereas Achebe and Ngugi have stayed recurring Nobel contenders in the public opinion long into the twenty-first century.

As we have seen, one of the earliest crises in the history of the prize had to do with a perceived failure to award the most-worthy author (see Chapter 2, p. 22): the loud Swedish protests against the decision to not appoint Russian writer Leo Tolstoy as the first-ever Nobel laureate in literature. In 1951, Lamont's experts mentioned Tolstoy as one of the great authors, but they thought that the Russian writer's most significant contributions to world literature belonged to the nineteenth century, and that his name therefore was rightly avoided by the early Nobel Committees. Instead, many of these critics argued that Anton Chekhov, Maxim Gorky, and Mikhail Sholokhov were overlooked by the Swedes. In fact, several of the individual responses to Lamont's questions in *Books Abroad* pointed out an "anti-Russian bias" on the part of the Swedish Nobel Committee (Seidlin 1951: 217). Up until 1951, Ivan Bunin was the sole author writing in Russian to have received the prize, and he had lived in French exile for many years when awarded. The second Russian prize, to Boris Pasternak in 1958, did little to improve the Nobel Prize's reputation in Moscow. Pasternak's most recent work at the time, the novel *Doctor Zhivago* from 1957, had been rejected by the Soviet publishers due to its critique of Stalinism.

Another early heated discussion concerned Norwegian playwright Henrik Ibsen. Later Permanent Secretary and Committee Chair Anders Österling thought, in retrospect, that the failure to award Ibsen was one of the greatest neglects in the history of the prize (Rydén and Westerström 2018: 478). Wirsén dismissed the Norwegian author for lacking in idealism. He found parts of Ibsen's work "repulsive" (Svensén 2001a: 32, my translation), and thought that his later plays were "desolate, enigmatic, confused, and misleading" (Rydén 2010: 593, my translation). In the 1903 prize negotiations, Wirsén accepted to recommend the playwright's compatriot Bjørnstjerne Bjørnson in order to block out Ibsen (Rydén 2010: 599).

Wirsén was even more hostile toward the most famous Swedish playwright of all times, August Strindberg. Strindberg and Wirsén were long-standing enemies, and the latter would never have accepted to honor his antagonist. The playwright was never formally nominated (the single proposal in 1911 arrived too late), but outside the Academy circle, money was collected to make Strindberg an alternative literary laureate and give him a "people's Nobel Prize," which was handed over on the writer's birthday in January 1912 (Rydén 2010: 632–5). International critics have also lamented the absence of Strindberg's name among the laureates. In 1951, German critic Lion Feuchtwanger thought that it was "impossible to understand why the Scandinavian judges declined to award the prize to the writer whom the whole world recognizes as Scandinavia's greatest: August Strindberg, although they bestowed it on a row of Scandinavian writers whom the world could never rank so high" (Feuchtwanger 1951: 115).

A third Scandinavian name that many critics have missed in the list of laureates is Danish prose writer Karen Blixen, author of *Out of Africa*, which was originally written in English. Blixen was a recurring top name during a period in the 1950s and was almost chosen in 1959, but eventually she had to stand back for Italian poet Salvatore Quasimodo (Rydén and Westerström 2018: 523).

Besides Rainer Maria Rilke, Theodore Ziolkowski mentioned Bertolt Brecht, Hermann Broch, and Hugo von Hofmannsthal as German lacunae in the prize history. In retrospect, Anders Österling regretted that he did not fight for Hofmannsthal before the Austrian poet and playwright died in 1929 (Rydén and Westerström 2018: 465). Germanist Ludwig Marcuse also mentioned Wilhelm Dilthey, Georg Simmel, Stefan George, Frank Wedekind, and Arthur Schnitzler as overlooked names—as well as Heinrich Mann, "the most unjustly neglected of all German authors" (Marcuse 1951: 118). Quite a few critics have also missed Sigmund Freud among the laureates (see for example Lang 1951: 116 and Marcuse 1951: 118). As to Swiss authors, several critics would have preferred Francophone novelist and poet Charles-Ferdinand Ramuz instead of Carl Spitteler, who wrote in German (see for example Perruchot 1951; Roditi 1951).

When it comes Spanish language laureates, Argentinian Jorge Luis Borges has been the most missed writer. In October 1970, for example, Milan newspaper *Corriere della Sera* asked a range of Italian critics about the Nobel Prize, and most interviewees agreed that Borges was the most-worthy author not yet awarded (Ratcliffe 1970). The Argentinian was nominated several times and was recurringly expected to be the next laureate until his death in 1986 (Espmark 1986: 167). One of the reasons why he was never awarded was Anders Österling's assessment of his playful narratives as "too artificial" (Rydén and Westerström 2018: 654). In not awarding Borges, the Nobel Committee went quite distinctly against the grain of world literary discourse and values. When Gabriel García Márquez was awarded in 1982, many critics concluded that his fellow Spanish-speaking and fellow Latin American author from Argentina would never receive the prize. The *Times* published quite a melodramatic report from Buenos Aires: "Señor Borges, aged 83, who has been blind for more than a quarter of a century, has waited in vain to be awarded the prize since 1963." Still, Borges is said to be a good sport in receiving the news from Stockholm: the choice of Márquez was "excellent, a notably good show," he says to the empathic correspondent (Howard 1982).

Apart from Borges, Spanish poet Federico García Lorca, Argentine-French novelist and short story writer Julio Cortázar, and Spanish philosopher and essayist José Ortega y Gasset have often been mentioned as overlooked by the Swedish Academy (see Feuchtwanger 1951: 115; Lang 1951: 116; Neumeyer 1951: 119; and Peyre 1951: 214). And no Catalan writer has yet been awarded, a lacuna pointed out by Manuel Durán in the 1988 survey (Durán 1988: 215).

Another giant in literary history who never received the Nobel Prize is the very productive French novelist Émile Zola. His name was an issue in relation to the 1902 decision, at a time when the novelist's relevance had been renewed in the widely known and heatedly discussed Dreyfus affair. But just like he did with Ibsen, Wirsén found Zola lacking in idealism. The Permanent Secretary and Committee Chair had never been a fan of Naturalism. In fact, he had been strongly opposed to this specific literary aesthetics for twenty years (Rydén 2010: 266). In 1902, Wirsén was prepared to fight for an alternative candidate, but there was no need. Before a decision had to be made, Zola died.

In 1951, Marcel Proust was mentioned as one of the most missed French names among the laureates, and so was François Mauriac, who received the award a year later (Lamont 1951: 13). Another repeatedly pointed out French lacuna is André Malraux, art theorist and author of the Goncourt winning novel *La Condition humaine* (*Man's Fate*) from 1933. His position as Minister of Cultural Affairs in Charles de Gaulle's governments between 1959 and 1969 made him a problematic candidate, but after his comeback to the literary scene with the autobiographical *Antimémoires* (*Anti-memoirs*), and after his retirement from political life, Malraux was a serious contender in 1969 (Espmark 1986: 168–9). But that year the Academy eventually decided upon Samuel Beckett instead.

Since Beckett wrote several of his most influential works in French, he is one of two Francophone laureates whom John L. Brown discussed in the 1988 survey. Brown found both Beckett and Claude Simon worthy of the prize, even though the latter decision did stir quite some criticism in 1985. Brown regretted that the recently deceased Louis Aragon, Marguerite Yourcenar, Henri Michaux, and René Char never received the prize, and he pointed out that the Swedish Academy still had the chance to honor Julien Green, Francis Ponge, and Yves Bonnefoy. He also drew attention to the possibilities of awarding Francophone African, Caribbean, and Canadian writers, and mentioned Senghor, Aimé Césaire, Marie-Claire Blais, Mohammed Dib, and Édouard Glissant as worthy candidates. None of these potential laureates were to be awarded, but of the three up-and-coming authors whom Brown found worthy of a future Nobel Prize, two have since then been honored: Jean-Marie Gustave Le Clézio and Patrick Modiano. Only one of Brown's young writers on the rise, Michel Tournier, who died in 2016, has been left unawarded (Brown 1988: 207–11).

In an article in the magazine *Collier's* from 1949, US best-selling author Irving Wallace accused the Swedish Academy for being anti-American (Wallace 1949). In this strong critique of the Nobel Prize, which was the initiating spark behind William F. Lamont's survey for *Books Abroad* a couple of years later, Wallace was probably mainly thinking of the first thirty years of the prize's history, since the 1930s saw three laureates from the United States and the following decade included an award to T.S. Eliot, who at least was a US citizen until the age of twenty-seven. Among the renowned authors from the United States, Henry James has often been mentioned as neglected by the Swedish Academy. James was nominated in 1911, but the Committee dismissed him due to a "lack of concentration" in his novels (Rydén and Westerström 2018: 43). In the 1951 survey, Berlin professor Édouard Roditi wrote that the Swedish

Academy could not be blamed for this lacuna in the history of the prize, because James "was granted almost no recognition in the U.S.A. or in England" during his lifetime. If he did not enjoy any real recognition in his own cultural contexts and language, Roditi argued, how could a Swedish group of intellectuals be expected to acknowledge the innovative greatness of the novelist? (Roditi 1951: 214) Another US-born influential writer who never was awarded is Ezra Pound, a name that was substantially discussed in the Nobel Committee but in the end was declared impossible for political reasons (see Chapter 5, p. 180). Lamont did not mention Pound, but his critics do miss Henry James, Robert Frost, and Carl Sandburg, as well as William Faulkner and Ernest Hemingway, who both received the prize shortly after the survey was conducted. The 1951 critics and scholars also missed novelist Theodore Dreiser among the laureates (Lamont 1951: 13). Dreiser was nearly selected instead of Sinclair Lewis in 1930 as the first-ever North American laureate (Svensén 2001b: 153–5).

James Joyce is another central figure in Anglophone Modernism that many critics have mentioned as a serious lacuna in the Nobel canon. Even though the author of *Ulysses* and *Finnegan's Wake* was never nominated, Anders Österling regretted in retrospect that the Irishman was not awarded (Rydén and Westerström 2018: 467). A prize to Joyce would indeed have improved the status of the Nobel institution. But the 1930s Committees were not very fond of experimental Modernism, and Joyce died in 1941, just when modernist aesthetics was on the verge of breaking through in the Committee work (Espmark 1986: 163). If Joyce would have lived through the 1940s, it is quite likely that he would have been awarded—probably at the expense of T.S. Eliot or William Faulkner.

Most loud calls of Nobel neglect have concerned British writers. Joseph Conrad, who was born in Poland as a Russian citizen but became a British national in 1886, was never discussed as a potential laureate, and it is probably not fair to be too critical of the absence of nominations to and recognition by the Academy. Apparently, Conrad hoped to be selected by the Swedish Academy after his breakthrough novel *Chance* in 1913 (Najder 2007: 512 and 550), but his reputation as a pivotal figure in the modern history of literature—especially due to the novella *Heart of Darkness*—has mostly been posthumous.

Algernon Charles Swinburne is a completely different case. The poet was nominated for the first time in 1903. In his prize recommendation address to the Swedish Academy, Carl David af Wirsén was genuinely sympathetic to what he called "England's sick nightingale." He admitted that Swinburne was an "immortal poet," but he also acknowledged that the author of "The Garden of Proserpine" and "The Leper" lacked nobility, which was why he was eventually dismissed in 1903 (Rydén 2010: 610). Four years later, Swinburne was nominated again. But in a strategic—and successful—attempt to block out Selma Lagerlöf, Wirsén instead favored Rudyard Kipling. Since he lacked his compatriot's "admittedly adorable, but morbid yearning" (Rydén 2010: 612, my translation), it was easier to convince the Academy members of Kipling's greatness. When the first Nobel Committee Chair finally came around to suggest Swinburne's name in 1908, and managed to convince his fellow Committee members of the poet's greatness, the Committee recommendation was voted down by the Academy (Rydén and Westerström 2018: 47). Instead of the Victorian poet, a compromise between Swinburne and Lagerlöf was selected—German philosopher Rudolf Eucken. When Swinburne died in 1909, Wirsén was sorry that the Academy never awarded him (Rydén 2010: 614).

A recurring name in the 1910s and 1920s discussions was the poet and novelist Thomas Hardy. Contemporary English academics and intellectuals expressed a recurrent critique of the Swedish Academy's unwillingness to award the author of *Tess of the d'Urbervilles, Jude the Obscure,* and *Wessex Poems*. When he was nominated in 1910 by six members of the Society of Authors in London, it was Erik Axel Karlfeldt's task to review the author's work and prepare the Committee discussion. Karlfeldt disliked Hardy's tendency toward "the most blatant ugliness of Naturalism" (Rydén and Westerström 2018: 43, my translation). A decade later, Karlfeldt had changed his mind and suggested the English writer as a rival candidate to William Butler Yeats in 1923, and then again to George Bernard Shaw two years later, but by then Hardy's work had found another skeptical reader in Per Hallström (Rydén and Westerström: 267 and 355–6).

Besides Conrad and Hardy, H.G. Wells was the most missed British author in the list of laureates by the 1951 experts (Lamont 1951: 13). The author of science-fiction classics like *The Time Machine* and *The War of the Worlds* was nominated several times, but his work failed to convince the Committees. In 1921, Committee Chair Per Hallström praised Wells' lively and innovative imagination, but criticized him for publishing too many insignificant works (Svensén 2001b: 13). Next time he was discussed, after being suggested by the newly appointed laureate Sinclair Lewis in 1932, the Committee thought that the British novelist's production since 1921 had not been substantial enough to change the last assessment—even though they admitted that Wells as an author was "doubtlessly a genius" (Svensén 2001b: 178, my translation). Another recurring name in discussions of overlooked British authors has been D.H. Lawrence (see for example Perruchot 1951: 120 and Peyre 1951: 213).

Most controversies have perhaps surrounded the fact that Graham Greene never received the Nobel Prize. Greene's work was a significant part of the Committee's discussion for several years, and the productive English writer was on the verge of earning the honors. Per Hallström was Greene's reviewer in the 1950s, filing written assessments of his œuvre in 1950, 1952, 1953, and 1956. These accounts were generally sympathetic toward the recurring nomination, especially in regards to Greene's "religious worldview," but in his later assessments Hallström regretted the writer's reduced interest in religious themes. His case in point was the latest novel *The Quiet American* from 1955, in which Greene's storytelling had become "completely modern with pure sensory impressions right into the void" (Rydén and Westerström 2018: 363 and 365). A decade later, however, Greene was the first choice of Hallström's successor as Permanent Secretary and Committee Chair, Anders Österling, and in the 1970s, the British novelist, playwright, film writer, travel writer, and poet was discussed once again. Lars Gyllensten's ambition as Permanent Secretary and Nobel Committee Chair to recognize literature from "small countries" has been seen as the main reason why Graham Greene was never awarded (cf. Espmark 1986: 112). In 1980, Academy member Artur Lundkvist publicly expressed two arguments why he was reluctant to contribute to awarding the British author: Greene was already too celebrated and esteemed, and his best works were written a long time ago (Espmark 1986: 169).

Another English writer from Greene's generation, poet W.H. Auden, has also been repeatedly seen as left out by the Academy. Auden was very close to earning the award in the 1960s. In 1967, the final decision stood between Auden, Greene, and Miguel Ángel Asturias. It is not unreasonable to interpret the choice of the Guatemalan writer as an early expression of Gierow's and Gyllensten's pragmatically pluralist view of the prize's main purpose.

Today, the absence of Virginia Woolf's name probably appears as one of the biggest lacunae in the list of Nobel laureates. Woolf's relevance as a modernist novelist beyond mere experimentation and—certainly—as one of the most important precursors of modern feminism, gender theory, and queer theory, is much more evident today than it was in the early and mid-1900s. Woolf was indeed mentioned as an overlooked author by the 350 experts in the 1951 *Books Abroad* survey—and Renée Lang thought that Woolf and French writer Colette should have been awarded instead of Grazia Deledda, Pearl Buck, and Gabriela Mistral (Lang 1951: 116)—but she was not one of the most endorsed missing authors in this early survey. Throughout the twentieth century, Woolf's absence from the list of Nobel laureates was not as heatedly discussed as Joyce's, Kafka's, and Proust's, which makes it very clear that retrospective assessments of prize decisions are always deeply entrenched in their own times, values, and customs.

In the 1951 *Books Abroad* survey, Herman Salinger of Grinnell College in Iowa efficiently and unceremoniously summed up all the Swedish Academy's missed opportunities to honor the most influential twentieth-century authors: "We seek in vain for several of those writers who have proved most influential on the succeeding literature of their own and other countries, whether it be through the discovery of new and relatively unexplored terrain of human living or thinking, or through the discovery or invention of a new style or recording experience, or both" (Salinger 1951: 251–2). Salinger shares this observation with many international critics, a fact that quite forcefully confirms the notion that the prize's influence on literary history is limited. The most influential authors of the twentieth century—internationally as well as nationally—have made literary history without any decisive help from the Nobel Prize.

The Already Canonized

The Nobel selections are often criticized for being belated. The honors have come too late, critics have pointed out, to have a real effect on world literature. In selecting Gabriela Mistral in 1945, Manuel Dúran argued forty years later, the Swedish Academy did award "a woman of exquisite personality and undeniable poetic talent," but her verse was "too reminiscent of the Rubén Darío *modernista* trend," which made the decision "twenty-five years behind the times" (Dúran 1988: 214–15). This tendency of belatedness has not only meant that the Swedish Academy often has awarded laureates whose works were outdated at the time, but also that authors have been awarded long after their prime, which has limited the prize's impact on their future work. Being too late has also meant that many prizes have been given to writers most people already knew, had read, and agreed were highly important. "Only with hesitation and restraint," Herbert Howarth argued in the 1967 survey, "should the Academy endorse a writer already widely recognized and rewarded" (Howarth 1967: 7). "What great virtue is there," George Steiner effectively summed up in 1984, "in acclaiming that which is already of global renown?" (Steiner 1984)

There have been many examples of already canonized authors in the history of the prize. François Mauriac and Mikhail Sholokhov were already discussed in 1951 as missing names in the list of laureates. When these authors were honored in 1952 and 1965, the Swedish Academy managed to silence a recurring criticism rather than point readers in a new direction. In an article in *The Atlantic* from 1966, Donald Fleming mentioned Pablo Neruda as an obvious candidate for the prize (Fleming 1966). Five years later, the Academy heeded his call for a second prize to a Chilean poet. Thomas Mann, T.S. Eliot, Ernest Hemingway, and Samuel Beckett were already viewed as three of the most important modern writers when they were honored, and both J.M. Coetzee and Kazuo Ishiguro were generally perceived as highly central contemporary authors when they received their prizes. Bertrand Russell's and Jean-Paul Sartre's respective reputations as indispensable contributors to contemporary philosophy were firmly established before they became laureates in 1950 and 1964, and Winston Churchill was, of course, one of the most famous heroes from the Second World War, having accepted his knighthood from Elizabeth II eight months before his wife received his Nobel medal and diploma from the Swedish king Gustaf VI Adolf in December 1953.

You could argue that these awards have had a very limited direct impact on literary and cultural history. Well, have they had any effect at all? Wouldn't T.S. Eliot's reputation as one of the most influential modernist poets be strong enough without the prize? And has Churchill's Nobel Prize in Literature really strengthened his position in the history books?

One way of measuring the level of pre-Nobel canonization is to find out if the laureates had won other highly profiled prizes before receiving the Swedish prize. Four of the Nobel laureates had already won the American Neustadt Prize, which has been awarded every second year since 1970, when receiving the Nobel honors: Gabriel García Márquez (Neustadt winner in 1972, Nobel laureate in 1982), Czeslaw Milosz (Neustadt 1978, Nobel 1980), Octavio Paz (Neustadt 1982, Nobel 1990), and Tomas Tranströmer (Neustadt 1990, Nobel 2011). Eighteen other laureates had been finalists for the Neustadt Prize before winning the Nobel: Pablo Neruda, Claude Simon, Harold Pinter, Wole Soyinka, Doris Lessing, Elias Canetti, V.S. Naipaul, Günter Grass, Kenzaburo Oe, Peter Handke, Nadine Gordimer, Omar Pamuk, Svetlana Alexievich, Seamus Heaney, Mo Yan, Mario Vargas Llosa, Alice Munro, and Bob Dylan. In addition to these names, Alexandr Solzhenitzyn and Eyvind Johnson were finalists for the Neustadt Prize the same year they won the Nobel. These numbers show why the Neustadt Prize is often regarded as "a 'waiting room' or 'antechamber' of the Nobel," as Manuel Dúran phrased it in 1988 (Dúran 1988: 216). Only three Nobel laureates had formerly been awarded the Prix Formentor, a prize given between 1961 and 1967, and then from 2011 onward—Samuel Beckett in 1961, Saul Bellow in 1965, and Annie Ernaux in 2019.

The Prix Goncourt is the oldest of the nationally domestic or language-restricted prizes comparable in stature with the Nobel Prize. Despite the fact that the Goncourt has been awarded since 1903, only one of the fifteen Francophone Nobel laureates had previously been Goncourt winners—the 2014 Nobel winner Patrick Modiano, whose novel *Rue des boutiques obscures* earned him the domestic French honors in 1978. Apart from Modiano, the Swedish Academy has totally avoided the choices of the Académie Goncourt, including Marcel Proust, who was awarded in 1919 for the second part of *À la recherche du temps perdu*; André Malraux, who earned the Goncourt in 1933 for *La Condition humaine*; Simone de Beauvoir, who was awarded the French prize in 1954 for her novel *Les Mandarins* (*The Mandarins*); Marguerite Duras, whose *L'Amant* (*The Lover*) won the prize in 1984; and Michel Houellebecq, who was awarded in 2010 for his novel *La Carte et le territoire* (*The Map and the Territory*).

In this respect, the Anglophone Nobel laureates are quite different from the French. Six of the US Nobel laureates had already won the Pulitzer Prize before receiving the Nobel. Eugene O'Neill had won three drama Pulitzers—for *Beyond the Horizon* in 1920, *Anna Christie* in 1922, and *Strange Interlude* in 1928—before earning the Nobel in 1936. A year before his Nobel honors in 1954, Ernest Hemingway had won a Pulitzer in the fiction category for *The Old Man and the Sea*. Saul Bellow was announced as that year's Nobel laureate in October 1976, only five months after he had won the fiction Pulitzer for the novel *Humboldt's Gift*. Toni Morrison won a Pulitzer for the novel *Beloved* five years before winning the Nobel in 1993, and Louise Glück had won a Pulitzer in the poetry category for *The Wild Iris* in 1993, twenty-seven years before being awarded in Stockholm. Also, when Bob Dylan surprisingly was announced as the 2016 Nobel laureate, he was already a Pulitzer-winner, having won a "Special Citations and Awards" distinction in 2008.

If we look at London-based consecration, we find that the Nobel laureates who had previously been awarded the Booker Prize are also six. V.S. Naipaul was honored for *In a Free State* in 1971, and also shortlisted in 1979 for *A Bend in the River*. Nadine Gordimer won the Booker Prize in 1974 for *The Conservationist*, and William Golding in 1980 for *Rites of Passage*. J.M. Coetzee had won the Booker twice—for *Life & Times of Michael K* in 1983 and for *Disgrace* in 1999—when he received the Nobel in 2003, and Kazuo Ishiguro had won the Booker for *The Remains of the Day* in 1989 and been shortlisted for three other novels—*An Artist in the Floating World* in 1986, *When We Were Orphans* in 2000, and *Never Let Me Go* in 2005—before becoming a Nobel laureate in 2017. Patrick White (*The Vivisector*, 1970), Doris Lessing (*Briefing for a Descent into Hell*, 1971; *The Sirian Experiments*, 1981; and *The Good Terrorist*, 1985), Alice Munro (*The Beggar Maid*, 1980), and Abdulrazak Gurnah (*Paradise*, 1994) had all been shortlisted for the Booker Prize before winning the Nobel. Additionally, two laureates had already won the International Booker Prize when receiving the call from Stockholm: Alice Munro in 2009 for her entire body of literary works, and Olga Tokarczuk in 2018 for the novel *Bieguni* in Jennifer Croft's translation *Flights*.

Awarding the already canonized authors with the most prestigious prize is of course not absolutely pointless. The literary works that have proven influential and highly important become consecrated as even more influential and important when acknowledged by the most recognized international prize institution. The earlier, more contemporary positive criticism of the work is confirmed from a little less contemporary perspective, making sure that the honored œuvre will survive and meet future readers. But the most important effect of these quite expected selections has not to do with the particular laureates and their respective works, but with the prize itself. Honoring the already highly esteemed literature brings as much prestige to the Nobel Prize as it does to the awarded writers. More than anything, these prizes reassure the world that the members of the Swedish Academy and its Nobel Committee know what they are doing, and confirm the notion that the selection process is reasonable. The prizes to Mann, Hemingway, Sartre, Beckett, García Márquez, and Ishiguro reinforce the Nobel's position as an important international consecrational institution.

An Alternative Literary History

If we were to rely on the Nobel Prize for an impression of German twentieth-century literary history, literary scholar Theodore Ziolkowski wrote in 1967, we would get a grotesquely distorted picture (Ziolkowski 1967: 13). Of the early German-language prizes, only that to Gerhart Hauptmann has turned out to be a fortunate choice from Ziolkowski's late 1960s perspective, whereas Mommsen, Eucken, Heyse, and Spitteler were all very unwise selections of authors soon to become thoroughly outdated. Ziolkowski had an important point that we must not ignore. The history of the Nobel Prize in Literature does not automatically reflect timeless literary greatness and foundational aesthetic influence. Its history is full of decisions that seem strange and unfortunate in retrospect.

Even though William F. Lamont's respondees in the 1951 survey were generally quite sympathetic and understanding toward the first fifty years of selections, they did raise quite a few critical issues. The Nobel Committee had generally made "good decisions," Lamont summed up, but "it could, nevertheless, have done considerably better" (Lamont 1951: 11). We shouldn't ignore that the eighteen individual responses to Lamont's questions were published under the headline "What's Wrong with the Nobel Prize?"

One of the points made in this survey was that "certain countries relatively rich in literary productivity" have been "entirely neglected" (Lamont 1951: 11). Lamont did not report any argument among the asked experts concerning a Western bias in the list of laureates. There was no call for Asian, African, or South American awards. The four overlooked nations mentioned by the 350 experts were all European: Iceland, Hungary, Austria, and the Netherlands. The first Icelandic award was to be given just a couple of years later, but the 1955 Halldór Kiljan Laxness prize remains the only Icelandic prize up until today. Hungary had to wait until 2001 until Imre Kertész received the first—and so far only—award. Two Austrian authors have been awarded since 1951, but both of these prizes came very late in the Nobel history: Elfriede Jelinek in 2004 and Peter Handke in 2019. Even today, no Nobel Prize in Literature has been awarded to a Dutch writer. In his individual response, Henri Peyre argued that Russia and Spain had been unfairly treated by the Committee, with too few awards and awards to the wrong authors (Peyre 1951: 213).

In his critical assessment from 1967 of the early German awards, Theodore Ziolkowski confirmed what the experts consulted by Lamont had said sixteen years earlier: Heyse and Spitteler were seen as unworthy of an award of this stature, and the works of historian Mommsen and philosopher Eucken were not literary enough to be considered "eligible for a literary prize" (Lamont 1951: 12). In his individual assessment in the 1951 survey, Ludwig Marcuse called the decisions to award Eucken and Heyse "flagrant errors": "These errors would have been serious even if there had been no abler candidates. But the jury failed to notice, or refused to notice, abler candidates" (Marcuse 1951: 117). The 1908 laureate was a candidate, Rydén and Westerström write, whom "almost nobody wanted," even at the time of the decision (Rydén and Westerström 2018: 48). Marcuse called Eucken an "amiable epigone of the German Idealists" without any influence on the rising generation after the turn of the century (Marcuse 1951: 118). Rudolf Eucken was nominated by Swedish philosopher Vitalis Nordström and suggested in the internal discussions by Academy member Harald Hjärne as a protest against the Committee Chair Carl David af Wirsén. The Academy's decision to overrule Wirsén's candidate, Algernon Charles Swinburne, did not include any particular enthusiasm for the German philosopher. Many of the Academy members wanted to give the honors to Selma Lagerlöf, but it was impossible for them to distance themselves that far from Wirsén's literary taste and his reluctance to award Swedish authors. The Paul Heyse award in 1910 belongs, Rydén and Westerström sweepingly conclude, to "the least successful" prizes in the Nobel history (Rydén and Westerström 2018: 274). For Ludwig Marcuse, Heyse is—just like Eucken—an obsolete epigone: "of his 50 plays not one outlived him," he brusquely concluded forty years after the prize decision (Marcuse 1951: 118).

Mommsen and Spitteler, on the other hand, have both been positively re-evaluated since Ziolkowski's harsh verdict, for example by George Steiner. The second ever laureate, Steiner wrote in 1984, was "a great historian and epigrapher of ancient Rome." Mommsen belongs to the "illustrious recipients" of the prize history whose works exist "outside normal definitions of literature" (Steiner 1984). And the Swiss 1919 laureate was, according to Steiner, one of the very few important discoveries made by the Swedish Academy.

Among the French laureates, Lamont's experts thought that five of the seven awards up until 1950 were mistakes: Sully Prudhomme, Frédéric Mistral, Romain Rolland, and Roger Martin du Gard were all unworthy laureates, and Henri Bergson was considered non-eligible. He was, the 1950s writers argued, a philosopher and not a literary author (Lamont 1951: 12). In 1967, Gene J. Barberet was more generous to the Swedish Academy, but he admitted that the works of Rolland, France, and Martin du Gard came forth as quite passé from a 1960s perspective (Barberet 1967: 8). George Steiner approved of France and Bergson, was critical of Prudhomme, and did not mention Mistral, Rolland, or Martin du Gard at all, which, of course, signals indifference toward these three French selections. Both Spanish laureates up until 1950—José Echegaray and Jacinto Benavente—were unfortunate choices according to Lamont's jury (Lamont 1951: 12). Angel del Río from New York University could think of "a dozen Spanish authors as well or better qualified for the prize" than these two playwrights (del Río 1951: 214).

The decision to award the first Russian prize to the exile writer Ivan Bunin was quite strongly criticized in 1951, and most Polish critics would have preferred novelist and short story writer Stefan Zeromski to Wladyslaw Reymont (Vlach and Filipoff 1967). In the 1988 survey, critics were quite skeptical as to the long-standing positive effects of the 1984 prize to Czech author Jaroslav Seifert (Ivask 1988: 198). Generally, the Nordic prizes have not gone down well with international critics and scholars. The only Finnish prize—to Frans Eemil Sillanpää in 1939—has been quite questioned, and among the (all too many, according to most external critics) Swedish prizes Verner von Heidenstam's in 1916 has often been seen as the most unnecessary internal decision (Espmark 1986: 160 and 162). In his individual response in *Books Abroad*, New York scholar Renée Lang placed Heidenstam (alongside Heyse, Karlfeldt, and Sillanpää) in the category of "respectable middlebrows" who should not have been awarded (Lang 1951: 116). But the 1951 jury of 350 experts did find Heidenstam worthy of the prize (Lamont 1951: 13).

The early Italian prizes have also been quite criticized. In 1951, Grazia Deledda was not seen as a worthy laureate (Lamont 1951: 11), and in the 1967 survey Italian critic Olga Ragusa described Giosuè Carducci's poetry as "merely erudite and coldly formal" (Ragusa 1967: 30). A negative view also seems to have been dominating regarding the 1959 award to Salvatore Quasimodo. "Few experts," Kjell Espmark wrote in 2021, "would today put Quasimodo above Ungaretti and Montale. But above all we may regret that Karen Blixen was thus set aside" (Espmark 2021: 31).

Several of the Anglophone prizes have been strongly criticized. Many critics have questioned the 1938 award to Pearl Buck, and some Academy members have in retrospect renounced responsibility for that decision (Rydén and Westerström 2018: 347). In the 1951 survey, there was a general rejection of the decisions to give Kipling, Galsworthy, and Buck the honors. And in the second *Books Abroad* survey, Robert E. Spiller criticized the 1953 Committee for awarding Winston Churchill. The British politician's prose, the expert of American literature wrote, only consists of "elaborate copies of by-gone literature" (Spiller 1967: 33).

But the Swedish Academy's failures to select the right laureates in the eyes of the literary experts do not necessarily diminish the impact of the prize. The institution of the Nobel Prize is by default continually creating a long-standing canon that is indestructible by the posthumous factors of literary consecration: the Nobel list of literary awards is a consecration for posterity that cannot be completely eradicated by posterior re-evaluations. The names of the laureates will always be there, whoever reads—if anyone—their works, and however they are understood and assessed. What Ziolkowski called a distorted perspective of German literary history is still a highly existing perspective, grotesque or not. And it only exists because of the Swedish

Academy. Whatever we think of particular prize decisions and how they were made, the distributed honors remain unperturbed. As Ludwig Marcuse writes in 1951: "The Nobel Prizes for science and literature are all-powerful. The man who gains one is no longer a physicist or a novelist, he is a Nobel Prize Winner" (Marcuse 1951: 117). There seems to be some kind of irrational, quasi-religious aura surrounding the selected authors—as Manuel Dúran's concepts of a "magic circle" and a "sacred space" of laureates suggest. The more or less extinguished metaphors "consecration" and "canonization" as words for high cultural status, borrowed as they are from the Christian processes of ordaining someone a sacred office and admission a dead person into sainthood, have never been more appropriate.

The semi-contemporary temporal distance between the discussed literary works and the Nobel Committee and the semi-peripheral cultural perspective of the Swedish Academy both contribute strongly to the prize's very special and influential role in world literary canon formation. But it cannot be denied that these two positions also make the Nobel's strong influence on international literary history quite problematic. Laureate selections are not based upon absolutely contemporary assessments of the discussed texts, nor on distinctly retrospective evaluations made with the help of another era's disinterested and wide perspective. The temporal in-between position in relation to the literary texts leads to an unevenly constructed canon, to which authors are selected for many different, disparate, and often unacknowledged reasons. This makes it hard to identify and interpret the aesthetic, cultural, and ideological mechanisms at work in the selection process. The same problem is at work in regards to the Nobel Committee's semi-peripheral position. The Swedish judges have very different kinds of relations to the literary traditions of the world, and these relations are rarely very clear from an international perspective. Any attempt at creating an overarching, general canon for all these literatures must be understood as a construction made from a particular position, and if this canon is constructed in one of the centers of world literature, this central, powerful outlook on things must be taken into account when evaluating the value and effects of the canon formation. The power structures and blindspots of the semi-periphery are much harder to recognize, acknowledge, and describe. As a result, there is an acute danger that the complexity of such a semi-peripheral position is confused with a neutral perspective, which it certainly is not.

No wonder, then, that the literary history of the Nobel Prize is seen by many critics as a grotesquely distorted version of our common literary past. The toughest critics see the list of laureates as obsolete at best, and misleading and destructive at worst. But aren't there also positive effects of such a canon? Yes, I think there are.

One constructive effect of the Nobel literary history is that its idiosyncracies make visible the constructed nature of all literary canons. Every assessment of literary quality is, of course, unavoidably a biased product of a particular historical context. The strangeness of the list of Nobel laureates reminds us of what we already know— that the literary canon that helps us read, learn, and teach literary history is a product of a complex combination of coincidences and subjective, ideologically entrenched collective decisions. A good reminder of this is the fact that one of the most canonized laureates in our twenty-first-century perspective, T.S. Eliot, was dismissed in 1951 as one of the authors who "should never have stood on a list of Nobel prize winners." Yale professor Henri Peyre put Eliot—alongside France, Galsworthy, and Gide—in the category of truly unworthy laureates: "none of them," he wrote, "was or is a truly important writer and our successors will laugh one day (and many of us already smile) at the lack of perspective which made them pass for talents of the very first order" (Peyre 1951: 213).

Another point of the Nobel canon is the very fact that it offers an alternative. This peculiarly constructed list of authors makes up a complement to other kinds of canonization. An imminent effect of every canon formation is a slimming down of the all-too-huge number of cultural phenomena produced. In national as well as comparative literary history we tend to return to the same literary texts again and again and again, in our teaching as well as in our research. We know that the Greek Antiquity produced much more stories, poetry, and dramatic works than *The Iliad*, *The Odyssey*, "Fragment 31," *King Oidipus*, and *Medea*, but we keep coming back to Homer, Sappho, Sophocles, and Euripides—because they are accessible, and because their texts make up a toolbox of cultural references that glues our civilization together, which is all very fine and necessary. But if we would also—as an additional activity—have access to, read, and teach all the plays that actually won the annual dramatic contests in fifth-century Athens, our general notion of the time would be much more nuanced, and much more adequate.

Unlike T.S. Eliot, many of the most questioned laureates have, since receiving their awards, been increasingly less reprinted, less read, and less discussed. Their long-standing significance in literary history has not become as central as their contemporaries in the Nobel Committees expected. But none of these criticized and less read laureates, I would argue, really belong to what Margaret Cohen calls "the great unread"—the mass of historical literary material not analyzed by scholars (Cohen 2009). Thanks to the Nobel Prize, all these names are indeed still mentioned here and there. Thanks to frequently criticized decisions by the Swedish Academy, they are saved from the oblivion of the great unread. Eucken, Heyse, and other laureates who seem obscure to us today are occasionally re-read by scholars, if only to confirm harsh verdicts from earlier critics.

Unlike many other writers who used to be read and discussed by their contemporaries, Nobel laureates are never completely forgotten by posterity. And sometimes they get upgraded and reprinted, like Grazia Deledda and Pearl Buck in the highly profiled Swedish book series "Women Nobel Laureates in Literature" from 2018, which includes new editions of works by Alice Munro, Herta Müller, Doris Lessing, Wislawa Szymborska, Toni Morrison, Nadine Gordimer, Selma Lagerlöf, Buck's *The Good Earth*, and Deledda's novel *Elias Portolu*. This kind of publication initiative—an action that updates, markets, and distributes rarely read older works of literature—is a distinct effect of prize decisions taken a long time ago. Buck is an excellent example of a laureate who has been losing and gaining in status, respect and recognition several times since she was awarded in 1938. In 2021 her works were, for example, relaunched in Italy (Lanfranchi 2022).

For Spanish scholar Manuel Durán, reading the list of Nobel laureates in the late 1980s was a "melancholy and depressing pastime" since most of the names "have long become passé" (Durán 1988: 214). But this reading could also be something else than a melancholy pastime—a tangible insight into literary history and its changing values, a new perspective that works against presentism and offers a necessary alternative to the most frequently told narratives of twentieth-century literature. Durán himself unintentionally illustrated this point when arguing that the first Nobel award to a Hispanic author was "squandered" on José Echegaray, whose "melodramatic and bombastic plays are unreadable and unperformable today." Many graduate students in Spanish literature, Durán wrote, have "complained bitterly about the inclusion of plays by Echegaray in the Ph.D. reading lists, where he had been placed due to his international reputation based upon his receipt of the Nobel." In this critique, the Spanish scholar described one of the most pregnant historical effects of the prize: even those Nobel-winning authors whose works are viewed as hopelessly outdated and irrelevant by posterity are and will stay included on mandatory reading list in different kinds of educational contexts. And these authors are there only because they once were honored by the Swedish Academy. Without the Nobel Prize, Echegaray would not be read at all. The embittered doctoral students may not like it, but the prize gives them an alternative access to literary history, a sort of constant structure in the ever-changing re-evaluations of literary values.

The Nobel Prize history forces us to read certain texts against our own tastes and desires. It thereby enlarges and variegates (if not necessarily aesthetically enriches) the effective life of literary history. And maybe this long-standing effect is the most important result of the prize: the list of laureates works against the inevitable mechanism of standardization and solidification of literary history writing. Maybe the least recognized, least understood, and most criticized prizes actually are—in the long run—the most important ones. As the expert of French literature, Gene J. Barberet wrote in his contribution to the 1967 survey in *Books Abroad*: "Although Rolland along with Anatole France and Martin du Gard may be considered passé today and writers of the secondary rank, they fruitfully reflected the preoccupations, the values, and the finest aspirations of their age" (Barberet 1967: 8). There is, Herbert Howarth argued in the same survey, "such a thing as a fertile mistake," but to "canonize the already-canonized fertilizes no one" (Howarth 1967: 7).

In his 1967 review of the prize history, Robert E. Spiller pointed out that "the Nobel Prize in literature is not really a literary award in the modern sense and was never intended to be" (Spiller 1967: 31). Yes, perhaps the prize shouldn't be regarded as modern at all, and perhaps not being modern is one of its central strengths and contributions. The history of the selections does indeed go beyond the normative focus on Modernism that has, according to Pascale Casanova, been so prevalent in European and North-American twentieth-century canon formation. Modernity—in the restricted Western sense of the concept—has been regarded as synonymous with the aesthetically complex and valuable (Casanova 2005: 73). The list of twentieth-century Nobel laureates can point to other values, other aesthetics, and other contexts than Pre-modernism, High Modernism, and Postmodernism;

this list includes—for those who feel the urge to look beyond their own historically conditioned literary tastes and preferences—an alternative history of literature from 1901 onward, in all its flaws and biases, complete with hidden gems alongside hopelessly outdated texts.

This way, the Nobel Prize is a central vehicle for the Swedish Academy to accomplish what Per Wästberg described in 2020 as their fundamental task—to "keep alive texts and thoughts that are not staggering new" (Wästberg 2020: 399, my translation).

Nobel Effects and the World Literary System

The Nobel does not only lead to recognition, it also increases the availability of the awarded œuvres. The prize decisions initiate new editions of older works in source languages, new translations of these works, and new editions of older translations. Providing distinct ignition for new translations and re-issued old translations is in itself quite a significant world literary effect. As Pascale Casanova phrases it, literary translation "is a kind of right to international existence" (Casanova 2015: 19, my translation). Being translated is to become legitimate in the eyes of the world. In 1951, Belgian critic Constant Burniaux expressed his wish that the Nobel Prize should lead to "the publication of Nobel Prize anthologies in all major languages" (Burniaux 1951: 115). This wish hasn't been fully fulfilled, but a couple of publication initiatives have made Nobel-prized œuvres collectively more accessible. One example is the Swedish Academy's and the Nobel Foundation's own ambitious project "La Collection des prix Nobel de littérature," a sixty-volume book series including one work each by all the laureates from Sully Prudhomme to Giorgos Seferis, either in the French original or in French translation, all of them accompanied by rich introductions.

Occasionally, the Nobel Prize has a more general publication effect. This happens when a particular decision not only leads to translations of the laureate's own works, but also to an increased number of translations from the honored author's country or language. In 1932, for example, the *New York Times* reported on a "new vogue abroad" for US novels. It was described as a "wave of interest first roused by Sinclair Lewis" and his Nobel Prize two years earlier, a commercial boost that "builds up new publics" for American authors ("Our Books Enjoy New Vogue Abroad," 1932). Four years later, the New York paper reported on a slightly different kind of effect when the second US award to Eugene O'Neill led to an "American week in London" ("American Week in London," 1936). The decision to honor the American playwright stirred a general British interest in US culture.

Swedish scholar Anna Gunder refers to the prize-triggered publications of translations as the "Nobel effect." Her research shows that this effect indeed is distinct in the months and years following each announcement, but also that the increased number of translations varies significantly between different kinds of laureates. The Nobel effect tends to be stronger, Gunder observes, for authors who were less known before the award (Gunder 2014). These observations seem to confirm the value of the pragmatic strategy in the 1970s and 1980s to honor formerly unknown writers, and

George Steiner's opinion that there is no point in giving the prize to authors who are already widely renown. But how is this effect of new or renewed availability related to what Johan Heilbron calls the "hierarchical structure" of "the international translation system" (Heilbron 1999: 433)? To what extent do the translational effects of the Nobel Prize follow the imbalanced pattern of literary exchange observed and analyzed by Heilbron and many others (cf. Maia et al 2015; Schwartz 2017; Brems et al 2017; Lindqvist 2019; Edfeldt et al 2022)?

Heilbron identifies four categories of languages with four different relations to the translational system. The hyper-central English is a very dominant language *from* which many literary texts are translated but *to* which relatively few texts are imported. The three central languages French, German, and Russian are not at all as dominant as English but they are still quite translated, and relatively few literary texts are translated into these languages. The semi-peripheral Spanish, Italian, Polish, Czech, Danish, and Swedish are not as frequently translated as the central literary languages, but they are much more translated than all the languages not specifically mentioned—that is, the vast number of what Heilbron calls "peripheral" literary languages that make up the fourth category. These categories have been discussed, adjusted, and updated many times over the last twenty years, but Heilbron's basic four-layered structure has been generally confirmed by later statistics.

Does the Nobel translation effect confirm this imbalanced system? Is the Nobel Prize an integral part of the global translation system or is it an anomaly that challenges its logic and works against its consequences? Let's look at two sets of chronologically closely connected prizes and compare their respective translational effects. The first set is four awards from the period 1968–74 representing all four language categories: Yasunari Kawabata and peripheral Japanese, Heinrich Böll and central German, Patrick White and hyper-central English, and Harry Martinson and his semi-peripheral Swedish. A digital search for translations published in the five years following the prize instantly reveals that all these prizes definitely *did* lead to a Nobel effect, but also that the extent of this effect varied quite significantly between the laureates.[1]

If we start with the translations of Harry Martinson's work from the year he was awarded, 1974, and five years onward, Heilbron's pattern seems to be confirmed. The prize led to a significant general Nobel effect, but if we only look for translations into English this increase is hardly noticeable. Between 1974 and 1979, more titles by Martinson were published in each of the central languages French and German, in the semi-peripheral language Italian and in each of the peripheral languages Norwegian, Finnish, Hungarian, and Slovenian than in hyper-central English. So far, then, the Nobel translation impact is totally in line with the general literary power-structures between languages as described by Heilbron. The availability effects of the Nobel Prize

---

[1] This search is done with the help of WorldCat and Index Translationum, and the lists in these digital sources cannot be completely trusted. They are, of course, not absolutely complete, and they include quite a lot of incorrect information, for example about the languages in which the listed books are written. Still, these two sources do provide information rigorous enough to get us a fairly correct overall picture.

seem to be dependent on the general structure of international literary traffic, and the impact of the prize seems to reinforce this hierarchy.

But if we compare these numbers with the translation effects of Kawabata and Böll, a distinct pattern fails to appear. Between 1968 and 1973, the Japanese author was translated significantly more into English than into any other language, which suggests, in contrast to both the Martinson effect and Heilbron's analyses, that English is more open for translations than other languages. An even more complex picture emerges from the Heinrich Böll translations published between 1972 and 1977. In one respect, Heilbron's model is confirmed by the Böll translations: as a writer in a central language, Böll was more translated in his post-prize period than both the semi-central Martinson and the peripheral Kawabata. But when it comes to what languages Böll was translated into during these five years, the pattern is no longer confirmed. The Nobel effect for Böll included more English translations than translations into any other language except Dutch and Spanish. WorldCat lists thirty-four English books and thirty-six Dutch, to be compared with thirty-three Danish, thirty-two Swedish, sixteen French titles, and as many as fifty-five Spanish translations.

This lack of pattern is confirmed by the translational effects of Patrick White's prize in 1973. Despite writing in hyper-central English, White is less generally translated in his five-year post-prize period than both Heinrich Böll and Yasunari Kawabata. The Nobel effect of this hyper-central prize is stronger than the semi-peripheral Martinson prize, but weaker than both the central and the peripheral prize. The Nobel impact on availability from the late 1960s and early 1970s is not in line with the general pattern of translation traffic. It seems to follow its own logic.

These observations are distinctly confirmed by another sample of four authors awarded in a period more or less contemporary with Heilbron's statistics—Claude Simon, writing in central French and winning the 1985 prize; Wole Soyinka, writing in hyper-central English and awarded in 1986; Naguib Mahfouz, writing in peripheral Arabic and winning in 1988; and Camilo José Cela, awarded in 1989 for his work in semi-central Spanish. Mahfouz was much more translated into English than into any other language between 1988 and 1993, and he was much more translated generally in his post-prize period than both Simon and Soyinka. Semi-central Cela was much less translated into English than peripheral Mahfouz, but more translated generally than the other three authors. Considering the total number of publications, the translation effect of the Simon prize was distinctly weaker than the other three awards, but when it comes to the number of different languages, Simon was more translated after his prize than both Soyinka and Mahfouz. Camilo José Cela enjoyed the strongest Nobel effect in reaching different languages. His work was translated into thirty-eight different languages between 1989 and 1994, whereas Simon's work reached twenty-five, Mahfouz' twenty and Soyinka's sixteen languages in their respective post-prize periods.

Just like in the 1968–74 period, it is the hyper-central prize that is most distinctly at odds with Heilbron's hierarchy in these awards from the late 1980s. Between 1986 and 1991, the prize to Soyinka led to fewer translations than the awards to Cela and Mahfouz in their equivalent periods, and, perhaps more significantly, Soyinka's

Nobel effect involved fewer languages than the equivalent effects of the three other laureates from this period.

The fact that English and the central languages fail to dominate in these numbers could perhaps be explained by the hypothesis that White, Soyinka, Böll, and Simon were already more translated than Kawabata, Martinson, Mahfouz, and Cela before becoming Nobel laureates. But this argument does not explain why new editions of already existing translations were not issued to a larger extent after the announcement of the prize. Another explanation of the lack of pattern in the Nobel effects could be that particularly close relations between some languages led to strong availability effects with a dominant impact on the overall statistics. The fact that the awards to Cela and Mahfouz, for example, led to more French than German translations could be seen as results of the Romance kinship between Spanish and French, and the intimate post-colonial relation between French and Arabic.

In other cases, a more complex picture emerges. The most distinct Nobel effects for Claude Simon were, for example, translations into Spanish and German. Only the many Spanish translations can be explained by language kinship, but both Spain and Germany are of course geographical neighbors of Simon's France. Some cases in my two sample sets of awards suggest that the Nobel effect of availability has less to do with language and more to do with culture. Neither Patrick White nor Wole Soyinka was, after all, British or US writers, which could contribute to the fact that their respective Nobel effects were limited.

Whatever explanations we find most valid, we can conclude that the Nobel translation effects are not in accordance with the strict and profound hierarchy of Johan Heilbron's world systems analysis. This does not mean that Heilbron's numbers are incorrect, or that all the studies of translation patterns that rely on his basic observations are misleading. Neither does my small study of two sample periods show that the Nobel translation effect follows its own unique logic and distinctly goes against the grain of dominant economic and political factors involved in intercultural and interlingual literary traffic. What it does show, however, is that it is difficult to detect a distinct pattern in the Nobel Prize's impact on translation.

Every laureate selection leads to translation activity and increased availability, but the factors involved in this process are numerous and disparate. As Pieter Vermeulen notes: "even if non-Anglophone winners are published by major publishers *after* winning the Nobel Prize (Simon & Schuster for Le Clézio; Macmillan for Hertha Müller; Random House for Svetlana Alexievich; Riverhead Books for Tokarczuk), their entrance into the American literary field typically occurs through independent publishers, and several of them return to indies when the Nobel effect wears off" (Vermeulen 2023: 11, italics in the original). Besides the world literary positions of source and target languages, several other factors affect the intensity and significance of the Nobel's translational impact: cultural and geographical relations, existing translations, earlier authorial positions, surprise effects of the selections, and market positions of different literary genres. There is, then, no single Nobel effect, but rather a range of different Nobel effects.

Shaping the Cosmopolitan Space

The Nobel Prize does not only bring attention to a set of single authors, making their work more accessible and discussed. The annual selections also have a more fundamental and general impact on the transcultural discussions and distribution of literature. They collectively contribute to shaping and re-shaping the literary landscape as such. Effects of this kind can be seen on different levels.

The cosmopolitan space encompasses smaller national spaces of renowned authors, and consecration into the cosmopolitan magic circle of Nobel laureates is also an entrance ticket to a national elite. A telling example of how transnational literary prestige trickles down to a national level is the way the French publishers Gallimard commemorated the passing of Roger Martin du Gard in 1958. In a special memorial issue of their literary magazine *La Nouvelle Revue Française*, Gallimard took the opportunity to market the late laureate's books. Apart from the author's most known works—the novel *Jean Barois* and the seven-volume narrative *Les Thibault*—the advertisement also tried to attract buyers to Martin du Gard's critical study of a fellow French laureate, *Notes sur André Gide*, and the Pléiade-edition of his *Œuvres complètes*, with a preface by a third Nobel Prize winner, Albert Camus (*La Nouvelle Revue Française* 1958: 6). This marketing strategy makes it evident that the French laureates of 1938, 1947, and 1957 belonged to a national power house of literary prestige, used by their publisher to acknowledge and market their separate bodies of work. In the late 1950s, then, Martin du Gard, Gide, and Camus formed a national circuit of Nobel laureates at the very center of the French literary scene.

A geographically broader example of a literary landscape partly shaped by the Nobel Prize is Latin America. Starting with the Gabriela Mistral prize in 1945, and the prize motivation stressing the poet's importance for "the entire Latin American world," the four awards to Spanish-language American authors reinforced a particular international space of quality literature at the highest level. The prize motivation for the second Chilean award in 1971 also underlined this large, supra-national cultural identity in pointing out that Pablo Neruda's poetry "brings alive a continent's destiny and dreams," and in his Nobel lecture Guatemalan laureate Miguel Ángel Asturias seizes the opportunity to educate his world audience on the "antecedents of Latin American literature" by describing "its three great moments: Maya, Aztec and Inca" (Asturias 2022).

Álvaro Santana-Acuña has shown that the fourth Latin American laureate, Gabriel García Márquez, was more or less obsessed with the Nobel Prize (Santana-Acuña 2020). The future Colombian laureate first came across the Swedish prize, Santana-Acuña suggests, when Mistral was honored, and in 1971 he was the first person to interview the newly appointed Neruda. When García Márquez finally received his long-awaited prize, many critics felt sorry for his South American colleague Jorge Luis Borges ("Nobel prize for García Márquez," 1982). In 1982, the newspaper logic went, time had come for a fourth prize to Latin America, and the choice stood between the Colombian and the Argentinian. It seemed quite impossible that there would be a fourth Latin American selection while the 83-year-old Borges was still alive. The literary space of the southern Americas was, for the time being, saturated with Nobels.

On a more fundamental level, the establishment of the Nobel Prize in Literature in the first half of the twentieth century strongly contributed to constructing the idea of a worldwide cosmopolitan literary scene. Since then, the Swedish prize institution has continuously taken an active part in continuously upholding this wide space. As the signature A.T. wrote in *Le Figaro* in 1948: every Nobel Prize is a "consécration mondiale," a world consecration of what is seen as the internationally most important literary works (A.T. 1948). The annual prize selection does not, then, only contribute to constructing an international canon of specific texts and writers, but also to shaping a discursive space where a transnational discussion of transculturally valuable literature is in play, in short what Pascale Casanova calls "the world literary space." The Nobel Prize is, of course, not the only institution that affects and upholds this space, but it is, Casanova writes, one of the most important institutions for maintaining such a "world republic of letters." From the very first prizes onward, Carl David af Wirsén's ability to execute Alfred Nobel's idea managed to "reform literary culture," Per Rydén and Jenny Westerström write. In its attempt to distinguish "a literature without boundaries," the Nobel Committee created "a new literary universe" (Rydén and Westerström 2018: 24, my translation). This kind of canonization is based on the idea that literature enjoys a position of relative autonomy from commercial and political power structures. In fact, it could be argued that the Nobel Prize is to a high extent responsible for creating, establishing, and maintaining such an independent position for literature.

From the first half of the nineteenth century onward, the concept of world literature had been successively established in European literary discourse. In 1827, Johann Wolfgang von Goethe's famously observed that "[n]ational literature means nothing now" and that "the age of Weltliteratur has begun" (Goethe 2013: 11). Twenty years later, Karl Marx and Friedrich Engels wrote, in the *Communist Manifesto*, that modern times brought "intercourse in every direction," including "intellectual production": "The intellectual creations of individual nations become common property. National one-sidedness and narrow-mindedness become more and more impossible, and from the numerous national and local literatures, there arises a world literature" (Marx and Engels 2013: 17). And at the very end of the century, Danish critic Georg Brandes observed a "new phenomenon": a kind of literature that was "universally recognized and read everywhere" that he thought would lead to a standardized and watered-down sort of world literature (Brandes 2013: 26). Through the course of some eighty years, then, the idea of a world stage of literature was established, even if the "world" thus far was more or less restricted to Western and Central Europe. The concept of world literature had successively become a literary equivalent to the world stage of innovation and technology arranged at the great exhibitions, the world stage of science administered by the increasing transnational collaboration at international conferences and journals, and the world stage of sports at the Olympic Games.

At the turn of the century, this idea of a world literature was given a medial platform when the Swedish Academy started to select Nobel Prize laureates. With their announcements and prize-giving ceremonies, the Swedish scholars and critics created a distinct stage for a continuous discussion of literary achievements and values beyond national ideals, domestic cultures, and particular languages. A list of canonical names of contemporary world literature was in construction. The world literary space as such was already there, but the Nobel Prize made it more tangible and stable; it created a concrete and fixed channel for the formation, discussion, and distribution of world literature.

In retrospect, we can trace this new medial scene of world literature in the way newspapers from different countries mirrored each other in their reactions to the early prize decisions. On several occasions, a news report in one country reacted to a decision by referring to a reaction in another. Part of the *Times*' national pride in relation to the Kipling prize was a report on how the Swedish decision was received in Paris ("The Nobel Prizes," 1907), and a significant part of the positive reaction in *Le Figaro* to the Rabindranath Tagore prize was a quote from the London paper *Daily Mail* (untitled article, *Le Figaro*, 1913). And when the first American prize was announced in 1930, the enormous attention given to Sinclair Lewis in the *New York Times* included several reports on how the decision was received in Sweden, Germany, and France ("Works Popular in Sweden," 1930; "Nobel Prize Winner a 'Best Seller' throughout Germany," 1930; "France and Sweden Laud Award to Lewis," 1930).

A more complex mirroring occurred when the *New York Times* reported from negative Swedish reactions to the Pearl Buck award in 1938. In this case, there were two opposite Swedish reactions (a very positive one from the Swedish Academy and a negative one in the criticism of the Academy's decision) to an American author's literary depiction of China ("Award Perturbs Swedes," 1938). These multilayered reflections sweep over and across very different cultural spaces and geographical places. The prize to Buck made the different literary cultures mirror and scrutinize each other in a way that constructed a cross-cultural space transcending their particular positions.

All through the decades of the twentieth century, the Nobel Prize has contributed to upholding and maintaining this international public sphere of literary discussion. The Stockholm award prompted the inquiries in *Books Abroad* and *World Literature Today* in 1951, 1967, and 1988 that resulted in a wide-ranging and multi-voiced discourse on literary values within and across languages and cultures. Without the Nobel, such a discourse would have been much more difficult to initiate and cultivate. The Nobel Prize, Henri Peyre wrote in the first of these surveys, "provides welcome material to critics and journalists for one whole month, and increases by a few thousands the number of book buyers" (Peyre 1951: 214). With this recurring provision of new material, the Swedish Academy has managed to shape a new kind of literary climate, Manuel Durán reflected thirty-seven years later: "By separating the writer from the social and cultural environment that nurtured him, the Nobel Prize has created an artificial climate, much like a lush tropical garden kept alive by glass and steam" (Durán 1988: 214). In this hothouse, new rules and a new logic apply, Henri Perruchot wrote, since "no man is a prophet in his own country." And "this merit of the Nobel jury," he added, "is not unimportant" (Perruchot 1951: 120).

With its annual selection, the Swedish Academy does not only successively maintain the space of world literature, but continuously re-shapes it. In the late 1980s, Ivar Ivask pointed to the prize's "salutary global side effect" of initiating a worldwide discussion that enlarges "our very understanding of what constitutes world literature today" (Ivask 1988: 199). This discussion has taken small steps and bigger leaps throughout the twentieth century. In awarding Rabindranath Tagore in 1913, the Swedish Academy made a first attempt to enlarge the scope of the world literary space. The prize invited the Bengali author to the cosmopolitan scene and thereby enriched this scene with a new cultural and geographic perspective. In the 1930s, the American awards to Lewis, O'Neill, and Buck strongly contributed to enlarging the cosmopolitan literary scene westward, and in the following decade the Gabriela Mistral prize made sure to add Latin America. The Nobel Prize has not been the only institution that has managed to expand the world literary space in the late twentieth century, far from it, but it has been an important agent in this process. The central position of the Swedish award is not least confirmed by Julia Lovell's account of a "Nobel complex." In her book *The Politics of Cultural Capital*, Lovell shows that Chinese authorities started a "quest for a Nobel Prize in Literature" in the 1980s (Lovell 2006). This ambition continued after the Gao Xingjian prize in 2000, which was not received as a proper Chinese award by Beijing authorities.

In the 1988 *World Literature Today* survey, William Pratt pointed out that several of the recent Anglophone Nobel Prizes had been awarded to "writers who enjoy bilingual audiences," and he referred to American-Polish authors Isaac Bashevis Singer and Czeslaw Milosz, as well as American-Russian writer Joseph Brodsky. In these prize decisions, Pratt recognized something new: these authors may be "harbingers of a more international tradition in literature generally, which the Nobel is uniquely situated to honor" (Pratt 1988: 227). Reading this observation today, in the midst of a boom of transcultural literature extensively discussed by revitalized world literary theories, Pratt's words seem to bear a trace of clairvoyance. Yes, transnational literature without any distinct and univocal anchorage in one single culture has indeed enjoyed a great increase in interest, distribution, and recognition since the late 1980s, not least in the form Rebecca L. Walkowitz calls "the transnational book" (Walkowitz 2013). If Pratt was right about the Nobel being unique in its mandate to identify, recognize, and acknowledge a less nationally rooted kind of literature, the Swedish Academy's impact on late twentieth- and early twenty-first-century literature and literary critical discourse has been vast.

The institution of the Nobel Prize is thus one of the main factors in constituting a cultural center that is partly independent from the economic and political global hierarchy. But only partly, of course. As poet, critic, and translator Édouard Roditi pointed out from his North American perspective in the 1951 survey: it is difficult for the Swedish Academy to "ignore the ballyhoo that reaches Sweden from our literary industry" (Roditi 1951: 215). It is in light of this powerful industry that we should interpret the then Permanent Secretary of the Swedish Academy Horace Engdahl's statement in 2008 that US literature was inferior to the cosmopolitan openness of European letters (see for example "Nobel judge attacks 'ignorant' US literature," 2008). Here, Engdahl expressed a strongly Eurocentrist universalism, but it is a universalism that resists another kind of cultural imperialism.

But the cosmopolitan space maintained by the Nobel Prize is also different from the literary texts and œuvres included in Casanova's Paris-based (and, to a lesser extent, London- and New York-based) literary world republic. Casanova's tendency to see the Nobel Prize institution as an integral part of the world republic of letters is reductive. The international Nobel Prize discussion and the works of Nobel laureates do not form exactly the same kind of cosmopolitan space as Casanova's abstract, general, and unrooted canon of modernist Western writers does. These two spaces stand close to each other, but are not identical. The Prousts and Kafkas in the world republic of letters are all de-rooted from the cultural specificities they originate from, they have left their respective home base and work in a higher dimension. The Nobel laureates have only one foot in this higher, transcultural dimension; the other remains firmly rooted in a specific and culturally limited space. No matter how international they want to be and how universal the Nobel Committee thinks their literary works are, practically all the Nobel Prize-winners remain cultural representatives of some kind.

The laureates' position can be described with the help of Alexander Beecroft's ecological metaphor for spaces of literary circulation. Based on Asian and European literary history from Antiquity to today, Beecroft identifies six kinds of literary ecologies with different ranges and logics: epichoric, panchoric, cosmopolitan, vernacular, national, and global (Beecroft 2015: 33–6). Whereas the world republic is distinctly cosmopolitan, Nobel Prize authors and œuvres are simultaneously cosmopolitan and national or vernacular.

From the start in 1901, the Nobel Prize literary space has continuously crossed the border between the cosmopolitan and the national. An important factor in establishing the world's first world literary prize was to try to create a balance between the big languages and literary cultures in Europe. In his 1899 essay "World Literature," Georg Brandes observed not only a new kind of standardized world literary address but also an opposite literary development in recent decades: "When Goethe coined the term *world literature*," he wrote, "humanism and the spirit of world citizenship were still ideas universally entertained. In the last decades of the 19th century, an ever stronger and more bellicose nationalism has pushed these ideas backward. The literatures of our day become ever more national" (Brandes 2013: 27).

These were the contemporary conditions that the Swedish Academy had to deal with in selecting their first laureates for the new literary prize, and that's why they had to—at odds with Alfred Nobel's expressed instructions not to pay any attention to national belongings—strike a balance between nationalities and reward a French writer in 1901, a German in 1902, a Scandinavian in 1903, a Spanish (and a second French) in 1904, a Polish in 1905, an Italian in 1906, and an English in 1907. In shaping such a nationally rooted cosmopolitan literary space, the Swedish Academy acted totally in line with Brandes' description of contemporary world literature. This is how he concluded his discussion on, on the one hand, a standardized form of world literature and, on the other, rising nationalist sentiments:

> I by no means, however, mean to suggest that nationalism and world citizenship are mutually exclusive. The world literature of the future will become all the more captivating the more the mark of the national appears in it and the more heterogeneous it becomes, as long as it retains a universally human aspect as art and science. That which is written directly for the world will hardly do as a work of art.
>
> (Brandes 2013: 27)

Many of the central elements in Carl David af Wirsén's strategy to establish the Nobel Prize—from the design of the nomination process to the ongoing discussion of cultural representation—directly considered this balance between the cosmopolitan and the distinguished European literary vernaculars.

A concrete example of how the Nobel Prize in Literature became a channel for this balance between the national and the cosmopolitan is the UK reactions to the first prize announcements (see, for example, the recurring reports from announcements and ceremonies in the *Times* 1901–1906). The lack of British awards created an atmosphere of urgency. The British press took for granted that its domestic literature really deserved a place in the world literary space, but that the international (or semi-peripheral) intellectuals in Stockholm had not come around to acknowledge it yet. The media reports showed no signs of direct resentment. Instead, British scholars and critics took action. They found a Nobel organization of their own with the distinct task to select the strongest British names to nominate for the prize. The British literati wanted to be part of the newly established scene of world literature, and they knew that they needed to be there in order to maintain their culture's international position. And in 1907, they finally managed to gain such a position when the Swedish Academy settled for Rudyard Kipling.

The early Nobel laureates were consecrated into a cosmopolitan sphere of transnationally valuable literature, but this process relied heavily on proposals from national academies and other nationally rooted organizations from different parts of the world. An important argument for giving the first Nobel Prize to Sully Prudhomme was to reward the French Academy for their eager response to the Swedish Academy's call for proposals. A prize to Prudhomme, Carl David af Wirsén wrote to a fellow member, would be "a tribute to the French Academy, who so willingly answered our invitation and from whom so many are united in proposing Sully" (Rydén 2010: 569, my translation). The award's basis in separate national cultures and intellectual contexts is very apparent in the early Nobel Committee reviews, addressed to the Swedish Academy, especially the recommendation texts from 1901, 1903, 1904, and 1905, all of which include a table of proposed authors and proposers divided into nationalities. This is how the 1905 table looks like:

	PROPOSED					PROPOSERS				
	1901	1902	1903	1904	1905	1901	1902	1903	1904	1905
Swedes	—	—	—	1	1	6	10	6	3	5
Norwegians	—	3	2	1	—	3	3	3	1	2
Danes	—	—	1	1	1	—	—	18	1	1
Finns	1	1	—	—	—	1	—	1	—	19
Germans	3	6	2	1	—	14	22	21	—	1
Austrians/ Hungarians	2	2	—	1	1	8	2	11	26	4
Englishmen	—	8	5	6	5	—	60	44	51	35
Swiss	3	—	—	—	—	5	—	—	—	1
Frenchmen	11	6	7	5	1	37	5	10	6	31
Belgians	—	—	1	1	—	—	—	4	15	—
Italians	1	2	1	—	1	—	2	1	—	—
Spaniards	1	3	3	1	1	1	16	20	1	24
Portuguese	1	—	—	—	—	1	—	—	—	—
Romanians	1	—	—	—	—	1	—	—	—	—
Russians	—	2	1	1	1	—	1	7	—	3
Poles	1	1	1	1	2	1	—	—	—	6
Greeks	—	—	—	1	1	—	—	—	1	1
Total	25	34	24	21	15	78	121	146	105	133

Svensén (2001a: 83, my translation).

Still today, the laureates' nationalities are very important in the discourse surrounding the prize. In their announcement of the prizes, the Swedish Academy always mentions the new laureate's national belonging, and on the Academy's webpage each winner from 1901 onward is linked to a country of residence and a country of birth. In several versions of Wikipedia—for example, the Swedish, the French, and the German— laureates' nationalities are stressed through national flags attached to their names.

Not everyone has thought that the Academy's attempts to balance between the national and the cosmopolitan have been successful and productive. Harry Slochower from Brooklyn College argued in the 1950s, for example, that the Committees had had an all-too-national mindset, and thereby had missed an opportunity to strengthen the cosmopolitan literary space. The Swedish Academy, Slochower wrote, had awarded too few authors "of universal apperception": "It has elected men with a local or national orientation over those whose folk base is widened towards an international perspective." As an example of this national mindset, he pointed out that Thomas Mann wasn't awarded for his cosmopolitan novel *Der Zauberberg* (*The Magic Mountain*), but for his "more purely German novel" *Buddenbrooks* (Slochower 1951: 217–18).

In the latter half of the twentieth century, the focus on the prize-winning authors' belongings somewhat shifted from the national to the vernacular. This had to do with the development William Pratt observed in 1988 toward a more international tradition of literature connected to bilingual and transcultural contexts rather than monocultural national spaces. More recent examples of this development were the prizes to Gao Xingjiang and V.S. Naipaul. These awards were "international" in the sense that the awarded works lacked single cultural and lingual traditions and contexts, but they were still connected to situated and specific vernaculars: Gao's œuvre to the Chinese-speaking minority in France, and Naipaul's to the Indian-Caribbean Anglophone culture. These prizes—along with quite a few others, such as the ones to Jean-Marie Gustave Le Clézio, Herta Müller, and Abdulrazak Gurnah—have contributed to establishing and maintaining a space overlapping cosmopolitan and vernacular ecologies rather than cosmopolitan and national ecologies.

This does not mean, however, that all laureates have been directly rooted in specific nations or vernaculars. Some of the awarded authors have been more cosmopolitan than most, for example Samuel Beckett, who is difficult to pin down to any particular vernacular, and whose works fit perfectly with Casanova's idea of a literary world republic. Another cosmopolitan laureate was Elias Canetti and his multi-cultural background in Bulgaria, Great Britain, Austria-Hungary, and Switzerland. Even stating his citizenship has been tricky: at Canetti's post in the Wikipedia-list of prize-winners, there must be room for three different flags (the Union Jack, the Swiss cross, and the Bulgarian flag of white, green, and red stripes). The continual oscillation between more or less cosmopolitan and more or less culturally rooted authors has added important nuances to the multi-layered mix of the Nobel Prize context.

What Pascale Casanova identifies as a transnational space of generally (if not globally and universally) and absolutely canonized texts and œuvres, is quite slim and uniform. Compared to this world republic of letters, the Nobel literary space includes a more complex set of conflicting aesthetic values, strong disagreement, cultural and national bickering, political frustration, national pride and hurt feelings, incomprehension, ridiculed authors, regrets, and outdated decisions. At the very foundation of the Nobel Prize discourse lies suspicion, mistrust, and criticism. In the 1988 survey, Bernth Lindfors pointed out that the Academy "will continue to be open to charges of bias, chauvinism, parochialism, and outright racism," and then quoted Nigerian author and critic Chinweizu Ibekwe's deep mistrust of "the conceit that a gaggle of Swedes, all by themselves, should pronounce on intellectual excellence for the whole wide world" (Lindfors 1988: 222).

The Nobel literary discourse is a space of continuous conflict. It is a biased but non-conform and fragmented transnational space that I would like to describe as a *pluralist centrality*. It clearly enjoys a central position with a strong and wide impact, and sometimes it certainly contributes to streamlining the global distribution of literature. But in their ambition of being inclusive, the Swedish judges also help to distribute cultural difference. Their attempts to include a wide range of cultures, languages, and literary traditions in the transnational Nobel literary space continually open up for discussion, criticism, protests, anger, and ridicule—not least because these attempts are paradoxically combined with a rather preposterous claim to select the neutrally most valuable œuvres. There is a distinct sense of impossibility in this complex gesture, in René Étiemble's positive sense of the word (Étiemble 2013: 102). At the very least, this impossible ambition has contributed to making the world literary space multidimensional, and not only instructed by economic and political hierarchies, cultural hegemonies of hyper-central and central literary languages, or a universalist aesthetics based on nineteenth- and twentieth-century European and North American ideas on modernity. Alongside a couple of similar international prize institutions, like the Neustadt Prize and the International Booker, the Nobel Prize makes sure that the world literary center is not as narrow and streamlined as it has been described.

This structural impact of the Nobel Prize is perhaps its most important contribution to twentieth- and twenty-first-century world literature. As E.J. Czerwinski, expert of Slavic literature and culture at SUNY, expressed it in 1988: "To try to imagine the twentieth century without the Nobel Prize is ultimately to concede that Alfred Nobel has, by personal design, made this world a different if not a better place to live in" (Czerwinski 1988: 212). No matter what we think of the consequences, the Nobel Prize has been and still is a key institution in shaping and re-shaping the international discourse of literature.

The Nobel Prize's contribution to a pluralist centrality of world literature was there from the very start, when the Committee tried to create a balance between the different literary traditions of Europe, rewarding a French poet, then a German historian, a Norwegian poet, a Spanish playwright, and so on. This effect was, however, intensified with Karl Ragnar Gierow's and Lars Gyllensten's pluralist principle of the 1960s, the 1970s, and the 1980s. For them, the Nobel's most important task was to widen and nuance the literary center. Gyllensten summarized this ambition in a 1971 declaration:

> The uses of a literary prize could be very different—for example, an original and innovative *author* is supported and urged to carry on; a neglected but fertile *literary genre* is acknowledged and supported; an insufficiently recognized language or cultural area or other human endeavours and concerns are promoted through a support of their *literary manifestations*.
> (Espmark 1986: 102, my translation, italics in the original)

Through contributing to such a plurality of world literature, the Nobel Prize was for Gyllensten a counterweight to commercial interests dominating the distribution of literature.

The Nobel Prize is, then, at least potentially, a force that resists what Erich Auerbach in his well-known article from 1952 identified as one of the central characteristics of twentieth-century international culture: "Today [...] human life is becoming standardized. The process of imposed uniformity, which originally derived from Europe, continues its work, and hence serves to undermine all individual traditions" (Auerbach 2013: 66). In their very rare, in some way unique, mandate to bring any kind of literature from every part of the globe to the world's central stage, the members of the Nobel Committee have the opportunity to support the kind of "*Weltliteratur*" that for Auerbach is the wonderful result of "a *felix culpa*": "mankind's division into many cultures."

Political Consequences

In establishing a cosmopolitan platform for literary assessment in the early twentieth century, the Nobel Committee and the Swedish Academy did their best to avoid political controversies. Neutral authors were favored over politically active ones, like Leo Tolstoy, Émile Zola, Henrik Ibsen, and August Strindberg. This strategy was at its peak during and immediately after the First World War, when outspokenly neutral French novelist Romain Rolland and writers from neutral Scandinavian countries (Heidenstam 1916, Pontoppidan and Gjellerup 1917, and Hamsun 1920) and Switzerland (Spitteler 1919) received the awards. But there were also exceptions from this rule. The 1903 laureate Bjørnstjerne Bjørnson was known for his involvement in the political struggle for Norwegian independence from the Swedish monarchy, and Polish novelist Henryk Sienkiewicz took the opportunity to use the 1905 prize ceremony in Stockholm to express his opinion on the ongoing political conflict between Poland, Russia, and Germany. "Poles are," he said, "strong enough to fight Russia, but not Germany" ("Sienkiewicz Fears Kaiser," 1905).

For many years, the fact that no Russian author had been awarded was a source of intercultural tension. This silent conflict intensified when Ivan Bunin became the first-ever Russian-language laureate in 1933. Bunin had lived in French exile for many years, and was described as a "stateless" writer. The first Russian prize, then, was certainly not an award to the Soviet Union. On the contrary, the Academy's motivation to award Bunin for continuing the "classical Russian traditions in prose writing" (www.nobelprize.org) was interpreted as an indirect critique of Soviet ambitions to deviate from a rich and time-honored literary civilization. And Bunin indeed used the international limelight of the prize. Despite the fact that he couldn't attend the ceremony, he took the opportunity to make a political statement against his country of birth. The *Times* reported from the festivities in the Swedish capital: "The winner of the Literature Prize, M. Ivan Bunin, owing to his dislike of the present Russian régime, had refused to ask the Soviet Minister in Stockholm to present him to the King, and this was done by the chairman of the Nobel section for literature" (untitled article, 1933).

Six years later, the Swedish Academy opened up the cosmopolitan stage for new protests against the Soviet Union in awarding the 1939 prize to Finnish writer Frans Eemil Sillanpää. From a wide international perspective, this selection was interpreted as strongly politically motivated. The so-called Winter War between Soviet and Finland didn't break out until November 30, 1939, when Stalin's troupes and air raids crossed the border and invaded the neighboring country, but the conflict was already boiling when the literary Nobel Prize laureate was announced on November 10. The *Times*' correspondent in Stockholm observed a general "gratification" from the Swedish public to the Academy "at a time when Finland is nearer to Swedish hearts than she has been for a long time" ("Nobel Literature Prize: Honour for Finnish Author," 1939). In a second article that day, the *Times* reported from the Finnish capital Helsinki on the award's effects on national morale ("A Great Patriot and Liberal," 1939). It is quite clear that the Sillanpää award helped to establish and uphold international sympathies with

Finland after the invasion had taken place. In a report from December 1939 on Soviet bombings of the cities Helsinki, Turku, and Tampere, the *Times* mentioned Sillanpää as an important figure of resistance, and the British journalist made it quite clear that the novelist was not a random intellectual representing the threatened Finnish culture: he was in fact the latest Nobel laureate ("Two Raids on Helsinki," 1939). In selecting Sillanpää, the Swedish Academy must have expected quite substantial political consequences.

The relations between the Swedish Academy and Soviet authorities were definitely not improved when it was announced that Boris Pasternak was selected for the 1958 prize. Pasternak was the first laureate who both wrote in Russian and lived in Russia or the USSR when awarded a Nobel Prize in Literature. Moscow had waited a long time, and when a Russian prize was finally given, it was awarded to an author whose latest novel, *Doctor Zhivago* (first published in Italy in 1957), had been refused publication in Soviet due to its criticism of Stalin's politics. Despite the fact that the Nobel Committee motivation focused on Pasternak's poetry and did not mention the banned novel, the selection resulted in the strongest political consequences of any Nobel decision until then. A contributing reason for the strong Soviet reactions was the fact that the 1956 Nobel Prize in Chemistry was awarded to USSR Professor Nicolay Semenov. Up until that decision, Moscow had showed indifference to the Nobel Prizes, but the award to Semenov had changed the attitude of the Soviet authorities. The Chemistry prize was received as a kind of redemption after a long lack of international recognition of scientific progress in the USSR. The Swedish Academy's decision two years later to give Boris Pasternak the first ever Soviet literary prize was received as an elaborate humiliation.

Soviet authorities saw the selection of Pasternak as a "hostile act," a reaction that strongly affected the author himself. A week after the announcement in October 1958, he was expelled from the Soviet Writers' Union, and just a couple of days later a bid was filed urging the authorities to deprive him of his USSR citizenship. Pasternak's first reaction to the award was joy and pride. He immediately expressed his intention of going to Stockholm later that year to collect the honors in person. But after being expelled from the Writers' Union, he changed his mind and publicly declined the Nobel, explaining that it was "undeserved." In early November, he appealed to the authorities and asked to be allowed to stay in the Soviet Union and keep his citizenship ("Mr. Pasternak Denounced in Moscow," 1958; "Telegram from Prizewinner," 1958; "Mr. Pasternak's Treason," 1958; "Bid to Deprive Mr. Pasternak of Citizenship," 1958; "Mr. Pasternak's Appeal to Be Allowed to Stay in Russia," 1958).

The Soviet treatment of Pasternak led to a strong wave of indignation in many countries. There were loud protests from Swedish and Norwegian writers and intellectuals ("Authors' Plea for Mr. Pasternak," 1958; "Norwegian Protest," 1958). Academy member (and later Nobel laureate) Harry Martinson was interviewed on national Swedish television where he came across as "one of the angriest men ever seen on a Swedish television screen" ("Mr. Pasternak's Refusal of Nobel Award," 1958). Polish writers posted an official message to Pasternak ("Polish Message to Mr. Pasternak," 1958), and in a Greek newspaper a cartoon showed the Soviet leader

Nikita Khrushchew sending the literary laureate, with his Nobel medal around his neck, to Siberia for having tasted the forbidden fruit called "Freedom of Thought" (cartoon reprint, 1958). The Indian Prime Minister Jawaharlal Nehru made a statement criticizing the Soviet persecution of Pasternak ("Naked Military Dictatorship," 1958), and in the UK, several loud protests were heard from British writers ("Writer's Concern for Fate of Mr. Pasternak," 1958). In January 1959, schemes were laid out in London by the exiled Spanish novelist José Luis de Vilallonga to establish a "Boris Pasternak Foundation" in order to help "writers of merit from any country in the world" ("A Boris Pasternak Foundation Plan," 1959).

Soviet authorities were somewhat compensated by the 1965 award to Mikhail Sholokhov, who was loyal to the Kremlin. It's easy to see this decision as an attempt to smooth the waves after the Pasternak prize and to restore the image of the Nobel as a purely aesthetic, non-political award. But we must not forget that the announcement of Sholokhov's name was not a total surprise. The Soviet novelist had been discussed as a potential candidate for quite some time and was missed in the list of laureates by several of the critics in William F. Lamont's survey for *Books Abroad* in 1951. The 1965 selection had two very different kinds of political consequences. It gave Sholokhov a mandate and an opportunity to argue that he was, in fact, the first Soviet writer to win the Nobel. He dismissed Pasternak as "an internal émigré" and Bunin as "a stateless person" ("Sharp Tongue of Mr. Sholokhov," 1965), and these statements were totally in accordance with official Moscow policies. On the other hand, the award to Sholokhov also led to a renewed recognition of the Kremlin's oppressive treatment of undesirable writers within the USSR ("Soviet Writers 3 Months in Detention," 1965).

The only decision in the history of the Nobel with stronger political consequences than the Pasternak prize was the selection of Aleksandr Solzhenitsyn in 1970. The announcement of the fourth Russian-language laureate was met with a sharp protest from Moscow. The Chair of the USSR Writers' Union, Sergey Mikhalkov, criticized the prize decision as an "anti-Soviet" act with "purely political aims" (Bonavia 1970a). And indeed, the prize initiated a political turmoil. At the Gum store in central Moscow, three young foreigners—one of them was French and one was Swedish—were arrested after distributing leaflets calling for the release of political prisoners in Russia (Bonavia 1970c). A month later, this manifestation was followed up by renowned Russian cellist Mstislav Rostropovich, who publicly defended Solzhenitsyn and protested against "the lack of cultural freedom in the Soviet Union" ("Solzhenitsyn Defended by Russian Cellist," 1970). And a couple of days later, Rostropovich gained support from quite a surprising direction when the very influential Hungarian Marxist philosopher and literary critic György Lukács criticized the Soviet reaction and praised Solzhenitsyn as "the paragon of true socialist realism" ("Lukács solo," 1970). In Sweden, plans were made to bypass the Soviet travel ban on Solzhenitsyn by honoring the writer at the Swedish Embassy in Moscow, but this arrangement was stopped by the Swedish government for diplomatic reasons. The government's decision was strongly criticized and led to a widely watched, thoroughly discussed and still today famous dispute on live television between Prime Minister Olof Palme and popular writer Vilhelm Moberg (cf. Gyllensten 2000: 269).

Solzhenitsyn was not permitted to leave the USSR in December 1970 to receive his Nobel Prize, a fact that only intensified the international indignation and prolonged the criticism of the Kremlin and the Soviet Writers' Union. In 1974, the laureate was finally allowed to go abroad and attend the ceremony in Stockholm. From an international perspective, the great domestically Swedish controversy that year concerning the joint award to Eyvind Johnson and Harry Martinson was greatly overshadowed by the presence of Aleksandr Solzhenitsyn. The news footage of the Russian writer receiving the medal from Carl XVI Gustaf of Sweden four years after the prize decision was nothing less than a Cold War propaganda boost for Western liberalism.

The political impact of the Nobel has not been limited to awards to Russian authors. Nor has it always been shown as direct consequences of prize announcements or selections as such. The Nobel honors establish a certain kind of medial platform and give a certain kind of mandate from and with which laureates can act and speak in regards to any kind of political issue. In the 1920s and the 1930s, Pearl Buck's novels were very popular in China. When she was surprisingly consecrated as a Nobel laureate in 1938, however, Chinese officials were urged to take a stand as to the way the American writer depicted their country. A couple of years later, her books were banned in China (Hudey 2023). In Germany, Nazi reviewers welcomed Buck's novels as authentic and ideologically correct narratives. Her novels on rural China were used to support the domestic tradition of "Echtdeutsche Volksbücher" (popular books regarded as properly and authentically German). But after receiving the Nobel, Buck used her new international position to make a firm stand against Nazi-Germany. She signed a petition to President Roosevelt urging him to officially protest against Adolf Hitler, and she refused to visit the Third Reich. After that, the Nazi officials did their best to diminish her position, and her novels weren't re-issued on the German market until after the Second World War (Hudey 2023).

Just a week after his Nobel Prize was announced in October 1957, Albert Camus collaborated with the 1952 laureate François Mauriac in writing a public appeal for the rights of Hungarian writers to the Prime Minister of Hungary. "Having learnt that," the two award-winning French authors wrote, "in spite of official denials, the case against Tibor Déry, Gyula Hay, Tibor Tardos, and Zoltan Zelk has just begun, we express the wish that the court discussions should be made public and that the international Press should be able to attend." ("Appeal for Hungarian writers", 1957). The timing was perfect for this kind of protest. Since the Nobel announcement in October, Camus' name was on everybody's lips. And in collaborating with the preceding French laureate, the Algerian-born novelist and moral philosopher also used the respect and recognition bestowed on Mauriac five years earlier. The Atheist Camus and the Catholic Mauriac joined troupes to pursue a common cause—the rights of writers in a totalitarian state.

In 1967, another political collaboration between two Nobel laureates took place in a process that has had many different names—the Stockholm Tribunal, the Russell Tribunal, the Russell-Sartre Tribunal, or the International War Crimes Tribunal. In the city where one of them was awarded by the Swedish king in 1950, and the other was announced as the 1964 laureate (an honor he declined), Bertrand Russell and Jean-Paul Sartre arranged an international tribunal to put the US government to justice for what they had done in Vietnam. Eighteen countries were represented in the hearings. The members of the Tribunal listened to testimonies from the war, evaluated other kinds evidence, and discussed the responsibility of the US government and its allies. In their eleven-point verdict, the Tribunal found the governments of Thailand, Philippines, Japan, Australia, New Zealand, and South Korea guilty of complicity, and the US government guilty of "aggression against Vietnam under the terms of international law," "bombardment of purely civilian targets, for example, hospitals, schools, medical establishments, dams, etc.," "aggression against the people of Laos," the use and experiment of "weapons prohibited by the laws of war," treatment of prisoners of war in ways "prohibited by the laws of war," "inhuman treatment" of "the civilian population," and, most notably, "genocide against the people of Vietnam."

Two years later, Samuel Beckett's new status as a Nobel scholar came in handy in a different kind of political struggle. On the very day of the Nobel ceremony in Stockholm, to which Beckett had sent his publisher, the *Times* reported from Paris: "Samuel Beckett, the author, who won the Nobel prize this year, Pablo Picasso, the painter, and Igor Stravinsky, the composer, are among some 50 international figures who appealed today for a 'gesture of clemency' towards Régis Debray, the French writer, and his friend, Ciro Bustos, who are imprisoned in Bolivia" ("World Figures Plead for Régis Debray," 1969). Three years later, Heinrich Böll declared—after the Swedish Academy's announcement of his award in 1972—that he would give part of his prize money to a fund for imprisoned writers and their families ("Nobel Prize Winner to Aid Jailed Writers," 1972). A couple of weeks later, Böll expressed his public support in the national election for the current Chancellor of West Germany, Social Democrat Willy Brandt, who had won the Nobel Peace Prize in 1971 (Spitzer 1972).

In 1980, the selection of Czeslaw Milosz managed to put the ongoing Polish democracy movement in a brighter international focus. "Solidarity"—or "Solidarnosc"—became the first independent trade union in Poland when founded in August 1980 at the Lenin Shipyard in Gdánsk. Two years later, its leader Lech Walesa was awarded the Nobel Peace Prize, but long before that—only a couple of months after the start of the union—the Swedish Academy awarded the exile author Milosz. This selection cast light on the heated situation in Poland, not least through reports on the laureate's Polish publisher, who was said to have been arrested forty-four times by Polish police up until 1976. In December 1980, this domestically controversial publisher accompanied Milosz at the ceremony in Stockholm, before visiting London where he was interviewed by the British press (Davy 1980). At first, the Polish ambassador to Stockholm didn't know how to react to this prize decision: Should he interpret the award as an anti-communist provocation or should he regard it as an honor to Polish culture and literature, in spite of the fact that Milosz had lived in exile since 1951? The 1980 award was, after all, the third prize given to an author writing in Polish, which made the literary tradition of Poland far more acknowledged by the Nobel institution than any other East European culture apart from the Russian. Shouldn't the Polish officials show national pride rather than ideological indignation? In the end, the Polish authorities decided on interpreting the award as an honor and not a provocation, at least officially (cf. Gyllensten 2000: 270–1).

The 1984 prize to Jaroslav Seifert led to a similar dilemma for the authorities in Czechoslovakia. But the reaction in Prague was different. The prize announcement in October was given a very limited recognition in Czech newspapers. The only report in the leading paper *Rudé právo* was a small notice on October 12—not on the front page, not even in the literary section, but amongst miscellaneous international news on page seven ("Nobelova cena J. Seifertovi," 1984). The Communist regime in Prague did its best to limit the political effects of the prize, and the Czech Embassy in Stockholm expressed an official protest against the "unacceptable formulations" on Czechoslovakia made by Permanent Secretary Lars Gyllensten in his Nobel speech to Seifert (Smejkalová 2022). A couple of years later, the political tension returned in relation to the laureate's funeral in Prague (cf. Gyllensten 2000: 271–2).

Another belated effect of a prize decision occurred when Wole Soyinka used his position eight years after becoming the first African literary Nobel laureate to protest against the Nigerian government. "After fleeing his homeland three weeks ago to avoid arrest," Steven Greenhouse reported in the *New York Times*, "Wole Soyinka, the Nigerian playwright and Nobel Prize winner, came to Washington today to publicize human rights abuses by his nation's military Government and to urge the United States to begin an economic boycott against his country" (Greenhouse 1994).

There are many cases of diplomatic crises and other political conflicts stirred by the Swedish Academy's laureate selections. Several decisions have led to direct political actions, statements, and protests. The first award to a Chinese-speaking author in 2000, for example, resulted in sharp criticism of the Swedish Academy from Gao Xingjiang's country of birth. The second Chinese selection, Mo Yan in 2012, was much more welcomed in Beijing, but strongly criticized by many European critics, journalists, and activists for justifying Chinese authorities and ignoring their restrictions of freedom of speech. However, Mo Yan used his Nobel mandate to urge the Chinese officials to release the imprisoned dissident writer Liu Xiaobo (Jacobs 2012). A more recent example is the 2015 laureate Svetlana Alexievich's opinions on Russia and Ukraine in the spring of 2022. In an interview on her work in progress about the 2020 Belarus revolution and on the ongoing war in Ukraine, the Nobel laureate, whose father was Belarusian and whose mother was Ukrainian, seized the opportunity to tell the international press what she thought of the anti-democratic authorities in Minsk and of Vladimir Putin. The President of Russia is a "war criminal," she said, who should be put to trial (Öberg Lindsten and Öberg 2022).

Later that year, French writer Annie Ernaux received the prize. A week after the announcement, the newly appointed laureate was seen in Paris participating in a big left-wing demonstration against the economic policies of President Emmanuel Macron. Her fresh Nobel Prize definitely increased the media attention of the demonstration, not least in Sweden (see for example Forsberg 2022).

A less direct political consequence of the Nobel Prize occurs when a selection changes how specific cultures and societies are seen from abroad. In a research report from 1954 on the presence and role of American literature on the Soviet literary market, Glenora and Deming Brown showed that Russian translations of American literature tended to confirm the Soviet stereotypes of the United States. Works by Howard Fast,

Jack London, Theodore Dreiser, Lincoln Steffens, Albert Maltz, and Sinclair Lewis that depict a decadent and politically indifferent United States were frequently published and discussed, whereas works that show a higher degree of political awareness (e.g., novels by Upton Sinclair, Ernest Hemingway, Erskine Caldwell, and John Steinbeck) were denounced or discarded (Brown and Brown 1954). It's easy to see how the Nobel Prize to Sinclair Lewis worked in favor of this kind of official control of the USSR image of the United States, whereas the later awards to Hemingway and Steinbeck may have helped to break through the biased selection of translated works, and thereby contribute to disrupting the politically charged stereotypes of US society and culture.

The Nobel Prize in Literature, then, not only contributes to the continuous forming and re-forming of world literature, but it also effects world politics. In fact, it must be seen as one of the most important channels connecting world literature with world politics. As German scholar Fritz Strich phrased it in 1930:

> World literary studies, then, sprang from national and cosmopolitan motives, and we cannot ignore that in our day this discipline has gained greater urgency and importance than ever before. Because it is this discipline that is able to help us resolve the battle now raging between the idea of the nation and that of humanity.
>
> (Strich 2013: 48)

The most urgent threat in Fritz Strich's 1930s Germany was violently resolved fifteen years later, but the battle between the idea of a culturally uniform nation and the notion of humanity still rages on. Every discussion of world literature is part of this battle, and so is every selection of Nobel Prize laureates in Literature.

Concluding Remarks

In his brief overview of the awards since 2000, Kjell Espmark summarized the problems and opportunities of the Nobel Prize in a very reasonable way. "These various arguments," he wrote in 2021 about the prize discussions within and outside the Academy, "some focusing on chronology, some on the abundance of candidates, some on the shifting perspective, make clear the difficulty in any attempt to create an up-to-date *Weltliteratur* with the help of the Nobel Prize. What the prize can in fact achieve is a substantial *contribution* to such a canon" (Espmark 2021: 46). Yes, the history of the Nobel Prize has indeed created a particular kind of literary canon—a list of names of authors who will probably enjoy a special kind of posthumous respect as Nobel laureates long into the future. These writers will remain in the history books, and their literary estates will continue to be stored in archives. Many of them will be read, re-issued, and discussed for many years to come. Some of them will be rediscovered by new generations of readers, critics, and scholars. This Nobel canon isn't at all identical with a more generally valid world literary canon, but the selection of laureates definitely contributes to it.

When it comes to the relation between the list of Nobel laureates and the world canon of what Pascale Casanova calls the world republic of letters, we can identify three different kinds of authors. Many of the most consecrated laureates already belonged to the world literary space before they were awarded, and they would have enjoyed a secured place amongst the most famous and respected international writers without the Nobel Prize. Works by, for example, Thomas Mann, T.S. Eliot, Ernest Hemingway, Gabriel García Márquez, and Bob Dylan do not have to be marketed as written by Nobel laureates. The Nobel label on their names is only a logical confirmation of their centrality. In these cases, the transmission of cultural prestige goes in the opposite direction: the reputation of the laureates contributes to keeping the Nobel Prize institution in the world literary space rather than the other way around.

Most of the Nobel laureates, however, belong to the world republic of letters partly because of the Nobel Prize. Many of these writers contribute to upholding the status of the prize, but they also gain crucial prestige from being Nobel laureates. Works by Selma Lagerlöf, Rabindranath Tagore, Isaac Bashevis Singer, Gao Xingjian, and Kazuo Ishiguro have met, and will continue to meet, more readers because of the Nobel Prize.

For the least consecrated laureates, the prize has a different function. In these cases, the Nobel label keeps the laureates' works from the abyss of the great unread. These authors do certainly not enjoy central positions in the world literary space, but rather inhabit some kind of limbo position just outside the internationally consecrated area. But all of these authors—the Paul Heyses, the Jacinto Benaventes, and the Eyvind Johnsons—have certainly once enjoyed a position in the world republic of letters, and the indelible Nobel Prize label makes sure that there will always remain a possibility for them to reclaim a position in the world literary space.

Nobel Prize decisions generally have a high impact on accessibility. Laureates will normally be translated into many languages, as an immediate effect of the prize announcement as well as in a longer perspective. But the level of increased access differs strongly between different laureates, and there is no clear and distinct pattern instructing these differences. The world literary hierarchy between languages, cultures, and markets is certainly a factor, but genre, pre-prize authorial positions, and relations between specific literary languages and cultures are just as important. It seems like each laureate enjoys a particular Nobel effect that follows its own logic, but it is difficult to deny that some kind of distributional effect always awaits a newly appointed Nobel Prize winner.

Even though the award was initiated and launched as an expressively non-political prize and despite the fact that many members of the Swedish Academy have recurringly denied any political intentions in the prize decisions, many awards have had distinct political consequences. These were most intense during the Cold War, when the decisions to honor Winston Churchill, Boris Pasternak, Aleksandr Solzhenitsyn, Czeslaw Milosz, and Jaroslav Seifert were seen as grounded in a Western ideology of Liberal Capitalism, but the awards to, for example, Pearl Buck, Frans Eemil Sillanpää, Mikhail Sholokhov, Gabriel García Márquez, Gao Xingjiang, and Peter Handke have prompted other kinds of manifestations and political actions.

A more generally important result of the Nobel Prize institution than its central part in consecrating particular authors is the way the award has contributed to the very infrastructure of world literary formation. Throughout its history, the Nobel Prize in Literature has been a central agent in establishing and maintaining a world literary space. The Swedish Academy and its Nobel Committee have created and kept open a network of channels between national literary ecologies and a cosmopolitan ecology, in Alexander Beecroft's terminology. The very traffic between these two kinds of ecologies, I would argue, is crucial for the existence of a world literary space. The transmission back and forth between the national and the supra-national needs to be continuously revitalized, and new channels must be opened up now and then in order for the cosmopolitan space to stay effective, vibrant, and relevant. The Nobel Prize is by no means the only institution that creates and maintains these channels, but it is one of the oldest and most powerful.

The Nobel Prize not only helps to maintain the existence of a world literary space, but also affects what this space looks like. The Nobel institution contributes to continuously reshaping the features and the scope of the world republic of letters. As long as the Swedish institution restricted the distribution of the awards—with the exception of the 1913 prize to Rabindranath Tagore—to writers from Western Europe, it confirmed and reinforced the world space position of the traditionally dominant literary cultures, not least through its universal pretentions. And the single exception to the limited distribution did little more than confirm this distinctly European universalism. But in redirecting—for a long time very slowly, cautiously, and hesitantly—the total focus of attention from France, Germany, Italy, Spain, Great Britain, and Scandinavia toward East European, North American, Latin American, Asian, and African literatures, the Swedish award has helped to make the cosmopolitan literary space a little bit more inclusive. The list of Nobel laureates creates a web of connections between different locations and cultural contexts. In its continuous prize-giving activity, the Nobel institution nurses a dream of making these consecrations non-biased and universally valid. We all know, however, that the honors are far from evenly distributed across the globe, and the deciding body's distinct anchorage in one single, European geocultural perspective strongly limits its possibilities of ever coming close to realizing such a grand ambition. But the very existence of the Nobel Prize at least keeps such a utopian idea alive.

5

Defining Literature: The Poetics of the Prize

Every mid-October the discussion starts again. When the Swedish Academy announces the name of that year's Nobel laureate, reactions are never univocal. Some critics and readers mean that the Academy this time around has made an excellent choice. Others shrug in a state of anticlimactic disappointment. Still others cannot believe their ears: Why on earth are they rewarding this particular author when that other one is still waiting to receive the honors? Arguments and opinions differ, but the fundamental attitude to literature is common in all these reactions: that literary values and merits can be justly compared, and that only the very best ones—the top-notch handful of all the world's men and women of letters—deserve to be awarded with the Nobel Prize.

These annual expressions of joy, pride, bewilderment, contempt, and frustration reveal an inescapable fact: that the group of eighteen Scandinavian intellectuals who call themselves the Swedish Academy form one of the most powerful institutions in the world in defining transculturally valid literary values. "The Nobel Prize," writes Pascale Casanova, "is today one of the few truly international literary consecrations, a unique laboratory for the designation and definition of what is universal in literature" (Casanova 2013: 278).

The Nobel Prize's focus on universal aesthetic values has been there right from the start. They were already mentioned in Alfred Nobel's last will. Just like the other four awards—in Physics, Chemistry, Medicine, and the Peace Prize—the literary prize was to be bestowed upon a person who had "conferred the greatest benefit to humankind" (Svensén 2001a: ix). This instruction was to be applied to all five prizes, even though it had and still has very different implications in the five different areas of achievements. What is universally beneficial in Physics, Chemistry, and Medicine cannot really be compared with wide, transcultural beneficial effects of literature and peace work, and putting human experiences and thoughts into poignant words is not at all similar to solving political and military conflicts between peoples and nations. As for literature, Alfred Nobel could not foresee the epistemologically problematic and ideologically charged navigation between languages and cultures, and the fundamentally imbalanced international power structures that instruct the recognition of different literary traditions. Nor could, of course, the writers of the Nobel Foundation's statutes and the early Nobel Committees.

In continually confirming, sanctioning, inventing, and adjusting what is seen as culturally and ideologically neutral literary values, the Swedish Academy is one of the key international and intercultural agents that define what literature as such is, and what it should and could do. What constitutes literary phenomena, effects, and qualities is defined differently in different languages and in different parts of the world, as well as in different contexts—commercial, political, professional, and educational. But with the Nobel Prize's important position comes a certain prescriptive, normative impact. The prize decisions collectively and individually sanction a definition of what prototypically high-brow literature should look like. What literary genres have a universal literary value? What styles, narrative techniques, and imagery are poignant and widely accurate? Although everyone knows that literature is a diverse field of many genres, styles, and functions, the annual selection of laureates by a powerful institution of international literary canonization continuously defines what is literary. The list of awarded œuvres forms a distinct but unformulated conception of prototypical literature. We can call this conception *Nobel Literature*—a literary prototype to protest against, despise, and ridicule, or (which is more common) compare with, try to appreciate, and strive toward.

Nobel Literature is predominantly shaped in three different ways: through the very selection of laureates and kinds of honored literary works, through the Swedish Academy's prize motivations, and through the actions and words of the laureates after they have been selected. This chapter will discuss these different kinds of social acts as prescriptive gestures that continuously form powerful ideas of what constitutes world literature.

The Poetics of Genre

The poetics of the Nobel Prize is partly a generic issue. Laureate selections recognize some literary genres more frequently and more intensely than others, and thereby successively construct an idea of what kind of literature is most valuable. The early Nobel Committees were well aware of this effect. Despite the fact that Alfred Nobel explicitly stated that the literary prize should be based on an inclusive definition of literature, and be awarded to all kinds of writing "that through form and style have a literary value," the Nobel Foundation early on decided that atypical literary genres should not dominate the awards. In order for the Nobel to be firmly established, it had to pursue a solid and general definition of literature that all the central European literary cultures could accept (Svensén 2001a: xi, my translation).

Which is, then, the most prototypical literary genre according to the Nobel Committees? In other words: what genre is Nobel Literature? Well, if we examine the generic characteristics of the awarded œuvres, a particular pattern appears. In the whole history of the prize, 1901–2022, the following four literary categories have been most frequently awarded: prose fiction (72); poetry (39); theatrical works (19); nonfiction prose (15). There is, thus, a strong focus on prose fiction, which is confirmed by the fact that titles of specific novels or, the words *novel* or *novels*, have been included in as many as eighteen different prize motivations. Poetry is the second most frequently awarded genre, distinctly more recognized than both dramatic works and nonfiction prose.

If we divide the history of the prize into twenty-year periods, we will directly notice that prose fiction has not always been at the forefront of the Nobel poetics. During the first period, 1901–20, poetry was slightly more awarded than prose fiction. In the interwar years, however, this relation was more than reversed: eleven prose fiction writers and only two poets. In this period, theatre was also more recognized than poetry, with the awards to distinctly dramatic authors Jacinto Benavente, George Bernard Shaw, Luigi Pirandello, and Eugene O'Neill. In the post-Second World War period, fiction and poetry were more or less equally honored. Theatrical works were less awarded, even though T.S. Eliot, Pär Lagerkvist, and Albert Camus were playwrights as well as poets and novelists. Between 1960 and 1990, novels and short stories enjoyed a comfortable pole position, and in the first twenty-year period of the new millennium, fiction was even more dominating than in the 1920s and 1930s, with fifteen awards compared to four for poetry and only three for theatrical works. So far, the 2020s have confirmed this pattern, with one poetry prize to Louise Glück, and two narrative fiction prizes to Abdulrazak Gurnah and Annie Ernaux.

In William F. Lamont's broad survey for *Books Abroad* in 1951, there was a general view that poets had been neglected and prose fiction writers favored by the Nobel Committees in the first fifty years of the prize (Lamont 1951: 11). In the follow-up survey in 1967, Herbert Howarth concluded that critics and scholars had not seen any improvement on this point in the 1950s and 1960s (Howarth 1967: 7), and in 1988, William Pratt still thought that poetry had been underrepresented in the prize selections (Pratt 1988: 226). Just after the 1988 survey, however, there was a boom of poetry awards. Between 1990 and 1996, as many as four out of seven laureates were poets. Since the turn of the millennium, however, the dominant position of prose fiction was restored. After the award to Wislawa Szymborska in 1996, Herta Müller, Tomas Tranströmer, Bob Dylan, and Louise Glück have been the only poets among the twenty-five laureates.

We can also determine that the Nobel institution defines literature as something written. Alfred Nobel's will did not include any restrictions on this point. It only stated that "the most outstanding work" was to be recognized. In the Nobel Foundation's statutes from 1900, however, literature was restricted to written texts. To be considered as merits by the Nobel Committee, the invoked literary texts had to be printed (Svensén 2001a: ix). Oral literature has indeed been almost nonexistent in the prize motivations and recommendations, but not completely. Three laureates have been distinctly awarded due to orally manifested texts: Winston Churchill for his "brilliant oratory," Dario Fo for his theatrical rather than dramatic work, and Bob Dylan for his contributions to "the American song tradition." The inaccessibility of the Committee reports from the last fifty years makes it impossible to know whether oral qualities have been substantially discussed in the selection processes during this most recent period, but the final selections and prize motivations do not reveal anything along these lines. Orally performed texts are not disqualified as Nobel Literature, but they remain exceptions to the rule of printed writing.

In the early prize discussions, the central generic issue was not the balance between oral and written literature or between poetry and prose, but between fiction and poetry on the one hand, and nonfiction on the other. The first selection in 1901 caused no generic problems. All the four major contenders were either novelists or poets: Italian novelist Antonio Fogazzaro, Provençal poet Frédéric Mistral, Polish novelist Henryk Sienkiewicz, and French poet Sully Prudhomme, who was recommended by the Committee and then selected by the Academy as the first Nobel Prize laureate in Literature (Svensén 2001a: 11–13). Next year, however, a generic discussion took up a central part of the Committee's lengthy report to the Swedish Academy. German biblical scholar Theodor Zahn was praised for his book on the New Testament, *Einleitung in das Neue Testament* (three volumes, 1897–1900), but the suggestion to give Zahn the prize was rejected by the Committee due to the fact that academic theological studies were seen as "relatively far from Nobel Prize literature" (Svensén 2001a: 21). Also in 1902, both French theologian and writer Paul Sabatier and Russian jurist and writer Anatoly Koni were celebrated for their biographical writings (Sabatier's on St. Francis of Assisi and Koni's on the legendary medical doctor Friedrich Joseph Haass), but the Committee preferred to award "more spontaneous products of the imagination or significant historical and philosophical academic studies" rather than biographies, "especially for the first prizes" (Svensén 2001a: 23).

The 1902 prize was eventually indeed awarded to a nonfiction writer, German historian Theodor Mommsen, for a work that was regarded as a significant historical study, *Römische Geschichte* (four volumes, 1854, 1855, 1856, and 1885). For this voluminous account of the history of Rome, Mommsen was praised by the Committee for his ability to combine genuine academic lore with artistic composition and style. In this work, the scholar showed "a force of imagination that from scrupulously studied facts shapes lively images" (Svensén 2001a: 35). Mommsen illustrated, the Committee concluded, how vast "the academic discipline of history is when it is also great historical art" (Svensén 2001a:37). Studies in history were, then, generically closer to central literary values than biographies and theological studies.

Awarding nonfiction writers was thus established early on in the history of the prize. But from the very start, the Nobel Committees were anxious not to deviate too much from poetry and fiction. In 1903, the Committee wrote that French historian Albert Sorel could very well have been recommended for the prize if it weren't for the fact that another historian had been awarded the year before (Svensén 2001a: 48). Next year, Sorel was rejected for the same reason, even though it was the poet Bjørnstjerne Bjørnson who won the 1903 prize (Svensén 2001a: 64). In none of the accessible reports from the Nobel Committees between 1901 and 1973 has a poet been rejected because another poet was awarded two years ago, and the same is true for prose fiction writers and playwrights.

Indeed, the underrepresentation of nonfiction prose is one of the strongest points made in the *Books Abroad* survey in 1951. What William F. Lamont called "littérateurs"—"especially essayists, critics, biographers"—were generally seen as "grossly neglected" by the Nobel Committee in the first fifty years of the prize. And yes, after Mommsen the two philosophers Rudolf Eucken and Henri Bergson and novelist and biographer Pearl Buck were the only genuinely (but only partly in Buck's case) nonfiction writers to be awarded up until Lamont's survey (which was conducted just before the 1950 prize to Bertrand Russell was announced). During these five decades, many other essayists, critics, biographers, and scholars had been proposed— for example German scholar of world literature Alexander Baumgartner (proposed in 1902 and 1903), English philosopher Herbert Spencer (proposed in 1902), Danish critic Georg Brandes (proposed twelve times between 1903 and 1925), the author of social utopias Godfrey Sweven (pen name for the Scottish-New Zealand academic John Macmillan Brown, proposed in 1905), Methodist preacher and founder of the Salvation Army William Booth (proposed in 1906), Belgian legal scholar and writer of several works on the legal rights of women Louis Franck (proposed in 1906), church historian Adolf von Harnack (proposed in 1908 and 1916), Scottish anthropologist James G. Frazer (proposed in 1926, 1928 and 1935), Italian philosopher Benedetto Croce (proposed nine times between 1929 and 1950), Sigmund Freud (proposed in 1936), Dutch historian Johan Huizinga (proposed seven times between 1939 and 1945), and Violet Clifton, who was proposed in 1935 for her biography of her husband John Talbot Clifton.

After the *Books Abroad* survey, Russell was awarded in 1950 and Winston Churchill in 1953. If we add Albert Camus to this list—since he did write the very influential essays *Le Mythe de Sisyphe* (*The Myth of Sisyphus*, 1942) and *L'homme révolté* (*The Rebel*, 1951) alongside his novels, plays, and short stories—the 1950s turns out to be quite a good decade for nonfiction. The 1964 award to Jean-Paul Sartre was another prize to a philosopher rather than a fiction writer, and in 1981 the Swedish Academy awarded Elias Canetti for the "broad outlook" most distinctly found in his memoirs *Die Provinz des Menschen* (*The Human Province*, 1973) and *Die gerettete Zunge* (*The Tongue Set Free*, 1977). In the motivation to the Joseph Brodsky prize in 1987, it was made obvious that the Russian-American author was awarded for his essays as well as for his poetry: Brodsky was honored "for an all-embracing authorship, imbued with clarity of thought and poetic intensity."

In his discussion of the prizes after 2000, Kjell Espmark pointed out a recent tendency to award what he calls "witness literature," that is, texts based on first- or second-hand experiences of historic events and social structures. He stressed the fact that the Swedish Academy arranged an international Nobel symposium in December 2001 dedicated to this kind of literature, and argued that the prizes to Gao Xingjian, V.S. Naipaul, Imre Kertész, Jean-Marie Gustave Le Clézio, Herta Müller, and Mo Yan were direct results of this focus on literature based on direct experiences, even though most of their works were fictionalized accounts of their lives (Espmark 2021: 13–20). In perfect line with this focus on literature's abilities to bear witness, a new kind of nonfiction Nobel Prize was awarded in 2015 when Belarus writer Svetlana Alexievich was honored for her journalistic books based on interviews. But the Alexievich award did not start a trend. Since 2015, fiction writers and poets have been dominating just as much as before the 2001 symposium.

Throughout the years, the Nobel Prize selections and motivations have continuously constructed a definition of literature that more or less has excluded texts written for non-adults. The exceptions are found in the beginning of the prize's history. In the argument leading up to the Committee's recommending Rudyard Kipling for the 1907 prize, the British author's tales about Mowgli, Baloo, and Bagheera in *The Jungle Book* (1894) and *The Second Jungle Book* (1895) were described quite thoroughly and very appreciatively. The author's skill in addressing children was put forward as a strong merit that helped him earn the award (Svensén 2001a: 141–2). Kipling's tales for children were not mentioned when the 1907 prize was discussed in *Le Figaro*, the *Times*, and the *New York Times*, but when Selma Lagerlöf was awarded two years later, Marc Hélys made quite a point in the French paper of the fact that the 1909 laureate shared a specific characteristic with Kipling:

> Everything she has written bears the mark of her noble soul; everything, from the minor short story to the delicious volume composed for children: *The Adventures of Nils Holgersson*, which rivals Rudyard Kipling's *The Jungle Book*. Swedish children will not be the last to applaud the choice of the Nobel Committee!
>
> (Hélys 1909, my translation)

After 1909, this inclusion of the child reader had disappeared, despite the fact that several laureates (e.g., T.S. Eliot and Juan Ramón Jiménez) also have written books for children. Since the Swedish Arts Council started to give out the Astrid Lindgren Memorial Award (ALMA) in 2002—an international prize to writers of books for children and young adults, often seen as the children's literature equivalent to the Nobel Prize in Literature—children's literature seems farther away from the Nobel discussions than ever before.

Rudyard Kipling's jungle tales for children were already mentioned in the 1903 Nobel Committee report on the nominated writers. In this early discussion, however, the Committee included a minor critical point. The jungle stories were praised for being "imaginative and entertaining," but "nature is elevated at the expense of the human" (Svensén 2001a: 51, my translation). This slight criticism of Kipling's tales for children sheds a light upon another general characteristic of the Nobel poetics: valuable literature is about humanity, not the cosmos, not the earth, and not other living beings on earth, which is, of course, quite in line with Nobel's will and its stress on "the benefit to humankind."

Throughout the years, the Nobel Prize motivations have been filled with references to specifically human issues. Often, these have remained on a very general level, as in the word "humanity" (2008) and a whole range of related phrases: "human reality" (1996), "human experience" (2019), "human values" (1953, 1975), "universal human conditions" (1978), "the human condition" (1983, 1985), "the human predicament" (1994), "human destinies" (1961, 2014), "human problems and conditions" (1947), "the problems of human conscience" (1957), "human conflict" (1937), "human beings" (1915), "the drama of human life" (1952), "man's condition in the cosmos" (1977), "man's vulnerability" (1989), and "the indomitable spirit and versatility of man" (1984). In many motivations, humankind has not been directly referred to, but rather taken for granted. The phrases "Northern life" (1928), "present-day life" (1917), "a form of life" (2018), "tragic experience of life" (1959), and "the drama of existence" (1986), for example, refer to human life, and "the individual" (2002, 2010), "the outsider" (2003), "the downtrodden" (1997), and "the dispossessed" (2009) are references to human positions. And when the Academy has talked about "a continent's destiny and dreams" (1971) and "a continent's life and conflicts" (1982), geographical categories were used as metonymies for the people living on these landmasses. When nonhuman phenomena have appeared in the motivations, they have often been treated as aspects of human conditions. Frédéric Mistral was, for example, praised for his depiction of the Provençal landscape, but only as a "natural scenery" surrounding the "native spirit of his people," and Sillanpää was awarded for his portrayal of "his country's peasantry," and "their way of life and their relationship with Nature."

From 1901 to 2022, there have only been three motivations that may be interpreted as directly referring to conditions and phenomena beyond a human focus. The "new continent" that Patrick White had introduced to literature could be a geographical or ecological entity rather than a cultural and social one, and the "reality" that Tomas Tranströmer's poetry was said to give access to is not necessarily human-based. Only one of the motivations has had a distinctly nonhuman focus: the praise of Swedish author Harry Martinson's ability to "catch the dewdrop and reflect the cosmos." One of the laureates, however, was explicitly selected because of a particular work on the relations between man and nature. Ernest Hemingway was awarded in 1954 "for his mastery of the art of narrative, most recently demonstrated in *The Old Man and the Sea*, and for the influence that he has exerted on contemporary style." The hard and long struggle in the Straits of Florida between fisherman Santiago and a marlin, depicted in Hemingway's story from 1951, also inspired that year's diploma artist. The American writer's Nobel diploma included, on the left-hand side, a painting of African animals, and, on the right, a painting of a colorful marlin dragging Santiago and his boat far out to the open sea. Nature itself, and the human individual's position within it, was indirectly stressed in the prize motivation and directly pointed out in the diploma as key elements of Ernest Hemingway's Nobel-winning works.

Generically speaking, Nobel Literature consists of written texts that are addressed to adults and concern humankind, predominantly in the form of prose fiction, but sometimes in the form of lyrical poetry and occasionally in dramatic or nonfiction genres. Despite the broad definition of literature in Alfred Nobel's will, the history of Nobel selections sends a very distinct generic signal: the most valuable, prize-worthy, and beneficial literature is prose fiction, predominantly novels. The prototype of quality literature is the lengthy fictional story.

Prize Motivations

A very distinct way in which the Swedish Academy prescribes literary quality is to accompany each laureate selection with a short prize motivation—an explanation of exactly what it is in the author's work that has made her or him worthy of the prize. The purpose of these motivations is to point out particular literary qualities in order to present each awarded author as unique and extraordinary. Even if Benedict Anderson is right when he calls these brief citations "one of the most mediocre genres of twentieth-century literature," filled with a "vapid humanism" and "accumulations of cliché" (Anderson 2013: 101), these descriptions of literary merits are, sometimes unwittingly, manifestations of the Nobel Committees' conception of general aesthetic values. Year by year, these prize motivations collectively and successively form a poetics. It is, in fact, through these brief texts that the members of the Nobel Committee most distinctly show themselves to the world.

What makes these annual motivations so potent as normative performative acts is the fact that they prescribe what literature is without using any kind of direct definitions: they distribute a general aesthetics through descriptions of particular œuvres. This way, the Academy's defining claims stay unpronounced and implied. Between the lines of these motivations, then, it is taken for granted that everybody shares the Academy's fundamental idea of literature, which is a continuous presumption that strengthens the award's normative contribution to what Casanova calls "the Greenwich Meridian of literature" (Casanova 2013: 278).

Looking back at the twentieth-century prizes in 2001, the sitting Permanent Secretary of the Swedish Academy, Sture Allén, identified the two most frequent elements in the motivations thus far: on the one hand, references to the laureates' regional, national, or cultural background, and, on the other, praises of the awarded authors' abilities to address existential human issues (Allén and Espmark 2001: 13–14). But, as another member of the Academy, Kjell Espmark, pointed out in the same publication, the Swedish Academy has not been one and the same during the 122-year history of the prize (40). Different Nobel Committees and different constellations of the Academy have recommended and selected laureates on the basis of very different aesthetic premises and appreciations. In order to get an overview of these changes in poetics, I have, quite mechanically, divided the history of the prize into six twenty-year periods. The rationale behind this crude division is to construct a neutral optic from which patterns can be recognized as free as possible from preconceptions.

The following discussion is fundamentally different from Kjell Espmark's substantial account of the history of prize decisions in his *Det litterära Nobelpriset* (Espmark 1986), *Litteraturpriset. Hundra år med Nobels uppdrag* (Espmark 2001), and *The Nobel Prize in Literature—a New Century* (Espmark 2021). First of all, in these studies Espmark focused on the discussions leading up to the decisions and the motivations, relying on discourses not publicly available until fifty years after being written. This means that the arguments Espmark interpreted and analyzed have not had any direct impact on the world literary discussion—until, that is, he published his accounts and assessments of these discussions. Secondly, when he wrote these historical accounts, Espmark was himself a central member of the Swedish Academy and the Nobel Committee. In his books, then, he analyzed the former prizes from a position not only within the Academy but, more importantly, within a particular constellation of the Academy that had distinct and sometimes conflicting relations to former constellations. This biased approach to the material studied is evident in Espmark's often quite personal evaluations of awarded œuvres and authors, and in his subjective remarks on laureate selections. From my point of view, Espmark's books are central parts of the 2001–21 period of Nobel history rather than neutral academic studies.

Unlike Espmark, I am—in the context of this chapter—not interested in the intentions behind to the finalized prize motivations, or what discussions in the Academy led up to the official formulation. No, in order to study the prescriptive gestures of the Nobel, I will only focus on the prize motivations as such and what they have been signaling—that is, what the actual phrases used to describe the laureates' works have told authors, critics, and readers about Nobel literary values. I will do this by looking at key concepts in the brief motivations, and by identifying the patterns of aesthetic evaluation created by recurring concepts in each of the twenty-year periods.

When Annie Ernaux, for example, was awarded in 2022 "for her courage and clinical acuity with which she uncovers the roots, estrangements and collective restraints of personal memory," the words "courage," "acuity," and "uncovers" entailed three different and distinct aesthetic dimensions, all of which resonated with the Abdulrazak Gurnah motivation from 2021 that stressed the Tanzanian-British novelist's "uncompromising and compassionate penetration of the effects of colonialism and the fate of the refugee in the gulf between cultures and continents." Both Ernaux's courage and Gurnah's uncompromising agenda acknowledged literary writing as a bold and determined activity, and their ability to uncover, penetrate, and show acuity forms a poetics of revealing hidden conditions and underlying structures.

The 2020 prize motivation for Louise Glück was quite different. When the American poet was said to be selected "for her unmistakable poetic voice that with austere beauty makes individual existence universal," the Swedish Academy stressed the literary qualities of beauty, originality, individuality, and universality—all values absent in relation to Gurnah and Ernaux. It is too early to speak of a distinct 2020s pattern as yet, but so far scrutiny and courage are leading concepts, with lyrical beauty and poetry's ability to express life's perpetual dynamic between the personal and the generally human as runners up.

1901–20: Nobility

Apart from its universal qualities, another distinct idea of literature evident in Alfred Nobel's will is that of usefulness. The focus on what is beneficial to humankind is quite logical in relation to science and peace, but in connection with literary achievements the call for usefulness implies a particular fundamental idea of literature's function in the world. Alfred Nobel wanted to award literary texts that have a positive effect on readers, societies, cultures, and, in effect, on humankind.

This doesn't mean that he was blind for other literary merits, like pure beauty and opportunities to enjoy temporary respites from reality, but in the context of his prize he wanted to stress psychologically and socially constructive texts—that is, what he called "idealist" literature. A frequent misunderstanding is that Alfred Nobel's notion of idealism necessarily entailed a conservative view of literature. That was simply not the case.

The Swedish engineer saw himself as politically radical, and in the last year of his life he completed the provocative anti-Catholic drama *Nemesis*, based on the same violent story as Percy Bysshe Shelley's *Le Cenci*. Nothing tells us that a radical literary provocation couldn't have been selected by Nobel himself as "the most outstanding work in an idealistic direction." Provocations can also, of course, lead to improvement. The distinct connections between idealism and conservatism have been made later on in the history of the Nobel Prize, by independent critics as well as by members of the Swedish Academy.

According to Kjell Espmark, the first selections were very much the results of Carl David af Wirsén's misinterpretation of the word "idealistic." The donor would not have agreed with the poetics behind these early selections, Espmark argued (Allén and Espmark 2001: 22). Wirsén was the first one to use the inclusion of idealism in Nobel's will to serve his own conservative ideals. This is manifested in the frequent use of the word "nobility" in the early prize motivations.

The twenty authors awarded in the first twenty-year period, 1901–20, were selected—according to the prize motivations—for having written literary works containing one or several of nine principally different values. The prize-winning œuvres were praised for being: *noble* (9 mentions in the motivations), *imaginative* (6), *versatile* (5), *grand* (5), *ingenious* (4), *skillful* (4), *vernacular* (3), *cosmopolitan* (3), *masterly* (1), and *communicative* (1). Communicative skills were only mentioned by the Academy in connection with Maurice Maeterlinck's ability to "appeal to the reader's own feelings."[1] Cosmopolitan qualities or successful transcultural distribution were mentioned three times: in pointing out Rudyard Kipling's international fame, praising Paul Heyse's "world-renowned short stories," and stressing Rabindranath Tagore's Asian contribution to Western literature. Opposite qualities were mentioned slightly more often when vernacular or culturally rooted values were identified in the works of Frédéric Mistral, José Echegaray, Verner von Heidenstam, and Henrik Pontoppidan.

The formal skills of the authors were only acknowledged four times in these early motivations. This kind of quality was, however, central in the very beginning of the history of the prize. The two first laureates were awarded for their brilliant craftsmanship: Sully Prudhomme for his "artistic perfection," and Theodor Mommsen for his ability to execute "the art of historical writing." A couple of years later, Italian poet Giosuè Carducci was awarded for rendering his works "lyrical force" and "freshness of style," and in 1910 Paul Heyse was acclaimed for his "consummate artistry." After Heyse, however, this quality was not noticed in the prize motivations. Quite a few motivations pointed out the grand scale of the works awarded. Mommsen, Bjørnson, Henryk

---

[1] Unless otherwise stated, all the English translations used are taken from the Swedish Academy's own homepage, https://www.nobelprize.org/prizes/literature. Occasionally, these translations differ quite distinctly from the words and phrases used in the original Swedish motivations, and it is unclear when these early motivations were translated into English. Several of them have certainly been distributed in other translations made by critics and correspondents, directly from the Swedish or via other translations by people outside the Academy. That's why my analysis is based on the Swedish motivations. I will point out significant dissimilarities between the original Swedish versions and the official English translations.

Sienkewicz, Carl Spitteler, and Knut Hamsun were all selected for the monumental, mighty, or magnificent qualities of their works. Just as acknowledged was the value of versatility, which was brought up as a special quality in the works of Bjørnson, Heyse, Maeterlinck, Gerhart Hauptmann, and Karl Gjellerup.

Two aesthetic qualities with distinctly Romantic dimensions were represented in these early motivations. Four of the authors were described as having some kind of ingenious abilities—Mistral, Echegaray, Kipling, and Rudolf Eucken. Another frequently invoked Romantic ideal was that of imagination. Six of these early laureates were acclaimed for possessing "freshness of inspiration" (Bjørnson), "true inspiration" (Mistral), "creative energy" (Carducci), "originality of imagination" (Kipling), "vivid imagination" (Selma Lagerlöf), and "wealth of imagination" (Maeterlinck).

However, the most praised literary quality in the prize motivations from this first period was nobility, a moral category in which thematic elements overlap with an assessment of the author's ethics. In stressing this quality, the early Nobel Committees saw writing as a moral endeavor. Literary quality was a successfully accomplished idealist intention. This kind of nobility had distinctly normative effects. The high moral standards were directly opposed to the literary values of provocation and critical accounts of cultural, political, and ideological hegemonies. The noble ethics of the authors reflected the ethics of the Swedish Academy, and thus of the dominant ideology and existing order.

To a certain extent it is fair to say that the extensive appreciation of nobility in this first period of the Nobel Prize illustrates how the poetic ideals of the nineteenth century lingered on in the Swedish Academy a couple of decades into the next century, which very much confirms Carl David af Wirsén's substantial power in the selection process. Wirsén held the positions as Permanent Secretary and Committee Chair until his death in 1912, and he contributed strongly to establishing the fundamental poetological standard of the prize.

The conservative poetics of the first twenty years of awarding the Nobel Prize must also, however, be related to the difficulties that the Nobel Committee and the Swedish Academy faced when given the task of selecting international literary laureates. Evident in the early reports from the Committee was a continual discussion on how closely the members must follow the exact words of Alfred Nobel's last will. When Alfred Nobel wrote about benefit and humankind, he was not describing specifically literary achievements, but the common idea behind all the five awards. In connection with the other four prizes, both the universalism and the utilitarian tendency in the will were easy to accept without fundamental reservations. Relating these qualities to literary texts was trickier. The early prize motivations were partly results of the Committees' interpretation of what universally useful literature looked like. After the first twenty years of awarding the literary prize, the Committees established a more independent relation to the will and Alfred Nobel's exact words.

After Wirsén's death in 1912, the moralistic tendency in the motivations successively ceased, but the focus on noble qualities in the first twenty-year period cannot altogether be seen as Wirsén's doing. The fact that nobility was also mentioned in both Tagore's and Gjellerup's motivations in 1913 and 1917 points to the fact that Wirsén was not the only Academy member to interpret Nobel's use of the adjective "idealistic" in a moral and ideological direction. The first Committee Chair initiated and established the first Nobel Prize poetics, but he was not the only Academy member promoting such a definition of literary greatness.

In what ways, then, were these awarded literary œuvres perceived as noble by the Swedish Academy? Well, the quality of nobility was invoked in two different ways. In six of the motivations, nobility was found in the literary texts themselves. Sully Prudhomme's "poetic composition" gave "evidence of lofty idealism," Bjørnstjerne Bjørnson's poetry was "noble" and characterized by the "rare purity of its spirit," and Rudolf Eucken's writings were described as showing "warmth and strength in presentation," whereas both Selma Lagerlöf's and Romain Rolland's writings were said to include a "lofty idealism," and Maurice Maeterlinck's poetry displayed a "poetic idealism."[2] In seven of the motivations, nobility was instead to be found in the attitudes or the characters of the authors themselves. Eucken, Heyse, Tagore, and Gjellerup were described as having a noble approach to their art: Eucken showed an "earnest search for truth," Heyse's artistry was "permeated with idealism," Tagore wrote with a deep and lofty "ambition,"[3] and Gjellerup's poetry was shaped by the Danish poet's "lofty ideals." Romain Rolland was rather displaying a noble attitude toward his literary characters. He was awarded because of the "sympathy and love of truth with which he has described different types of human beings." In the Eucken motivation, the author's attitude to life—his "idealistic philosophy of life"—was seen as an integral part of the nobility of his œuvre. The same is true for Rudyard Kipling, whose perception of the world displayed a "male strength of conception."[4] In the very first prize motivation, nobility was directly described as a personal moral quality in the author's character. The "lofty idealism" of Prudhomme's work, we are told, stems from the French author's "quality of […] heart."

Taken together, these eight accounts of literary nobility acclaimed a human characteristic as much as a literary quality. The members of the Swedish Academy took on the task to not only evaluate the quality of literary texts, but also judge the moral character of authors. This is perhaps most evident in the dismissal of Georg Brandes in 1903. When the Danish writer and literary critic was rejected, the Committee's critique of his œuvre seamlessly turned into a disqualification of his very person: Brandes' knowledge was "shallow," his tone was "ruthless," "sardonic," and "scornful," his judgments were "very unfair," and his opinions were "adventurous" and "licentious" (Svensén 2001a: 47, my translations). He was, in sum, not a good guy.

---

[2] The phrase "poetic idealism" is my translation. The Swedish Academy's own translation of the Swedish "poetisk idealitet" in the motivation of Maurice Maeterlinck's prize is "poetic fancy." The word "fancy" does not, however, cover the idealistic poetics evident in the Swedish word "idealitet."

[3] My translation. The Swedish Academy has translated the Swedish description of Tagore's works' "djup och höga syftning" with "his profoundly sensitive, fresh and beautiful verse," thereby removing the denotation of ambition and intention in "syftning" as well as the idealistic connotation in the adjective "höga" (high, lofty).

[4] My translation. The Academy's translation "virility of ideas" does not cover the tangibly gendered Swedish description of high moral standards: "manlig styrka i uppfattning."

1921–40: Skill

By 1920, the Swedish Academy had undergone a significant rejuvenation (Allén and Espmark 2001: 25), which led to a distinct shift of poetics—in the recommendations from the Nobel Committee as well as in the prize motivations. As a result, nobility lost its position as the most frequently invoked literary quality. In its place a very different literary characteristic appeared in the motivations as the most acknowledged and praised quality in the laureates' achievements. The most invoked literary qualities in the prize motivations from the 1920s and the 1930s were: *skillful* (10 mentions), *vernacular* (9), *noble* (6), *grand* (4), *ingenious* (3), *widely recognized* (1), *humorous* (1), *contemporary* (1), *imaginative* (1), *universal* (1), and *masterly* (1).

These qualities included a couple of characteristics that were not at all referred to in the 1900s and 1910s. The universalism of Grazia Deledda, whose writings dealt with "human problems in general," the "wit and humour" of Sinclair Lewis, and Roger Martin du Gard's ability to depict "contemporary life," all represented new aesthetic categories in the prize motivations. Also, the idea to award Thomas Mann partly because of the fact that *Buddenbrooks* had "won steadily increased recognition" since the novel's publication in 1901 was a new quality. Furthermore, the characterization of Pearl Buck's biographies as "masterpieces" added the idea of literary mastery to the qualities invoked by the Swedish Academy.

Nobility was not at all abandoned as an award-winning quality during this period. It was no longer a dominant category, but was still referred to in as many as six different motivations. Anatole France's writings were characterized by a "nobility of style," a "profound human sympathy," and "grace." George Bernard Shaw's works were "marked by both idealism and humanity." Deledda was awarded because of her "idealistically inspired writings" composed "with depth and sympathy." Eugene O'Neill's dramatic works were written with "honesty and deep-felt emotions," Martin du Gard showed "artistic power and truth," and Buck was celebrated for her "true epic descriptions."[5]

But noble qualities were surpassed by two quite different literary characteristics. The laureates' ability to nurture national or regional traditions or depict domestic ways of life were occasionally referred to in the motivations from the first twenty years of the prize, but it was much more frequently invoked in the 1920s and the 1930s. Jacinto Benavente was awarded for continuing "the illustrious traditions of the Spanish drama," and Ivan Bunin was selected because of the way he had "carried on the classical Russian traditions in prose writing." And as an author inspired by "a true Gallic temperament," Anatole France could not have had a more suitable name. Whereas Benavente, Bunin,

---

[5] My translation. The Swedish Academy's English version of the Buck motivation includes a mistranslation. The Swedish formulation "rika och äkta episka skildringar" is ambiguous. Read in isolation, it can mean, on the one hand, "rich and truly epic descriptions" (which is how the Academy translates it), and, on the other, "rich and true epic descriptions." In the Committee's lengthy recommendation to the Swedish Academy, however, Pearl Buck's prose was celebrated for its authenticity and truthfulness, which characterized her narratives as true and epic rather than truly epic (Svensén 2001b: 284).

and France were characterized by their ability to cultivate respective national literary traditions, other laureates were celebrated for depicting regional or national life. Deledda depicted "the life of her native island" Sardinia, Buck's narratives included "descriptions of peasant life in China," Finnish writer Frans Eemil Sillanpää showed a "deep understanding of his country's peasantry," Irish poet William Butler Yeats gave "expression to the spirit of a whole nation," and Polish author Wladyslaw Reymont was awarded for "his great national epic, *The Peasants*." The vernacular space in the works of the Norwegian Sigrid Undset was more extensive: she was praised for her depiction of "Northern life during the Middle Ages."

The most frequently invoked literary characteristic in the prize motivations from the period 1921–40 was, however, a more technical quality. Ten out of a total of eighteen writers (since no prizes were given in 1935 and 1940) were at least partly awarded because of their formal skills. Technical talents of describing, characterizing, and structuring were stressed in relation to poetry, dramatic works, philosophical prose, and fiction. Yeats' poetry was awarded because of its "highly artistic form," Shaw was praised for his skillful combination of "stimulating satire" and "poetic beauty," and Luigi Pirandello was acknowledged for his "revival of dramatic and scenic art." The philosopher Henri Bergson was awarded because of his "rich and vitalizing ideas," but also because of "the brilliant skill with which they have been presented." France's prose works were deemed "brilliant," and Deledda's writings were praised for their "plastic clarity." Sinclair Lewis was acknowledged for his "vigorous and graphic art of description," and for his "ability to create [...] new types of characters," John Galsworthy for his "distinguished art of narration," Bunin for his "strict artistry," and Sillanpää for "the exquisite art with which he has portrayed" Finnish peasantry.

Considering the fact that it was during this period that experimental modernist prose flourished in many European literatures, one would guess that the focus on formal skill in the Nobel Prize motivations corresponded with the contemporary tendency to explore and stretch the borders of literary style and structure. But it is a well-known fact that the most notorious modernist prose writers—Marcel Proust, Virginia Woolf, James Joyce, and Franz Kafka—never received the prize, and that literary Modernism was only acknowledged by the Swedish Academy after it had petered out or become a stylistic norm, most notably with the awards to T.S. Eliot and William Faulkner in the late 1940s. To be fair, the Academy did not totally ignore literary Modernism. In awarding Luigi Pirandello in 1934, for example, the Nobel institution did recognize experimental dramatic innovations in contemporary theater. Furthermore, the Swedish Academy and its Nobel Committee were by no means the only ones whose recognition of experimental modernist prose was belated. On the contrary, in not acknowledging Proust, Woolf, Joyce, and Kafka in the unambiguous way they have been canonized in hindsight, the Swedish Academy rather expressed a dominant poetics among the international literati of the 1920s and the 1930s.

Rather than an acknowledgment of contemporary literary Modernism, the focus on formal skill during this period of the Nobel Prize was an appraisal of literary efficiency and craftsmanship. Many of the laureates from the 1920s and the 1930s were awarded for widely accessible literary works, more so than during the first twenty years of the prize, which supports Kjell Espmark's observation that the ability to appeal to "the ordinary reader" became a central quality in the 1930s discussions (Allén and Espmark 2001: 26). The awards from this second twenty-year period of Nobel history were thus quite at odds with contemporary classics to-be. The prose of France, Undset, Mann, Lewis, Galsworthy, and Buck, and the broadly appreciated rhyming poetry of Erik Axel Karlfeldt, can indeed be seen as contrasts to the elaborately esoteric styles and structures of *À la recherche du temps perdu*, *Ulysses*, *The Waves*, *Der Prozess*, and *The Waste Land*. What the Nobel Committee recognized as important formal achievements in France's best-selling novels, Undset's "powerful" trilogy *Kristin Lavransdatter*, Mann's widely read family chronicle *Buddenbrooks*, Lewis' satirical *Babbitt*, Galsworthy's *The Forsyte Saga*, and Buck's "rich" and "epic" (and best-selling Pulitzer Prize winner) *The Good Earth*, was their capacity to elegantly and efficiently address a large reading public. For the Nobel Committees of the 1920s and 1930s, formal skill was understood as an ability to expertly make use of the well-tried instruments in the toolbox of literature rather than to tear down the conventions and create totally new ways of writing.

From 1921 to 1940, then, the Swedish Academy tacitly defined literature as a craft used to reach a significant number of readers. According to the prize motivations from this period, valuable and important literary works were expertly written and efficiently composed. The aesthetics of this period stands out in the history of the prize. In his discussion of authorial positions in the cultural space, Americanist Günther Leypoldt identifies two axes: one that stretches from a "communal régime" to a "singularity régime," and one between a "vocation régime" and a "trade régime" (Leypoldt 2022). Nobel laureates, Leopoldt argues, enjoy a position combining a high singularity and a high vocation, whereas genre-fiction writers, at the other end of the spectrum, combine communal and trade values. When Nobel poetics shifted from lofty nobility to skillful accessibility in the 1920s and the 1930s, the position of the laureates in the cultural space also changed. Nobel Literature moved toward a mid-cultural position in which communal and trade values were as important as vocation and singularity.

1941–60: Mastery

In the two decades following the Second World War, there was another distinct shift in the aesthetics of the prize motivations. It is an illustrative fact that a decision was made to award Paul Valéry in 1945, even though the French modernist poet died in July and the Academy did not want to have a second posthumous prize after Karlfeldt's in 1931 (Svensén 2001b: 355–6). In earlier discussions, Valéry had been rejected for being "intentionally inaccessible" (1930), "exclusive" (1933), "esoteric" (1935), and "too obscure" (1937), and for writing a "tremendously obscure verse" (1936) in an "exclusively peculiar form" (1931) with "unusually high inaccessibility" (1932). (Svensén 2001b: 150, 161, 178, 196, 227, 242, and 265, my translations) But in 1945, then, the Swedish Academy was ready to appreciate Modernism. Despite Valéry's untimely death, the 1940s belonged to modernist writers: Hermann Hesse, André Gide, T.S. Eliot, and William Faulkner. This change in poetics probably had to do with a strengthened position in the Academy for fiction writers and poets, at the expense of university professors and literary critics (cf. Allén and Espmark 2001: 28).

The most invoked literary qualities in the prize motivations between 1941 and 1960 were the following: *masterly* (8 mentions), *noble* (6), *grand* (5), *universal* (5), *vernacular* (5), *influential* (4), *contemporary* (3), *original* (3), *skillful* (2), *inspired* (2), *sharp-sighted* (1), and *versatile* (1).

The merit of having had a great impact was a new category, a fact that confirms the notion that experimental modernist poetics was normalized in the latter half of the 1940s—a tendency most tangibly evident in the Eliot motivation in 1948 and its recognition of the poet's "pioneer" achievements. Ernest Hemingway was also awarded for being hugely influential to modern literary prose. On the other hand, the fact that both Albert Camus and Boris Pasternak were acknowledged as authors of "important" works had probably more to do with philosophical and political significance than modernist narrative techniques.

Another new category had to do with inspiration. The fact that both Gabriela Mistral and Hermann Hesse were praised for their "inspired" writings seems to reveal an underlying Romantic poetics, perhaps caused by a need to reenchant the world after six years of war. A second category with Romantic dimensions, also invoked for the first time, was that of originality. In praising Johannes V. Jensen's "bold, innovative style,"[6] Eliot's "pioneer contribution" to modern poetry, Faulkner's "artistically unique contribution to the modern American novel," and Pär Lagerkvist's "true independence of mind," the Academy repeatedly stressed the fundamental value of independent literary creativity.

The fresh experience of Adolf Hitler's fascism may explain why the category of nobility was still one of the most invoked literary qualities in the postwar period. In awarding Winston Churchill for his defense of "exalted human values," the Swedish Academy expressed gratitude for the British Prime Minister's wartime efforts, and a clear retrospective rejection of the defeated Nazi ideology was also indirectly evident in the praise of Mistral's "idealistic aspirations," Hesse's "classical humanitarian ideals," André Gide's "fearless love of truth," Bertrand Russell's "humanitarian ideals and freedom of thought," and Juan Ramón Jiménez' "example of high spirit." Interpreted as more contemporary and forward-looking gestures, the acknowledgments of these noble qualities in authors and texts can also be read as indirect protests against the Soviet Union and the communist dictatorship of Joseph Stalin.

The frequent praise of grandness in these motivations was also related to the recently unfolded violent drama of the Second World War. The feeling of having just come out of a human catastrophe—and being on the verge of racing into a new one—strongly influenced the Academy's choice to award Lagerkvist's attempts "to find answers to the eternal questions confronting mankind," François Mauriac's "artistic intensity with which he has in his novels penetrated the drama of human life," and

---

[6] My translation. The Academy's phrase "freshly creative style" does not really cover the aspects of originality evident in the original "djärv, nyskapande stilkonst."

Camus' dramatization of "the problems of the human consciousness in our times." The fact that the ability to address and depict the contemporary world was more invoked in this period than in the two preceding ones also reveals a feeling of living in dramatic times. But since this literary quality only appeared at the very end of the period in question, the likely real-world background was rather the threat of a new devastating military conflict than the Second World War. Apart from Camus' ability to discuss "human consciousness in our times," Italian poet Salvatore Quasimodo was praised for the way he expressed "the tragic experience of life in our own times," and French author Saint-John Perse was awarded for a poetry "which in a visionary fashion reflects the conditions of our time."

In my understanding of the 1940s and 1950s prize motivations, the quality of formal skill was not as directly invoked in this period as in the preceding one, but skill is difficult to distinguish from two other categories. It is quite close to the quality of originality, which was directly mentioned in three motivations during this period. It is also difficult to separate formal skill from the most invoked literary quality in the motivations from this period: mastery. Both skill and mastery have to do with craftsmanship, but in stressing the latter rather than the former, I would argue, the prize motivations from these decades focused on a literary quality in its own right that involved a certain kind of aesthetics. You can be skillful without being a master, but you must be skillful in order to become a master. Extreme skill can be executed in a solitary act of inspiration by a very talented writer. But if you're a master, you need to be able to use your talent in a controlled and systematic way. When the Nobel motivations praised mastery rather than skill, they lifted up the best literary achievements to a higher level. Nobel-worthy texts were not only very well written—they were masterpieces, normative models to learn from and follow. To master an art requires total control of means and materials, as when Ernest Hemingway shows "his mastery of the art of narrative," and when Winston Churchill executes "his mastery of historical and biographical description."

Another element that distinguished the postwar idea of mastery from earlier praises of formal skill was a wider focus. The masterly quality of the 1940s and the 1950s wasn't necessarily a matter of writing and composition. It might just as well be a category of perception, thinking, and knowledge, as in Gide's "keen psychological insight," Mauriac's "deep spiritual insight," Quasimodo's "classical fire," and the way in which Russell "champions humanitarian ideals and freedom of thought." In this focus on the laureates themselves and their capacities, the postwar prize motivations were closer to the dominating nobility discourse in the first two decades of the Nobel than to the more technical poetics in the 1920s and 1930s.

The idea of mastery had quite strong connections to the notion of competition. This is a discourse that still today often instructs the critical commentaries of the Nobel announcements. In discussing the Academy's choices, media reactions often involve opinions on whether the laureate really is *the best* author, writer, or poet, as if the Nobel Prize is a kind of World Cup in Literature, a competition in which literary achievements and qualities can be strictly ranked. The metaphor of mastery includes the idea of something highest up in the hierarchy: a master is the most distinguished practitioner of his or her art, a role model for all the apprentices to follow. But, as Per Wästberg put it in his book on the Academy from 2020, the Swedish judges do not have access to any "hollow Olympic yardstick" in comparing the nominated œuvres (Wästberg 2020: 401). Literary achievements cannot be neutrally measured.

On this issue, Academy members have sometimes communicated paradoxical signals. In Sture Allén's and Kjell Espmark's book *Nobelpriset i litteratur* from 2001, Allén rejected the idea of the prize as a "world championship" of literature, whereas Espmark later on in the same book discussed the laureates as "masters" (Allén and Espmark 2001: 7, 30, and 32). Whereas Allén described the Nobel distinction as a singular reward to a particular achievement and not a prize earned in a competition, Espmark's appellation suggested a direct comparison between abilities and qualities leading to the designation of the best contender. When it comes to the prize motivations, however, 1941–60 was the only period in which the latter discourse has been central. The conception of literary champions was thus just a historical parenthesis in the poetics expressed and suggested by the official prize motivations.

In the prize motivations from the 1940s and the 1950s, then, valuable literature was first and foremost writings produced by a master—either of language, description, narrative, tradition, philosophy, psychology, spirituality, or ideals. The most important literary works were read as masterpieces. Seen through the lens of Günther Leypoldt's two axes of cultural positions, Nobel Literature was again firmly and distinctly placed within the régimes of vocation and singularity, having enjoyed a more mid-cultural position in the preceding twenty-year period.

1961–80: Vernaculars

In the 1960s and the 1970s, references to the concept of mastery were more or less dropped. Instead, a new set of recurring key words appeared in the prize motivations. These were the most prize-winning literary values between 1961 and 1980: *vernacular* (14 mentions), *universal* (7), *grand* (7), *noble* (6), *contemporary* (5), *sharp-sighted* (4), *imaginative* (4), *original* (3), *skillful* (2), *humorous* (1), and *impactful* (1). Of these qualities, the one closest to the mastery discourse was the value of sharpness and perceptive analysis, as in John Steinbeck's "keen social perception," Saul Bellow's "subtle analysis of contemporary culture," Odysseus Elytis' "intellectual clear-sightedness," and Czeslaw Milosz' "uncompromising clear-sightedness." The qualities of nobility, grandness, and contemporaneity were all somewhat more invoked here than in the preceding period, but creative originality and formal skill were as scantily referred to in both periods.

The most invoked literary quality in this period was the authors' capacity to continue and develop culturally specific literary traditions. In 2001, Espmark described this change as a process in which the praised pioneering and inventive literary qualities were successively more connected to specific languages and cultures rather than to the cosmopolitan literary space (Allén and Espmark 2001: 29). In acknowledging, praising, and encouraging vernacular literary elements and functions, the Swedish Academy systematically embraced a pluralist perspective of cultures and literatures.

This dominance closely corresponded with a widening of the laureates' cultural backgrounds. Despite the earlier prizes to Tagore and Gabriela Mistral, it was not until the 1960s that the Nobel Prize in Literature really managed to reach beyond Europe and North America, to Israel (Shmuel Agnon), Guatemala (Miguel Ángel Asturias), Japan (Yasunari Kawabata), Chile (Pablo Neruda), and Australia (Patrick White). The vernacular elements in the award-winning œuvres from the 1960s and the 1970s were often described in the motivations as nationally conditioned. In more than half of these fourteen brief texts, the authors' writings were directly anchored in national contexts. Ivo Andric was praised for drawing "themes" and "human destinies" "from the history of his country," Yugoslavia, whereas Mikhail Sholokhov had "given expression to a historic phase in the life of the Russian people," and Nelly Sachs was praised for interpreting "Israel's destiny with touching strength." Alexandr Solzhenitzyn had pursued the "tradition of Russian literature," and Elytis' poetry was written "against the background of Greek tradition." Two of the laureates were awarded for their capacity to renew their respective national traditions: Heinrich Böll had revitalized German literature, and Vicente Aleixandre had renewed the tradition of Spanish poetry. In the Kawabata motivation, the invoked national context was described as a vague, psychologically defined ethnic identity when the author was said to express "the essence of the Japanese mind."

There was only one case in which the invoked vernacular context was more limited than a nation, and that was the Isaac Bashevis Singer motivation, which positioned the author in "a Polish-Jewish cultural tradition." Larger cultural entities were much more common. The conception of a distinct but transnational people was evident in connection with Agnon, who was praised for his "motifs from the life of the Jewish people." A cultural rather than ethnic transnational context was referred to when Giorgos Seferis was described as being "inspired by a deep feeling for the Hellenic world of culture." In three of the motivations, the larger context was geographical. Neruda's poetry "brings alive a continent's destiny and dreams," whereas White's "narrative art has introduced a new continent into literature." Asturias' writings, being "deep-rooted in the national traits and traditions of Indian peoples of Latin America," were described as both nationally and transnationally conditioned. There is of course a big difference between national traditions, minority cultures within nations (like the Polish-Jewish one), and the cultural context of a whole continent, but all three categories were described in a similar vein in these motivations, namely, as distinct cultural entities, separated from some kind of cosmopolitan center.

The tendency in the motivations to confirm and stress the borders of such entities was not only a result of the ambition to enlarge the geographical scope of the prize. It was also a confirmation of an earlier tendency in the history of the prize motivations. The culturally rooted and particular didn't appear as a new category in the 1960s and 1970s. Vernacular qualities were also quite extensively acclaimed in the two earliest twenty-year periods. They were, however, totally nonexistent in the 1940s and the 1950s. After that two-decade pause, the vernacular returned as the most dominant literary quality in any of the six twenty-year periods. But in the earlier acknowledgments of vernacular traditions, the motivations mostly vernacularized European and North American cultures and literary traditions. What was new in the 1960s was the recurring vernacularizations of cultures beyond Western traditions.

Throughout the history of the prize motivations, several cultures have been vernacularized more than once. South America, Spain, and Russia have been invoked in four motivations each, and United States in three, whereas Chinese, Greek, Polish, Danish, and Jewish vernaculars have been referred to in two motivations each. The cultural histories of Spain and Russia have thus been as vernacularized as South American traditions, and the US vernacular has not been far behind. Even French literature underwent a vernacularization when the 1921 motivation referred to Anatole France's "charming Gallic temperament."

The motivations from the 1920s were an early stronghold of vernacular qualities. As many as six laureates from this decade were praised as cultural representatives (France, Benavente, Yeats, Reymont, Deledda, and Undset), which was slightly more frequent than the references to formal skill during this decade. According to the Nobel Committees of the 1920s, 1960s, and 1970s, then, literature was predominantly a culturally restricted affair. For them, important and valuable literature belonged to a specific culture or literary tradition that it depicted, cultivated, or reinvigorated.

1981–2000: the Universal

While vernacular aspects were the most frequently awarded literary qualities in the 1960s and 1970s, the second most praised literary element during that period was a seemingly opposite value: universal relevance. This is not as paradoxical as it may sound, since it was often the very dynamic between the culturally distinct and the generally human that was acclaimed as an important literary value. Still, vernacular qualities were mentioned twice as often as universal significance during these decades.

In the 1980s and the 1990s, the relation between these two literary qualities was reversed: universal relevance was mentioned in nine motivations whereas only four included praise for vernacular distinctness. Being universally significant was, in fact, the single most awarded literary quality from the last two decades of the twentieth century, and the pattern of dominance comes forth as even stronger if we connect it to the neighboring aspect of cultural inclusiveness. Other than that, the qualities praised in these decades were quite diverse. These were the values most mentioned in the motivations: *universal* (9 times), *grand* (7), *sharp-sighted* (6), *skillful* (6), *imaginative* (5), *noble* (5), *culturally inclusive* (4), *vernacular* (4), *contemporary* (3), *versatile* (2), *influential* (1), and *oppositional* (1). The merit of being universal was recognized in several of the awarded non-European œuvres during this period. Naguib Mahfouz, Nadine Gordimer, Kenzaburo Oe, and Gao Xingjian were all described as having a universal appeal or depicting universal issues. But universalism was also detected in Jaroslav Seifert's and Wislawa Szymborska's East-European works, in José Camilo Cela's Spanish novels, and in the Anglophone and Francophone centers. William Golding's novels were awarded for their use of the "universality of myths," and Claude Simon was praised for his "depiction of the human condition."

Even though "cosmopolitan" was already recognized in three motivations from the earliest twenty-year period of the prize, distinctly universal qualities were not introduced in the motivations until the Henri Bergson award in 1927, and this was the only motivation that included universalism in the period 1921–40. The frequency of the quality then increased in the 1941–60 period (five mentions), and in the 1961–80 period (seven mentions). It reached an all-time high during the 1980s and 1990s, and then became less important again in the first two decades of the new millennium (only three mentions between 2001 and 2022).

There were two new aesthetic categories in the motivations from the period 1981–2000. One of them was the quality of being culturally inclusive, a category very much in line with the recurring praises of universalism in its stress on literature's ability to unite and go beyond cultural, social, and individual limitations. The other new category was literature's capacity to be oppositional. When Dario Fo was awarded in 1997 for "scourging authority and upholding the dignity of the downtrodden," literature was, for the first time in the history of the motivations, perceived as a vector for societal change. Of course, Albert Camus' illuminations of "the human consciousness in our times," John Steinbeck's "keen social perception," Vicente Aleixandre's ability to illuminate "man's condition [...] in present-day society," and Odysseus Elytis' depictions of "modern man's struggle for freedom," may all lead to social change, but their strengths as authors were connected to *showing* social realities rather than fighting the agents of injustice.

Similarly, Jean-Paul Sartre's "spirit of freedom," Aleksandr Solzhenitsyn's "ethical force," Eyvind Johnson's "service of freedom," and Jaroslav Seifert's "liberating image of the indomitable spirit and versatility of man" may all give readers the strength to stand up for what they believe in, but in the motivation texts, these œuvres were not described as integral parts of the struggle itself. When Toni Morrison was awarded for giving "life to an essential aspect of American reality," the obvious reference to domestic US politics remained unexpressed, and when the Academy reused a phrase from Alfred Nobel's last will in praising Nadine Gordimer's stories for being "of great benefit to humanity," they only indirectly invoked the laureate's political activism against Apartheid in South Africa. None of these motivations identified literature's possibility of being a direct gesture of political protest as directly as in the description of Dario Fo's tendency to scourge authority in his performing art.

The last two decades of the twentieth century, then, were dominated by a stress on universal literary qualities, equally valid for all humans. In a way, this new focus was a turning back to the universal scope of Alfred Nobel's original vision.

2001–20: Examination

In the prize motivations from the first two decades of the twenty-first century, references to universal dimensions in the laureates' literary works decreased significantly, and so did the references to vernacular rootedness. Only Jean-Marie Gustave Le Clézio (2008) and Kazuo Ishiguro (2017) were praised for their universalism, the former for exploring "humanity" and the latter for uncovering "the abyss beneath our illusory sense of connection with the world," in which "our" refers to all human beings. And only Bob Dylan (2016) was distinctly situated within a specific culture, namely, "the great American song tradition."

The oppositional power of literature that was introduced as a valuable aesthetic quality in the Dario Fo motivation in 1997 was, to a certain extent, followed up in the 2000s and the 2010s. Ideological or political opposition was acknowledged in connection with several laureates, but in abstract and general ways that stressed its philosophical significance and implications. Hertha Müller was awarded in 2009 for depicting "the landscape of the dispossessed," Mario Vargas Llosa in 2010 for his "cartography of structures of power and his trenchant images of the individual's resistance, revolt, and defeat," and Harold Pinter in 2005 for forcing "entry into oppression's closed rooms." When Imre Kertész's testimonies from Nazi deportations and concentration camps were awarded in 2002, his ideological stance was existentially phrased: his writing was said to uphold "the fragile experience of the individual against the barbaric arbitrariness of history."

The literary category most referred to in the motivations between 2001 and 2020 was, however, an aesthetic quality not mentioned in any earlier period. The literary values most awarded in this period were: *examining* (11 mentions), *skillful* (6), *impactful* (5), *oppositional* (4), *passionate* (4), *contemporary* (3), *universal* (3), *influential* (2), *original* (2), *versatile* (2), *noble* (2), *vernacular* (1), *grand* (1), *female* (1), *sharp-sighted* (1), *imaginative* (1), *ingenious* (1), *transboundary* (1), and *compassionate* (1). The prize motivations from these recent decades thus identified the ability to examine something as the most valuable literary quality. The different verbs used to describe literary examination varied—some of the authors *explored*, others *uncovered*, *discovered*, *revealed*, or *scrutinized* the world. It is, of course, not exactly the same thing to explore, uncover, reveal, and scrutinize, but the differences between these actions are quite subtle and much less significant than their similarities. What examining authors had in common—according to the prize motivations—was their honest attempts to reveal the real state of things without reducing any complexity.

These motivations referred to two different kinds of truth at the end of the examining laureates' literary efforts. Their texts either led to an uncovering of life's complexities, or a revealing of deficiencies. When V. S. Naipaul was said to show us "the presence of suppressed histories," and Peter Handke was praised for exploring "the periphery and the specificity of human experience," the Swedish Academy argued that the authors offered more nuanced pictures of the world than we usually are confronted with. Similarly, when Le Clézio was awarded for examining "a humanity beyond and below the reigning civilization," he was said to contribute with new aspects to our understanding of the world, and when Patrick Modiano was praised for evoking "the most ungraspable human destinies," his texts were awarded for their acknowledgment of new depths of life. In discovering "new symbols for the clash and interlacing of cultures," the works of Orhan Pamuk were seen as offering new perspectives on a very complex issue, and in uncovering the "abyss beneath our illusory sense of connection with the world," Ishiguro's novels were read as contributions to our understanding of human complexity.

The œuvres of Pinter and Vargas Llosa were awarded for revealing societal and human deficiencies, but from two very different perspectives. So were Elfriede Jelinek's works, when she was praised for revealing "the absurdity of society's clichés and their subjugating power," and Doris Lessing's for subjecting "a divided civilisation to scrutiny." In a way, this poetological shift toward literature as a kind of examination already started in 1999, when that year's laureate Günter Grass was called "the great prober of the history of this century" in the Academy's press release, a formulation not included in the prize motivation ("Günter Grass," 2022).

As we have seen, the acknowledgment of literary scrutiny has continued in the early 2020s, when Abdulrazak Gurnah was awarded for his "penetration of the effects of colonialism," and Ernaux was praised for the acuity "with which she uncovers [...] personal memory." In the 2021 motivation, the Swedish Academy introduced a new synonym for literary examination, and in 2022 they reused the one that described Ishiguro's work in 2017.

A literary quality that was seldom mentioned in the motivations before 2000 was the ability to write with passion. Quasimodo's "classic fire," Singer's "impassionate narrative art," and Paz's "impassioned writing" stood alone—perhaps along with Prudhomme's "quality of the heart"—in the twentieth-century motivations on passionate qualities. When the Swedish Academy awarded Elfriede Jelinek's "extraordinary linguistic zeal," Doris Lessing's "fire and visionary power," Le Clézio's "sensual ecstasy," and Olga Tokarczuk's "encyclopedic passion," they acclaimed, to a certain extent, opposite literary values to the examining qualities that dominated the motivations from this latest twenty-year period. But the two abilities to explore through literature and write passionately also have a distinct similarity: both the painstaking search for truth and a passionate attitude to the world reject every kind of quiescence, inaction, apathy, and carelessness. Interpreted as gestures, both of these literary qualities can be seen as calls for action.

These two literary gestures are very much in line with another frequent quality in the 2001–20 motivations that was almost, but not completely, new. In earlier motivations, authors' abilities to be influential had often been acclaimed, but apart from Jean-Paul Sartre's "far-reaching influence on our age," the influence referred to was always expressively literary. Authors were awarded for finding new ways to write or for reinvigorating and developing literary traditions, and thereby establishing new paths for other writers to follow. In the first decades of the twenty-first century, however, Nobel Prize motivations stressed the awarded authors' ability to have an impact on *readers* rather than fellow writers. In the list of values above, I have thus distinguished this quality from literary influence by calling it "impactful" rather than "influential." When the literary examinations of Jelinek, Pinter, and Ishiguro were said to "reveal" and "uncover" truths, they were praised for making their readers see the world in a new light, just like Naipaul's works "compel us to see" suppressed histories, and Tomas Tranströmer's poetry "gives us fresh access to reality."

The list above shows that the quality of literary nobility was still around in the early twenty-first century. After being a dominant reference in the first twenty-year period of the prize's history, nobility has had a stable position during the years: six references each in the 1921–40, 1941–60, and 1961–80 periods, and five references between 1981 and 2000. Of course, the fact that the motivations from the 2000s and 2010s only included two distinct references to noble aims and endeavors reveals a decline in the centrality of this literary quality, but the many acclaiming mentions of examination and opposition in this period were often close to the category of nobility.

What did it mean, then, to be noble in the first two decades of the twenty-first century, according to the Nobel Prize motivations? Well, the two motivations that included the category of nobility referred to two moral qualities also evident in many of the other motivations from the 2000s and the 2010s. Imre Kertész was awarded for an œuvre that upheld "the fragile experience of the individual against the barbaric arbitrariness of history," and Svetlana Alexievich was praised for erecting a literary "monument to suffering and courage in our time." These motivations strongly acclaimed the literary courage to detect, describe, and fight injustice, as well as the strength to align with the human individual in facing collective or structural forces of oppression. Whereas the "lofty idealism" frequently invoked in the earliest period of the prize had an abstract, general, and collective quality, the references to nobility in the early-twenty-first-century motivations involved an individualist stance against mighty power structures.

The Role of the Author and the Purpose of Literature

The changing tendencies in the Swedish Academy's prize motivations reveal a continuous development of poetics. For each period described above, there has been a specific dominant view of what societal and cultural position an author has, and what his or her fundamental function is in the public life of a certain culture or on the international literary stage. Each period has also held a dominant idea—seldom expressed, more often taken for granted—of what a valuable literary text is and what cultural, societal, and personal effects it should lead to. These mostly tacitly communicated ideas on the roles and functions of authors and literary texts have always taken part of larger aesthetic contexts. To be sure, each prize motivation has not only expressed the particular poetics of eighteen Swedish intellectuals, but has also, more importantly, been manifestations of the historical situation from which the Academy members selected and presented the particular laureate.

In awarding literary nobility during the first twenty-year period of the prize, the Swedish Academy indirectly communicated the idea of the author as a sage or a secular priest—a wise and morally impeccable person who intends to make the world a better place through spreading his or her wisdom. According to this poetics, the literary text is a vehicle for communicating a morally coded wisdom, which makes it a kind of guide for the particular reader and, in effect, society at large. The desirable effect of this literature is improvement. The receptive reader is morally and intellectually enriched, which makes him or her a better person who can contribute to the betterment of society. The desirable literary mixture of moral goodness, objective truth, and convincing rhetoric gives this kind of literature a homiletic dimension. When distributing such a definition of literary purpose in the first decade of the prize's history, the Swedish Academy was deeply rooted in the bourgeois idealism of the West European nineteenth century, in which the true, the good, and the aesthetically valuable were thoroughly intertwined.

In the period 1921–40 the sage was replaced by the literary craftsman as the dominant kind of author in the prize motivations. Rather than a thinker or a guide, this kind of author is first and foremost a writer, someone who knows his or her language very well, who can use it in an efficient and original way and is able to experiment with it and expand its usage. According to this poetics, the ideal literary text is a platform for improving the distinctness and efficiency of language and for developing new ways of using it. The objective of literature is thus to develop more adequate linguistic tools for describing and depicting life. Although this poetological development toward formal aspects of literature was not, as with have seen, directly linked to literary Modernism but rather to narrative efficiency and aesthetic effects in accessible novels and poetry, the focus on formal skill was still very much in line with the development of different kinds of formalist literary criticism during the first half of the twentieth century. The title of Viktor Shklovsky's highly influential article "Art as Technique" from 1917 poignantly sums up the Nobel poetics of the 1920s and 1930s.

The dominant authorial role in the motivations from the next twenty-year period, 1941–60, was a development of the concept of the literary craftsman. The masterly text is written by a master, that is, the recognized expert of a certain craft. But the literary masters praised in the selections and prize motivations of the 1940s and the 1950s were masters not only of language, but also of perception and thinking. What these different kinds of experts had in common was their top position: in their respective fields, these authors were the best. The desirable effect of this literature was to establish a model literature for others to learn from and follow, and the overall purpose of literature, then, was to uphold and cultivate the quality of our common culture. Whereas the formal focus of the 1920s and the 1930s was language-oriented, the motivations in the 1940s and the 1950s presupposed and tacitly communicated a broader cultural purpose of literature. In these motivations, the Swedish Academy was establishing a canon of contemporary writing and thinking.

During the period 1961–80, when the motivations were mostly focused on vernacular traditions, the awarded authors were predominantly seen as representatives of their particular cultures. The laureates were first of all praised for their capacity to cultivate specific literary traditions or give voice to a part of the world. According to this aesthetics of representation, the texts themselves are given the role of literary ambassadors for their source cultures, or channels of access to certain cultural spaces. The desirable general effect of these œuvres was to contribute with new perspectives on life and the world. Through this kind of literature, the individual reader was invited to enlarge his or her epistemic and emotional scope. In effect, the world community would become more multifaceted, and its cultural representation more inclusive and democratic. In this period, more than during any earlier periods, highly valuable and widely significant literature—Nobel Literature, if you like—was defined as a palette of different literatures: it became a plurality of voices and distinct contributions, not unlike what we today tend to call "world literatures," with a plural s.

This ambition toward inclusiveness was very much in line with the left-wing tendency among many west European intellectuals during the period, and their engagement against political violence around the world, for example the war in Vietnam and Augusto Pinochet's regime in Chile. On a more domestic level, Sweden's quite prominent position in international affairs during these decades—particularly through United Nation's Secretary-General Dag Hammarskjöld and, later, Prime Minister Olof Palme—was an important nonliterary context for the vernacular motivations. Via these leading figures, Swedish citizens were prompted to recognize the multitude of cultural belongings in the world and its implications. Another significant background was the fact that the 1970s saw the first wave of political migrants to Sweden—Chilean dissidents.

When the dominant literary quality shifted from "vernacular" to "universal" in the next twenty-year-period, the author as a cultural representative was replaced by the idea of the author as a literary philosopher. During the 1980s and the 1990s, then, laureates represented humankind as a whole rather than a geo-culturally specific community or tradition. Read collectively, however, the sets of motivations from the two periods were not oppositional. The quality of literary universality was the second most referred to quality in the prize motivations between 1961 and 1980, and vernacular merits were mentioned in four motivations during the following twenty years. Moreover, these two qualities were occasionally referred to as different aspects of the same phenomena, as in the assessment of Naguib Mahfouz's having "formed an Arabian narrative that applies to all mankind." If prize-worthy authors were, during the period 1981–2000, predominantly seen as literary philosophers, the most valuable literature was the kind that provided general visions of the human condition. The desirable effect of these visions was a widened perspective—the purpose of literature was to remind the readers of the commonality of being human.

This was, then, the period in which the prize motivations most distinctly confirmed the notion of a world literary space. According to this poetics, the most valuable texts had a worldly character that made them speak to all of us. An important context for this view of literature was the philosophical turn in literary criticism during the period, with poststructuralist ideas prompting deconstructivist methods and influencing Marxist, feminist, and postcolonial literary theories. From a strictly Swedish perspective, the universalized poetics was connected to a renewed interest in French and German culture and philosophy in Sweden around 1980, after a period of predominantly domestic literary discussions and concerns. On a more general level, I do not think it is unreasonable to see the perestroika movement in the Soviet Union during the 1980s, the Reykjavik summit meeting between Ronald Reagan and Mikhail Gorbachev in 1986, and the demolition of the Berlin wall in 1989 as important political changes inspiring a call for a universal literature.

After 2000, the dominant authorial role amongst the Nobel laureates changed from literary philosopher to examiner. This role combined two slightly different identities with slightly different assignments: the author as researcher, which borders on the role of the academic, and the author as reporter, which is close to the investigating journalist. According to the first of these perspectives, the literary text is a kind of dissertation or study, whereas in the latter the literary text is a kind of report. The study and the report have a common purpose—that of finding and showing the truth. The literary examination is written in order to show complexities beyond simplifications, reveal deficiencies beneath the polished surface, and find the real state of affairs behind the fake front.

The Nobel poetics between 2001 and 2020, then, saw literature as a means to obtain and distribute substantial and real knowledge of the world. Why did the quality of examination suddenly appear as a highly esteemed literary value in the 2000s and the 2010s? Well, it is not far-fetched to connect this poetics to the increasing importance of the internet during these two decades, and its overflow of unverified digital information based on opinions, emotions, and personal search histories. In light of this global development, it seems like the Swedish Academy regarded literature as a counterforce to the negative effects of the new, digitized media landscape, an antidote to the forces threatening the notion of objective truth. The laureates were awarded, it seems, for being thorough, nuanced, and accurate in a time characterized by the shallow, the simplified, and the false.

Which literary qualities, then, have been most referred to during the whole history of the prize, 1901–2022? Well, if we ignore the historical shifts and look at the motivations generally, four values stand out as distinctly most invoked: *vernacular* (with 36 references), *noble* (34), *skillful* (30), and *grand* (29). According to the collected constellations of the Swedish Academy and its Nobel Committees, the most valuable literary quality is the ability to represent, preserve, renew, or ennoble a particular literary tradition, a specific cultural affiliation, or a distinct geographical position. From this point of view, the Nobel Prize comes forth as a champion of cultural and literary diversity. If you want to be awarded, it also helps if your œuvre subscribes to a specific set of moral standards, demonstrates technical skills according to the Academy's taste in style and narration, and has a certain level of aesthetic magnitude. The merits of being vernacular, noble, and skillful have each dominated during particular periods of the prize, but they also enjoy a recurring presence throughout the history of the prize. Grandiosity has never been the most invoked literary quality in any given period, but it has kept coming back throughout the twentieth century as a central characteristic of the most valuable literature.

What is then *not* Nobel Literature? Is there a particular literary poetics that has been absent from the history of the prize motivations? Well, one specific literary quality that has been quite rare in these short texts is the category of aesthetic beauty. The words "beauty" and "beautiful" have only appeared in four motivations from 1901 to 2022: in describing Tagore's "beautiful verse," Shaw's "singular poetic beauty," Heaney's "lyrical beauty," and Glück's "austere beauty." In addition, Prudhomme's "artistic perfection," Jiménez' "artistic purity," and Seifert's "sensuality" may also qualify as belonging to this category. Only 7 out of 119 motivations, then, have invoked the textual quality that corresponds with the role of the literary aesthete or charmer, and the desirable effect of aesthetic pleasure. Nobel Literature is far from the tradition of art-for-art's-sake.

Throughout the years, there has thus been a tendency in the Nobel Prize motivations to suppress the "sweetness," the "dulci," and the "prodesse" from the literary enterprise—to use three of the best-known slogans of literary purposes, Philip Sydney's "sweetness and light," and Horate's "utile dulci" and "prodesse et delectare." Instead, the motivations have generally stressed its opposites: the insightful, the useful, and the educational. Compared with the two most invoked literary qualities in the motivations—cultural representativity and nobility—the rarity of beauty also confirms the Academy's fidelity with the donor's last will and Alfred Nobel's stress on selecting laureates who have contributed with the greatest "benefit to humankind." Literary benefit has been, on the whole, interpreted in correspondence with scientific benefit as concerning some kind of pragmatic use, some kind of improvement. It is thus clear that the exact words used by Nobel in his will did not only have an impact on the first two decades of the prize, but have been instructive throughout its history. The two other very frequently invoked qualities in the motivations—skill and grandiosity—are less pragmatic and closer to the category of aesthetic beauty. But whereas beauty and pleasure concern effects on the reader, skill focuses on the ability of the author, and grandiosity is a matter of scale, volume, and quantity rather than the exquisite and subtle quality implied in the category of literary beauty.

The aesthetic value of beauty is close to another literary quality very rarely referred to in prize motivations and selection discussions—that of musicality. Many aspects of literary beauty are related to the time-honored overlap between literature and music: rhythm, euphony, and composition. Musical qualities of this kind have rarely been brought up as decisive in the prize motivations. The poetry of Bjørnson, Frédéric Mistral, Heyse, Heidenstam, Tagore, Gjellerup, Yeats, Karlfeldt, Gabriela Mistral, Eliot, Lagerkvist, Jiménez, Pasternak, Quasimodo, Perse, Seferis, Sachs, Martinson, Montale, Aleixandre, Elytis, Seifert, Brodsky, Paz, Walcott, Heaney, Szymborska, Müller, and Tranströmer were described without any references whatsoever to rhythmical, euphonic, or compositional elements. Not even poets like Frédéric Mistral and Erik Axel Karlfeldt, whose poetry and poetics are distinctly associated with musical genres and effects, were explicitly rewarded for their musical dimensions.

The motivations bring up other poetic qualities. Many of the early ones included references to inspiration. Frédéric Mistral's lyrical poetry was characterized by "true inspiration," Yeats' was "always inspired," and Gabriela Mistral's was "inspired by powerful emotions." Another recurring lyrical quality has been that of sensitivity. Tagore's poetry was "sensitive," Montale's was characterized by a "great artistic sensitivity," Elytis' by a "sensuous strength," and Paz's by a "sensuous intelligence." The aesthetic quality most often referred to in the prize motivations for lyrical poets, however, has been that of reflection and representation. Frédéric Mistral's poetry "faithfully reflects the natural scenery and native spirit of his people," Martinson's writings "catch the dewdrop and reflect the cosmos," Aleixandre's œuvre "illuminates man's condition in the cosmos," Elytis' "depicts [...] modern man's struggle for freedom and creativeness," Seifert's "provides a liberating image of the indomitable spirit and versatility of man," and Müller's "depicts the landscape of the dispossessed."

There have been only minor exceptions to this lack of musical qualities. The aesthetic category of force in the motivations of Carducci ("lyrical force"), Neruda ("elemental force"), and Oe ("poetic force") could be interpreted as referring to some kind of musical effects, and so could the category of voice and voicing when the works of Milosz (he "voices man's exposed condition") and Glück (celebrated for her "unmistakable poetic voice") were praised. But the only motivation of poetic quality that has directly brought up musical elements was the very first one. Sully Prudhomme's verse was rewarded "in special recognition of his poetic composition." Apart from this first text, a direct musical reference has only been included once in the history of Nobel Prize motivations: when Elfriede Jelinek's prose was awarded for its "musical flow of voices and counter-voices in novels and plays."

The 2016 prize to Bob Dylan could definitely be seen as a late compensation for the lack of advocating musical qualities in poetry—a double reminder pointing out that most traditions of written poetry have their roots in oral literary cultures, and stressing that much contemporary poetry is still composed in order to be orally performed. The Dylan prize motivation did not mention any distinct musical qualities in the laureate's verse, but it did position his work "within the great American song tradition," thereby underlining the oral and musical characteristics of his poetry. As Sara Danius—who was the Permanent Secretary in 2016—wrote two years later, "Bob Dylan writes poetry for the ear. Moreover, his poetry is part of something larger: the song, the record, the concert, the radio, YouTube and Spotify. We are supposed to listen to his texts, not read them, at least not initially" (Danius 2018: 14, my translation). This is also how the prize announcement was received in October 2016. The first reactions in the *New York Times* expressed a slight shock, but they were not unsympathetic to the selection. The decision was interpreted as an expansion of the "Nobel Pantheon" ("Expanding the Nobel Pantheon," 2016). By including Dylan in this very special assembly of canonical writers, the Swedish Academy had actively made a "Redefining" of the "Boundaries of Literature" (Sisario et al 2016).

A frequent critique in the reception of the Nobel Prize has been that the Academy has avoided to award morally challenging literature. In William F. Lamont's 1951 survey for *Books Abroad*, this opinion was expressed by several scholars. Renée Lang wrote that the Swedish Academy had been all too cautious in their first fifty years of selections (Lang 1951: 40), Oskar Seidlin criticized the Nobel Prize for being all too respectable and conservative (Seidlin 1951: 60), and Édouard Roditi wrote that "the Swedish Academy's tastes are stuffy, uninformed, very middle-class and oddly Germanic." (Roditi 1951: 215) On the same note, Ernst Waldinger saw a strong tendency in the Academy to award "respectable mediocres" (Waldinger 1951: 218). A recurring thought in this criticism has been that the Academy's decisions have been generally based on moral rather than aesthetic aspects. This is an effect, Herman Salinger argued, of the Swedish Academy having been too loyal to Alfred Nobel's idealist literary ideal (Salinger 1951: 216). Lars Gyllensten agreed with this view, at least regarding the early period in the prize's history (Gyllensten 2000: 260).

To be sure, Hugo von Hofmannsthal, Thomas Hardy, and Georg Brandes were all turned down on moral grounds (Rydén and Westerström 2018: 43, 267, 69). And five years before he was rewarded, Thomas Mann was dismissed because his famous short novel *Der Tod in Venedig* (*Death in Venice*) brought up a subject matter "too uncomfortable and dangerous to be literary suitable" (Rydén and Westerström 2018: 275). And the notion that the Nobel Prize is a fundamentally conservative institution was still around in the 1980s. In the *World Literature Today* survey, Bernth Lindfors did not believe that the Cameroonian writer Mongo Beti would ever receive the prize. Beti's work was, he argued, "too iconoclastic" to "satisfy the Swedish Academy's directive to reward writers who produce work of an ideal, or idealistic, tendency" (Lindfors 1988: 223).

Some critics have argued that the Swedish Academy's tendency to ignore morally challenging literature has been more or less unavoidable. "All academies tend to be conservative," Henri Peyre concluded in the 1951 survey, pointing out an immanent problem with all kinds of institutional consecration (Peyre 1951: 214). Herman Salinger agreed: "Academicians do not like nightmares," which is why the Nobel Prize committees have, in their prize selections, excluded "anything that smacks of materialism, skepticism, cynicism, agnosticism, sex, or the other base preoccupations of the all-too-human race" (Salinger 1951: 216). For other critics, scholars, and writers, this is a simplistic view of the prize. When Sinclair Lewis was awarded in 1930, for example, he accepted the prize because he thought that the Nobel was different from the Pulitzer. Whereas the American award was morally normative in rewarding "the highest standard of American manners and manhood," Sinclair argued, the Swedish prize was "an international prize with no strings tied" ("Nobel Prize Goes to Sinclair Lewis," 1930).

There have been significant exceptions to the morally conservative ideal amongst the prize selections. In 1951, the expert in French literature, H.R. Lenormand, hoped that the 1947 prize to André Gide marked the beginning of a new, less conservative, and less moralist direction for the Swedish Academy's prize decisions:

> Since the day when André Gide received the Nobel Prize it has become evident that what you call 'distinguished literary achievement' has prevailed over previous criteria which rewarded idealism and benefaction to mankind. The awarding of the Nobel Prize to the author of *L'immoraliste* should spare us, at least in the future, from seeing moralists, philosophers, and humanists destined for oblivion hailed as artistic geniuses.
>
> (Lenormand 1951: 117)

The decision to award Gide didn't, perhaps, lead to a revolutionary change in the Academy's attitude toward challenging texts, but the prize remained an important gesture for many years. In the 1967 survey, Lenormand's interpretation of the symbolic value of the 1947 award was repeated by his colleague Gene J. Barberet: André Gide, he wrote, "claimed that his function as a writer was to disturb, and he disturbed by challenging all dogmas, moral or aesthetic, searching constantly for his true self beneath the layers of convention and civilization" (Barberet 1967: 9). Twenty-one years later, William Pratt argued that the awards to the "nihilistic" Samuel Beckett and the "atavistic" William Golding proved that the "liberal humanitarian bias in the literary awards" had been laid to rest. These decisions showed, he concluded, that "idealism, at any rate of the patently uplifting variety [...] is no longer a requirement for the Nobel Prize in Literature." (Pratt 1988: 226–7)

The 1969 prize to Beckett was controversial within the Swedish Academy. Breaking the tradition, Nobel Committee Chair Anders Österling did not present the laureate at the festivities on December 10. In his place, Karl Ragnar Gierow held his first Nobel speech. Österling's decision to stand down from this honorable task should be interpreted, as Kjell Espmark has pointed out, as a gesture of distance. For the eighty-five-year-old Chair, Beckett's works were too far from the idealism stipulated by the donor (Espmark 1986: 93).

The latest example of a morally (rather than politically) challenging award led to far stronger reactions within the prize-giving institution itself. In October 2005, Academy member Knut Ahnlund publicly declared that he left the Swedish Academy in protest against the preceding year's prize to Elfriede Jelinek. "After Jelinek, the prize is devastated," he argued, and pointed to the Austrian author's literary "orgies" in "sadism and masochism," the "excess of horror" in her work, and her tendency toward "violent porn" (Ahnlund 2005, my translations). The 2004 prize was definitely not an award to morally conservative idealism.

Poetics and Politics

The vague borders between literary aesthetics and politics have been a complicated and heated issue ever since the start of the Nobel Prize. Alfred Nobel's instruction to the prize-givers not to take national backgrounds and belongings into consideration when deciding whom to award, distinctly commissioned the Swedish Academy to stand clear of international politics. Politics was reserved for the Peace Prize. And as the first Nobel Committee Chair, Carl David af Wirsén declared that the Academy should "never use these awards as political means and transactions" (Espmark 1986: 116).

But it is one thing to express such a guiding principle, quite another to apply it when evaluating specific literary texts, œuvres, and achievements. On several occasions, Wirsén was indeed political in his reports on prize candidates. Leo Tolstoy, for example, was not only dismissed because of his nonliterary political writings. The famous Russian writer's radical ideology also had a demeaning effect on his novels and short stories. The otherwise-great *War and Peace*, Wirsén wrote in the report for the 1905 prize decision, was tainted by a firm belief in "blind coincidence," *The Kreutzer Sonata* expressed a disturbing antipathy toward "sexual intercourse between spouses," and in "a vast number of texts" Tolstoy "dismisses not only the church, but also the state, well, even property rights" (Svensén 2001a: 85, my translations).

One of the other well-known authors who were not awarded in the early days of the Nobel Prize's history, Norwegian playwright Henrik Ibsen, was disqualified due to his "negativity" in relation to traditional institutions in works like *Samfundets støtter* (*Pillars of Society*), *Gengangere* (*Ghosts*), *En folkefiende* (*An Enemy of the People*), and

Et dukkehjem (*A Doll's House*) (Svensén 2001a: 32). And a couple of years before Giosuè Carducci was awarded, Wirsén had reservations about the Italian poet's paganism and republican sympathies (Svensén 2001a: 29–30). These examples confirm the nuanced view on poetics and politics that Academy member Bishop Gottfrid Billing expressed in a letter to Wirsén in 1902: "It is true that the prize must not be a matter of state politics. But it is just as undeniable and unavoidable that it has and will have a political dimension" (Österling 1949: 94, my translation). For Billing, poetics and politics were intertwined and impossible to separate from each other.

During the First World War, the Academy had distinct diplomatic reasons to separate aesthetics from politics. Wirsén's successor as Nobel Committee Chair, Harald Hjärne, saw it as the task of the Committee to confirm and reinforce the Swedish government's neutral position in the European conflict. The Swedish Academy, Hjärne wrote, was internationally regarded as representing Sweden, and it should act accordingly: "It is impossible for us to give any public motivations that could lead to unfavorable interpretations of how Sweden acts in this affair" (Svensén 2001a: 315). The poetics of literary autonomy—what Hjärne calls "literature's elevation above the current political turbulence" (Svensén 2001a: 314)—proved to be a pragmatic way out of this dilemma. Selecting laureates from the neutral nations Sweden (Heidenstam 1916), Denmark (Gjellerup and Pontoppidan 1917), Switzerland (Spitteler 1919), and Norway (Hamsun 1920) was a concrete result of this policy.

In 1986, Kjell Espmark also pointed out that the 1915 prize to Romain Rolland was an effect of this strive for literary and political neutrality: Rolland was a pacifist who lived in Swiss exile and whose work "includes both German and French elements without favoring any of them" (Espmark 1986: 44, my translation). In effect, of course, these attempts from the Swedish Academy to strictly separate politics from literary values fundamentally confirmed the opposite: that literary texts and the ways in which they are produced, distributed, and understood are always deeply affected by political conditions and implications.

Sometimes, political reservations have been raised in generally positive reports on specific candidates. In the report leading up to Rudyard Kipling winning the 1907 prize, for example, expert reader Erik Axel Karlfeldt brought up many strengths in the works of the English author, but he also pointed to a disturbing tendency to glorify the colonial British "policy of conquest" (Rydén and Westerström 2018: 44, my translation). More often, however, political opinions have stood in the way of an award. In 1928, a prize to Maxim Gorky was seriously discussed, but the proposal was eventually dismissed due to the risk that a prize to his autobiographical books would be interpreted as a political praise of the Soviet Union (see Rydén and Westerström 2018: 391).

But political dimensions have also worked in favor of candidates. The award to Frans Eemil Sillanpää has, for example, been interpreted as a distinctly political prize. In the 1980s, Finnish writer Ingmar Björkstén could not understand why the Swedish Academy honored the "aesthetically totally insignificant" Sillanpää if it wasn't a political gesture in face of the military threat to Finland from Soviet (Björkstén 1984, my translation). This notion had already been confirmed by Anders Österling, who admitted in 1949 that the Academy was probably affected, "consciously or unconsciously," by "the Finnish Republic's ongoing heroic struggle against the superior power on the other side of the Baltic Sea" (Österling 1949: 60, my translation).

Hermann Hesse's connection to the Nobel Prize institution was deeply affected by the Second World War. As Paulus Tiozzo has shown in a recent dissertation on the German Nobel Prizes between 1901 and 1971, Per Hallström was strongly against awarding Hesse in the 1930s. The Permanent Secretary had right-wing sympathies and thought that the author of *Siddhartha* and *Der Steppenwolf*, who was born in Germany but gained Swiss citizenship in 1923, was too critical of Adolf Hitler (Tiozzo 2023; Rosch 2023). In 1941, however, Hallström was replaced as Permanent Secretary by Anders Österling, who had very different political beliefs and supported Hesse. By honoring Hesse, Österling wrote to the Nobel Committee, the Academy would seize the opportunity to "reinstall the connection to the German language as a poetic medium and finely strung instrument" in the wake of Adolf Hitler's destruction of cultural life in Germany (Svensén 2001b: 365, my translation). When the Swiss novelist was awarded in 1946, the reporter in the *New York Times* saw this selection as a political gesture. In fact, he could only understand the decision on political grounds. Hermann Hesse's novels, poems, and essays, he argued, were not "widely known," but "[i]f, as Secretary Anders Oesterling of the Swedish Academy suggests, this honor recognizes an early revolt against German anti-humanism, we can understand it" ("Six Americans Win Nobel Prizes," 1946; "For Service to Mankind," 1946).

The John Steinbeck prize is a similar case, albeit with a very different kind of ideological tension. In the latter part of the 1940s, the American novelist was firmly dismissed as a genuine candidate due to his official support of the Soviet Union's invasion of Finland in 1939 (Rydén and Westerström 2018: 584). But when the feelings of indignation had cooled down, Steinbeck could be awarded in 1962.

In the latter half of the twentieth century, the Swedish Academy was frequently criticized for too political prize decisions. More than once, members have reminded their critics that the Academy is not subordinated to the Swedish government and does not have to cooperate with the Swedish Foreign Office (cf. Espmark 1986: 114; Rydén and Westerström 2018: 720; Espmark 2021: 37). In the Alexandr Solshenitsyn crisis, Swedish Prime Minister Olof Palme considered handing out the prize to the curfewed Russian novelist at the Swedish Embassy in Moscow, but decided not to because he didn't want his political administration to interfere with the independent Academy's affairs (Rydén and Westerström 2018: 628). During Dag Hammarskjöld's years in the Swedish Academy—from 1954 to his premature death in 1961—the borders between literary evaluations and international diplomacy looked more blurred than ever before. Already in Alfred Nobel's will, Per Rydén and Jenny Westerström writes, there is a notion of the Nobel Prize as some kind of world conscience—not only in connection with the Peace Prize, but also in the selections of "idealist" literary writers (Rydén and Westerström 2018: 510). When the sitting Secretary-General of the United Nations (Hammarskjöld had occupied this post since April 1953) took an active part in selecting the Nobel Prize for Literature, political negotiations and world literary consecration definitely looked like overlapping diplomatic endeavors.

In 1959, François Mauriac (laureate in 1952) wrote an article for *Le Figaro* in which he criticized the Swedish Academy for favoring a politically and ideologically engaged literature, a "littérature engagée," at the expense of authors with purely aesthetic ambitions. Morally concerned writers like Romain Rolland, Anatole France, André Gide, and Albert Camus had been favored, he argued, over artistically refined poets like Paul Valéry and Paul Claudel (Mauriac 1959). Several of the participants in the 1967 *Books Abroad* survey shared this opinion. Herbert Howarth noticed many "divagations from pure literature" among the selections (Howarth 1967: 6), Gene J. Barberet found it significant that Rolland, France, and Roger Martin du Gard were all involved in the Dreyfus affair (Barberet 1967: 9), Theodore Ziolkowski argued that many of the Nobel Committees had seemed to confuse Alfred Nobel's notion of idealism with conservatism (Ziolkowski 1967: 15), and Richard Vowles argued that "[p]olitics and the sociology of taste have been such powerful factors in the history of the Prize that any retrospective appraisal like this one must be a very impure kind of literary criticism" (Vowles 1967: 17).

In this context, one of the post-war Anglophone selections stands out as particularly political: Winston Churchill. In 1953, this laureate was not only a sitting political leader of one of the most powerful European nations and the most famous political hero of the recently finished Second World War. The prize motivation also expressly praised his oral, rhetoric skills, which he, of course, had almost exclusively been practicing in political speeches. To separate Churchill's mastery of public speech from his political beliefs and achievements was a difficult task indeed. After being elected in 1954, UN Secretary-General Hammarskjöld was the Academy member who worked most strongly against prizes with distinct political implications (Rydén and Westerström 2018: 517, 528, 554). As a reaction to the Churchill award, he sarcastically wondered if the Swedish Academy had become "one of the committees of the Foreign Office" (Espmark 2001: 182). It's also telling that former Permanent Secretary of the Academy, Per Hallström, who had sympathies for Germany during the war, was opposed to the prize—but in his case for political rather than aesthetic reasons (Rydén and Westerström 2018: 361–2).

The most distinctly political dismissal from the post-war period was the decision not to award Ezra Pound. The American author's significant contributions to the history of modern poetry were presented by several Academy members as worthy of a Nobel Prize, but Pound's fascist opinions, publicly and famously expressed during the Second World War, made him an impossible candidate most of them agreed in the end (Espmark 1986: 123; Gyllensten 2000: 269; Rydén and Westerström 2018: 530–6).

The strongest accusations of a political tendency in the prize decision have come from the left. In the 1951 *Books Abroad* survey, Oskar Seidlin detected an "anti-Russian bias" in the history of the literary Nobel awards (Seidlin 1951: 217), and Ernst Waldinger pointed out that the Swedish decisions had generally been "Rightist rather than Leftist" (Waldinger 1951: 218). The negative reactions to the Pasternak prize in 1958 did not only come from Moscow. In his diary, sitting Swedish Prime Minister Tage Erlander expressed his anger toward the decision, which he interpreted as a direct political gesture: "General exasperation with the Swedish Academy's demonstration against the Soviet Union in their choice of this year's Nobel laureate." The selection of Pasternak significantly disturbed the Swedish government's diplomatic relations to the Kremlin. It strongly disrupted the diplomatic balance and reciprocal respect between the nations, especially since Moscow saw the Swedish Academy as officially representing the Swedish state. A couple of days later, Erlander added: "The Swedish Academy as a politician right now stages a pitiful show" (Erlander 2008: 260, 264). The Permanent Secretary Anders Österling's attempt in national Swedish radio to defend the decision did little to convince the Prime Minister that the selection was purely based on aesthetic qualities. "It should be noted," Österling said, "that [Pasternak] does not narrate in order to accuse or protest. He does not criticize the revolution, only its followers and collaborators" (Espmark 1986: 125, my translation).

In light of the turbulence of 1958, commentators saw the prize to Mikhail Sholokhov seven years later as a compensation made to please the officials in Moscow. The intense, appreciative, and prolonged responses in the *New York Times* to the Boris Pasternak award strongly confirmed that the prize decision was received as a Cold War gesture. Seven years later, the Sholokhov prize was seen as an opposite statement, trying to make diplomatic amends between Stockholm and Moscow. The *New York Times* dedicated almost twenty articles to the 1965 award, and several of the headlines revealed the American paper's difficulty in accepting this prize decision: "Prize Acclaimed in Moscow," "Sholokhov Accepts Prize 'Gratefully,'" "Sholokhov 'Happy' for Soviet." One of the headlines paid a mournful tribute to an earlier award: "Pasternak Lies in a Lonely Grave." With the prize to Sholokhov, the American paper argued, the Swedish Academy had ruined what they achieved with the bold Pasternak prize.

Jean-Paul Sartre had refused to accept the Nobel Prize in 1964 for political reasons, pointing out what he thought was ideologically biased selections of Russian laureates (Rydén and Westerström 2018: 610). When it comes to Sholokhov, even Dag Hammarskjöld, who was generally opposed to any kind of political reasons to award or dismiss an author, had shown strong political reservations. In 1955, he wrote in a letter to fellow Academy member Sten Selander: "I would vote against Sholokhov with a conviction not only grounded in aesthetic arguments and a spontaneous resistance to social pressure, but also because a Soviet prize today appears to be, for exactly those widely expressed political reasons, a very bad idea" (Espmark 1986: 121, my translation). But in 1965, Hammarskjöld was no longer around.

All the accusations of a biased approach to the Soviet Union returned with the announcement of the Alexandr Solzhenitsyn prize in 1970. The laureate was not allowed to leave his country in order to receive the prize in Stockholm, but he sent a letter to be read at the banquet, with a very direct concluding sentence: "I hope that you, at this rich table, do not forget the political prisoners who are on hunger strikes for their strongly restricted and totally suppressed rights." When reading this letter at the ceremony, Permanent Secretary Karl Ragnar Gierow skipped this last sentence, and when he later on addressed the absent laureate in his Nobel speech, he made a diplomatic effort in pointing out that Solzhenitsyn was not only appreciated abroad but also praised in his homeland, quoting the Moscow newspaper *Pravda*. But Gierow's speech also included quite a strong critique of the Soviet system and its authorities: "We have honored a great humanist author," he said at the banquet, "whose moral stance has political implications in a society where human dignity is violated" (Rydén and Westerström 2018: 625–6). A couple of months later, Swedish journalist Stig Fredrikson smuggled Alexandr Solzhenitsyn's acceptance speech out of Moscow so it could be published in international media (Rydén and Westerström 2018: 629).

After having lost his Soviet citizenship, Solzhenitsyn was finally able to come to Stockholm in December 1974. From an international perspective, his attendance at the ceremonies totally overshadowed that year's two Swedish laureates, Harry Martinson and Eyvind Johnson, but domestically the fact that the Academy was honoring two of their own was a proper media scandal. What hasn't been very acknowledged, however, is the political directness included in Karl Ragnar Gierow's speech to the Swedish laureates. They were honored as "representatives of that huge number of proletarian writers or working-class authors" that had strongly affected Swedish twentieth-century literature. Martinson's and Johnson's literary success was a symbol of the development of a certain kind of modern society:

> The fact that these two, having started from such an unprivileged initial position, today earn their places on this stage, is the visible testimony of a societal change that is still ongoing, step by step, around the world. It came especially early to us; it is perhaps the greatest blessing of our country, perhaps also the most extraordinary achievement made during the last thousand years.
> (Rydén and Westerström 2018: 649, my translation)

It is not at all far-fetched to interpret these sentences as an intense celebration of the Social-Democratic welfare state. The shared award to Martinson and Johnson was a political stand, domestically as well as internationally.

From the last two decades of the twentieth century up until today, stronger attempts have been made by Academy members to separate aesthetic values from politics. These attempts have shown a successive change toward a new, more formalist poetics in the Academy that has tied well into the return to a universalist rather than a pluralist view on literary values (see Chapter 3, pp. 67–78). Central accounts of this poetics can be found in Nobel Committee Chair Kjell Espmark's books on the history of the Nobel Prize for Literature, *Det litterära Nobelpriset* (The literary Nobel Prize, 1986), *Litteraturpriset* (The Literary Prize, 2001), and *The Nobel Prize in Literature—a New Century* (2021). In his work in the Committee, Espmark wanted to avoid what he calls a "politicizing" of the prize (Espmark 2021: 22). He stressed the importance of "political integrity" and expressly defined "literary" qualities as separate from politics, ideology, morality, and world views, and he certified that "literary qualities" were "paramount" in the prize decisions he was involved in (Espmark 2021: 37, 40). He defended the 1999 award to Günther Grass as "a *literary* prize," not a moral one, and he pointed out that the Committee, in making the decision to honor the German novelist, ignored his politically controversial—and recently published—novel *Ein weites Feld* from 1995 (Espmark 2021: 12, italics in the original). Political intention, Espmark concluded, "has been expressly banned by the Academy" (Espmark 2021: 37).

One quite acknowledged and certainly damaging result of the Swedish Academy's reluctance to politicize literature and literary values was the Salman Rushdie scandal in February and March 1989. In the wake of the Iranian Ayatollah Khomeini's fatwa on the British author's head, as retribution for his novel *The Satanic Verses*, the Swedish Academy decided not to condemn the fatwa and thereby not to officially and univocally support Rushdie. The reasons for this were clear: "The Swedish Academy," read the official statement, "has as a principle never to express any opinion in political issues, partly in order to avoid suspicions that the distribution of the Nobel Prize would have political reasons" (Gyllensten 2000: 255). Three Academy members—Kerstin Ekman, Werner Aspenström, and Lars Gyllensten—expressed a public protest against this collective decision and announced that they refused to continue their work in the Academy. If they could have, they would have resigned from their positions. But since it was impossible to officially resign from the Academy, Aspenström's and Gyllensten's chairs remained empty until their deaths in 1997 and 2006. Kerstin Ekman's chair remained empty until the rules were changed in 2018.

In 2001, Sture Allén admitted that the praxis to draw a distinct dividing line between literature and politics has often been at odds with dominant definitions of literature and literary purposes outside the Swedish Academy (Allén and Espmark 2001: 9). The Academy's recurring attempts to avoid politics have often been either criticized as an impossible endeavor or ignored as an empty rhetoric used to avoid scrutiny. What are, then, the reasons for this formalist, apolitical approach to literature? Well, for one thing I think this successive change should be seen as a reaction—deliberate or not—to a recurring international critique against earlier prizes, motivations, and statements. In the last decades of the twentieth century, the Swedish Academy made a long-standing effort to avoid coming across as representing the Swedish government, and as giving out an aesthetically framed Peace Prize. Secondly, I think stressing the honored works' textual values has been a way for later days' Academy and Committee constellations to distance themselves from Alfred Nobel's fuzzy category of "idealism." Thirdly, I also think that the dominant poetics in recent decades has had a generational dimension. Most of the writers and literary scholars who were elected into the Academy between 1970 and 2000 matured as intellectuals in an age when a formalist approach to literature—especially in the form of New Criticism—was successively established at Swedish universities as the norm of studying, discussing, and evaluating literature. Leaving aside biographical, moral, and political issues when analyzing literary texts has been part of many Swedish literary scholars' cultural DNA up until quite recently.

But this expressed apolitical poetics has not prevented many of the more recent prizes from having strong political dimensions. Far from it. The award to Vicente Aleixandre, for example, was announced two years after the death of the Spanish dictator Franco. The *Times* reported on a more or less explicit political gesture from the Swedish Academy to the liberated Spain: "In poems spanning half a century he had emerged as a rallying figure for 'what remained of spiritual life' under the rule of the late General Franco, the panel of 18 scholars and author of the Swedish Academy said" ("Spanish poet winner of Nobel prize," 1977). That is also how American poet Robert Bly understood the prize decision: "For the Nobel Prize to come to Aleixandre now is fitting, not only because of the energy and intensity of his own poetry, but because it comes at this moment in Spanish history. Spain is waking up after years of sleep, and Aleixandre's poetry and stubborn presence have a strong part in that awakening" (Bly 1977).

The issue of political timing has been acknowledged in many cases: Czeslaw Milosz's and the Polish Solidarnosc movement in 1980; Nadine Gordimer's 1991 award and the South African Apartheid system, which had formally been abolished earlier that year; the praise of Olga Tokarczuk's stories of migration in the midst of a rising nationalist sentiment in Poland in the last years of the 2010s. One of Kjell Espmark's arguments when insisting on the prize being unpolitical has been that laureates generally have been candidates for quite some time before being awarded. Just like Pasternak and Sholokhov, Espmark wrote in both 1986 and 2021, Milosz had been a candidate for many years when the Nobel Committee finally recommended him in 1980 (Espmark 1986: 124–6; Espmark 2021: 38). It wasn't, in other words, the Solidarnosc movement in Poland that made the Academy start to acknowledge Milosz's writings. This argument does not account for the actual decisions in the falls of 1958, 1965, 1980, 1991, and 2019 to honor these politically charged œuvres at exactly these very moments in time. The process toward the final prize decisions is not inevitable: the Academy has never been forced to honor a certain writer just because he or she has been nominated several times. Their hands have never been tied to any author standing first in line. On the contrary, all the actual decisions have been based on a conviction that now is the time to acknowledge this very author.

In the *Times*, the 1982 prize to Gabriel García Márquez was also interpreted politically. The Columbian novelist was "a militant socialist, and a friend of Fidel Castro," and before breaking his literary silence with *Crónica de una Muerte Anunciada* in 1981 he had sworn never to write any more literary stories until "General Pinochet was removed from power in Chile" ("Nobel prize for García Márquez," 1982). A spicy diplomatic aftermath of this prize decision was reported by the *Times* in December:

> Sweden has protested to Cuba over the gift of 1,500 bottles of tax-free rum for distribution as a party here for Señor Gabriel García Márquez, the Columbian author and winner of this year's Nobel Prize for Literature.
> Mr Jan af Sillén, head of protocol at the foreign ministry, said the gift by President Fidel Castro, of Cuba, was a violation of Swedish alcohol restrictions. Señor Pino Machapo, the Cuban Ambassador, has been told of Sweden's displeasure.
> ("Castro's rum handout vexes Swedes," 1982)

The selection of Márquez, doubtlessly interpreted by Castro as at least partly a political gesture from the Swedish Academy, led to a diplomatic clash between two very different national policies on alcohol distribution.

Just like the selection of Milosz, the award to Czech poet Jaroslav Seifert in 1984 was received in London as a "Cold War prize." The literary editor of the *Times*, Philip Howard, pointed out that the laureate "broke with the Communist Party after a visit to the Soviet Union in 1929," and that he "has been silenced by the authorities since the brief 'Prague Spring' of 1968" (Howard 1984). And three years later, yet another dissident from behind the Iron Curtain was honored: Russian émigré in the United States, Joseph Brodsky. The title piece of Brodsky's most recent book when receiving the prize, the essay collection *Less Than One*, was a sharp castigation of the Soviet society that the author was deported from in 1972. A couple of pages into the book, we find this memory from his childhood in 1940s and 1950s Leningrad:

> All that had very little to do with Lenin, whom, I suppose, I began to despise even when I was in the first grade—not so much because of his political philosophy or practice, about which at the age of seven I knew very little, but because of his omnipresent images which plagued almost every textbook, every class wall, postage stamps, money, and what not, depicting the man at various ages and stages of his life. There was baby Lenin, looking like a cherub in his blond curls. Then Lenin in his twenties and thirties, bald and uptight, with that meaningless expression on his face which could be mistaken for anything, preferably a sense of purpose. This face in some ay haunts every Russian and suggests some sort of standard for human appearance because it is utterly lacking in character.
>
> (Brodsky 1986: 5)

Honoring an author with such a strong antipathy toward the founder of the whole system was of course to add fuel to the ongoing process of perestroika and glasnost in Mikhail Gorbachev's changing Soviet Union at the end of the 1980s.

It is also difficult to understand the prizes to Naguib Mahfouz (1988), Nadine Gordimer (1991), Derek Walcott (1992), Toni Morrison (1993), and then, a bit later, V.S. Naipaul (2001) and J.M. Coetzee (2003), as unrelated to the, at that time, growing field of postcolonial theory in literary studies, as manifested in Edward Said's *Orientalism* from 1978, *The Empire Writes Back* by Bill Ashcroft, Gareth Griffith, and Helen Tiffin from 1989, and Homi K. Bhabha's *The Location of Culture* from 1994. Similarly, it is impossible to avoid seeing the return of female laureates—after a twenty-five-year all-male period since the Nelly Sachs prize in 1966—in 1991 (Gordimer), 1993 (Morrison), and 1996 (Wislawa Szymborska) as a response to the fields of feminist criticism and gender studies that were firmly established in many Western universities in the 1970s and 1980s. In both these cases, the rise of ideologically charged discourses of literary studies and literary criticism strongly affected the Nobel selections. As William Pratt wrote in 1988, a couple of years before this change toward a more equal distribution: "To predict that a woman will win the next prize is to admit that the Nobel is often political and social as well as literary, and any honest survey would have to concede that fact [...]" (Pratt 1988: 227).

The 2022 award to Annie Ernaux confirmed the notion that the struggle for equal gender rights must continue. By the time her prize was announced, the French writer was very active in protesting against the new anti-abortion regulations in the United States and in expressively supporting the loud public demonstrations in Tehran against the systematic oppression of women in Iran. In France, Ernaux was seen as a very political writer. Her works clearly followed the tradition of "littérature engagée" (Leyris 2022; Nykvist 2022). The Swedish Academy's selection was not only a gesture that generally supported this kind of politically engaged literature, but also an acknowledgment of Annie Ernaux's particular political opinions. By many, the prize decision was received as an indirect stand against US anti-abortion laws and the Iranian regime's violent reactions to the protests in the streets of central Tehran.

In his recent study *Critical Responses to the Nobel Prize in Literature: An Analysis of 22 Awards*, Karl Ågerup emphatically shows how politically controversial many of the most recent Nobel Prize selections have been. Several of the Swedish Academy's choices between 2000 and 2021 have roused anger and resentment, and this critique has come from various ideological and geopolitical positions. The most common objection, Ågerup writes, has had to do with treason and misrepresentation of a nation or a culture. Gao Xingjian, V.S. Naipaul, Imre Kertész, Orhan Pamuk, Herta Müller, Mario Vargas Llosa, and Mo Yan were been accused of painting a false picture of their home countries—and the Swedish Academy was criticized for ignoring or reinforcing these false representations (Ågerup 2022).

The opposite political implications of the two first Chinese prizes to Gao Xingjian in 2000 and Mo Yan in 2012, mirrored the Pasternak and Sholokhov awards in the 1950s and 1960s, but on a less intense level. The selection of Gao was criticized by Chinese officials, who accused the Academy for "hidden political motives" (Espmark 2021: 40), and the selection of Mo Yan was considered by some, among them recent laureate Herta Müller, as a prize to a loyal member of the undemocratic ruling party. Accordingly, the 2012 selection was met with pride and joy by Chinese authorities (cf. Jacobs and Lyall 2012). The 2015 award to Svetlana Alexievich was also seen as a distinct political gesture against the totalitarian political system of the laureate's homeland Belarus, a gesture made more or less manifest in the prize motivation that praised Alexievich's "monument to suffering and courage in our time."

The latest intense political controversy stirred by a laureate selection occurred in 2019 when Peter Handke was awarded. The Austrian writer was accused of genocide apologetics in the aftermath of the 1990s Balkans War and was strongly criticized for speaking at Serbian leader Slobodan Milosevic's funeral in 2006. In his 2021 account of the process leading up to the selection, Kjell Espmark certified that the decision was made because "the well-known political implications could be left behind," but he also pointed out that former Permanent Secretary Peter Englund objected to the decision and "marked his position by being absent from all of the ceremonies connected with the prize" (Espmark 2021: 40, 36). The Handke prize thus created a distinct rift within the Academy between those who wanted to separate poetics from politics, and Englund who couldn't disregard the political dimensions in or around the Austrian writer's literary œuvre. The 2019 choice of laureate was met with strong international protests. After the announcement, PEN America posted a very straightforward statement: "We are dumbfounded by the selection of a writer who has used his public voice to undercut historical truth and offer public succor to perpetrators of genocide" (PEN America 2019).

Apart from the issue of timing, these examples relate to at least five different dimensions of the apolitical poetics expressed in recent decades by representatives of the Swedish Academy. One of them is the matter of intention and effect. Following a long tradition in the Swedish Academy, Espmark wanted to make a strict distinction between these two, and he argued that the Nobel Committees and the Academy did not have any kind of political intentions when selecting laureates, but that these selections of course often have had political effects (Espmark 2021: 37). A counter-argument would be that it is often quite easy to predict that a certain prize decision will have political consequences. Carrying on making the decision with these expected effects in mind could very well be seen as an intentional political act.

Another argument for a strict separation between poetics and politics, often unspoken but perfectly detectable between the lines in Espmark's accounts, has been the concept of absolute aesthetic quality, the "unique artistic force" in the writings of the most-worthy authors (Espmark 1986: 134). Some prize decisions have come across as more or less predestined because the laureate has simply been seen as the best author of all available candidates. For people who do not see literary value as an absolute and universal quality but a relative phenomenon, there are no acute problems in regarding objectionable political elements as a disadvantage. If there are many authors around the world who are, for different reasons, equally worthy of a Nobel Prize in Literature, why settle on a politically problematic one? Unless, of course, part of your agenda is to provoke politically and ideologically charged questions and discussions.

The awards from the 1980s onward related to postcolonialism and feminist literary theory prompt another important issue of literary evaluations: that of an ideologically changing world. Today's authors, readers, critics, and Academy members live in another world than Alfred Nobel and the early Nobel Committee members did. Struggles for equal gender equality, large-scale liberation from colonial oppression, civil rights movements—all of these fundamental ideological changes started to happen in the twentieth century, and they were and still are political projects. It is impossible to imagine a literary prize that could exist and survive without adjusting to these distinct changes of what most people in large parts of the world believe is right. In close relation to this issue, the Gao Xingjian and Svetlana Alexievich prizes exemplified—just like the prizes to Hesse, Pasternak, Solzhenitsyn, Aleixandre, Milosz, Seifert, and Brodsky had done previously—that there seems to be a basic ideology underscoring all the Swedish Academy's Nobel work: an anti-totalitarian belief in democracy and freedom of speech.

Even Kjell Espmark sometimes used a political rhetoric when he described these particular prizes: "A prize motivation," he wrote in 1986 apropos Czeslaw Milosz, "that focuses on the author's interpretation of the human predicament and on top of that marks his integrity, is simply not understandable from a 'Marxist-Leninist' aesthetics—other than as camouflage for political intentions" (Espmark 1986: 132). In this critique of a dogmatically political view on literature, Espmark himself ended up being political, conveying the values of individualism and personal integrity as opposed to obedience to a collective system. Even when the prize decisions have signaled something else (e.g., the selections of Sholokhov and Mo Yan), these announcements have led to international political debates that in themselves are expressions of democracy.

The discrepancy between the outspoken unpolitical policy of the Swedish Academy and the strong political implications of many of their selections reflects the most central discussion in twenty-first-century world literary theory. In a comparison from 2011, Robert J.C. Young finds distinct contrasts between postcolonial criticism and contemporary world literary studies. Whereas postcolonialism is a fundamentally ideological project and thereby focuses on the political dimensions of literary texts, world literature stresses the aesthetic dimensions of literature and follows the tradition of the Comparative Literature discipline in its methodological focus on close textual analysis (Young 2011). Many studies in postcolonial criticism and world literary studies—empirical as well as theoretical—have been conducted since Young wrote this piece, and the two fields have developed an expanded common, overlapping area. The unpolitical approach of Kjell Espmark was very close to the more aesthetically oriented versions of contemporary world literary studies, whereas many actual selections from recent decades have rather exemplified the possible combination of, on the hand, formal and textual complexity, and, on the other, political and ideological gestures and effects. Several decisions and motivations seem to confirm that politics can be acknowledged as an integral part of an aesthetically grounded poetics.

Nobel Lectures

The poetological impact of the annual prize decisions has not been restricted to prize motivations and what kind of literature has been selected. In connection with each ceremony in Stockholm, the honored work has also been presented by a member of the Swedish Academy, and the laureate has been given the opportunity to deliver a public lecture. The Academy's introductions to the laureates' literary achievements have often been expansions of the prize motivations and have generally had a very limited reach. The laureates' Nobel lectures, on the other hand, have been widely distributed. Written versions of these talks have often been printed afterward—in newspapers (like André Gide's in *Le Figaro* in 1947 [Gide 1947]), separate books (like Albert Camus' *Discours de Suède* from 1958 [Camus 1958]), or in anthologies such as Horst Frenz's *Nobel Lectures: Literature, 1901–1967* from 1969 (Frenz 1969). Nowadays, many of these speeches are also available online on the Nobel Foundation's home page (www.nobelprize.org). In these addresses—totally free in form as well as content—each selected writer has had a unique opportunity to speak his or her mind. And a large part of the world has been listening.

Most of these Nobel lectures were given in Stockholm a couple of days before the actual prize-giving ceremony, but there have been variations. Lectures by absent laureates have been either prerecorded, like Elfriede Jelinek's, or written and printed, like André Gide's. A special case was 2013 laureate Alice Munro, who instead of a speech gave an interview with Swedish journalist Stefan Åsberg in her home in Victoria, Canada. Some of these talks have been given via the laureates' representatives in Stockholm, like Doris

Lessing's lecture in 2007, which was read by her publisher Nicholas Pearson. Several of the speeches have also been given afterwards, like Bob Dylan's Nobel lecture, which was made public in June 2017, six months after the prize ceremony.

The importance of these Nobel lectures was stressed in Robert E. Spiller's discussion of the William Faulkner prize in the 1967 *Books Abroad* survey:

> It came as a surprise to hear the author of *Sanctuary* proclaiming that man would not only survive, he would prevail, apparently in spite of both Popeyes and bombs. The frantic re-reading of his major work which was provoked by this acceptance speech revealed an entirely new Faulkner, but one that a few critics like Malcolm Cowley had long before recognized.
>
> (Spiller 1967: 35)

The Nobel lectures have not only expanded the time in the spotlight for already highly praised writers, they have also been a chance for them to change the way their works are read—and an opportunity to express any kind of thought on any matter important to them.

What views on literature, then, have the laureates distributed in these lectures? Well, needless to say, it has varied deeply. In his contribution to the genre, 1908 laureate Rudolf Eucken was loyal to the donor's poetics and stressed the necessity of idealism in a modern world. "The superiority of man to mere nature," the German philosopher argued, "is also proved by modern technology, for it demands and proves imaginative anticipation and planning, the tracing of new possibilities, exact calculations, and bold ventures. How could a mere natural being be capable of such achievements?" (Eucken 2022). Other laureates have rather used this platform to disconnect literature from the task of being idealistically beneficial to humankind. In contrast to Alfred Nobel's literary ideal, Claude Simon took the opportunity in his lecture to defend the "artificial" in literature, and thereby also distancing himself from the preceding French laureate, Jean-Paul Sartre, and his ideal of the engaged writer. "As you see," Simon summed up, "I've nothing, in Sartre's sense, to say." According to Simon's poetics, an author doesn't have to want to say anything special to the world; he or she doesn't have to have any kind of message (Simon 2022).

Along the same lines as Simon, Eugenio Montale argued in 1975 that his poetry was not only "useless," but also an incurable "sickness." In thus positioning himself very far from the healthy and robust idealism of Nobel's will, the Italian poet stressed a literary dimension that has—as we have seen—very rarely been addressed in prize motivations from the Swedish Academy: musical elements. Poetry is, Montale argued, "born of the necessity of adding a vocal sound (speech) to the hammering of the first tribal music," and modern, written poetry "makes itself felt" with effects "common with music" (Montale 2022). Forty years later, Patrick Modiano expanded the central role of music to the realm of prose fiction in his Nobel address: "I believe the world of music has an equivalent to this intimate and complementary relationship between the novelist and the reader. I have always thought that writing was close to music, only much less pure [...]" (Modiano 2022).

Far from Alfred Nobel's idealism, we also find Isaac Bashevis Singer's stressing the entertaining qualities of literature. "The storyteller and poet of our time, as in any other time," he said when receiving the prize in 1978, "must be an entertainer of the spirit in the full sense of the word, not just a preacher of social and political ideals." There is no paradise, Singer continued, "for bored readers and no excuse for tedious literature" (Singer 2022). A related poetics was expressed by Mo Yan when he said that his ideal as a writer was that of "the marketplace storyteller" of his childhood in Northeast Gaomi Township, China (Mo Yan 2022).

Several laureates have expressed a more philosophical view of literature. Pablo Neruda talked in 1971 of poetry as part of life's essentials. He placed the writing and reading of verse alongside "bread, truth, wine, dreams," and compared the poet with the local baker "who prepares our daily bread" (Neruda 2022). Eight years later, Odysseus Elytis phrased another philosophical poetics when he argued that poetry's task is to offer "luminosity and transparency," to make us see and genuinely acknowledge the world we live in (Elytis 2022), and in 1991, Nadine Gordimer expanded this task to prose fiction and art as a whole: "Perhaps there is," she said in a lecture entitled "Writing and Being," "no other way of reaching some understanding of being than through art?" (Gordimer 2022) A couple of years later, Seamus Heaney had a more psychological approach to literature's existential dimension: "I credit poetry [...] for making possible a fluid and restorative relationship between the mind's centre and its circumference" (Heaney 2022).

Several of these Nobel addresses have been political. Gabriel García Márquez used his lecture to call the sitting Chilean leader Augusto Pinochet a "diabolic dictator" (García Márquez 2022), Mario Vargas Llosa criticized all kinds of "fanaticism" resulting in gruesome terrorist attacks (Vargas Llosa 2022), and both Imre Kertész and Herta Müller took the opportunity to denounce the totalitarian systems of Nazi-Germany, Hungary, and Romania, in which they grew up (Kertész 2022; Müller 2022). Wole Soyinka used his Nobel lecture to describe and support African resistance to colonial rule through a detailed presentation of the Mau-Mau liberation struggle in Kenya. His address thus made an important contribution to the political and theoretical project of postcolonialism that was rapidly expanding in the mid-1980s (Soyinka 2022).

Most directly political was, however, 2005 laureate Harold Pinter's speech. In his lecture "Art, Truth & Politics," Pinter started with a discussion of political theatre and then moved on to discuss the US, UK, Australian, and Polish invasion of Iraq in 2003, the US intervention in Nicaragua in 1985, as well as the political position of the United States more generally since the Second World War:

> The United States supported and in many cases engendered every right wing military dictatorship in the world after the end of the Second World War. I refer to Indonesia, Greece, Uruguay, Brazil, Paraguay, Haiti, Turkey, The Philippines, Guatemala, El Salvador, and, of course, Chile. The horror the United States inflicted upon Chile in 1973 can never be purged and can never be forgiven.
> (Pinter 2022)

Far from stating such direct and particular political opinions, Bertrand Russell discussed, in 1950, politics as such in his theoretical lecture entitled "What Desires Are Politically Important?" (Russell 2022) Albert Camus' talk seven years later was also devoted to political philosophy, but the French writer had a clear focus on literature's direct political potential. The author has a responsibility, he argued, to serve truth and freedom. As a tool to execute this task, literature is two things, both fundamentally important for any society: "the refusal to lie about what you know and the resistance to oppression" (Camus 1958, my translation).

The idea of literature as a resistance has appeared in many Nobel addresses. Some of these have been, like Camus', political. In his 1997 lecture, Italian playwright Dario Fo expressed a strong kinship with the Medieval jester, and discussed a Sicilian law from 1221 that allowed anyone to "commit violence against jesters without incurring." To select Dario Fo as a Nobel laureate, Fo himself argued, was to do the opposite: with this prize, the Swedish Academy officially honored the outcast whose art constantly resists the political power. "Yours is an act," he said at the ceremony in Stockholm, "of courage that borders on provocation." (Fo 2022)

In her talk in 1993, Toni Morrison pointed to a language-oriented resistance. Literature, she stressed, is an attempt to stop the "systematic looting of language," an antidote to the violent manifestations of political and cultural power: "Oppressive language does more than represent violence; it is violence" (Morrison 2022). Aleksandr Solzhenitsyn had followed the same line of thought twenty-three years earlier, when he argued that literature "conveys irrefutable condensed experience" that resists untruthful official constructions of history and expresses the actual "living memory of a nation" (Solzhenitsyn 2022).

This task of resistance was also underlined in 2021 when Abdulrazak Gurnah told the story of how he became a writer. Early on he knew that "there was something [he] needed to say, that there was a task to be done, regrets and grievances to be drawn out and considered." He noted how a complex chain of events—the "detentions, executions, expulsions, and endless small and large indignities and oppressions" in and around the 1964 revolution in Zanzibar—was officially summed up into a "new, simpler history" by the victors. The young Gurnah saw the necessity "to refuse such a history." He realized that his task as an author was to put the complexity of history into truthful words that could let "both the ugliness and the virtue come through" (Gurnah 2022).

Other kinds of literary resistance have been broader and not specifically political. Salvatore Quasimodo argued in 1959 that poetry is "a threat to the existing cultural order" that is "lethal to the inert." Poetic language is thus the opposite of political discourse: "The politician judges cultural freedom with suspicion, and by means of conformist criticism tries to render the very concept of poetry immobile" (Quasimodo 2022). Olga Tokarczuk expanded this view in her talk held in 2019 to also include the "commercialization of culture." "He who has and weaves the story is in charge," the Polish novelist said in her address. Therefore, Tokarczuk continued, it is of uttermost importance that we constantly find "new ways of telling the story of the world." Since they limit "authorial freedom" and "completely exclude from the creative process any of the eccentricity without which art would be lost," commercial restraints on literature diminish the author's ability to contribute with genuinely new stories (Tokarczuk 2022). Twenty-three years earlier, Tokarczuk's compatriot Wislawa Szymborska had described poetry as a resistance to all kinds of firm beliefs and convictions, political or philosophical. "Poets," she said in her 1996 lecture, "if they're genuine, must also keep repeating 'I don't know'" (Szymborska 2022).

Tokarczuk's praise of "eccentricity" and Quasimodo's notion of the "nonconformist" poet working "in his own obscure sphere," are examples of an individualist stance frequently expressed in the Nobel lectures. In 2000, Gao Xingjian pointed out that real literature expresses "the voice of an individual." This voice is "inevitably weak," but it is "authentic" and therefore extremely valuable:

> Once literature is contrived as the hymn of the nation, the flag of the race, the mouthpiece of a political party or the voice of a class or a group, it can be employed as a mighty and all-engulfing tool of propaganda. However, such literature loses what is inherent in literature, ceases to be literature, and becomes a substitute for power and politics.
>
> (Gao Xingjian 2022)

In his written lecture published in *Le Figaro* in 1947, André Gide expressed the same idea. Literature is the expression of "the independent spirit," a spirit that "in our age" is "being fought from every angle and every side" (Gide 1947, my translation). This notion of independence was also stressed by Orhan Pamuk in 2006. In order to retain this independence, the Turkish laureate argued, the author must always guard his or her solitude. An author is "a person who shuts himself up in a room, sits down at a table, and alone, turns inward; amid its shadows, he builds a new world with words" (Pamuk 2022). Spanish novelist Camilo José Cela described the writing life in exactly the same way in 1989: "from my solitude I think, work, and live" (Cela 2022). "If art teaches anything," Joseph Brodsky had concluded two years earlier, "it is the privateness of the human condition" (Brodsky 2022).

In her address, Belarusian writer and journalist Svetlana Alexievich did not share this vision of the necessarily lonely author. But she did agree that the writer should be a vessel for the voice and experience of the individual human being: "Flaubert called himself a human pen; I would say that I am a human ear." In this lecture, Alexievich made clear that her work did not express her own perspective of the world, but the perspectives of all the people she had listened to. She thus described her occupation as the opposite of the solitary poet's isolated work, but she still saw it as her task to acknowledge and distribute personal testimonies (Alexievich 2022).

Frequently, these Nobel lectures have discussed issues that have been absolutely central in twenty-first-century world literature theories. This fact indicates that these theories really are important if we are to understand how literature is discussed and valued internationally, but it also shows that the most central issues in recent literary theory are far from new. World literary questions have been there all along, even though they haven't been discussed in a very theoretical way. When T.S. Eliot, in his Nobel lecture, showed his gratitude to the Swedish Academy and described the award as a recognition that "an author's reputation has passed the boundaries of his own country and his own language" (Frenz 1969: 501), his words were very similar to David Damrosch's definition in *What Is World Literature?* of world literature as "literary works that circulate beyond their culture of origin" and are "actively present" there (Damrosch 2003: 4). And when Aleksandr Solzhenitsyn gratefully describes the prestigious context into which he had been selected, he put early words to the notion of what Pascale Casanova calls "the world literary space" in *La République mondiale des Lettres*: "I am cheered by a vital awareness of WORLD LITERATURE as of a single huge heart, beating out the cares and troubles of our world, albeit presented and perceived differently in each of its corners" (Solzhenitsyn 2022).

In his lecture from 2006, Orhan Pamuk expressed his acknowledgment of how imbalanced and hierarchical this world literary space is:

> As for my place in the world—in life, as in literature, my basic feeling was that I was "not in the centre." In the centre of the world, there was a life richer and more exciting than our own, and with all of Istanbul, all of Turkey, I was outside it. Today I think that I share this feeling with most people in the world. In the same way, there was a world literature, and its centre, too, was very far away from me. Actually what I had in mind was Western, not world, literature, and we Turks were outside it. My father's library was evidence of this. At one end, there were Istanbul's books—our literature, our local world, in all its beloved detail—and at the other end were the books from this other, Western, world, to which our own bore no resemblance, to which our lack of resemblance gave us both pain and hope.
> (Pamuk 2022)

Just like Casanova, Johan Heilbron, and many other scholars have done since the turn of the millennium, Pamuk pointed to the fact that what is perceived as cosmopolitan or universal literature is often restricted to Western literary texts and traditions. The "world literary space" does not include an even representation of all literature written in the world, far from it. This is also what William Golding admitted in his 1983 address to the Swedish Academy. "I do not speak in a small tribal language," he said. English writers "need not fear comparison with those of any other language." But this privileged position is not only beneficial, Golding continued. The dominant literary language "may suffer from too wide a use rather than too narrow a one." English literature runs the risk of being too general, losing its particularity. (Golding 2022)

In recent years, a branch of world literary theory has focused on the vernacular rather than the cosmopolitan, and seen the relation between these two positions as a reciprocal dynamic central for the production, distribution, and understanding of many different kinds of literature (Kullberg and Watson 2022; Helgesson et al 2022). Several Nobel lecture titles reveal the laureates' fundamental ambitions to inform the world of their particular literary backgrounds and how they relate to the rest of the world. William Butler Yeats' lecture "The Irish Dramatic Movement," Sinclair Lewis' "The American Fear of Literature," Giorgos Seferis' "Some Notes on Modern Greek

Tradition," Yasunari Kawabata's "Japan, the Beautiful and Myself," and Gabriel García Márquez' "The Solitude of Latin America" belong to this category.

Along these lines, José Saramago positioned his own work in the Portuguese literary tradition (Saramago 2022), and Miguel Ángel Asturias placed his novels in a long Latin American tradition dating back to the cultures of Maya, Aztec, and Inca (Asturias 2022). Vicente Aleixandre presented himself as being "born under the protection of benign stars" growing up to be a poet in the rich Spanish literary tradition of Antonio Machado, Miguel de Unamuno, Juan Ramón Jiménez, Gustavo Adolfo Bécquer, and José Ortega y Gasset (Aleixandre 2022). Similarly, Jaroslav Seifert talked about "the great love of poetry" among the Czech people and in the Czech culture (Seifert 2022), and Bob Dylan placed his songs in the rich tradition of American twentieth-century popular music ("country western, rock'n'roll, and rhythm and blues"), particularly stressing his personal influences from Buddy Holly and Lead Belly (Dylan 2022). In his contribution to this genre, Octavio Paz pointed to what he saw as the special characteristics of literatures from the Americas: "they are literatures written in transplanted tongues," based on European languages that "took root in new lands" (Paz 2022). Naguib Mahfouz positioned himself and his work in two different traditions, the Pharaonic civilization and the Islamic civilization, thereby informing the Swedish Academy and the rest of the world about the particularities of the Egyptian cultural space (Mahfouz 2022).

Several laureates have stressed their double or multiple cultural backgrounds and belongings in their Nobel addresses. In 1976, Saul Bellow talked about his kinship with Joseph Conrad—"an uprooted Pole sailing exotic seas, speaking French and writing English with extraordinary power and beauty"—himself being a Canadian-born son of Lithuanian-Jewish parents "who grew up in one of Chicago's immigrant neighborhoods" (Bellow 2022). Derek Walcott, who was born in Saint Lucia to a family with English, Dutch, and African descent, described Port of Spain in Trinidad and Tobago, where he moved as a young man, as "mongrelized, polyglot, a ferment without a history, like heaven." Yes, he added with a poetological turn, this multicultural place was indeed "a writer's heaven" (Walcott 2022).

Nine years later, V.S. Naipaul returned to Trinidad in his Nobel lecture, when he told the Academy his life story. Naipaul was born to Indian parents in a small Trinidadian village, where he grew up before leaving for university studies in the UK. The 2001 laureate stressed how Asia, the Caribbean, and Europe all added cultural dimensions to his literary work (Naipaul 2022). Kazuo Ishiguro also stressed his "mixed cultural heritage" in 2017, in the story of how his literary imagination took off when he started to write about Japan, a country he had not visited since he and his parents moved to the UK when he was five (Ishiguro 2022). Complex cultural belongings were also central for Svetlana Alexievich. "I have three homes": she said in her lecture, "my Belarusian land, the homeland of my father, where I have lived my whole life; Ukraine, the homeland of my mother, where I was born; and Russia's great culture, without which I cannot imagine myself" (Alexievich 2022).

Migration and multicultural belongings have been very important issues in contemporary world literary theory, often with a backdrop in postcolonial theory.

Conceptual contributions such as Evelyn Nien-Ming Ch'ien's "weird English" and Rebecca L. Walkowitz's "comparison literature" (Ch'ien 2005; Walkowitz 2009) have been instructive in scholarly attempts to analyze a literary phenomenon that has been central for several decades in the history of the Nobel Prize. In her account of the migrant experience, Pearl Buck touched upon another important approach in recent world literary theory. Despite being "American by birth and by ancestry," she said in her Nobel address in 1938, "it is the Chinese and not the American novel which has shaped [her] own efforts in writing" (Buck 2022). The way Buck thus positioned her own work within the dynamic relation between early-twentieth-century Chinese and US cultures, would be a grateful starting point for a "distant reading" of the intercultural movement of genres, as proposed and performed by Franco Moretti in many studies (Moretti 2013), as well as for Shu-mei Shih's method of "relational comparison" (Shih 2015).

Another branch of twenty-first-century world literary studies has been very concrete and material, focusing on print cultures and book history. Here, Isabel Hofmeyr's exploration from 2004 of different African editions of John Bunyan's seventeenth-century story *The Pilgrim's Progress* has been very influential (Hofmeyr 2004), and so has B. Venkat Mani's work on what he calls "bibliomigrancy"—"the accessibility or inaccessibility to imaginary texts from elsewhere" (Mani 2011 and 2017). Studying the actual existence of literary works from different parts of the world in libraries, bookstores, homes, schools, journals, and digital services has become a very central contribution to any discussion of world literature.

Several Nobel lectures have stressed the importance of having access to literature from elsewhere. In her address, Doris Lessing gave a glimpse of Zimbabwe in the 1950s, where the young author was asked to help out: "Everybody I met, everyone, begged for books." Lessing made the point of her story very clear: "Writing, writers, do not come out of houses without books" (Lessing 2022). This point has been thoroughly confirmed by several personal stories in the Nobel lectures. Jean-Marie Gustave Le Clézio described the treasure of books in his father's library. As a child, the future laureate especially appreciated the works of Miguel de Cervantes, Jonathan Swift, Victor Hugo, and Honoré de Balzac, but also *The Ingoldsby Legends* by nineteenth-century British writer Richard Harris Barham and the anonymously written sixteenth-century Spanish novella *La vida de Lazarillo de Tormes y de sus fortunas y adversidades*. Le Clézio also stressed the importance of travel books for his imagination and world curiosity as a young boy (Le Clézio 2022).

In her 2020 lecture, Louise Glück told the story of how she as a young girl had considered William Blake's "The Little Black Boy" to be the best poem ever written. She was not sure, however, how she came across the works of the British Romantic poet. "I think there were a few poetry anthologies in my parents' home," she guessed, "among the more common books on politics and history and the many novels" (Glück 2022). Besides the American tradition of popular music, Bob Dylan traced his literary interest back to his "grammar school reading," of *Don Quixote, Ivanhoe, Robinson Crusoe, Gulliver's Travels*, and *The Tale of Two Cities*, but especially Herman Melville's *Moby Dick* and the English translations of Erich Maria Remarque's *Im Westen Nichts Neues* and Homer's *The Odyssey* (Dylan 2022).

A couple of Nobel lectures have stressed the power and importance of translated children's literature. Czeslaw Milosz pointed out in 1980 that Selma Lagerlöf's *The Wonderful Adventures of Nils* was one of his favorites as a child in Poland (Milosz 2022), and Kenzaburo Oe mentioned both Lagerlöf's Swedish classic and Mark Twain's *The Adventures of Huckleberry Finn* as formative stories for his development as a person and author (Oe 2022). And in Stefan Åsberg's interview with Alice Munro, the Canadian laureate had a very distinct memory of what ignited her literary interest. Her fascination with reading started when somebody read Danish author H.C. Andersen's nineteenth-century tale "The Little Mermaid" for her when she was a little girl (Munro 2022). From all these personal accounts by newly or soon-to-be honored laureates, it is quite clear that winners of the Nobel Prize in Literature do not come out of homes, schools, and cultures without books.

Concluding Remarks

Handing out the Nobel Prize in Literature is a performative act that not only affects the selected laureates and their publishers. If the award is, as Pascale Casanova insists, a "unique laboratory" for "the definition of what is universal in literature," the act of selection has a normative quality. This prescription of what literature is and should be is not primarily based upon what the members of the Swedish Academy actually say about or think of literature, but what their prize decisions signal. The Nobel Prizes collectively form a literary ideal, an international prototype of quality literature. It's a prototype that is slightly changing all the time, but that circles around a specific set of literary values. I would like to call this cluster of literary norms Nobel Literature. This poetics is by no means the only set of internationally distributed literary norms, but it is a quite powerful one.

Nobel Literature follows a logic of standardization with distinctly imperialist effects. Firmly based on European definitions of literary functions and values, this set of norms cast a biased prescription of high-quality storytelling, versification, and dramatization to all corners of the world, thereby reinforcing the cultural dominance of Western Europe and Northern America. In line with Emily Apter's critique of many proponents of twenty-first-century world literary studies, the Nobel Prize in Literature indeed runs the risk of zooming over "the speed bumps of untranslatability" with a "reflexive endorsement of cultural equivalence and substitutability" (Apter 2013: 2–3). To treat Nobel Literature as something even remotely close to a universal model for quality literature is to ignore the fact that its administration is firmly situated in a particular north-European institution with a very specific history.

But the normative logic of the Nobel Prize does not only have potential destructive consequences. If the prize is seen, in line with Casanova's metaphor, as a *laboratory* of universal values—that is, as a cultural space in which transcultural and translingual literary values are continuously tested and explored—the Swedish award may work quite productively in prompting questions and urging discussions on commonalities and differences in the varied world of literature. Just like the world literary ideas of David

Damrosch, Franco Moretti, and Pascale Casanova provoked Apter—as it prompted several other heated reactions, not least from postcolonial scholars—into the lengthy and substantial response *Against World Literature*, and made possible a complex and expanded clarification of the different theoretical and ideological positions at stake in reading and studying literature across borders, Nobel Prize selections may function as productive provocations. And the award has indeed been surrounded by conflict, from the very first prize decision onward. If nothing else, the annual reminders of Nobel Literature make us talk about literary values.

A central element in the Nobel poetics is the fact that its literary values are not directly formulated. What constitutes Nobel Literature is almost always indirectly expressed. Another important aspect of this aesthetics is that it is not always intentional. It cannot be totally controlled by the Swedish Academy, nor its Nobel Committee. The Nobel poetics is distributed in many ways, but three kinds of value distribution stand out as especially important: the selections themselves, prize motivations, and Nobel lectures given by the newly selected laureates.

Regarding the selections as such and their poetological signals, Nobel aesthetics has historically been quite biased. Until the 1930s, Nobel Literature was predominantly European. The only exception to this rule—the award to Rabindranath Tagore in 1913—did little more than confirm the rule. Between the early 1930s and the latter half of the 1960s, Nobel Literature was, with very few exceptions, a European and US set of literary norms. From 1966 onward, however, the Nobel poetics has slowly and successively become more culturally, geographically, and linguistically inclusive. The gender bias has been even more significant. Up until the 1990s, Nobel Literature was a very male affair. The six exceptions in 1909, 1926, 1928, 1938, 1945, and 1966 didn't manage to produce a positive trend of evening out the distribution, but since the Nadine Gordimer award in 1991, more than a third of the prizes have gone to women writers.

When it comes to politics, critics have frequently interpreted the selections as opposed to the Swedish Academy's recurring statement that the Nobel Prize in Literature is not political. Quite a few prize decisions have been praised or (which has been more usual) criticized—from several different ideological positions—as being indirect political statements made by the Swedish institution.

Generically speaking, Nobel Literature predominantly consists of prose fiction, with occasional excursions to lyric poetry, and, to a much lesser extent, to theatre and nonfiction. Overall, the laureates' authorial positions have been that of aesthetic vocation and singularity. There have been exceptions, but Nobel Literature is generally seen as deeply ambitious, distinctly serious, aesthetically innovative, and original.

The continually constructed and reconstructed poetics distributed by the prize motivations has shifted significantly—and sometimes quite dramatically—since the first prize in 1901, but if we sum up all the 119 motivations, we can conclude that even though these short evaluations acclaim several universally construed literary qualities, the most frequently praised literary value has been the ability to represent a particular literary or cultural tradition. The aesthetics expressed by Nobel lectures has also been very varied. Many laureates have gone against the fundamental poetics of Alfred Nobel and the first Nobel Committee in advocating a non-idealist, political, rebellious, or individualist view of literature and its purpose. On one account, however, most of these Nobel lectures have included a poetics shared with the donor and all the Nobel Committees—the value of internationally distributed literary imagination, the absolute necessity of world literature. This is a frequently expressed idea in the laureate addresses, and it confirms the fundamental aesthetics of the whole literary Nobel Prize project.

If we sum up all the selections, prize motivations, and lectures, we can conclude that the Nobel poetics says—in line with Aleksandr Solzhenitsyn's metaphor from 1970—that transnationally valuable literature has a common beating heart, but this heart is located in many different individual bodies. Nobel Literature means many things, but predominantly it is a prescription for a collective, literary balance between the small and the vast, the cosmopolitan and the vernacular, the particular and the universal, the individual and the generally human. It is a poetics that resonates very well with the 1974 motivation to award the Swedish poet and novelist Harry Martinson "for writings that catch the dewdrop and reflect the cosmos."

6

Looking Ahead:
The Survival of the Prize

What kind of world-literary discourse has, then, been formed and confirmed by the Nobel Prize institution? What is world literature according to the Nobel Committees' suggestions, the Swedish Academy's decisions, and the international reactions to the selections? Well, this discourse hasn't been stable over the years. It has rather been constantly changing—sometimes slowly and successively, sometimes more drastically. There have, however, been distinct patterns in the Nobel Prize version of world literature.

In the early period of the prize, world literature was predominantly seen—in the decision process as well as in the reactions—as a consecration of national literatures. World literature was a gilded, transnational space into which national literary cultures could gain access. France, Germany, and Spain were invited early. Great Britain had to wait a couple of years, whereas the US literary tradition was left out for decades, and the Soviet Union even longer. In this early period, the particular laureates were representatives of their backgrounds and belongings. Later in the history of the prize, the logic of representation was widened from national identities to larger geocultural spheres or more abstract and complex cultural belongings—like Latin America, the Australian continent, or different kinds of exile positions.

All from the start of the Nobel Prize, this concept of representation was challenged by the idea of world literature as a list of very important and illustrious individuals. The laureates have been seen as outstanding in different ways. Some of them were praised for their high moral standards, others for their intellectual depth or genial literary innovations. Representation and individual qualities have existed side by side throughout the history of the prize, but on a general level there has been a historical shift of focus from the former to the latter. But even after this change, the values of representation have tended to dominate in relation to laureates whose backgrounds are remote from the cultural position of the Nobel. The representational dimension has been more evident, for example, in relation to Mo Yan than to Patrick Modiano.

Another fundamental opposition in the Nobel discourse of world literature has been that between laureate characteristics and autonomous values of texts. Closely linked to this dichotomy has been the opposition between ideological and technical qualities of literary works. Many laureates have been honored for their nobility and decency as public figures, and opposite personal qualities have sometimes disqualified candidates, for example Ezra Pound. But the advocates for literature's autonomy from political situatedness and personal circumstances have also been numerous, not least within the Swedish Academy and its Nobel Committee. Within the Nobel institution, there has been a successive historical shift in focus from morals to autonomy, but if we include the international reactions to the prizes, ideology has always slightly overshadowed technical brilliance. An author must, it seems, show more than just artistic writing skills in order to be accepted as an altogether worthy Nobel laureate.

But how robust is the Nobel Prize's position in the formation of world literature? Will it remain a relevant factor in twenty-first-century international canon consecration? How has the boom of world literary theory in the last two decades affected the position of the Swedish award? Has the Nobel gained from this intensified attention to intercultural literary traffic, or have new theoretical perspectives made the prize institution outdated, rooted as it is in a nineteenth-century European concept of cosmopolitanism? One way of starting to answer these questions is to take a step back and consider how the prize institution has survived this far.

Crises Endured

Through the years, the Nobel Prize has endured several serious crises. The first one was the reactions to the very first prize decision. When it was announced in December 1901 that the first literary Nobel was awarded to Sully Prudhomme, forty-two Swedish writers, artists, and intellectuals signed an open letter to Leo Tolstoy, in which they took a firm stand against the Swedish Academy and expressed their opinion that the Russian novelist "first of all authors should have been considered" for the new international award (Rydén 2010: 581, my translation). A decade later another strong domestic sentiment reached the boiling point. Plenty of Swedish readers, critics, and public figures couldn't understand why playwright, novelist, and poet August Strindberg hadn't been awarded, and when it was announced in December 1910 that the Academy had yet again left out the opinionated author, the Swedish Social Democratic Party's youth association took the initiative to constitute an alternative literary award, an anti-elitist "people's Nobel Prize" (Rydén 2010: 634–5, my translation).

These domestic crises didn't, however, spread beyond the Swedish borders. The outbreak of the First World War in 1914 led to a much more fundamental crisis. Laureates and other dignitary people couldn't travel to Stockholm, the recognition of the prize was overshadowed by headlines from the front, and any prize decision would be critically scrutinized as taking a stand for either of the two fighting sides. Another problem was that the war had, according to the Nobel Committee, a degrading effect on the aesthetic value of many potentially worthy œuvres. In "our days," the Committee wrote in 1914, authors have a tendency to "express generally human ambitions and qualities" in "distinctly national forms and themes" that appear as "offensive from other national perspectives" (Svensén 2001a: 310, my translation). The war politicized and nationalized literature, removed it from that overarching level of human literary achievements that Alfred Nobel wanted to award, and this resulted in a lack of worthy laureates. Despite these different problems, the awards for 1915, 1916, and 1917 were given, whereas the prizes for 1914 and 1918 were canceled by the Swedish Academy.

In the early period of the prize's history, there were recurring complaints from the Nobel Committee that they lacked nominated authors worthy of the prestigious honor and the large sum of prize money. The Committee members struggled with the task of finding a new laureate every year. Almost always, they managed to deal with this challenge and ended up suggesting a name to the Swedish Academy. In 1935, however, they simply could not find any worthy candidate amongst the thirty-eight nominated authors. The ones that had been discussed before hadn't strengthened their positions. Eugene O'Neill's plays were still met with skepticism by the majority of the Committee, James G. Frazer was dismissed for representing and outdated strand of Religious History, Paul Valéry's poetry was too esoteric to be awarded the widely relevant Nobel Prize, and Frans Eemil Sillanpää's new novel wasn't yet available in translation (Svensén 2001b: 225–8). And none of the fourteen new nominations were seen as living up to the Nobel standard. Spanish author Miguel de Unamuno came close, with a poetry that had "a simple and great style" as well as "concrete beauty and firmness," but his narrative prose was too abstract and his dramatic works too randomly experimental (Svensén 2001b: 232, my translation). The Committee eventually decided to suggest that no prize would be given for 1935. One of the members, Hjalmar Hammarskjöld, filed a reservation from this decision, in which he expressed his opinion that the Committee's demands on literary works were "too strict, so strict that if they are kept they will surely make the distribution of the Nobel Prize a rare event in the future" (Svensén 2001b: 237, my translation). The Swedish Academy listened to the Committee majority and postponed the award one year. Next year, the 1935 prize was canceled, and the 1936 prize was given to O'Neill (Svensén 2001b: 259).

The Second World War brought the same kind of challenges to the Swedish Academy as the First World War had done, but on an even more fundamental level. Even though the Nobel Committee kept having their meetings in which they annually evaluated the nominated authors, the awards for four consecutive years, 1940–43, were canceled. This Second World War also had a prolonged negative effect on the Swedish Academy, since some of the members had openly supported Nazi-Germany before and during the war. One of them, Sven Hedin, refused to change his position even after Adolf Hitler's defeat. Several members tried to make Hedin formally excluded from the Academy, but they didn't succeed (Rydén and Westerström 2018: 485–6). Before he died in November 1952, Sven Hedin strongly objected to the plans to award Winston Churchill the Nobel Prize in Literature, but that last struggle turned out to be another losing battle for the old explorer.

Another political conflict started with the 1958 prize to Boris Pasternak and continued with the awards to Mikhail Sholokhov and Aleksandr Solzhenitsyn in 1965 and 1970—well, it was prolonged until Solzhenitsyn finally was able to come to Stockholm and receive his prize in 1974. In relation to these awards, the Swedish Academy was accused, domestically as well as internationally, for using the selections of laureates to take political sides—by the Soviet Union and its followers in the cases of Pasternak and Solzhenitsyn, and by Western liberals in the case of Sholokhov. But these controversies also stirred a renewed interest in the Nobel Prize, and the upset voices revealed that the Swedish literary award was an important institution, not only in a world literary context but also in a broader context of international politics.

From an international perspective, Solzhenitsyn's presence at the 1974 prize ceremony overshadowed another crisis that domestically was far more serious than the awards to the Russian authors. When the two Swedish authors and Academy members Eyvind Johnson and Harry Martinson jointly received the 1974 Nobel Prize, several Swedish literary critics and journalists strongly criticized the fact that the Swedish Academy had awarded two of their own. The prize decision resulted in an infected debate in Swedish newspapers and national television that strongly affected the two laureates. Lars Gyllensten even argued that it led to Harry Martinson's suicide in 1978 (Gyllensten 2000: 272-4). This discussion deeply wounded the domestic reputation of the Swedish Academy. The intense criticism was a strong blow of weakened respect that the institution arguably still has not completely recovered from.

One of the members of the Swedish Academy, Lars Forssell, publicly criticized the 1974 prize decision, which revealed an internal conflict that didn't help when the reputation of the institution needed to be restored (Gyllensten 2000: 222). Similar events have happened a couple of times since then. Academy member Artur Lundkvist distanced himself from the award to William Golding in 1983 (Gyllensten 2000: 218), and Peter Englund, former Nobel Committee Chair, declared in 2019 that he didn't support the decision to award Austrian author Peter Handke (Espmark 2021: 36). These controversies have, of course, had a negative effect of the position of the Nobel Prize, but they have also, perhaps, made the Academy appear as less aloof. Internationally, these internal conflicts have not had any substantial effect. But one of the controversial prizes has definitely had a negative international impact: the selection of Peter Handke in 2019. The gesture to award Handke despite his public support for former Serbian president Slobodan Milosevic was received by many international authors, intellectuals, and critics as either an intentionally offensive provocation or the result of a naïve, unworldly idea of aesthetic autonomy.

In 1989, the Swedish Academy experienced a huge crisis in relation to the Iranian Ayatolla Khomeini's fatwa on Salman Rushdie for his novel *The Satanic Verses*. The question whether the Academy should—in support of free speech and literary freedom—openly condemn Khomeini's fatwa, or decline to make a public statement on the matter in order to mark that they, as an institution, never make political statements, created a deep rift between the members. When it was finally decided that the Academy's official approach was to not condemn the fatwa, three members left their positions for good in a loud protest. Since the statutes of the Academy said that a member could not resign, Werner Aspenström's seat remained empty until his death in 1997, and Lars Gyllensten's wasn't filled until his death in 2006. Kerstin Ekman's seat remained empty until the rules for resignation were changed in 2018. This controversy did not have a direct relation to the task of selecting Nobel Prize laureates, but in a wider perspective the very visible internal controversy and the Swedish Academy's official stand in such an important and medial affair, affected the prize's international reputation in a negative way.

The deepest crisis so far for the Nobel Prize in Literature, however, occurred in the late 2010s. As part of the #MeToo campaign, eighteen women stepped forward in the Swedish newspaper *Dagens Nyheter* in November 2017 accusing an anonymous man for sexual assaults. When it was revealed that the man in question was Jean-Claude Arnault, husband of Academy member Katarina Frostenson, the scandal exploded. In a long series of scrutiny, the Academy was accused of having suspected Arnault's unacceptable behavior for a long time without intervening. The scandal also involved several cases of corruption where, it was argued, Arnault and Frostenson had systematically used money from the Academy to fund their own institution of cultural performance, Forum in central Stockholm. Frostenson and Arnault were also accused of having leaked names of future Nobel laureates to the public. In December 2018, Arnault was found guilty of rape and sentenced to prison (Henley 2018; see also Gustavsson 2019 and Wästberg 2020: 388–97 for more substantial accounts of the affair).

The scandal led to catastrophic consequences for the learned Swedish assembly. A couple of years after the event, Per Wästberg, who was Nobel Committee Chair at the time, wrote that he witnessed "the Academy's disintegration" from November 2017 and a year forward 2018 was a "fatal year" for the reputation of the institution, and for the Nobel Prize (Wästberg 2020: 392–3, my translation). During the investigation, the Academy was split in two, especially in relation to the question of Frostenson's future in the Academy. This conflict made several members leave their work in the Academy, among them writer and literary scholar Sara Danius, who until then had been the first female Permanent Secretary. Many people saw what had happened to Danius as a symbol of fundamental patriarchal structures: a man stood accused of rape and sexual assault on a large number of women, and a woman was forced to leave her powerful position. The heated atmosphere reached far beyond Academy meetings, and far beyond the culture news pages. On April 13, 2018, the day after Danius' decision to leave, a large crowd of people gathered outside the Academy's premises at Stortorget in central Stockholm to support her and to voice their protest against the way the rest of the Academy had handled the scandal.

The Arnault affair eventually resulted in a change in the statutes of the Swedish Academy that allowed members to formally resign from the learned assembly. Several members made use of this adjustment. One of them was Frostenson; another one was Kerstin Ekman, who hadn't been present since 1989. The scandal made it impossible to finish the process of finding a laureate in 2018. Instead, a completely different organization called the "New Academy"—rapidly formed in the wake of the feminist reactions in support of Danius—handed out an alternative prize to Guadeloupean novelist Maryse Condé (cf. Edfeldt et al 2022: 113–18). This event mirrored—in quite a complex way—the "people's Nobel Prize" to August Strindberg in 1912. There was by no means a seamless match between the feminist protests of the late 2010s and Strindberg's reputation, but both manifestations of alternative prizes supported a democratization of literary taste and a flattening out of cultural power. As a sign of the scope and depth of the Arnault scandal, it is telling that the "New Academy Prize in Literature," as it was called, was the first anti-elitist manifestation of this kind in 106 years of laureate selections.

To rescue the reputation and position of the Nobel Prize in Literature, the Nobel Foundation decided to intervene. The structure of the Nobel Committee was changed to include three members from outside the Swedish Academy (Espmark 2021: 33–6). The 2018 Nobel Prize in Literature was postponed, something that hadn't happened since the 1949 award was belatedly given to William Faulkner in 1950. When it was revealed in October 2019 that Olga Tokarczuk was to be awarded the 2018 prize, it was also announced that the 2019 prize would go to Peter Handke. It is not far-fetched to argue that the fact that this latter decision resulted in quite another kind of political controversy helped the Nobel Committee and the Swedish Academy to move on from the catastrophe of the #MeToo scandal. Before she stepped down and left the Academy, Sara Danius suggested that they should introduce an age limit of seventy years for active Academy members. The suggestion as such wasn't implemented, but it did contribute to a fundamental discussion that eventually resulted in new regulations limiting a particular member's individual influence in the Nobel Committee (Wästberg 2020: 216).

The reputation of the Nobel Prize has survived all these crises. Indeed, despite the catastrophic dimension of the latest scandal and its very serious allegations against the Swedish Academy and the Nobel Committee, the international acknowledgment and recognition of the prize have not seemed to fade. A quick look around in the bookstores of Paris in the summer of 2022 supported this notion, albeit with an anecdotal rather than a systematic confirmation. The label "Prix Nobel de littérature" was used as a selling point on many book covers in the publishers' attempts to attract buyers with this signal of literary quality. And it was printed on a range of different kinds of books. Information of the award appeared, unsurprisingly, on books by more or less newly appointed laureates, for example the publisher Denoël's edition of Abdulrazak Gurnah's *Adieu Zanzibar* (*Desertion* 2005) and Noir sur blanc's edition of Olga Tokarczuk's *Maison de jour, maison de nuit* (*House of Day, House of Night*; *Dom dzienny, dom nocny* 1998). The Nobel label was also used to sell new editions of older, but still-contemporary laureates, for example Folio's paperback editions of Mario Vargas Llosa's *La tante Julia et le scribouillard* (*Aunt Julia and the Scriptwriter*; *La tía Julia y el escribidor* 1977) and Orhan Pamuk's *Istanbul* (*Istanbul: Memories and the City*; *Istanbul: Hatiralar ve Sehir* 2003). The Nobel quality sign was also printed on the covers of classics, like Folio's two-volume edition of Roger Martin du Gard's *Les Thibault*, originally published between 1922 and 1940. Also, the prize was used to sell formerly unpublished stories by Isaac Bashevis Singer, on Biblio's paperback edition of *Le charlatan* (*The Charlatan*) and Stock's edition of *Retour rue Krockmalna* (*The Visitors*).

A fifth kind of book on which the Nobel award was used to attract readers and buyers this summer was scholarly nonfiction with contributions from laureates. The publisher CNRS's ambitious, new study *Lettres européennes* (European literature), edited by Annick Benoit-Dusausoy, Guy Fontaine, Jan Jedrzejewski, and Timour Muhidine, had this information printed into the cover image reproduction of Pablo Picasso's lithograph *Don Quixote*:

Préface de
Olga Tokarczuk
Prix Nobel de littérature

After 121 years, the Nobel Prize in Literature is certainly still viewed, in one of the geo-cultural centers of world literature, as a distinct token of literary quality and intellectual depth. The question is if this label will survive in future landscapes of world literature.

The Balancing Act

Maintaining the prestige and importance of the Nobel Prize in a complex and ever-changing international cultural landscape is a perpetual act of balance. The continually constructed list of authors needs to be poised between expected and surprising laureates, and between safe and bold decisions. And in the twenty-first century, the balance between male and female authors—as well as between European, North American, South American, Asian, and African laureates—has been increasingly important for the prize institution's credibility. But the Swedish Academy needs to manage this navigating act *without* giving the impression that balance is their first priority when selecting laureates. Such an impression would be catastrophic for the award's grand aspirations.

But in selecting, presenting, and discussing Nobel laureates in the twenty-first century, the Swedish Academy also needs to negotiate between two more fundamental oppositional literary and cultural values: tradition and contemporary relevance. The Nobel must come across as a time-honored institution that follows stable, well-proven procedures—a constant and recognizable feature in a capricious and erratic modern world. At the same time, the prize has to adjust to new ideological, medial, and aesthetic circumstances to avoid being seen as irrelevant or even harmful to the common, transnational literary discourse. Prize selections and motivations need to negotiate between the timeless and the timely, which is, of course, a very difficult balancing act with several different implications.

The Nobel Prize in Literature has a distinct conservational function. The list of former laureates guarantees some kind of cultural relevance and presence. Sully Prudhomme's name is still occasionally mentioned in our literary discussions, if only as a reminder of another time with another set of aesthetic values. The tastes of the late nineteenth century and early twentieth century are preserved by the early selections. And this important function instructs the whole annual process of finding laureates. The Nobel Committee is supposed to lift up the most valuable contemporary or semi-contemporary literary works from the chaotically vast maelstrom of modern publishing, distribution, and reception, and preserve these works for the future. But the Nobel Prize cannot only be conservational. It also needs to be the direct opposite—constructive and formative at the front of literary history. The Committee and the Academy have on several occasions made distinct attempts to redirect the transnational literary discourse or, at least, support such a redirection. Some of these attempts have been successful and appreciated, others have not. In the 1930s, for example, many laureate selections supported a more accessible and widely attractive literature than earlier prize decisions, a redirection that has been frequently criticized in retrospect. The support in the 1940s of Modernist innovators of poetry and prose fiction, and the consecration of French existentialist philosophy in the 1950s and 1960s have been more appreciated by later generations of critics and scholars.

The selections of Shmuel Agnon, Miguel Ángel Asturias, Yasunari Kawabata, Pablo Neruda, and Patrick White between 1966 and 1973 helped to form a new geo-cultural scope of world literature, or at least slightly shift the focus of that scope. One result of such a change of focus, postcolonialism, was firmly supported twenty years later when the Academy decided to give the prize to Derek Walcott. The *New York Times* was thrilled with the selection: "Readers of the poet Derek Walcott have predicted for years that the Nobel Prize would one day be his. The prize has arrived. It is richly deserved. It also honors a writer who was a 'multiculturalist' long before the term was invented" ("Derek Walcott's Embrace," 1992). Even if Walcott's supporters had to wait for years, the actual decision was very important when it finally came. The selection of the Saint Lucian poet lifted up the discourse of multiculturalism to another level of discussion and evaluation. And the consecration of a postcolonial perspective on literature was thoroughly confirmed by the fact that the Walcott prize had been preceded by the award to Nadine Gordimer and succeeded by the selection of Toni Morrison. In 1991, 1992, and 1993, then, three central literary contributions to the intense discussion of colonialism, imperialism, and systematic racism were said to belong to the absolutely most valuable works of world literature. This gesture was not only a consecration of three particular literary œuvres, but also a consecration of a whole perspective on history.

The Nobel Prize work involves the tasks of constructing a literary canon, upholding such a canon, as well as revitalizing the structure of this canon. The latter task necessarily includes an indirect criticism of the existing canon. The best-known example of such an indirect criticism is the Bob Dylan prize in 2016. In explaining the rationale behind this decision to the British newspaper *The Guardian*, Permanent Secretary Sara Danius said that Dylan's work was "not just high literature, but also low literature" (Ellis-Petersen and Flood 2016). With these words, Danius declared that the highest kind of consecration had been intentionally given to a kind of literature that at least partly was not considered high, but rather had been written, distributed, and received as a popular and subcultural phenomenon. This explanation was quite close to the Nobel Committee's attempts in the 1930s to lift up Sinclair Lewis, John Galsworthy, Roger Martin du Gard, and Pearl Buck to the literary Mount Olympus—not despite the fact that they were popular, but because they were.

The Dylan award can be discussed in relation to the apocalyptic idea of the decline of literature's important role in society, an idea that recurs from time to time and that has been intensely discussed in recent years. In such an apocalyptic view of current and future states of literature, critics often think about literature as a written phenomenon produced to be read. And yes, perhaps the cultural importance of traditional books is threatened in the new, digital media landscape, but if literature is slightly redefined to also include song lyrics, audio books, e-books, and manuscripts written for the screen, the future looks distinctly brighter. This kind of redefinition of the literary object itself needs to be done all the time, and the Nobel Prize institution must take part in that work. But the Swedish Academy has to contribute to this necessary revitalization without giving up its strong support for the written canon and the importance of traditional reading. These two ambitions do not exclude each other, but it is a real challenge to find a balance between them.

If James F. English is right when he argues that the very idea of the Nobel Prize is intimately connected to a universalist belief in literary values (English 2005: 49), the Swedish Academy needs to support this belief in order to maintain the award's credibility. If the prize no longer is perceived as at least someone's idea of the absolutely best literature there is, a significant part of its raison d'être wanes. But the Nobel judges must also respect and listen to perspectives on literature that significantly differ from their own. In his study of critical responses to Nobel selections from 2000 until today, Karl Ågerup shows that the most common objection to a prize decision in the first two decades of the new millennium had to do with a perceived misrepresentation of the protesting person's home country or culture (Ågerup 2022). But it was not the literary texts themselves that upset the critics, Ågerup writes, but the political positions with which the authors were connected. The Swedish Academy should not, of course, change their views according to every objection. An international literary prize that did not prompt any protests would rapidly become uninteresting. But in order to stay widely relevant, the Nobel cannot afford to be seen as being administered by a self-sufficient North European assembly who ridiculously pretends to know it all.

The Committee members need to listen to critical opinions from afar and be perceptive, which is a distinct ambition behind a recent change in procedures. Since 2021, there are ten formally appointed external experts from different parts of the world directly connected to the Committee work (Espmark 2021: 36). The Committee has asked for help before. Indeed, the very procedure of inviting nominations from all over the world is such a gesture. A more urgent call for help was sent in 1949. When the Academy declared that they had to postpone that year's prize announcement, they also publicly asked international critics, scholars, and institutions for help to find a worthy laureate ("Nobel Prize Rule Revised," 1949). Another important change in the early 2020s is the new rule that a Committee member is appointed on a three-year tenure, with a possibility to earn the trust to stay for another three years after the first period. Both these changes may turn out to form a very constructive counterweight to the universalist claims made by the members.

But the concept of universalism is also challenged from a more fundamental perspective—that of personal experience. In advocating the value of literary testimony (in a 2001 Nobel symposium, in several prize motivations, and in Espmark's discussion of twenty-first-century awards), the Swedish Academy had adhered to a poetics of subjectivity and particularism. To give witness is to challenge general notions of life with an absolutely specific and individual account. Acknowledgment of this value was very scarce in earlier periods of the prize. The 1947 award to André Gide was a possible exception. The praise of the French author's "fearless love of truth" may have referred to his published diaries, in which he describes his homosexuality. In the discussion leading up to the decision, Committee member Hjalmar Gullberg wrote that Gide least of all should "be dismissed for openly showing his nature in his confessional texts" (Svensén 2001b: 381, my translation). After Gide, testimonial values have perhaps been relevant in several internal discussions, but they haven't been openly expressed until the turn of the millennium. Since the Gao Xingjian prize in 2000, however, these literary values have been addressed in relation to several different kinds of experiences, for example migration (Gao, Gurnah), war (Kertész, Alexievich), and belonging to an ethnic minority (Naipaul).

After the movements of #MeToo and Black Lives Matter at the end of the 2010s, the discourse of witnessing has been strongly intensified and gained a new kind of acute relevance. It is not at all surprising that Nobel Prize discussions haven't as yet been able to address these changes, but maybe they must in the near future in order to stay relevant. A very important function of twenty-first-century literature is to express nonnormative and minority experiences, in other words to contribute with a "*world-imagining from below*," as Jennifer Wenzel calls it (Wenzel 2019: 9, italics in the original). The world's most influential literary prize must be able to acknowledge this central value in contemporary literature.

At the basis of several of these balancing acts lies a fundamental opposition between, on the one hand, charming aspects and, on the other, inattractive dimensions of the Nobel Prize's old-world aura. The historical roots of the Swedish Academy, which dates back to the late eighteenth century, and its Nobel Committee, initiated by Alfred Nobel's nineteenth-century cosmopolitanism, give the award a weight and a glory beyond contemporary politics, academic theories, literary markets, and tastes, but the fact that the Swedish monarch is the official protector of the Academy, and hence of the whole Nobel Prize process, is bizarrely outdated in the eyes of many domestic and international critics. It is no coincidence that on both occasions when an alternative Nobel Prize has been given as a protest against the Academy (in 1912 to August Strindberg and in 2018 to Maryse Condé), these events have been manifestations of anti-elitism.

In this context, the lack of transparency of the prize decision process adds a particular dimension. Some critics argue that the secrecy around the short list and the internal discussions infers a necessary mysticism to the prize process, and thereby contributes to making the Nobel award special. Others criticize this custom for being undemocratic. The members of the Nobel Committee should, these critics argue, recognize their powerful position and be openly responsible for its actions. To stay relevant, the Nobel Prize institution needs to retain some of its old aura without being dismissed as a hopelessly obsolete ivory tower. That is a tricky challenge.

Literary Canonization in an Age of Polarization

For four years in the early 1940s, no Nobel laureates in Literature were selected and no ceremonies were arranged in Stockholm. The Second World War had disrupted the cosmopolitan space of transcultural literary and scientific communication. As a replacement for the first canceled prize in 1940, the Common Council for American Unity arranged its own Nobel Dinner in New York City on Alfred Nobel's birthday, December 10. The specific purpose of the dinner was to honor "the twenty-eight Nobel prize winners now in this country, most of them refugees," the *New York Times* reported. But the gesture was much wider than honoring particular laureates. The overall aim was to give praise to the donor and his vision of a world in peace:

> Alfred Nobel expressly declared that not the slightest attention was to be paid to nationality. Did he foresee the rising tide of the narrow nationalism that has given us the Germany, Italy and Japan of today? Certainly he realized that great thinking and great discovery belong to the world and that neither is possible under tyranny.
> ("The Nobel Dinner," 1940)

The world was on fire. The Western civilization was threatened to its very core by fascism. For the American organizers, Alfred Nobel and the fruit of his endeavors, the Nobel Prize, represented everything valuable that Adolf Hitler and Benito Mussolini wanted to destroy:

> In this war the fate of a whole culture is at stake—a culture which gave us the Nobel prize winners, a culture based on knowledge of the atom, on electric machines, on automobiles, on television, on theories of evolution and relativity, on great novels, plays and philosophies of life. If the world is ever socially unified the way must be prepared by scientists and writers who may work and speak freely. Last night's dinner was a liberty dinner, a protest against the blasphemies and the tyrannies that have quenched in Fascist countries the spirit embodied by Alfred Nobel and by those who have been honored in accordance with his precepts.

Science and literature paved the way, the *New York Times* reporter argued, toward liberty, peace, and intercultural respect. And the Nobel Prize was the prime international infrastructure for these vital endeavors.

Three years later, in December 1943, the American council arranged a second replacement dinner at the Hotel Astor in central New York ("Nobel Anniversary Celebrated Here," 1943), but in November 1944 it looked like the Swedish Academy would resume its laureate selections. In the *New York Times*, there were speculations on the Swedish intellectuals' first choice after the three-year break. Ernest Hemingway, Willa Cather, John Steinbeck, and Gabriela Mistral were mentioned as possible winners. One thing was for certain: it would not be a German author. Permanent Secretary Anders Österling was quoted declaring that German culture "has been decaying under Adolf Hitler and the country has been unable to produce a literary figure of any stature" ("Nobel Board Studies Literature Nominees," 1944). It is not difficult to conclude that such a statement was exactly what the New York newspaper and most of its readers wanted to hear. In the 1940s United States, the Nobel Prize was a bastion of anti-fascism.

Eighty years later, democratic ideals and aspirations toward intercultural communication and cooperation are under threat again. As always, progress is disturbed by conflicts between nations and cultures, but this time around a huge threat also comes from rising nationalist attitudes *within* numerous countries and cultures—in the West as well as in the East, South, and North. Could the Nobel Prize be a call for democracy, tolerance, and humanity in this alarming situation? Could the award be an antidote to intolerant nationalism, cultural seclusion, and increasing racism?

Well, it has been understood as such an antidote before, and not only in the early 1940s. In his 1967 assessment of the history of the prize, American scholar Robert E. Spiller argued that the Nobel was not a literary award in the ordinary sense, but rather a prize guided by an overall ambition to promote world peace (Spiller 1967). In the prize discussion in 1914, the Nobel Committee had a hard time finding an appropriate laureate. Many of the nominated authors took active parts in the ongoing European conflict, promoting nationalist sentiments at odds with the Nobel Prize institution's "purpose of promoting humanism" (Svensén 2001a: 310). The Committee decided to postpone the prize decision, and next year the decision was made to cancel the 1914 award altogether. This cancelation was perhaps not a strong gesture for democracy, humanity, and tolerance in itself, but it did show the Swedish Academy's refusal to promote opposite values and attitudes.

In the early 1960s, the heated discussion on whether the Academy should select Ezra Pound as a laureate or not resulted in the clear decision that even if politics wasn't supposed to instruct the selections, the Nobel Prize couldn't possibly be awarded to an author who is or has been promoting fascist values (cf. Espmark 1986: 122–4). A decade later, the suggestion to award Jorge Luis Borges was dismissed at least partly because of the Argentinian author's connections to Chilean dictator Augusto Pinochet. In 1979, Committee member Artur Lundkvist wrote: "His hasty political gestures, now with fascist tendencies, make him in my view an improper Nobel laureate, for ethical and humane reasons" (Lundkvist 1979). And in-between these two ideologically charged issues, the prize to Aleksandr Solzhenitsyn was definitely interpreted as a firm stand against the totalitarian Soviet system in support of the "indelible dignity of the individual human being," as Permanent Secretary Karl Ragnar Gierow phrased it (Espmark 1986: 128, my translation).

The Nobel Prize institution could, then, be used as supporting more fundamental values than those recognized by political trends and current opinions. It could stand for a continuity of acknowledging democratic human rights, promoting freedom of speech, and supporting a tolerant attitude toward different perspectives of life. The Nobel Prize could provide an ideological space for long-term, cross-generational, and cross-cultural values. In this light, Alfred Nobel's idea to award authors for outstanding works written "in an idealistic direction" is perhaps not that out-of-date after all. As a late-nineteenth-century word for a combination of democracy, humanity, and tolerance, idealism is perhaps exactly what the twenty-first-century world urgently needs. Swiss-German literary historian Fritz Strich's famous words from 1930 are, sadly enough, just as relevant in the 2020s as they were in 1930s Germany: "World literary studies, then, sprang from national and cosmopolitan motives, and we cannot ignore that in our day this discipline has gained greater urgency and importance than ever before. Because it is this discipline that is able to help us resolve the battle now raging between the idea of the nation and that of humanity" (Strich 2013: 48). If the Nobel Prize can contribute, in any way, to making people reflect upon humankind at large as much as on the interests of their own particular nations and cultures, much has been gained.

We must not, however, ignore the basic problems with the Nobel Prize in Literature. The selection of laureates is an active act of canonization, and such an act will always be elitist in one way or another. Secondly, the Nobel will always be a European prize that will never be able to completely balance out the hierarchy between cultures, languages, and literatures. This hierarchy is rather reinforced by the international importance of the Nobel Prize. Furthermore, the Swedish Academy is fundamentally an elitist and undemocratic assembly. It was founded by the Swedish king Gustav III a decade after he secured more power for himself in a coup d'état and significantly restricted freedom of speech. And the learned assembly administrating the Nobel Prize in Literature still falls under the protection of the Swedish monarch, whose position as a hereditary Head of State does not merge well with core democratic values.

To a certain extent, these problems are immanent and inescapable. But in order for the Nobel Prize to stay relevant in the twenty-first century, the Swedish Academy must, I argue, reduce its undemocratic dimensions to a minimum. And to achieve that, a lot of work remains to be done, especially when it comes to transparency. A central part of the lingering undemocratic dimension of the Nobel Prize institution is what I would like to call its culture of secrecy. The uncompromising reluctance of the Academy members to show any part of their internal discussions to the outside world—including the rule that critics and scholars have to wait for fifty years until Committee discussions of nominated authors are made public—is firmly rooted in eighteenth-century Freemasonry. This ceremonious secrecy is a leftover from the cultural practice of closed circles of power, a social practice in which the actual decisions important for all were made behind closed doors far from the scrutinizing eye of the public. Not only does this culture of secrecy run the risk of appearing archaically ridiculous—with its cloak-and-dagger customs of fake book covers and mysteriously veiled shelves in the Nobel Library (cf. Rydén 2010: 542, 547, 566–7; Rydén and Westerström 2018: 500)—but it also, and more importantly, supports the dangerous idea of self-sufficient, opaque cultural power.

The problematic aspects of this secrecy culture were blatantly revealed in relation to the Jean-Claude Arnault affair in 2018 and 2019. Facing the allegations of having downplayed, ignored, and even hushed down suspicions against Katarina Frostenson's husband, the Swedish Academy's reactions were too late, too ambiguous, and too weak. Many critics argued that in their inaptitude to take necessary action, both before the scandal erupted and after the allegations against Arnault had been made public, the Academy revealed that they thought that they stood above the law and the moral rules of ordinary people. Their passivity was seen as a closing of ranks intended to obstruct insights into what had actually taken place.

Indeed, the culture of secrecy was one of Arnault's central tools in his systematic exploitation of Frostenson's position. Frostenson leaked the names of soon-to-be-announced laureates to Arnault, who used this information to "convince impressionable young women that he was close to the Academy and could guide their futures in the cultural world," as Per Wästberg poignantly phrased in 2020 (Wästberg 2020: 388, my translation). The culture of secrecy produces power, and this power can be misused.

To mitigate the loss of respect for the Swedish Academy in the public eye, the Nobel Foundation had to intervene and require adjustments in the formation of the Academy and its Nobel Committee. It is obvious that the Swedish Academy was unable to solve the problem as an autonomous, secret circle. In order to survive as an internationally important body of literary consecration, the members of this Academy need to lose their desire for cultural autonomy. They do not stand above the law or any other moral rules, and their literary decisions do not stand above ideology, politics, cultural situatedness, or other readers' aesthetic tastes, values, and opinions. The eighteen members of the Academy do not work from any Olympic heights, but from a position amongst fellow humans and fellow readers.

As we have seen, the secrecy surrounding laureate selections has been far from strict in earlier periods of the prize. In fact, letting out information on the Nobel Committee's suggestion before the final decision was made by the Academy was for decades a very successful media stunt, securing at least two days of intense attention. But yes, since these leaks stopped and the secrecy started to be held to the very end, the prize announcement has gained two other media benefits: the dramatic moment of the Permanent Secretary stepping out of his office to announce the name of that year's laureate, and the betting community's ability to upheld a financial interest in the announcement. But endorsing a more transparent view of cultural consecration would perhaps be worth the risk of losing some dramatic effects.

And perhaps there are other benefits to be gained from a more open prize-decision process, more in line with the contemporary cultural landscape. In 1994, Sarah Lyall wrote this report on the reactions to that year's prize announcement:

> American publishers of Kenzaburo Oe's novels had heard so often that Mr. Oe was about to win the Nobel Prize in Literature that they'd stopped listening to the rumors. But Mr. Oe (pronounced OH-ay) did indeed win this year, and now the taken-by-surprise publishers have another problem: how to get copies of the books into bookstores quickly enough to capitalize on the news.
>
> (Lyall 1994)

If they had been taken less by surprise, the laureate's publishers might have earned more money on the decision by making it possible for more American readers to get to know the Japanese novelist.

A process toward increased transparency has indeed started, both regarding the Swedish Academy's economy and its administration. In 2019, a first public activity report was published, and a new, stricter practice of documentation started. Nowadays, anyone can gain insight into most of the Academy's activities. But meeting minutes and discussions of domestic awards and grants are still classified—and so are the procedures, documents, and evaluations concerning the Nobel Prize in Literature (Wästberg 2020: 399). Maybe it's time to let go of some of these secrets too.

In order to survive as an important factor in international literary canonization, the Nobel Prize must also, I think, be able to take a firm, direct, and unambiguous stand in the ideological battles that plague the world of today. Some traces of such a stand are definitely noticeable. In an official tweet explaining the choice of Abdulrazak Gurnah in 2021, the Swedish Academy distinctly referred to one central aspect of the current ideological polarization: the laureate was honored for his "dedication to truth and his aversion to simplification" (cf. Vermeulen 2023: 5). And being asked about the general election in Sweden in September 2022, Permanent Secretary Mats Malm expressed his concerns about the increasing need to support "language, thought and facts" in the current political situation (Beckman and Voss Gustavsson 2022). Malm's statement was not totally unambiguous, but the way he stressed the importance of "thought" and "truth" was hardly in line with the fiercely nationalist sentiments instructing the election campaign. A more poignant example is the international symposium "Thought and truth under pressure," which was arranged in Stockholm in March 2023 by the Swedish Academy and initiated by Malm.

Most people acknowledge that the members of the Swedish Academy want to support humanist ideals everywhere and for everyone. But it wouldn't hurt if they made this ideologically charged position absolutely clear now and again. In fact, recurring direct gestures of this kind will probably be necessary if the Nobel Prize is to retain its importance in an age of renewed battles between, on the one hand, violent self-sufficiency and, on the other, what is beneficial to humankind.

Acknowledgment

The research for this book was made possible by Sven och Dagmar Saléns Stiftelse.

Appendix: Nobel Laureates in Literature 1901–2022

1901	Sully Prudhomme	1938	Pearl Buck
1902	Theodor Mommsen	1939	Frans Eemil Sillanpää
1903	Bjørnstjerne Bjørnson	1940	—
1904	Frédéric Mistral and José Echegaray	1941	—
		1942	—
1905	Henryk Sienkiewicz	1943	—
1906	Giosuè Carducci	1944	Johannes V. Jensen
1907	Rudyard Kipling	1945	Gabriela Mistral
1908	Rudolf Eucken	1946	Hermann Hesse
1909	Selma Lagerlöf	1947	André Gide
1910	Paul Heyse	1948	T.S. Eliot
1911	Maurice Maeterlinck	1949	William Faulkner
1912	Gerhart Hauptmann	1950	Bertrand Russell
1913	Rabindranath Tagore	1951	Pär Lagerkvist
1914	—	1952	François Mauriac
1915	Romain Rolland	1953	Winston Churchill
1916	Verner von Heidenstam	1954	Ernest Hemingway
1917	Karl Gjellerup and Henrik Pontoppidan	1955	Halldór Kiljan Laxness
		1956	Juan Ramón Jiménez
1918	—	1957	Albert Camus
1919	Carl Spitteler	1958	Boris Pasternak
1920	Knut Hamsun	1959	Salvatore Quasimodo
1921	Anatole France	1960	Saint-John Perse
1922	Jacinto Benavente	1961	Ivo Andric
1923	William Butler Yeats	1962	John Steinbeck
1924	Wladyslaw Reymont	1963	Giorgos Seferis
1925	George Bernard Shaw	1964	Jean-Paul Sartre
1926	Grazia Deledda	1965	Mikhail Sholokhov
1927	Henri Bergson	1966	Nelly Sachs and Shmuel Agnon
1928	Sigrid Undset	1967	Miguel Ángel Asturias
1929	Thomas Mann	1968	Yasunari Kawabata
1930	Sinclair Lewis	1969	Samuel Beckett
1931	Erik Axel Karlfeldt	1970	Aleksandr Solzhenitsyn
1932	John Galsworthy	1971	Pablo Neruda
1933	Ivan Bunin	1972	Heinrich Böll
1934	Luigi Pirandello	1973	Patrick White
1935	—	1974	Harry Martinson and Eyvind Johnson
1936	Eugene O'Neill		
1937	Roger Martin du Gard	1975	Eugenio Montale

1976	Saul Bellow	2000	Gao Xingjian
1977	Vicente Aleixandre	2001	V.S. Naipaul
1978	Isaac Bashevis Singer	2002	Imre Kertész
1979	Odysseus Elytis	2003	J.M. Coetzee
1980	Czeslaw Milosz	2004	Elfriede Jelinek
1981	Elias Canetti	2005	Harold Pinter
1982	Gabriel García Márquez	2006	Orhan Pamuk
1983	William Golding	2007	Doris Lessing
1984	Jaroslav Seifert	2008	Jean-Marie Gustave Le Clézio
1985	Claude Simon	2009	Herta Müller
1986	Wole Soyinka	2010	Mario Vargas Llosa
1987	Joseph Brodsky	2011	Tomas Tranströmer
1988	Naguib Mahfouz	2012	Mo Yan
1989	Camilo José Cela	2013	Alice Munro
1990	Octavio Paz	2014	Patrick Modiano
1991	Nadine Gordimer	2015	Svetlana Alexievich
1992	Derek Walcott	2016	Bob Dylan
1993	Toni Morrison	2017	Kazuo Ishiguro
1994	Kenzaburo Oe	2018	Olga Tokarczuk
1995	Seamus Heaney	2019	Peter Handke
1996	Wislawa Szymborska	2020	Louise Glück
1997	Dario Fo	2021	Abdulrazak Gurnah
1998	José Saramago	2022	Annie Ernaux
1999	Günter Grass		

References

"1926 Nobel Prize for Literature" (1927), the *Times*, November 11, 1927.
"1940 Nobel Prizes Canceled" (1941), *New York Times*, October 18, 1941.
"1970 Nobel Prize Presented to Solzhenitsyn" (1974), the *Times*, December 11, 1974.
"2 U.S. Scientists Win Nobel Prizes" (1944), *New York Times*, November 10, 1944.
"£7,500 Nobel Prize Surprises Yeats, Who Will Invest It" (1923), *New York Times*, December 2, 1923.
Adams, Mildred (1945), "The 1945 Winner of the Nobel Award," *New York Times*, December 9, 1945.
advertisement (1929), the *Times*, November 22, 1929.
advertisement (1934), the *Times*, November 17, 1934.
advertisement (1937), the *Times*, November 15, 1937.
advertisements (1930), the *Times*, December 5 and 12, 1930.
Ågerup, Karl (2022), *Critical Responses to the Nobel Prize in Literature: An Analysis of 22 Awards*, Lewiston and Lampeter: Edwin Mellen Press.
"A Great Patriot and Liberal" (1939), the *Times*, November 11, 1939.
"Albert Camus prix Nobel de littérature" (1957), *Le Figaro*, October 18, 1957.
"Albert Camus prix Nobel de littérature 1957" (1957), *Le Figaro*, October 18, 1957.
Aleixandre, Vicente (2022), https://www.nobelprize.org/prizes/literature/1977/aleixandre/lecture/, June 20, 2022.
"A Letter of Rejection: The Case Against 'Dr. Zhivago'" (1958), *New York Times*, December 7, 1958.
Alexievich, Svetlana (2022), "On the Battle Lost," https://www.nobelprize.org/prizes/literature/2015/alexievich/lecture/, translated by Jamey Gambrell, June 21, 2022.
"Alfred Nobels testamente" (1896), *Svenska Dagbladet*, December 31, 1896.
"Alfred Nobels testemente" (1897a), *Nya Dagligt Allehanda*, January 2, 1896.
"Alfred Nobels testamente" (1897b), *Dagens Nyheter*, January 4, 1897.
"Alfred Nobels testamente" (1897c), *Svenska Dagbladet*, January 4, 1897.
"Alfred Nobel's Will" (2022), https://www.nobelprize.org/alfred-nobel/alfred-nobels-will/, read in September 2022.
Alguazils, Les (1926), "Bernard Shaw. Prix Nobel de Littérature," *Le Figaro*, November 12, 1926.
Alguazils, Les (1928), "M. Henri Bergson lauréat du Prix Nobel," *Le Figaro*, November 14.
Allen, Roger (1988), "Nobel Prize Symposium II: Choices and Omissions 1967–1987. Arabic Literature and the Nobel Prize," *World Literature Today* 1988: 2, pp. 201–3.
Allén, Sture, and Kjell Espmark (2001a), *Nobelpriset i litteratur. En introduktion*, Stockholm: Svenska Akademien.
Allén, Sture, and Kjell Espmark (2001b), *The Nobel Prize in Literature: An introduction*, translated by Erik Frykman, Stockholm: Svenska Akademien.
Allén, Sture, and Kjell Espmark (2006), *The Nobel Prize in Literature: An introduction*, translated by Erik Frykman, Stockholm: Svenska Akademien.

Allén, Sture, and Kjell Espmark (2014), *The Nobel Prize in Literature: An introduction*, translated by Erik Frykman, Stockholm: Svenska Akademien.
Alph. B. (1908), "Le prix Nobel," *Le Figaro*, December 11, 1908.
Alph. B. (1928), "M. Henri Bergson lauréat du Prix Nobel," *Le Figaro*, November 14, 1928.
Amanuddin, Syed (1988), "Nobel Prize Symposium II: Choices and Omissions 1967–1987. South Asian Writers and the Nobel Prize," *World Literature Today* 2, pp. 204–7.
"A Master Every Year" (1965), the *Times*, October 16, 1965.
"American Week in London" (1936), *New York Times*, November 29, 1936.
"Anatole France" (1921), *Le Figaro*, November 11, 1921.
Anderson, Benedict (2013), "The Unrewarded: Notes on the Nobel Prize for Literature," *New Left Review* 80, pp. 99–108.
"André Gide and Communism" (1947), *New York Times*, November 16.
"ANDRÉ GIDE obtient le Prix Nobel de Littérature" (1947), *Le Figaro*, November 14, 1947.
"André Gide Ordered to Rest" (1947), *New York Times*, November 26, 1947.
Angioletti, G.B. (1948), untitled article, *New York Times Book Review*, November 21, 1948.
"A Nobelist Delves into the Language" (1993), *New York Times*, October 10.
"Appeal for Hungarian Writers" (1957), the *Times*, October 31, 1957.
"Approve Award to Shaw" (1926), *New York Times*, November 13, 1926.
Apter, Emily (2013), *Against World Literature: On the Politics of Untranslatability*, New York and London: Verso.
A.R. (1947), "Une consécration française," *Le Figaro*, November 14, 1947.
A.R. (1948), "Le poète britannique T.S. ELIOT reçoit le Prix Nobel de littérature," *Le Figaro*, November 5, 1948.
"Assails Award to Lewis" (1930), *New York Times*, December 6, 1930.
Asturias, Miguel Ángel (2022), "The Latin American Nobel: Testimony of an Epoch," https://www.nobelprize.org/prizes/literature/1967/asturias/lecture/, translated by the Swedish Trade Council Language Services, June 20, 2022.
Atkinson, J. Brooks (1926), "Burden of Success," *New York Times*, November 21, 1926.
"Attribution aujourd'hui du prix Nobel de littérature" (1957), *Le Figaro*, October 17, 1957.
Auerbach, Erich (2013), "Philology and *Weltliteratur*," in *World Literature: A Reader*, ed. by Theo D'haen, César Domínguez, and Mads Rosendahl Thomsen, London and New York: Routledge.
"Aujourd'hui prix Nobel de Littérature" (1970), *Le Figaro*, October 8, 1970.
"Award Perturbs Swedes" (1938), *New York Times*, November 12, 1938.
"Award to Churchill Assailed in Sweden" (1953), *New York Times*, October 17, 1953.
"Award to Eliot" (1948), *New York Times*, November 5, 1948.
"Award to Maeterlinck" (1911), *New York Times*, November 10, 1911.
"Award to Sir W. Churchill" (1953), the *Times*, December 11, 1953.
Baldensperger, Fernand (1951), "What's Wrong with the Nobel Prize?," *Books Abroad* 2, p. 114.
Barberet, Gene J. (1967), "France and Belgium," *Books Abroad* 1, pp. 8–13.
"Beckett to Accept Prize" (1969), the *Times*, October 27, 1969.
Beckman, Åsa, and Matilda Voss Gustavsson (2022), "25 kulturpersonligheter om känslorna inför dagens val," *Dagens Nyheter*, September 11, 2022.
Beecroft, Alexander (2015), *An Ecology of World Literature: From Antiquity to the Present Day*, London and New York: Verso 2015.
Bell, Clive (1948), untitled article, *New York Times Book Review*, November 21, 1948.

Bellow, Saul (2022), https://www.nobelprize.org/prizes/literature/1976/bellow/lecture/, June 20, 2022.
"Bergson Surprised to Get Nobel Prize" (1928), *New York Times*, December 2, 1928.
Bernstein, Richard (2012), "In China, a Writer Finds a Deep Well," *New York Times*, October 11, 2012.
Beslic, Isidor (2020), "Nobelstiftelsen höjer prissumman: 'Viktigt för Nobelpriset,'" *Dagens Industri*, September 24, 2020.
Birch, Cyril (1967), "China: Lu Hsün," *Books Abroad* 1, p. 42.
"Biographie de François Mauriac" (1952), *Le Figaro*, November 7, 1952.
Björkstén, Ingmar (1984), *Titel*, 1984:4.
Bloom, Harold (1994), *The Western Canon: The Books and School of the Ages*, New York: Harcourt Brace.
Bly, Robert (1977), "The Man Who Stayed Behind," *New York Times Book Review*, October 30, 1977.
Bonavia, David (1970a), "Nobel Award to Disgraced Writer Certain to Give Grave Offence to Soviet Establishment," (1970), the *Times*, October 9, 1970.
Bonavia, David (1970b), "Writers condemn award to Solzhenitsyn," the *Times*, October 10, 1970.
Bonavia, David (1970c), "Three Demonstrators Are Arrested after Protest in Moscow Store," the *Times*, October 15, 1970.
Bonavia, David (1970d), "Solzhenitsyn Defended by Russian Cellist," the *Times*, November 13, 1970.
"Book Notes" (1932a), *New York Times*, November 11, 1932.
"Book Notes" (1932b), *New York Times*, November 21, 1932.
"Books and Authors" (1933), *New York Times*, November 26, 1933.
"Books and Authors" (1936), *New York Times*, November 29, 1936.
"Books and Authors" (1938), *New York Times*, December 4, 1938.
"Books and Authors" (1939), *New York Times*, December 3, 1939.
"Boris Pasternak prix Nobel de Littérature" (1958), *Le Figaro*, October 23, 1958.
"Boris Pasternak n'ira sans doute pas à Stockholm" (1958), *Le Figaro*, October 27, 1958.
Brandes, Georg (2013), "Weltliteratur," in *World Literature: A Reader*, ed. by Theo D'haen, César Domínguez, and Mads Rosendahl Thomsen, London and New York: Routledge.
Breit, Harvey (1953), "In and Out of Books," *New York Times*, October 25, 1953.
Brems, Elke, Orsolya Réthelyi, and Ton Van Kalmthout (eds.) (2017), *Doing Double Dutch: The International Circulation of Literature from the Low Countries*, Leuven: Leuven University Press.
Brodsky, Joseph (1986), *Less Than One: Selected Essays*, New York: Farrar, Straus & Giroux.
Brodsky, Joseph (2022), https://www.nobelprize.org/prizes/literature/1987/brodsky/lecture/, translated by Barry Rubin, June 21, 2022.
Brown, Deming B., and Glenora W. Brown (1954), *A Guide to Soviet Russian Translations of American Literature*, King's Cross Press: New York.
Brown, John L. (1988), "Nobel Prize Symposium II: Choices and Omissions 1967–1987. Twenty Years and Two Lauraetes: Francophone Nobel Prizes, 1967–1987," *World Literature Today* 2, pp. 207–11.
Buck, Pearl (2022), "The Chinese Novel," https://www.nobelprize.org/prizes/literature/1938/buck/lecture/, June 21, 2022.
"Bunin Is Acclaimed in Nobel Ceremony" (1933), *New York Times*, December 11, 1933.

Burniaux, Constant (1951), "What's Wrong with the Nobel Prize?," *Books Abroad* 2, pp. 114–15.
Camus, Albert (1958), *Discours de Suède*, Gallimard: Paris.
Carlberg, Ingrid (2019), *Nobel. Den gåtfulle Alfred, hans värld och hans pris*, Stockholm: Norstedts.
Carter, Albert Howard (1967), "Rabindranath Tagore," *Books Abroad* 1, pp. 36–7.
cartoon reprint (1958), the *Times*, November 8, 1958.
Casanova, Pascale (1999), *La République mondiale des Lettres*, Paris: Seuil.
Casanova, Pascale (2004), *The World Republic of Letters*, translated by M.B. DeBevoise, Cambridge, Mass., and London: Harvard University Press.
Casanova, Pascale (2005), "Literature as a World," *New Left Review* 31, pp. 71–90.
Casanova, Pascale (2013), "Literature as a World," in *World Literature: A Reader*, ed. by Theo D'haen, César Domínguez, and Mads Rosendahl Thomsen, Routledge: London and New York.
Casanova, Pascale (2015), *La Langue mondiale: Traduction et domination*, Seuil: Paris.
"Castro's rum handout vexes Swedes" (1982), the *Times*, December 15, 1982.
Cela, Camilo José (2022), "Eulogy to the Fable," https://www.nobelprize.org/prizes/literature/1989/cela/lecture/, translated by Mary Penney, June 21, 2022.
Chatelain, Nicolas (1958), "Pasternak m'a dit," *Le Figaro*, October 25, 1958.
Cheuk, Michael Ka-chi, and Takashi Inoue (2022), "The Nobel Complex in Japan and China," "Literature in the Nobel Era: Regimes of Value," German Literature Archive, Marbach, August 24–6, 2022.
Ch'ien, Evelyn Nien-Ming (2005), *Weird English*, Cambridge, MA: Harvard University Press.
"Churchill Bars Trip To Sweden" (1953), *New York Times*, November 11, 1953.
"Churchill Creed: 'Old Words Best'" (1953), *New York Times*, October 16, 1953.
"Churchill Reported Nobel Prize Winner" (1953), *New York Times*, October 14, 1953.
"Churchill's Wife Reveals He Is Writing a New Book" (1953), *New York Times*, December 9, 1953.
"Churchill Wins Nobel Prize" (1953), *New York Times*, October 16, 1953.
Churchill, Winston (1953), "The Second World War," *New York Times*, published in 30 parts between October 23 and November 26, 1953.
"Claude Simon prix Nobel de littérature" (1985), *Le Figaro*, October 18, 1985.
Coppola, Carlo (1967), "Urdu Possibilities," *Books Abroad* 1, pp. 44–5.
"Critical Award to Sinclair Lewis" (1930), *New York Times*, December 28, 1930.
"Crowd Hears Lewis Talk at Gothenburg" (1930), *New York Times*, December 20, 1930.
Czerwinski, E.J. (1988), "Nobel Prize Symposium II: Choices and Omissions 1967–1987. For Whom the Nobel Tolls: The Nationless," *World Literature Today* 2, pp. 211–4.
Damrosch, David (2003), *What Is World Literature?*, Princeton and Oxford: Princeton University Press.
"Danes Get Nobel Prize" (1917), *New York Times*, November 10, 1917.
"Danes and the Nobel Prize" (1917), *Times Literary Supplement*, December 19, 1917.
Danius, Sara (2018), *Om Bob Dylan*, Stockholm: Bonniers 2018.
Delerm, Philippe (2016), "Mon adolescence nobélisée, ça fait bizarre," *Le Figaro*, October 14, 2016.
"DEMAIN: François Mauriac" (1952), *Le Figaro*, October 20 and 27, 1952.
de Vogüé, E.M. (1907), "Le prix Nobel á Rudyard Kipling," *Le Figaro*, December 11, 1907.

"Dernières nouvelles" (1903), *Le Figaro*, December 11, 1903.
"Des académiciens nous disent …" (1964), *Le Figaro*, October 23, 1964.
"Dimnet Deplores Honoring of Lewis" (1930), *New York Times*, December 22, 1930.
"Distrubution of Nobel Prizes" (1928), the *Times*, December 11, 1928.
"Dr. Phelps Praises Lewis Prize Speech" (1930), *New York Times*, December 15, 1930.
Durán, Manuel (1988), "Nobel Prize Symposium II: Choices and Omissions 1967–1987. The Nobel Prize and Writers in the Hispanic World: A Continuing Story," *World Literature Today* 2, pp. 214–7.
Durán, Manuel, and Michael Nimetz (1967), "Spain and Spanish America," *Books Abroad* 1, pp. 23–5.
Dutourd, Jean (1954), "Hemingway," *Le Figaro*, October 29, 1954.
Dylan, Bob (2022), https://www.nobelprize.org/prizes/literature/2016/dylan/lecture/, June 21, 2022.
Edfelt, Johannes (1975), "Elias Canetti," *Artes* 4, s. 40–1.
Edfeldt, Chatarina, Erik Falk, Andreas Hedberg, Yvonne Lindqvist, Cecilia Schwartz and Paul Tenngart (2022), *Northern Crossings: Translation, Circulation and the Literary Semi-periphery*, New York and London: Bloomsbury 2021.
Edström, Vivi (2002), *Selma Lagerlöf. Livets vågspel*, Stockholm: Natur och Kultur.
Ekelund, Bo G., Adnan Mahmutovic, and Helena Wulff (2022), *Claiming Space: Locations and Orientations in World Literatures*, New York and London: Bloomsbury.
Eliot, T.S. (1969), "Banquet Speech," in *Nobel Lectures, Literature 1901–1967*, ed. by Horst Frenz, Amsterdam: Elsevier.
Ellis-Petersen, Hannah, and Alison Flood (2016), "Bob Dylan Wins Nobel Prize in Literature," the *Guardian*, October 13, 2016.
Elytis, Odysseus (2022), https://www.nobelprize.org/prizes/literature/1979/elytis/lecture/, June 20, 2022.
"Engdahl i AP-intervju" (2008), https://www.svt.se/kultur/engdahl-i-ap-intervju-europa-litteraturens-centrum.
Engdahl, Horace (2013), "Canonization and World Literature: The Nobel Experience," in *World Literature: A Reader*, ed. by César Domínguez and Mads Rosendahl Thomsen, London and New York: Routledge.
English, James F. (2005), *The Economy of Prestige: Prizes, Awards, and the Circulation of Cultural Value*, Cambridge, MA, and London: Harvard University Press.
"Ennobel-ling O'Neill" (1936), *New York Times*, November 22, 1936.
Erlander, Tage (2008), *Dagböcker 1958*, Stockholm: Gidlunds.
"Ernest Hemingway reçoit le prix Nobel de littérature 1954" (1954), *Le Figaro*, October 29, 1954.
Espmark, Kjell (1986), *Det litterära Nobelpriset. Principer och värderingar bakom besluten*, Stockholm: Norstedts 1986.
Espmark, Kjell (2001), *Litteraturpriset. Hundra år med Nobels uppdrag*, Stockholm: Norstedts 2001.
Espmark, Kjell (2021), *The Nobel Prize in Literature: A New Century*, Stockholm: Svenska Akademien 2021.
Étiemble, René (2013), "Do We Have to Revise the Notion of World Literature?," in *World Literature: A Reader*, ed. by Theo D'haen, César Domínguez, and Mads Rosendahl Thomsen, translated by Theo D'haen, London and New York: Routledge 2013.
Eucken, Rudolf (2022), "Naturalism or Idealism?," https://www.nobelprize.org/prizes/literature/1908/eucken/lecture/, June 20, 2022.

"Eugene O'Neill, laureate" (1936), *New York Times*, November 14, 1936.
"Eugene O'Neill Mentioned for Nobel Literary Prize" (1936), *New York Times*, November 11, 1936.
"Expert on Atoms Win Nobel Prizes" (1945), *New York Times*, November 16, 1945.
"Faulkner and Bertrand Russell Get Nobel Awards for Writings" (1950), *New York Times*, November 11, 1950.
"Festivities Tire Lewis" (1930), *New York Times*, December 17, 1930.
Feuchtwanger, Lion (1951), "What's Wrong with the Nobel Prize?," *Books Abroad* 2, p. 115.
"Finds 'Main Street' Unfair" (1930), *New York Times*, December 29, 1930.
Fleming, Donald (1966), "Nobel's Hits and Errors," *The Atlantic*, October 1966.
Fo, Dario (2022), "Contra Jogulatores Obloquentes," https://www.nobelprize.org/prizes/literature/1997/Fo/lecture/, translated by Paul Claesson, June 21, 2022.
"For Service to Mankind" (1946), *New York Times*, November 16, 1946.
Forsberg, Emil (2022), "Nobelprisvinnaren demonstrerar mot Macron i Paris," *Aftonbladet*, October 16, 2022.
Foster, David William (1967), "The 'Modernistas' of Brazil," *Books Abroad* 1, pp. 41–2.
"Four Nobel Prizes Presented by King" (1932), *New York Times*, December 11, 1932.
"France and Sweden Laud Award to Lewis" (1930), *New York Times*, November 7, 1930.
"François Mauriac" (1952), *Le Figaro*, November 7, 1952.
Frank, Bruno (1929), "Thomas Mann, Winner of the Nobel Prize for Literature," *New York Times*, November 24, 1929.
"Frederic Passy Interviewed" (1901), *New York Times*, December 24, 1901.
"French Author Honoured" (1957), the *Times*, October 18, 1957.
Frenz, Horst (ed.) (1969), *Nobel Lectures, Literature 1901–1967*, World Scientific: Singapore.
Fries, A.E.B. (1915), "Famous Swedish Poet May Win Nobel Prize," *New York Times*, December 12, 1915.
"Galsworthy Ill With Chill" (1932), *New York Times*, December 11, 1932.
"Galsworthy Will Not Go to Sweden" (1932), *New York Times*, December 6, 1932.
Garner, Dwight (2016), "Bob Dylan the Writer: An Authentic American Voice," *New York Times*, October 13, 2016.
G.D. (1901), "Le Prix Nobel et M. Sully-Prudhomme," *Le Figaro*, December 10, 1901.
"Gerhart Hauptmann" (1912), the *Times*, November 14, 1912.
"Gerhart Hauptmann Writes on the New Religion" (1912), *New York Times*, December 8, 1912.
Gide, André, "Réflexions sur un prix" (1947), *Le Figaro*, December 11, 1947.
"Gide Gets Nobel Literature Prize" (1947), *New York Times*, November 14, 1947.
Gierow, Karl Ragnar (1970), "Nobelpriset i litteratur," *Les Prix Nobel 1969*, Stockholm: The Nobel Foundation.
"Giosuè Carducci" (1907), *Times Literary Supplement*, February 1, 1907.
"Gives Nobel Prize to Polish Author" (1924), *New York Times*, November 14, 1924.
Golding, William (2022), https://www.nobelprize.org/prizes/literature/1983/Golding/lecture/, June 21, 2022.
Glissant, Édouard, and Betsy Wing (1997), *Poetics of Relation*, Ann Arbor: University of Michigan Press.
Glück, Louise (2022), https://www.nobelprize.org/prizes/literature/2020/gluck/lecture/, June 21, 2022.

"Godot Has Arrived" (1969), the *Times*, October 24, 1969.
Goethe, Johann Wolfgang von (2013), "On World Literature," in *World Literature: A Reader*, ed. by Theo D'haen, César Domínguez, and Mads Rosendahl Thomsen, translated by Theo D'haen, London and New York: Routledge.
Goodman, Grant K. (1967), "Japan's Candidates," *Books Abroad* 1, p. 43.
Gordimer, Nadine (2022), "Writing and Being," https://www.nobelprize.org/prizes/literature/1991/Gordimer/lecture/, June 21, 2022.
Gorman, Herbert S. (1921), "Anatole France, Nobel Prize Winner," *New York Times*, November 20, 1921.
Grimes, William (1993), "Toni Morrison Is '93 Winner of Nobel Prize in Literature," *New York Times*, October 8, 1993.
Gunder, Anna (2014), "Nobelpriset är ingen dödskyss," www.rj.se, published January 1, 2014, read March 21, 2022.
Gün, Güneli (1992), "The Turks Are Coming: Deciphering Orhan Pamuk's Black Book," *World Literature Today* 1.
"Günter Grass" (2022), www.nobelprize.org/prizes/literature/1999/press-release/, read September 2022.
Gurnah, Abdulrazak (2022), "Writing," https://www.nobelprize.org/prizes/literature/2021/Gurnah/lecture/, June 21, 2022.
"Gustav Presents Nobel Prizes to 3" (1936), *New York Times*, December 11, 1936.
Gustavsson, Matilda (2019), *Klubben: en undersökning*, Stockholm: Bonniers.
Gyllensten, Lars (1984), "Bara några få av de förtjänta kommer att få nobelpriset," *Göteborgs-Posten*, 24 juni 1984.
Gyllensten, Lars (2000), *Minnen, bara minnen*, Stockholm: Bonniers.
Hackett, Francis (1944), "Books of the Times," *New York Times*, November 23, 1944.
Hallström, Per (1914), *Levande dikt. Essayer*, Stockholm: Bonniers.
"Hauptmann" (1912), *New York Times*, October 6, 1912.
"Hauptmann's Prize" (1912), *New York Times*, November 16, 1912.
Heaney, Seamus (2022), "Crediting Poetry," https://www.nobelprize.org/prizes/literature/1995/heaney/lecture/, June 21, 2022.
Heilbron, Johan (1999), "Towards a Sociology of Translation: Book Translations as a Cultural World-System," *European Journal of Social Theory*, 2, pp. 429–44.
Helgesson, Stefan, Helena Bodin, and Annika Mörte Alling (2022), *Literature and the Making of the World: Cosmopolitan Texts, Vernacular Practices*, New York och London: Bloomsbury.
Hélys, Marc (1909), "Le Prix Nobel," *Le Figaro*, December 11, 1909.
"Hemingway Is the Winner of Nobel Literature Prize" (1954), *New York Times*, October 29, 1954.
"Hemingway's Quality Built on a Stern Apprenticeship" (1954), *New York Times*, October 29, 1954.
Henley, Jon (2018), "Jean-Claude Arnault, man at centre of Nobel scandal, jailed for rape," the *Guardian*, October 1, 2018.
Hofmeyr, Isabel (2004), *The Portable Bunyan: A Transnational History of The Pilgrim's Progress*, Princeton and Oxford: Princeton University Press.
Hollinger, David A. (2001), "Not Universalists, Not Pluralists: The New Cosmopolitans Find Their Own Way," *Constellations* 8, pp. 236–48.
"Hors Paris" (1904), *Le Figaro*, December 11, 1904.

Howard, Philip (1982), "Nobel prize for García Márquez," *The Times*, October 22, 1982.
Howard, Philip (1984), "Nobel prize for silenced Czech poet," the *Times*, October 12, 1984.
Howarth, Herbert (1967), "A Petition to the Swedish Academy," *Books Abroad* 1, pp. 4–7.
"How to Rewrite a Play" (1934), *New York Times*, December 9, 1934.
Hudey, Katrin (2023), forthcoming book.
Hutchison, Percy (1932), "John Galsworthy in His Most Acidly Ironical Vein," *New York Times*, November 13, 1932.
Hwang, Tsu-Yü (1984), "Det största språkets litteratur utan chans till nobelpriset?," *Göteborgs-Posten*, May 29, 1984.
"Incidents in European Conflict" (1939), *New York Times*, December 13, 1939.
"India's Poet" (1914), *New York Times*, January 25, 1914.
Ishiguro, Kazuo (2022), https://www.nobelprize.org/prizes/literature/2017/ishiguro/lecture/, June 21, 2022.
Iwamoto, Yoshio (1988), "Nobel Prize Symposium II: Choices and Omissions 1967–1987. The Nobel Prize in Literature, 1967–1987: A Japanese View," *World Literature Today* 2, pp. 217–21.
"Ivan Bounine lauréat du Prix Nobel" (1933), *Le Figaro*, November 11, 1933.
Ivask, Ivar (1988), "Nobel Prize Symposium II: Choices and Omissions 1967–1987. Introduction," *World Literature Today* 2, pp. 197–9.
Jacobs, Andrew (2012), "Chinese Nobel Winner Calls for Dissident's Release," *New York Times*, October 12, 2012.
Jacobs, Andrew, and Sarah Lyall (2012), "After Fury over 2010 Peace Prize, China Embraces Nobel Selection," *New York Times*, October 11, 2012.
"Jean-Paul Sartre a-t-il d'avance refusé le Prix Nobel?" (1964), *Le Figaro*, October 21, 1964.
"Jean-Paul Sartre prix Nobel de littérature" (1964), *Le Figaro*, October 23, 1964.
"John Galsworthy in His Most Acidly Ironical Vein" (1932), *New York Times*, November 13, 1932.
Jonsson, Stefan (2013), "Tagore är ett alibi för Nobelprisets eurocentrism," *Dagens Nyheter*, June 1, 2013.
J.P. (1929), "Thomas Mann/Lauréat du Prix Nobel," *Le Figaro*, November 13, 1929.
Kämpchen, Martin (2011), *Rabindranath Tagore und Deutschland*, Marbach am Neckar: Deutsche Schillergesellschaft.
Karaganis, Joe (2020), "About That Nobel Prize ...," blog.opensyllabus.org/about-that-nobel-prize, November 13, 2020.
Kakutani, Michiko (1993), "Lifting the Memory of Slavery into the Realm of Myth," *New York Times*, October 8, 1993.
Kemény, Franz (1901), *Entwurf einer internationalen Gesammt-Academie, Welt-Academie*, Dresden: Pierson 1901.
Kertész, Imre (2022), "Heureka!," https://www.nobelprize.org/prizes/literature/2002/kertesz/lecture/, translated by Ivan Sanders, June 21, 2022.
Khoury-Gatha, Vénus (1988), "Les contes de la rue," *Le Figaro*, October 14, 1988.
"King Gustaf Gives Prizes" (1934), *New York Times*, December 11, 1934.
"King Gustaf Fetes Nobel Prize Men" (1930), *New York Times*, December 12, 1930.
"King Gustaf of Sweden Presenting 1945 Nobel Prizes" (1945), *New York Times*, December 19, 1945.
"Kipling to Get the Prize," *New York Times*, November 26, 1907.
Knud (1902), "Distribution des Priz Nobel à Stockholm," *Le Figaro*, December 11, 1902.

Krajewski, Markus (2014), *World Projects: Global Information before World War I*, translated by Charles Marcrum II, Minneapolis: University of Minnesota Press.
Kreuder, Ernst (1951), "What's Wrong with the Nobel Prize?," *Books Abroad* 2, pp. 115–16.
K.S. (1970), "Alexandre Soljenitsyne à accepté le prix Nobel de littérature," *Le Figaro*, October 9, 1970.
Kullberg, Christina, and David Watson (eds.) (2022), *Vernaculars in an Age of World Literatures*, Bloomsbury: New York 2022.
Kummerle, Josef (1913), "Rabindranath Tagore's Fame," *New York Times*, December 2, 1913.
Lacontre, Robert (1970), "Silence à Moscou," *Le Figaro*, October 9, 1970.
"Lady Churchill To Accept Prize" (1953), *New York Times*, November 13, 1953.
"L'affaire Sartre" (1964), *Le Figaro*, October 22, 1964.
Lagerkvist, Johan (2012), "A Chinese Laureate's Tale of Free Speech," *New York Times*, October 19, 2012.
Lamont, William F. (1951), "The Nobel Prizes in Literature," *Books Abroad* 1, pp. 11–14.
Lanfranchi, Anna (2022), "The Nobel and Back Again: Re-evaluating Mondadori's Translation Strategy for Pearl S. Buck," "Literature in the Nobel Era: Regimes of Value," German Literature Archive, Marbach, August 24–6, 2022.
Lang, Renée (1951), "What's Wrong with the Nobel Prize?," *Books Abroad* 2, pp. 116–17.
La Nouvelle Revue Française (1958), 1958: 6, special issue titled *Hommage à Roger Martin du Gard 1881–958*.
"L'attribution des Prix Nobel" (1933), *Le Figaro*, November 10, 1933.
Le Clec'h, Guy (1988), "Un visionnaire minutieux," *Le Figaro*, October 14, 1988.
Le Clerc Phillips, R. (1924), "Tale-Teller of the Soil and Nobel Prize Winner," *New York Times*, November 30, 1924.
Le Clézio, Jean-Marie Gustave (2022), "In the forest of paradoxes," https://www.nobelprize.org/prizes/literature/2008/clezio/lecture/, translated by Alison Anderson, June 21, 2022.
"L'écrivain le refuse et s'en explique" (1964), *Le Figaro*, October 23, 1964.
"L'écrivain suisse Hermann HESSE Prix Nobel de Littérature" (1946), *Le Figaro*, November 15, 1946.
"L'Egyptien Naguib Mahfouz prix Nobel de littérature" (1988), *Le Figaro*, October 14, 1988.
Lemarchand, Jacques (1957), "Albert Camus," *Le Figaro*, October 18, 1957.
Lenormand, H.-R. (1951), "What's Wrong with the Nobel Prize?," *Books Abroad* 2, p. 117.
"Le prix Nobel" (1916), *Le Figaro*, November 10, 1916.
"Le prix Nobel de Littérature" (1922), *Le Figaro*, November 11, 1922.
"Le Prix Nobel de Littérature" (1932), *Le Figaro*, November 11, 1932.
"Le Prix Nobel de Littérature" (1936), *Le Figaro*, November 13, 1936.
"Le prix Nobel de Littérature" (1952), *Le Figaro*, November 7, 1952.
"Le prix Nobel de littérature à été décerné à Sir Winston Churchill" (1953), *Le Figaro*, October 16, 1953.
"Le prix Nobel de littérature à Sir Winston Churchill" (1953), *Le Figaro*, October 16, 1953.
"Le Prix Nobel de Littérature à la poétesse chilienne Gabriela Mistral" (1945), *Le Figaro*, November 17, 1945.
"LE PRIX NOBEL DE LITTÉRATURE attribué à François Mauriac" (1952), *Le Figaro*, November 7, 1952.
"Le Prix Nobel de Littérature est décerné à l'écrivain américain O'Neill" (1936), *Le Figaro*, November 11, 1936.

"Le Prix Nobel de Littérature est décerné à l'écrivain américain Mme Pearl Buck" (1938), *Le Figaro*, November 13, 1938.
"Le Prix Nobel de Littérature est décerné à Luigi Pirandello" (1934), *Le Figaro*, November 9, 1934.
"Le Prix Nobel de Littérature Est Décerné À M. Roger Martin du Gard" (1937), *Le Figaro*, November 12, 1937.
"Le prix Nobel de Littérature est décerné à un Polonais" (1924), *Le Figaro*, November 14, 1924.
"Le romancier américan FAULKNER et le philosophe anglaise RUSSELL reçoivent le prix Nobel de littérature" (1950), *Le Figaro*, November 11, 1950.
"Les lauréats du Prix Nobel" (1901), *Le Figaro*, December 11, 1901.
"Les premiers commentaires" (1970), *Le Figaro*, October 9, 1970.
"Les prix Nobel" (1905), *Le Figaro*, December 11, 1905.
"Les prix Nobel" (1906), *Le Figaro*, December 11, 1906.
"Les prix Nobel" (1910), *Le Figaro*, December 11, 1910.
"Les prix Nobel" (1911), *Le Figaro*, December 11, 1911.
"Les Prix Nobel" (1913), *Le Figaro*, December 11, 1913.
"Les Prix Nobel" (1920), *Le Figaro*, November 13, 1920.
"Les prix Nobel" (1927a), *Le Figaro*, November 11, 1927.
"Les prix Nobel" (1927b), *Le Figaro*, December 11, 1927.
"LES PRIX NOBEL 1947" (1947), *Le Figaro*, December 11, 1947.
"Les prix Nobel 1949" (1949), *Le Figaro*, November 4, 1949.
Lessing, Doris (2022), "On not winning the Nobel Prize," https://www.nobelprize.org/prizes/literature/2007/lessing/lecture/, June 21, 2022.
letters to the editor (1902), the *Times*, January 7 and 11, 1902.
Leudet, Maurice (1913), "Rabindranath Tagore/PRIX NOBEL," *Le Figaro*, November 14, 1913.
"Lewis Finds Irony in 'Serious' America" (1930), *New York Times*, November 26, 1930.
"Lewis Holds Books Do Not Prevent Wars" (1930), *New York Times*, December 30, 1930.
"Lewis Indifferent to Coolidge Criticism" (1930), *New York Times*, December 21, 1930.
"Lewis Is Lionized By All Stockholm" (1930), *New York Times*, December 14, 1930.
"Lewis Takes Swedish Curse for Nobel Prize Acceptance" (1930), *New York Times*, November 20, 1930.
Lewis, Sinclair (2022), "The American Fear of Literature," https://www.nobelprize.org/prizes/literature/1930/lewis/lecture/, June 21, 2022.
"Lewis Would Exile All Our Reformers" (1930), *New York Times*, December 23, 1930.
"Le vote de l'Académie Suédoise" (1937), *Le Figaro*, November 12, 1937.
Leypoldt, Günther (2022), "Civil Sacred: The Nobel and the Laureate Position in Cultural Space," *Poetics*, forthcoming autumn 2022.
Leyris, Raphaëlle (2022), "Annie Ernaux, une Nobel don't le 'je' dit l'expérience commune," *Le Monde*, October 8, 2022.
"L'homme et son œuvre" (1964), *Le Figaro*, October 23, 1964.
Lindfors, Bernth (1988), "Nobel Prize Symposium II: Choices and Omissions 1967–1987. Africa and the Nobel Prize," *World Literature Today* 2, pp. 222–4.
Lindsten Öberg, Kajsa, and Johan Öberg (2022), "Svetlana Aleksijevitj: 'Den ryska fascismen hotar hela världen,'" *Dagens Nyheter*, April 2, 2022.
Lindqvist, Yvonne (2019), "Translation Bibliomigration: The Case of French Caribbean Literature in Sweden," *Meta: International Journal for Translation Studies*, 3, pp. 90–104.

"Literature Award" (1962), *New York Times*, October 26, 1962.
"Lost in Leaking Dory, Pursued by Big Shark" (1926), *New York Times*, November 13, 1926.
Lovell, Julia (2006), *The Politics of Cultural Capital: China's Quest for a Nobel Prize in Literature*, Honolulu: University of Hawaii Press.
Lovell, Julia (2012), "Mo Yan's Creative Space," *New York Times*, October 15, 2012.
"Luigi Pirandello Wins Nobel Prize" (1934), *New York Times*, November 9, 1934.
"Lukacs solo" (1970), the *Times*, November 16, 1970.
Lundegård, Axel (1901), "Ideell värnplikt," *Svenska Dagbladet*, May 24, 1901.
Lundkvist, Artur (1979), "Nobelprisets vedersakare," *Svenska Dagbladet*, December 20, 1979.
Lyall, Sarah (1994), "Book Notes," *New York Times*, October 19, 1994.
Määttä, Jerry (2010), "Pengar, prestige, publicitet. Litterära priser och utmärkelser i Sverige 1786–2009," *Samlaren*, pp. 232–329.
"Maeterlinck Founds Prize" (1912), *New York Times*, January 12, 1912.
Mahfouz, Naguib (2022), https://www.nobelprize.org/prizes/literature/1988/mahfouz/lecture/, translated by Mohammed Salmawy, June 21, 2022.
Maia, R.B., M.P. Pinto, and S.R. Pinti (2015), "Introduction: Portugal and Translation Between Centre and Periphery," in *How Peripheral Is the Periphery? Translating Portugal Back and Forth*, ed. by R.B. Maia, M.P. Pinto, and S.R. Pinti, Newcastle-upon-Tyne: Cambridge Scholar Publishing.
"M. Anatole France's Nobel Prize" (1921), the *Times*, December 9, 1921.
"M. André Gide Awarded Literature Prize" (1947), the *Times*, November 14, 1947.
Mani, B. Venkat (2011), "Bibliomigrancy: Book series and the making of world literature," in *The Routledge Companion to World Literature*, ed. by Theo D'haen, David Damrosch and Djelal Kadir, London and New York: Routledge.
Mani, B. Venkat (2017), *Recoding World Literature: Libraries, Print Culture, and Germany's Pact with Books*, New York: Fordham University Press.
"Mann Deeply Moved on Hearing of Award" (1929), *New York Times*, November 13, 1929.
"Many Congratulation" (1953), the *Times*, October 17, 1953.
Marcus, Greil (2016), "Bob Dylan, Master of Change," *New York Times*, October 13, 2016.
Marcuse, Ludwig (1951), "What's Wrong with the Nobel Prize?," *Books Abroad* 2, pp. 117–18.
Márquez, Gabriel García (2022), "The Solitude of Latin America," https://www.nobelprize.org/prizes/literature/1982/marquez/lecture/, June 21, 2022.
Marx, Karl, and Friedrich Engels (2013), from *The Communist Manifesto*, *World Literature: A Reader*, ed. by Theo D'haen, César Domínguez and Mads Rosendahl Thomsen, translated by Theo D'haen, London and New York: Routledge.
"Master of English Prose" (1953), the *Times*, October 29, 1953.
Maulnier, Thierry (1964), "Médaille d'or quand meme," *Le Figaro*, October 23, 1964.
Mauriac, François (1952a), "Le Revenant," *Le Figaro*, October 13, 1952.
Mauriac, François (1952b), "Les Deux bouts de la chaine," *Le Figaro*, October 21, 1952.
Mauriac, François (1952c), "L'homme adore," *Le Figaro*, October 28, 1952.
Mauriac, François (1959), "Les 'prix Nobel' français," *Le Figaro littéraire*, October 10, 1959.
McDonald, Mark (2012), "'Garlands and Mud' for New Nobel Laureate from China," *New York Times*, December 9, 2012.
Milosz, Czeslaw (2022), https://www.nobelprize.org/prizes/literature/1980/milosz/lecture/, June 20, 2022.
"Mistral and the Nobel Prize" (1905), *New York Times*, January 15, 1905.

Mizener, Arthur (1962a), "Does a Moral Vision of the Thirties Deserve a Nobel Prize?," *New York Times*, December 9, 1962.
Mizener, Arthur (1962b), "Evaluating an Author's Vision of the Thirties," *New York Times*, December 10, 1962.
"Mme. Sigrid Undset Wins Nobel Prize" (1928), *New York Times*, November 14, 1928.
Modiano, Patrick (2022), https://www.nobelprize.org/prizes/literature/2014/modiano/lecture/, translated by James Hardiker, June 21, 2022.
Montale, Eugenio (2022), "Is Poetry Still Possible?," https://www.nobelprize.org/prizes/literature/1975/montale/lecture/, June 20, 2022.
Morand, Paul (1936), "Eugene O'Neill," *Le Figaro*, November 14, 1936.
Moretti, Franco (2013), *Distant Reading*, Verso: London and New York.
Morgan, Charles (1926), "Molière and Shaw," *New York Times*, December 5, 1926.
Morrison, Toni (2022), https://www.nobelprize.org/prizes/literature/1993/morrison/lecture/, June 21, 2022.
Mossu, René (1947), "A Neuchâtel, André GIDE parle de son Prix Nobel," *Le Figaro*, November 16, 1947.
"Mr. Hemingway's Nobel Award" (1954), the *Times*, October 29, 1954.
"Mr. Hemingway's Prize" (1954), *New York Times*, October 29, 1954.
"Mr. Lewis At Stockholm" (1930), *New York Times*, December 15, 1930.
"Mr. Lewis Mentions the Drama" (1930), *New York Times*, December 21, 1930.
"Mr. Lewis' Nobel Prize" (1930), *New York Times*, November 6, 1930.
"Mr. Shaw and the Nobel Prize" (1926), the *Times*, November 19, 1926.
"Mr. W.B. Yeats. Award of Nobel Prize" (1923), the *Times*, November 15, 1923.
"Mrs. Buck Guest at King's Dinner" (1938), *New York Times*, December 12, 1938.
"M. Sinclair Lewis lauréat du Priz Nobel" (1930), *Le Figaro*, November 6, 1930.
Muir, Edwin (1948), "An Interview with T.S. Eliot," *New York Times Book Review*, November 21, 1948.
Müller, Herta (2022), "Every Word Knows Something of a Vicious Circle," https://www.nobelprize.org/prizes/literature/2009/muller/lecture/, translated by Philip Boehm, June 21, 2022.
Munro, Alice (2022), https://www.nobelprize.org/prizes/literature/2013/munro/lecture/, June 21, 2022.
Naipaul, V.S. (2022), "Two Worlds," https://www.nobelprize.org/prizes/literature/2001/naipaul/lecture/, June 21, 2022.
Najder, Zdzislaw (2007), *Joseph Conrad: A Life*, London: Camden House.
Nathan, George Jean (1951), "What's Wrong with the Nobel Prize?," *Books Abroad* 2, pp. 118–19.
Nazaroff, Alexander (1933), "Ivan Bunin, Nobel Prize Winner," *New York Times Book Review*, November 26, 1933.
Neruda, Pablo (2022), "Towards the Splendid City," https://www.nobelprize.org/prizes/literature/1971/neruda/lecture/, June 20, 2022.
Neuberger, Richard L. (1936), "O'Neill Turns West to New Horizons," *New York Times*, November 22, 1936.
Neuhoff, Éric (2016), "Sois Nobel et tais-toi!," *Le Figaro*, October 14, 2016.
Neuman, Ricki (2012), "Graham Greene var nära Nobelpris 1961, *Svenska Dagbladet*, January 3.
Neumeyer, Alfred (1951), "What's Wrong with the Nobel Prize?," *Books Abroad* 2, p. 119.

"Newman Praises Lewis As Crusader" (1930), *New York Times*, November 17, 1930.
"New Yorker Shares Nobel Prize for Proof of Wave-Particle Today" (1937), *New York Times*, November 12, 1937.
"Nobel" (1988), *Le Figaro*, October 14, 1988.
"Nobel Anniversary Celebrated Here" (1943), *New York Times*, December 11, 1943.
"Nobel Awards. Literature Prize for Chilean Authoress" (1945), the *Times*, November 16, 1945.
"Nobel Board Studies Literature Nominees" (1944), *New York Times*, November 9, 1944.
"Nobel ceremony attack on Solzhenitsyn" (1970), the *Times*, December 11, 1970.
"Nobel judge attacks 'ignorant' US literature" (2008), the *Guardian*, October 1, 2008.
"Nobel Literature Prize. Honour for Finnish Author" (1939), the *Times*, November 11, 1939.
"Nobelova Cena J. Seifertovi" (1984), *Rudé právo*, October 12, 1984.
"Nobel Prize" (1905), the *Times*, November 16, 1905.
"Nobel Prize Awarded to Anatole France" (1921), *New York Times*, November 11, 1921.
"Nobel Prize Awarded to Dead Swedish Poet" (1931), *New York Times*, October 9, 1931.
"Nobel Prize Awarded to M. Maeterlinck" (1911), the *Times*, November 10, 1911.
"Nobel Prize Awarded to O'Neill" (1936), *New York Times*, November 13, 1936.
"Nobel Prize Awarded To William B. Yeats" (1923), *New York Times*, November 15, 1923.
"Nobel Prize Awards" (1908), *New York Times*, December 10, 1908.
"Nobel Prize Awards" (1928), the *Times*, November 14, 1928.
"Nobel Prize Awards" (1929), the *Times*, November 13, 1929.
"Nobel Prize Awards Announced in Oslo" (1931), *New York Times*, December 11, 1931.
"Nobel Prize Award to Lewis Is an 'Insult' to America, Says Van Dyke, Hitting Scoffers" (1930), *New York Times*, November 29, 1930.
"Nobel Prize Checks to be Paid Today" (1930), *New York Times*, December 10, 1930.
"Nobel Prize for Carducci" (1906), *New York Times*, November 25, 1906.
"Nobel Prize for Einstein" (1922), *New York Times*, November 10, 1922.
"Nobel Prize for Guatemalan" (1967), the *Times*, October 20, 1967.
"Nobel Prize for Hardy" (1913), *New York Times*, December 18, 1913.
"Nobel Prize for Heyse" (1910), *New York Times*, November 15, 1910.
"Nobel Prize for Icelander" (1955), the *Times*, October 28, 1955.
"Nobel Prize for Kipling" (1907), *New York Times*, November 25, 1907.
"Nobel Prize for Literature" (1932), the *Times*, November 11, 1932.
"Nobel Prize for Literature" (1953), the *Times*, October 14, 1953.
"Nobel Prize for Literature" (1956), the *Times*, October 26, 1956.
"Nobel Prize for Mr. Pasternak" (1958), the *Times*, October 24, 1958.
"Nobel Prize Given to a Hindu Poet" (1913), *New York Times*, November 14, 1913.
"Nobel Prize Given to Finnish Writer" (1939), *New York Times*, November 11, 1939.
"Nobel Prize Goes to Bunin, Russian" (1933), *New York Times*, November 10, 1933.
"Nobel Prize Goes to Sinclair Lewis" (1930), *New York Times*, November 6, 1930.
"Nobel Prize in Literature Awarded" (2016), *New York Times*, October 13, 2016.
Nobel Prize Library: Yasunari Kawabata, Rudyard Kipling, Sinclair Lewis (1971), Gregory and CRM, New York 1971.
"Nobel Prize Presented" (1948), *New York Times*, December 11, 1948.
"Nobel Prize Rule Revised" (1949), *New York Times*, November 12, 1949.
"Nobel Prizes" (1936), the *Times*, November 13, 1936.
"Nobel Prizes" (1937), the *Times*, November 12, 1937.

"Nobel Prizes" (1948), the *Times*, November 5, 1948.
"Nobel Prizes Awarded" (1903), *New York Times*, December 11, 1903.
"Nobel Prizes. Award for Literature to Pearl Buck" (1938), the *Times*, November 11, 1938.
"Nobel Prizes Distributed" (1905), *New York Times*, December 11, 1905.
"Nobel Prizes Distributed" (1912), *New York Times*, December 11, 1912.
"Nobel Prizes for Literature" (1950), the *Times*, November 11, 1950.
"Nobel Prizes for Only Few" (1902), *New York Times*, March 14, 1902.
"Nobel Prizes Reported Suspended" (1940), *New York Times*, October 12, 1940.
"Nobel Prizes Suspended" (1943), *New York Times*, October 23, 1943.
"Nobel Prize Surprise" (1920), the *Times*, November 13, 1920.
"Nobel Prizes Withheld" (1925), *New York Times*, November 18, 1925.
"Nobel Prize to Hauptmann" (1912), *New York Times*, November 16, 1912.
"Nobel Prize to Maeterlinck" (1911), *New York Times*, October 15, 1911.
"Nobel Prize To M. France" (1912), *New York Times*, November 3, 1912.
"Nobel Prize Rule Revised" (1949), *New York Times*, November 12, 1949.
"Nobel Prize Winner" (1938), *New York Times*, November 11, 1938.
"Nobel Prize Winner Beloved By Swiss" (1920), *New York Times*, November 14, 1920.
"Nobel Prize Winner Sails for Germany" (1930), *New York Times*, November 25, 1930.
"Nobel Prize Winners Receive Awards" (1911), *New York Times*, December 11, 1911.
"Nobel Science Prize Won by Dr. Langmur" (1932), *New York Times*, November 11, 1932.
"Nobel Winner to Los Angeles" (1945), *New York Times*, December 18, 1945.
"No Nobel Prizes For 1918 and 1919" (1919), *New York Times*, December 11, 1919.
"No Nobel Prize This Year" (1915), *New York Times*, December 11, 1915.
"No Nobel Prize This Year" (1942), *New York Times*, October 17, 1942.
"Nomination Archive" (2022), www.nobelprize.org/nomination/archive/list.php?prize=4&year, read in September 2022.
Nuc, Olivier (2016), "Bob Dylan, rockeur littéraire," *Le Figaro*, October 14, 2016.
Nuridsany, Michel (1985), "Sous le regard de Claude Simon," *Le Figaro*, October 18, 1985.
Nykvist, Karin (2022), "Jakten på en okänd pristagare," *Sydsvenskan*, October 9, 2022.
"O'Brien To Discuss André Gide" (1947), *New York Times*, November 17, 1947.
Oe, Kenzaburo (2022), "Japan, the Ambiguous, and Myself," https://www.nobelprize.org/prizes/literature/1994/oe/lecture/, June 21, 2022.
Ogliastro, Jacques M.J. (1953), "La carrière littéraire du nouveau laureate," *Le Figaro*, October 16, 1953.
Olsson, Anders (2022), "Reading for Nobel and the Idea of the Universal," paper given at "(World) Literature and the Problem of the Universal: Philosophical and Philological Approaches," Nobel Symposium 14, Stockholm, August 17–9, 2022.
Orsini, Francesca (2021), "World Literature and Minorisation," keynote address at "World Literature and the Minor: Figuration, Circulation, Translation," KU Leuven, May 5–7, 2021.
Osipova, Natalia V., and Jon Pareles (2016), "Bob Dylan and His Poetic Gift," *New York Times*, October 13, 2016.
Österling, Anders (1950), "Litteraturpriset," in *Nobelprisen 50 år. Forskare, diktare, fredskämpar*, ed. by Henrik Schück, Stockholm: Sohlmans 1950.
Österling, Anders (1967), *Minnets vägar*, Stockholm: Bonniers 1967.
"Our Books Enjoy New Vogue Abroad" (1932), *New York Times*, December 20, 1932.
Ovize, "Le Testament de M. Nobel," *Le Figaro*, January 7, 1897.

Pamuk, Orhan (2022), "My Father's Suitcase," https://www.nobelprize.org/prizes/literature/2006/pamuk/lecture/, translated by Maureen Freely, June 21, 2022.
"Pasternak Cited at Nobel Session" (1958), *New York Times*, December 11, 1958.
"Pasternak exclu de l'Union des écrivains soviétiques" (1958), *Le Figaro*, October 29, 1958.
"Pasternak Lies in a Lonely Grave" (1965), *New York Times*, October 18, 1965.
Paz, Octavio (2022), "In Search of the Present," https://www.nobelprize.org/prizes/literature/1990/paz/lecture/, translated by Anthony Stanton, June 21, 2022.
"Pearl Buck Proud of Her 'Backing Exit'" (1938), *New York Times*, December 24, 1938.
"Pearl Buck Wins Nobel Literature Prize" (1938), *New York Times*, November 11, 1938.
PEN America (2019), "Statement: Deep Regret over the Choice of Peter Handke for the 2019 Nobel Prize in Literature," https://pen.org/press-release/statement-nobel-prize-for-literature-2019/, October 10, 2019.
Perruchot, Henri (1951), "What's Wrong with the Nobel Prize?," *Books Abroad* 2, pp. 119–20.
Peyre, Henri (1951), "What's Wrong with the Nobel Prize?," *Books Abroad* 3, pp. 213–14.
photo gallery (1932), the *Times*, November 11, 1932.
photograph (1934), the *Times*, November 9, 1934.
photograph (1939), *New York Times*, November 26, 1939.
photographs (1947), the *Times*, November 14, 1947.
Pinter, Harold (2022), "Art, Truth & Politics," https://www.nobelprize.org/prizes/literature/2005/pinter/lecture/, June 21, 2022.
"Pirandello Play Opens" (1934), *New York Times*, December 20, 1934.
"Pirandello Play Welcomed in Dublin" (1934), *New York Times*, December 5, 1934.
"Pirandello to Visit U.S." (1934), *New York Times*, December 19, 1934.
"Poetry in Prose: A Morrison Sampler" (1993), *New York Times*, October 8, 1993.
"Poet's Ethological Museum. Frederic Mistral Will Devote Nobel Prize Money to His Project" (1904), *New York Times*, December 31, 1904.
"Poland's Nobel Prize" (1924), *New York Times*, November 16, 1924.
Poore, Charles (1950), "Books of the Times," *New York Times*, November 16, 1950.
"Posthumous Award of Nobel Prize" (1931), the *Times*, October 9, 1931.
"Potter Assails Van Dyke" (1930), *New York Times*, December 1, 1930.
Prasteau, Jean (1952), "François Mauriac prix Nobel de littérature," *Le Figaro*, November 7, 1952.
Prasteau, Jean (1957), "Le lauréat à l'ambassadeur de Suède," *Le Figaro*, October 18, 1957.
Pratt, William (1988), "Nobel Prize Symposium II: Choices and Omissions 1967–1987. Missing the Masters: Nobel Literary Prizes in English, 1967–1987," *World Literature Today* 2, pp. 225–8.
"Presentation of Nobel Prizes" (1923), the *Times*, December 11, 1923.
"Prix Nobel" (1921), *Le Figaro*, December 12, 1921.
"Prix Nobel de littérature" (1958), *Le Figaro*, October 24, 1958.
"Prix Nobel de littérature à Boris Pasternak" (1958), *Le Figaro*, October 23, 1958.
"Prize Acclaimed in Moscow" (1965), *New York Times*, October 16, 1965.
"Prizes are Given to Nobel Winners" (1947), *New York Times*, December 11, 1947.
"Prizes for 'Service to Humanity'" (1953), the *Times*, June 13, 1953.
"Prof. Mommsen Writes on German Political Aspect" (1903), *New York Times*, January 14, 1903.
"Protest Withholding of All Nobel Prizes" (1925), *New York Times*, November 19, 1925.

Quasimodo, Salvatore (2022), "The Poet and the Politician," https://www.nobelprize.org/prizes/literature/1959/quasimodo/lecture/, June 20, 2022.
"Quatre livres traduits en français" (1970), *Le Figaro*, October 9, 1970.
Quinn, Susan (1995), *Madame Curie: A Life*, New York: Simon and Schuster.
Raffel, Burton (1967), "Indonesia and the Nobel Prize," *Books Abroad* 1, pp. 42–3.
Ragusa, Olga (1967), "Carducci; Deledda; Pirandello; Quasimodo," *Books Abroad* 1, pp. 28–30.
Raine, Kathleen (1948), untitled article, *New York Times Book Review*, November 21, 1948.
Ramras-Rauch, Gila (1988), "Nobel Prize Symposium II: Choices and Omissions 1967–1987. The Nobel Prize: The Jewish/Hebraic Aspect," *World Literature Today* 2, pp. 228–31.
Ramsaran, John (1967), "African Potential," *Books Abroad* 1, pp. 39–40.
Ratcliffe, Michael (1970), "World Reputation: The Progress of Borges and the Beasts," the *Times*, December 24, 1970.
Recouly, Raymond (1928), "Honors Come to Bergson, Philosopher," *New York Times*, December 16, 1928.
"Reinhardt Praises American Theater" (1936), *New York Times*, December 14, 1936.
Reis, Roberto (1988), "Nobel Prize Symposium II: Choices and Omissions 1967–1987. Who's Afraid of (Luso-)Brazilian Literature?," *World Literature Today* 2, pp. 231–4.
Rendirome, Renzo (1927), *New York Times*, December 18, 1927.
Reuter, Gabriele (1929), "Thomas Mann as Revealed in His Work," *New York Times*, December 22, 1929.
Rexine, John E. (1967), "Seferis," *Books Abroad* 1, pp. 37–8.
Richter, Max (2023), "What Is a 'World Academy'? On One of the Nobel Prize Committees First Rejections," forthcoming 2023.
Río, Angel del (1951), "What's Wrong with the Nobel Prize?," *Books Abroad* 3, p. 214.
Robbins, Bruce, and Paolo Lemos Horta (2017), "Introduction," in *Cosmopolitanisms*, ed. by Bruce Robbins and Paolo Lemos Horta, New York: New York University Press.
Roditi, Édouard (1951), "What's Wrong with the Nobel Prize?," *Books Abroad* 3, pp. 214–15.
Rosch, Jonna (2023), "Så påverkade nazismen Nobelpriset och synen på tysk litteratur," Göteborgs universitet, https://www.expertsvar.se/pressmeddelanden/sa-paverkade-nazismen-nobelpriset-och-synen-pa-tysk-litteratur/, February 10, 2023.
Rosendahl Thomsen, Mads (2022), "Distant Reading the Nobel," paper given at "Literature in the Nobel Era: Regimes of Value," German Literature Archive, Marbach, August 24–6, 2022.
"Rostropovich Is Silent on Letter" (1970), the *Times*, November 14, 1970.
Rousseaux, André (1937), "Le prix Nobel de littérature a été décerné à M. Roger Marrtin du Gard," *Le Figaro*, November 12, 1937.
Ruger, F. White (1914), "Zangwill and Tagore," *New York Times*, January 4, 1914.
Rule, Sheila (1992), "Walcott, Poet of Caribbean, Is Awarded the Nobel Prize," *New York Times*, October 9, 1992.
Russell, Bertrand (2022), "What Desires Are Politically Important?," https://www.nobelprize.org/prizes/literature/1950/russell/lecture/, June 20, 2022.
"Russell Envisions a World at Peace" (1950), *New York Times*, November 17, 1950.
"Russian Author Given Nobel Prize" (1965), the *Times*, October 16, 1965.
"Russian Rush" (1970), the *Times*, October 15, 1970.
Rydén, Per (2010), *Den framgångsrike förloraren. En värderingsbiografi över Carl David af Wirsén*, Stockholm: Carlssons.

Rydén, Per, and Jenny Westerström (2018), *Svenska Akademiens modernisering 1913-1977*, Stockholm: Carlssons.
Salinger, Herman (1951), "What's Wrong with the Nobel Prize?," *Books Abroad* 3, pp. 215–16.
"Samuel Beckett Goes into Hiding" (1969), the *Times*, October 25, 1969.
"Samuel Beckett Wins Nobel Prize" (1969), the *Times*, October 24, 1969.
Santana-Acuña, Álvaro (2022), "García Márquez and the Nobel Prize: Genealogy of a Professional Obsession," paper given at "Literature in the Nobel Era: Regimes of Value," German Literature Archive, Marbach, August 24–6, 2022.
Saramago, José (2022), "How Characters Became the Masters and the Author Their Apprentice," https://www.nobelprize.org/prizes/literature/1998/saramago/lecture/, translated by Tim Crosfield and Fernando Rodrigues, June 21, 2022.
"Sartre tackar nej till Nobelpriset" (1964), *Dagens Nyheter*, October 20, 1964.
Schoolfield, George C. (1988), "Nobel Prize Symposium II: Choices and Omissions 1967–1987. Might-Have-Beens: The North and the Nobel Prize, 1967–1987," *World Literature Today* 2, pp. 235–9.
Schück, Henrik (1939), *Svenska Akademiens historia 7. Interregnum: de sista femtio åren*, Stockholm: Norstedts.
Schueler, Kaj (2018), "Hemliga dokument visar kampen om Nobelpriset," *Svenska Dagbladet*, January 2, 2018.
Schwartz, Cecilia (2017), "Semi-peripheral Dynamics: Inclusion Modalities of Italian Literature in Sweden," *Journal of World Literature* 2, pp. 488–511.
"Scooped" (1970), the *Times*, December 9, 1970.
Seferis, Giorgos (2022), "Some Notes on Modern Greek Tradition," https://www.nobelprize.org/prizes/literature/1963/seferis/lecture/, June 20, 2022.
Seidlin, Oskar (1951), "What's Wrong with the Nobel Prize?," *Books Abroad* 3, pp. 216–17.
Seifert, Jaroslav (2022), "On the Pathetic and Lyrical State of Mind," https://www.nobelprize.org/prizes/literature/1984/seifert/lecture/, June 21, 2022.
"Selma Lagerloef Is 70" (1928), *New York Times*, November 21, 1928.
"Selma Lagerlöf och vår fest" (1909), *Dagny* 1909: 48, pp. 575–6.
"Sharp Tongue of Mr. Sholokhov" (1965), the *Times*, December 1, 1965.
"Shaw Agrees with Lewis about Us" (1930), *New York Times*, December 19, 1930.
"Shaw Prize Ruling to Be Made Today" (1926), *New York Times*, November 20, 1926.
"Shaw's Refusal of Prize Money May Be 'Transient', He Says" (1926), *New York Times*, November 25, 1926.
"Shaw Takes Honor, but Not Nobel Cash" (1926), *New York Times*, November 19, 1926.
"Shaw Wants Subject Thrashed Out" (1926), *New York Times*, November 20, 1926.
"Shaw Will 'Hold' Nobel Prize Money" (1926), *New York Times*, November 21, 1926.
Shih, Shu-mei (2015), "World Studies and Relational Comparison," *PMLA* 2, pp. 430–8.
"Sholokhov Accepts Prize 'Gratefully'" (1965), *New York Times*, October 17, 1965.
"Sholokhov 'Happy' for Soviet" (1965), *New York Times*, October 22, 1965.
"Sidelights of the Week" (1936), *New York Times*, December 13, 1936.
Siems, Larry, and Jeffrey Yang (2012), "China's Nobels," *New York Times*, October 17, 2012.
"Sienkiewicz Fears Kaiser. Says Poles Are Strong Enough to Fight Russia, but Not Germany" (1905), *New York Times*, December 11, 1905.
Silberschlag, Eisig (1967), "Four Hebrew Writers," *Books Abroad* 1, pp. 38–9.
Simon, Claude (2022), https://www.nobelprize.org/prizes/literature/1985/simon/lecture/, June 21, 2022.

Simon, Sacha (1970), "Fragile et indomptable," *Le Figaro*, October 9, 1970.
"Sinclair Lewis Hits Old School Writers, Champions the New" (1930), *New York Times*, December 13, 1930.
"Sinclair Lewis in Films" (1930), *New York Times*, November 10, 1930.
"Sinclair Lewis Off for Sweden Today" (1930), *New York Times*, November 29, 1930.
"Sinclair Lewis Off, Hits Back at Critic" (1930), *New York Times*, November 30, 1930.
Singer, Isaac Bashevis (2022), https://www.nobelprize.org/prizes/literature/1978/singer/lecture/, June 20, 2022.
"Sir Winston Churchill grand favori du prix Nobel de littérature" (1953), *Le Figaro*, October 14, 1953.
Sisario, Ben, Alexandra Alter, and Sewell Chan (2016), "Bob Dylan Wins Nobel Prize, Redefining Boundaries of Literature," *New York Times*, October 13, 2016.
"Six Americans Win Nobel Prizes" (1946), *New York Times*, November 15, 1946.
Sjoestedt, Erick (1901), "Les instituts Nobel," *Le Figaro*, December 11, 1901.
Slochower, Harry (1951), "What's Wrong with the Nobel Prize?," *Books Abroad* 3, pp. 217–18.
Smejkalová, Jirina (2022), "Manufacturing Values behind the Iron Curtain: Czech Publishers and Their Jaroslav Seifert," "Literature in the Nobel Era: Regimes of Value," German Literature Archive, Marbach, August 24–6, 2022.
Snow, Charles Percy (2001), *The Two Cultures*, London: Cambridge University Press.
"Soljenitsyne a accepté le prix Nobel de littérature" (1970), *Le Figaro*, October 9, 1970.
"Soljenitsyne renouvelle son intention de se rendre à Stockholm" (1970), *Le Figaro*, October 12, 1970.
Solzhenitsyn, Aleksandr (2022), https://www.nobelprize.org/prizes/literature/1970/solzhenitsyn/lecture/, June 20, 2022.
"Solzhenitsyn Has No Passport" (1970), the *Times*, November 27, 1970.
"Solzhenitsyn Is Not Going to Stockholm" (1970), the *Times*, November 28, 1970.
"Solzhenitsyn will go to Stockholm" (1970), the *Times*, October 12, 1970.
Sorel, Albert-Émile (1901), untitled article, *Le Figaro*, December 10, 1901.
Soyinka, Wole (2022), "The Past Must Address Its Present," https://www.nobelprize.org/prizes/literature/1986/soyinka/lecture/, June 21, 2022.
Spiller, Robert E. (1967), "English, Anglo-Irish, and American Literature," *Books Abroad* 1, pp. 30–6.
Spitzer, Gretel (1972), "Authors Tell Berliners Why They Back the SPD," the *Times*, November 14, 1972.
"Steinbeck Candidate for Nobel Award" (1945), *New York Times*, November 8, 1945.
"Steinbeck Named Winner of 1962 Nobel Prize for Literature" (1962), *New York Times*, October 26, 1962.
Steiner, George (1984), "The Scandal of the Nobel Prize," *New York Times*, September 30, 1984.
Stevic, Aleksandar, and Philip Tsang (eds.) (2019), *The Limits of Cosmopolitanism: Globalization and Its Discontents in Contemporary Literature*, New York and London: Routledge 2019.
"Stockholm Ceremony" (1927), the *Times*, December 12, 1927.
Strich, Fritz (2013), "World Literature and Comparative Literary History," in *World Literature: A Reader*, ed. by Theo D'haen, César Domínguez and Mads Rosendahl Thomsen, translated by Theo D'haen, London and New York: Routledge.

Stromberg, Kjell (1951), "PAER LAGERKVIST," *Le Figaro*, November 16, 1951.
Stromberg, Kjell (1964), "Articles élogieux," *Le Figaro*, October 23, 1964.
Suttner, Bertha von, "Alfred Nobel," *Neue Freie Presse*, January 12, 1897.
Svegfors, Mats (2010), *Hjalmar Hammarskjöld, Sveriges statsministrar under 100 år*, ed. by Mats Bergstrand and Per T. Ohlsson, Stockholm: Bonniers 2010.
"Swedish Academy's Tribute" (1953), the *Times*, October 16, 1953.
"Swedish King Gives Mrs. Buck Nobel Prize" (1938), *New York Times*, December 11, 1938.
"Swedish Tribute to Mr. Tagore" (1913), the *Times*, November 14, 1913.
Svensén, Bo (ed.) (2001a), *Nobelpriset i litteratur. Nomineringar och utlåtanden 1901–1950. Del I: 1901–1920*, Stockholm: Svenska Akademien.
Svensén, Bo (ed.) (2001b), *Nobelpriset i litteratur. Nomineringar och utlåtanden 1901–1950. Del II: 1921–1950*, Stockholm: Svenska Akademien.
Szymborska, Wislawa (2022), "The poet and the world," https://www.nobelprize.org/prizes/literature/1996/szymborska/lecture/, translated by Stanislaw Baranczak and Clare Cavanagh, June 21, 2022.
"Tagore" (1913), *New York Times*, November 30, 1913.
Tatlow, Didi Kirsten (2012a), "The Writer, the State and the Nobel," *New York Times*, October 12, 2012.
Tatlow, Didi Kirsten (2012b), "In 3 Awards, 3 Ways of Seeing China," *New York Times*, October 17, 2012.
telegram (1933), the *Times*, December 12, 1933.
Tenngart, Paul (2016), "Local Labour, Cosmopolitan Toil: Geo-Cultural Dynamics in Swedish Working-Class Fiction," *Journal of World Literature* 1, pp. 484–502.
Tenngart, Paul (2020), "The Dislocated Vernacular in Translated Swedish Working-Class Fiction," *Interventions: International Journal of Postcolonial Studies* 3, pp. 382–99.
"Text of Sinclair Lewis's Nobel Prize Address at Stockholm" (1930), *New York Times*, December 13, 1930.
"The Critics View of the American Theatre" (1934), *New York Times*, December 2, 1934.
"The Essence of Toni Morrison" (1993), *New York Times*, October 8, 1993.
"The Hindu Poet" (1913), *New York Times*, November 23, 1913.
"The Literary Scene in Scandinavia" (1940), *New York Times*, December 8, 1940.
"The Magazines" (1901), *New York Times*, December 28, 1901.
"The Nobel Awards" (1948), the *Times*, November 5, 1948.
"The Nobel Dinner" (1942), *New York Times*, December 11, 1942.
"The Nobel Literary Prize" (1911), *New York Times*, October 15, 1911.
"The Nobel Literature Prize" (1913), the *Times*, November 14, 1913.
"The Nobel Prize" (2022), www.nobelprize.org/prizes/lists/all-nobel-prizes-in-literature/.
"The Nobel Prize Awarded to Roosevelt" (1906), *New York Times*, December 11, 1906.
"The Nobel Prize for Anatole France" (1921), the *Times*, November 11, 1921.
"The Nobel Prize for literature" (1902), the *Times*, January 15, 1902.
"The Nobel Prize for Literature" (1930), the *Times*, November 6, 1930.
"The Nobel Prize for Literature" (1944), the *Times*, November 10, 1944.
"The Nobel Prizes" (1904), the *Times*, December 12, 1904.
"The Nobel Prizes" (1907), the *Times*, December 12, 1907.
"The Nobel Prizes" (1908), *New York Times*, December 11, 1908.
"The Nobel Prizes" (1913), *New York Times*, December 19, 1913.
"The Nobel Prizes" (1941), *New York Times*, December 14, 1941.

"The Nobel Prizes. Award to Mr. Rudyard Kipling" (1907), the *Times*, December 11, 1907.
"The Nobel Prize Winner" (1953), the *Times*, October 16, 1953.
"The Pen Is Mightier" (1953), *New York Times*, October 16, 1953.
Thody, Philip (1957), "Albert Camus," *Times Literary Supplement*, December 1957.
"Thomas Mann to Build House" (1929), *New York Times*, November 24, 1929.
"Thomas Mann Wins Nobel Prize for 1929" (1929), *New York Times*, November 13, 1929.
Tiozzo, Paulus (2023), *Der Nobelpreis und die deutschsprachige Literatur. Eine Studie über die Vergabekriterien des Literaturnobelpreis 1901–1971*, University of Gothenburg: Gothenburg 2023.
"To Get Nobel Prizes" (1905), *New York Times*, December 10, 1905.
Tokarczuk, Olga (2022), "The Tender Narrator," https://www.nobelprize.org/prizes/literature/2018/tokarczuk/lecture/, translated by Jennifer Croft and Antonia Lloyd-Jones, June 21, 2022.
Toksvig, Signe (1944), "The Story of a Nobel Prize Winner," *New York Times Book Review*, December 10, 1944.
"Topic of the Times" (1932), *New York Times*, November 11, 1933.
"Topic of the Times" (1936), *New York Times*, December 12, 1936.
"Topic of the Times. Nobel prizes awarded" (1903), *New York Times*, December 13, 1903.
"Topics of the Times" (1934a), *New York Times*, November 9, 1934.
"Topics of the Times" (1934b), *New York Times*, December 11, 1934.
"Topics of the Times" (1936), *New York Times*, December 11, 1936.
"Topics of the Times" (1939), *New York Times*, November 16, 1939.
"To Select Nobel Prize Winners" (1942), *New York Times*, October 7, 1942.
"Triumph and Tragedy" (1953), *New York Times*, October 23, 1953.
"Trois lauréats des Prix Nobel" (1946), *Le Figaro*, November 16, 1946.
"T.S. Eliot Receives 1948 Nobel Award" (1948), untitled article, *New York Times*, November 5, 1948.
"Two Raids on Helsinki" (1939), the *Times*, December 12, 1939.
"Une Allocution de M. Henry Bergson" (1928), *Le Figaro*, December 12, 1928.
"Un français d'Afrique du nord" (1957), *Le Figaro*, October 18, 1957.
untitled article (1888), *Le Figaro*, April 15, 1888.
untitled article (1906), the *Times*, December 13, 1906.
untitled articles (1907a), the *Times*, February 15 and 18, 1907.
untitled article (1907b), the *Times*, December 11, 1907.
untitled article (1907c), *New York Times*, December 11, 1907.
untitled articles (1908), the *Times*, December 10 (two articles) and 11, 1908.
untitled article (1910), the *Times*, December 12, 1910.
untitled article (1911), the *Times*, December 11, 1911.
untitled articles (1912a), *Le Figaro*, November 16, 1912.
untitled article (1912b), the *Times*, November 16, 1912.
untitled article (1913a), *Le Figaro*, November 14, 1913.
untitled article (1913b), the *Times*, December 11, 1913.
untitled article (1917a), the *Times*, November 9, 1917.
untitled article (1917b), *Le Figaro*, November 10, 1917.
untitled article (1921), the *Times*, November 12, 1921.
untitled article (1922), the *Times*, November 10, 1922.
untitled articles (1924a), the *Times*, November 14 and 15, 1924.

untitled article (1926), the *Times*, November 22, 1926.
untitled article (1930), the *Times*, December 11, 1930.
untitled article (1931), *Le Figaro*, October 10, 1931.
untitled articles (1932), the *Times*, December 2, 6 and 12, 1932.
untitled article (1936), the *Times*, December 11, 1936.
untitled article (1937), *Le Figaro*, November 12, 1937.
untitled article (1938), the *Times*, November 24, 1938.
untitled article (1939), *New York Times*, November 13, 1939.
untitled article (1945), the *Times*, December 15, 1945.
untitled article (1948), the *Times*, November 5, 1948.
untitled article (1953a), the *Times*, December 1, 1953.
untitled article (1953b), the *Times*, December 8, 1953.
"Van Dyke Explains Nobel Prize Attack" (1930), *New York Times*, December 1, 1930.
Vargas Llosa, Mario (2022), "In Praise of Reading and Fiction," https://www.nobelprize.org/prizes/literature/2010/vargas_llosa/lecture/, translated by Edith Grossman, June 21, 2022.
Vermeulen, Pieter (2023), "The Indie Nobel? Stockholm, New York, and Twenty-First-Century Literary Value," *Journal of World Literature*, forthcoming.
Vlach, Robert, and Boris Filipoff (1967), "The Slavic Awards and Some Candidates," *Books Abroad* 1, pp. 26-8.
Vowles, Richard B. (1967), "Twelve Northern Authors," *Books Abroad* 1, pp. 17-23.
V.S. (2016), "6 000 objets aux enchères," *Le Figaro*, October 14, 2016.
Walcott, Derek (2022), "The Antilles: Fragments of Epic Memory," https://www.nobelprize.org/prizes/literature/1992/walcott/lecture/, June 21, 2022.
Waldinger, Ernst (1951), "What's Wrong with the Nobel Prize?," *Books Abroad* 3, p. 218.
Walkowitz, Rebecca L. (2009), "Comparison Literature," *New Literary History*, 3, pp. 567-82.
Walkowitz, Rebecca L. (2013), "The Location of Literature: The Transnational Book and the Migrant Writer," in *Global Literary Theory: An Anthology*, ed. by Richard J. Lane, London and New York: Routledge.
Wallace, Irving (1949), "Those explosive Nobel prizes," *Collier's*, April 9.
Warburg, Karl (1901), "En svensk världsinstitution. Alfred Nobels stiftelse," *Ord och bild*.
Wenzel, Jennifer (2019), *The Disposition of Nature: Environmental Crisis and World Literature*, New York: Fordham University Press.
Westerström, Jenny (2013), *Den unge Anders Österling*, Stockholm: Atlantis.
"What French Readers Find in William Faulkner's Fiction" (1950), *New York Times*, December 17, 1950.
"What Nobel Intended by the Prizes Awarded in His Name" (1911), *New York Times*, December 3, 1911.
Wickens, G.M. (1967), "Persia," *Books Abroad* 1, pp. 43-4.
Wilhelm, Gertraude (1983), *Die Literatur-Nobelpreisträger: ein Panorama der Weltliteratur im 20. Jahrhundert*, Düsseldorf: Econ.
Willson, A. Leslie (1988), "Nobel Prize Symposium II: Choices and Omissions 1967-1987. The German Quandary," *World Literature Today* 2, pp. 239-41.
"Winner Rules Out Trip to Stockholm" (1954), *New York Times*, October 29, 1954.
Wirsén, Carl David af (1901), *Post- och Inrikes Tidningar*, May 31, 1901.

Wiskari, Werner (1962), "Steinbeck Wins Nobel Prize for His 'Realistic' Writing," *New York Times*, October 26, 1962.
"Wit and Wisdom in Pirandello" (1934), *New York Times*, November 25, 1934.
Woodbridge, Benjamin M. (1951), "What's Wrong with the Nobel Prize?," *Books Abroad* 3, pp. 218-19.
Woolf, S.J. (1930a), "Back on Main Street with Mr Lewis," *New York Time Magazine*, November 16, 1930.
Woolf, S.J. (1930b), "Mr Chesterton Walks on Main Street," *New York Times*, November 30, 1930.
Woolf, S.J. (1938), "Pearl Buck Finds That East and West Do Meet," *New York Times*, November 20, 1938.
Wormhoudt, Arthur (1967), "The New Arabic Literature," *Books Abroad* 1, p. 40.
WReC (2015), *Combined and Uneven Development: Towards a New Theory of World-Literature*, Liverpool: Liverpool University Press.
Wastberg, Per (2015), "Priset som är kulturell dynamit," *Svenska Dagbladet*, October 4.
Wastberg, Per (2020), *Utsikt från stol 12*, Svenska Akademien: Stockholm.
Xingjian, Gao (2022), "The Case for Literature," https://www.nobelprize.org/prizes/literature/2000/gao/lecture/, translated by Mabel Lee, June 21, 2022.
Yan, Mo (2012), "Excerpts from His Work," *New York Times*, October 12, 2012.
Yan, Mo (2022), "Storytellers," https://www.nobelprize.org/prizes/literature/2012/yan/lecture/, translated by Howard Goldblatt, June 21, 2022.
Ybarra, T.R. (1921), "Anatole France Has a Boswell," *New York Times*, December 25, 1921.
"Yeats Is 'Delighted' at Award to O'Neill" (1936), *New York Times*, November 15, 1936.
Yeats, William Butler (2022), "The Irish Dramatic Movement," https://www.nobelprize.org/prizes/literature/1923/yeats/lecture/, June 21, 2022.
Yildiz, Hülya (2022), "Politics of Location and the Making of a Nobel Prize Laureate," "Literature in the Nobel Era: Regimes of Value," German Literature Archive, Marbach, August 24-6, 2022.
Young, Robert J.C. (2011), "World Literature and Postcolonialism," in *The Routledge Companion to World Literature*, ed. by Theo D'haen, David Damrosch, and Djelal Kadir, London and New York: Routledge.
Ziolkowski, Theodore (1967), "German Literature and the Prize," *Books Abroad* 1, pp. 13-17.

Index

Abbott, Wilbur Cortez 91
Achebe, Chinua 67, 111
Adams, Mildred 41, 217
Adonis (Ali Ahmad Said Esber) 84
Ågerup, Karl 186, 207, 217
Agnon, Shmuel 2, 96, 97, 99, 165, 206, 215
Aharonian, Avetis 91
Ahnlund, Knut 177
Ajneya, Sachidananda Vatsyayan 110
Aleixandre, Vicente 18, 165, 167, 174, 183, 184, 187, 194, 216, 217
Alexievich, Svetlana 18, 117, 128, 143, 151, 170, 186, 187, 192, 194, 208, 216, 217
Alguazils, Les 31, 32, 217
Allen, Roger 110, 217
Allén, Sture 3, 75, 76, 154, 156, 159, 161, 162, 164, 183, 217, 218
Allende, Isabel 85
Alph, B. 218
Alter, Alexandra 234
Amanuddin, Syed 110, 218
Andersen, H.C. 196
Anderson, Alison 225
Anderson, Benedict 154, 218
Andrade, Drummond de 110
Andreiev (Andreyev), Leonid 5
Andric, Ivo 3, 18, 66, 95, 96, 109, 165, 215
Angioletti, G.B. 218
Appleton, Edward 42
Apter, Emily 100, 101, 196, 197, 218
Aragon, Luis 113
Arnault, Jean-Claude 203, 204, 212, 223
Arvelo, Clotilde de 92
Åsberg, Stefan 188, 196
Ashcroft, Bill 185
Aspenström, Werner 183, 202
Asturias, Miguel Ángel 3, 18, 52, 72, 96, 99, 116, 129, 165
Atkinson, J. Brooks 31, 218
Auden, W.H. 66, 116

Auerbach, Erich 16, 85, 137, 218
Aurobindo, Sri 93

Bagryana, Elisabeta 93
Baldensperger, Fernand 218
Balzac, Honoré de 195
Baranczak, Stanislaw 235
Barberet, Gene J. 106, 120, 124, 176, 180, 218
Barham, Richard Harris 195
Baudelaire, Charles 63
Baumgartner, Alexander 151
Beauvoir, Simone de 118
Beckett, Samuel 18, 52, 72, 73, 107, 109, 113, 117, 118, 119, 136, 142, 176, 177, 215, 218, 233
Beckman, Åsa 213, 218
Bécquer, Gustavo Adolfo 194
Beecroft, Alexander 16, 133, 218
Bell, Clive 218
Bellow, Saul 72, 76, 118, 164, 194, 216, 219
Benavente, Jacinto 30, 66, 79, 121, 145, 149, 159
Benerjee, H.M. 92
Benoit-Dusausoy, Annick 205
Bergman, Bo 71
Bergson, Henri 32, 38, 105, 106, 120, 150, 160, 167, 215, 217, 218, 219, 232, 236
Bergstrand, Mats 235
Bernstein, Richard 54, 219
Beslic, Isidor 6, 219
Beti, Mongo 111, 176
Bhabha, Homi K. 185
Bialik, Chajim Nachman 92
Bibesco, Marthe 93
Bildt, Carl 87
Billing, Gottfrid 178
Birch, Cyril 110, 219
Björkstén, Ingmar 178, 219

Bjørnson, Bjørnstjerne 17, 23, 65, 90, 96, 97, 111, 138, 150, 156, 157, 174, 215
Bjurström, C.J. 82
Blackett, P.M.S. 43
Blais, Marie-Claire 113
Blake, William 195
Blanco-Fombona, Rufino 91, 92
Blixen, Karen 97, 112, 121
Bloom, Harold 109, 219
Bly, Robert 183, 184, 219
Böll, Heinrich 126, 127, 128, 142, 165, 215
Bonavia, David 53, 140, 219
Bonnefoy, Yves 113
Booker Prize 5, 9, 16, 118, 137
Booth, William 151
Borges, Jorge Luis 53, 110, 112, 129, 130, 210
Bowne, Borden Parker 90
Brandes, Georg 10, 130, 133, 134, 151, 158, 175, 219
Brandt, Willy 142
Brecht, Bertolt 112
Breit, Harvey 49, 219
Brems, Elke 126, 219
Brink, André 111
Brlic-Mazuranic, Ivana 92
Broch, Hermann 112
Brodsky, Joseph 7, 73, 76, 94, 96, 132, 151, 174, 185, 187, 192, 216, 219
Brown, Deming B. 143, 144, 219
Brown, Glenora W. 143, 144, 219
Brown, John L. 82, 107, 113, 219
Brown, John Macmillan (Godfrey Sweven) 89, 90, 151
Bush, George W. 76
Buck, Pearl 37, 38, 40, 43, 56, 57, 71, 72, 75, 87, 92, 95, 99, 116, 121, 123, 131, 132, 141, 145, 151, 159, 160, 161, 195, 206, 215, 219, 225, 226, 228, 230, 231, 235, 238
Bunin, Ivan 39, 51, 66, 94, 95, 99, 111, 121, 138, 140, 159, 160, 215, 219, 228, 229
Bunyan, John 195, 223
Burniaux, Constant 125, 220
Bustos, Ciro 142

Calderón, Francisco García 92
Calderón, Ventura García 92
Caldwell, Erskine 144

Camus, Albert 45, 48, 50, 51, 66, 95, 96, 106, 129, 141, 144, 149, 151, 162, 163, 167, 180, 188, 191, 215, 217, 220, 225, 236
Canetti, Elias 73, 83, 107, 117, 136, 151, 216, 221
Carducci, Giosuè 18, 24, 25, 77, 87, 105, 121, 156, 157, 175, 178, 215, 222, 229, 232
Carl XVI Gustaf 15, 141
Carlberg, Ingrid 1, 6, 10, 220
Carossa, Hans 93
Carter, Albert Howard 106, 220
Carvalho, Flávio de 92
Casanova, Pascale 9, 12, 13, 15, 16, 17, 56, 57, 64, 71, 76, 85, 100, 124, 125, 130, 133, 136, 145, 147, 154, 193, 196, 197, 220
Casanova, Sofía 91
Castro, Fidel 184, 220
Cather, Willa 41, 210
Cavanagh, Clare 235
Cela, Camilo José 127, 128, 166, 192, 216, 220
Cervantes, Miguel de 195
Césaire, Aimé 113
Chan, Sewell 234
Chapman, William 89
Char, René 113
Charasson, Henriette 93
Chatelain, Nicolas 51, 220
Chaudhuri, Sanjib 92
Chekhov, Anton 5, 111
Cheuk, Michael Ka-chi 85, 220
Ch'ien, Evelyn Nien-Ming 195, 220
Churchill, Clementine 14, 47, 49, 225
Churchill, Winston 14, 45, 46, 47, 48, 49, 50, 53, 56, 88, 95, 117, 121, 145, 149, 151, 162, 163, 180, 201, 215, 218, 220, 225, 234
Claesson, Paul 222
Clark, J.P. 111
Claudel, Paul 180
Clifton, Talbot 92, 151
Clifton, Violet 92, 151
Coelho Neto, Henrique Maximiano 69, 70, 92
Coetzee, J.M. 104, 108, 111, 117, 118, 185, 216
Cohen, Margaret 123

Colette, Sidonie Gabrielle 93, 116
Comte, August 8
Condé, Maryse 203, 208
Congwen, Shen 109
Conrad, Joseph 5, 114, 115, 194, 228
Cooper, A. Duff 50
Coppola, Carlo 110, 220
Cortázar, Julio 110, 112
Costa, Afonso 70
Coubertin, Pierre de 59, 60
Cowley, Malcolm 189
Croce, Benedetto 151
Croft, Jennifer 118, 236
Czerwinski, E.J. 109, 137, 220

Dabrowska, Maria 93
Damrosch, David 16, 24, 64, 76, 101, 193, 197, 220, 227, 238
Danius, Sara 175, 203, 204, 206, 220
Darío, Rubén 116
Datta, Roby 90
Davids, Thomas William Rhys 90
Debray, Régis 142
Deledda, Grazia 31, 32, 87, 90, 91, 99, 116, 121, 123
Delerm, Philippe 55, 220
Déry, Tibor 141
Desai, Anita 110
Dib, Mohammed 113
Dickinson, Emily 76
Dilthey, Wilhelm 112
Diop, Birage 111
Domet, Asis 92
Dong-Ho 89
Douglas, R. Langton 88
Dreiser, Theodore 66, 114, 144
Dreyfus, Alfred 113, 180
Dunant, Henri 21
Durán, Manuel 103, 112, 116, 117, 122, 124, 131, 221
Duras, Marguerite 118
Dutourd, Jean 50, 221
Dylan, Bob 54, 55, 117, 118, 145, 149, 168, 175, 189, 194, 195, 206, 207, 216, 220, 221, 222, 227, 230, 234

Ebner-Eschenbach, Marie von 90
Echegaray, José 2, 23, 24, 25, 65, 82, 121, 124, 156, 157, 215

Edfeldt, Chatarina 12, 16, 82, 84, 104, 126, 203, 221
Edfelt, Johannes 83, 221
Einstein, Albert 30, 33, 229
Eisenhower, Dwight 47, 49
Ekelund, Bo 16, 221
Ekman, Kerstin 183, 202, 203
El-Hakim, Tawfik 93
Eliot, T.S. 43, 44, 56, 71, 83, 95, 103, 105, 106, 113, 114, 117, 123, 145, 149, 152, 160, 161, 162, 174, 192, 215, 218, 221, 228, 236
Elizabeth II 117
Ellis-Petersen, Hannah 205, 221
Elytis, Odysseus 164, 165, 167, 174, 190, 216, 221
Engdahl, Horace 3, 76, 133, 221
Engels, Friedrich 130, 227
English, James F. 3, 4, 6, 7, 57, 60, 67, 207, 221
Englund, Peter 186, 202
Erlander, Tage 180, 181, 221
Ernaux, Annie 118, 143, 149, 155, 169, 185, 186, 216, 226
Esfani, Mohammad-Ali Jamalzadeh 93
Espina, Concha 91
Espmark, Kjell 3, 4, 5, 40, 60, 62, 65, 66, 68, 69, 70, 71, 72, 73, 74, 75, 76, 77, 82, 83, 87, 95, 96, 97, 108, 109, 112, 113, 114, 115, 116, 121, 137, 144, 151, 154, 155, 156, 159, 161, 162, 164, 177, 178, 179, 180, 181, 182, 183, 184, 186, 187, 188, 202, 204, 207, 208, 210, 217, 218, 221
Étiemble, René 81, 137, 221
Eucken, Rudolf 26, 29, 87, 115, 119, 120, 123, 150, 157, 158, 189, 215, 221
Euripides 123

Faiz, Faiz Ahmed 110
Falk, Erik 221
Fast, Howard 143
Faulkner, William 43, 44, 51, 56, 71, 95, 105, 106, 108, 114, 160, 161, 162, 189, 204, 215, 222, 226, 237
Feuchtwanger, Lion 5, 112, 222
Figueroa, Pedro Pablo 90
Filipoff, Boris 121, 237
Fisher, Dorothy Canfield 93
Fleming, Alexander 41

Fleming, Donald 117, 222
Fletcher, Joseph 16
Flood, Alison 206, 221
Fo, Dario 18, 82, 149, 167, 168, 191, 216, 222
Fogazzaro, Antonio 150
Fogelqvist, Torsten 71
Fontaine, Guy 205
Forsberg, Emil 143, 222
Forssell, Lars 202
Forster, E.M. 88
Förster-Nietzsche, Elisabeth 90, 91
Foster, David William 110, 222
France, Anatole 27, 30, 105, 107, 120, 123, 124, 159, 160, 161, 166, 180, 215, 218, 223, 227, 229, 230, 235, 238
Franck, Louis 151
Franco, Francisco 183
Frank, Bruno 33, 222
Franko, Ivan 90
Frazer, James G. 151, 201
Fredrikson, Stig 182
Freely, Maureen 231
Frenz, Horst 188, 193, 221, 222
Freud, Sigmund 112, 151
Fries, A.E.B 29, 222
Frost, Robert 114
Frostenson, Katarina 203, 212
Frykman, Erik 76, 217, 218
Fuentes, Carlos 110
Fugard, Athol 111

Galdames, Luis 70
Galsworthy, John 38, 56, 75, 83, 87, 105, 121, 123, 160, 161, 206, 215, 222, 224
Gálvez, Manuel 69, 70, 92
Gambrell, Jamey 217
Gandhi, Mahatma 110
Gao Xingjian 56, 76, 83, 96, 132, 136, 143, 145, 151, 166, 186, 187, 192, 208, 216, 238
García Lorca, Federico 112
Garibaldi, Giuseppe 88
Garner, Dwight 55, 222
Gaulle, Charles de 50, 113
George, Stefan 112
Ghods-Nakhai, Hossein 93
Gide, André 42, 43, 51, 66, 95, 105, 106, 123, 129, 161, 162, 163, 176, 180,

188, 192, 208, 215, 218, 222, 227, 228, 230
Gierow, Karl Ragnar 67, 68, 72, 73, 74, 75, 77, 116, 137, 177, 181, 182, 210, 222
Gjellerup, Karl 2, 17, 29, 30, 65, 68, 90, 96, 138, 157, 158, 174, 178, 215
Glissant, Édouard 16, 43, 222
Glück, Louise 118, 149, 155, 173, 175, 195, 216, 222
Goethe, Johann Wolfgang von 10, 63, 64, 130, 133
Golding, William 72, 96, 118, 166, 177, 193, 202, 216, 222
Goodman, Grant K. 110, 223
Gorbachev, Mikhail 172, 185
Gordimer, Nadine 96, 99, 111, 117, 118, 123, 166, 167, 184, 185, 190, 197, 206, 216, 223
Gorky, Maxim 5, 111, 178
Gorman, Herbert S. 30, 223
Grass, Günter 117, 169, 182, 216, 223
Green, Julien 113
Greene, Ernst S. 88
Greene, Graham 3, 115, 116, 229
Greenhouse, Steven 143
Griffith, Gareth 185
Grimes, William 54, 223
Grossman, Edith 237
Gullberg, Hjalmar 82, 83, 208
Gün, Güneli 85, 223
Gunder, Anna 125, 223
Gunnarsson, Gunnar 90
Gurnah, Abdulrazak 108, 118, 136, 149, 155, 169, 191, 204, 208, 213, 216, 223
Gustaf V 35, 38, 41, 71, 223, 224
Gustaf VI Adolf 117
Gustav II Adolf 20
Gustav III 2, 7, 62, 211
Gustavsson, Matilda (Matilda Voss Gustavsson) 203, 213, 218, 223
Gyllensten, Lars 3, 4, 6, 19, 33, 34, 39, 40, 67, 73, 74, 75, 77, 81, 86, 94, 115, 116, 137, 140, 142, 143, 175, 180, 183, 202

Haass, Friedrich Joseph 150
Hackett, Francis 41, 223
Hallström, Per 22, 62, 63, 64, 65, 68, 69, 70, 71, 79, 80, 81, 95, 109, 115, 179, 180, 223

Hammaskjöld, Dag 10, 13, 63, 66, 72, 83, 172, 179, 180, 181
Hammarskjöld, Hjalmar 10, 69, 70, 72, 201, 235
Hamsun, Knut 17, 30, 57, 68, 87, 96, 138, 157, 178, 215
Handke, Peter 117, 120, 145, 168, 186, 202, 204, 216, 231
Hardy, Thomas 28, 30, 115, 175, 229
Harnack, Adolf von 151
Hauptmann, Gerhart 27, 55, 91, 105, 106, 108, 119, 157, 215, 222, 223, 230
Haworth, W.N. 36, 37
Hay, Gyula 141
Heaney, Seamus 18, 96, 117, 173, 174, 190, 216, 223
Hedberg, Andreas 221
Hedin, Sven 71, 72, 92, 201
Heidenstam, Verner von 17, 22, 29, 60, 62, 65, 68, 69, 96, 97, 121, 138, 156, 174, 178, 215
Heilbron, Johan 15, 16, 17, 76, 84, 126, 127, 128, 193
Helgesson, Stefan 16, 193, 223
Hélys, Marc 26, 152, 223
Hemingway, Ernest 41, 45, 46, 48, 49, 50, 51, 95, 106, 114, 117, 118, 119, 144, 145, 153, 162, 163, 210, 215, 221, 223, 228
Hemingway, Mary 49
Henley, Jon 203, 223
Hesse, Hermann 43, 70, 83, 93, 105, 161, 162, 179, 187, 215, 225
Heyse, Paul 26, 28, 119, 129, 121, 123, 145, 156, 157, 158, 174, 215, 225
Hitler, Adolf 141, 162, 179, 201, 209, 210
Hjärne, Harald 62, 73, 120, 178
Hofmannsthal, Hugo von 112, 175
Hofmeyr, Isabel 101, 195, 223
Hollinger, David 67, 100, 223
Holly, Buddy (Charles Hardin Holley) 194
Holst, Henriëtte Roland 92
Homer 123, 195
Houellebecq, Michel 118
Howarth, Herbert 110, 117, 124, 149, 180, 224
Howard, Philip 112, 184, 185, 224
Howes, Edith 91
Hristic, Jovan 109

Huch, Ricarda 91, 93
Hudey, Katrin 141, 224
Hugo, Victor 195
Huidobro, Vicente 91
Huizinga, Johan 151
Hussein, Taha 93
Hutchison, Percy 38, 224
Hwang, Tsu-Yü 81, 84, 86, 224

Ibekwe, Chinweizu 136
Ibsen, Henrik 5, 64, 111, 113, 138, 177
Inoue, Takashi 85, 220
Iqbal, Mohammed 110
Ishiguru, Kazuo 104, 117, 118, 119, 145, 167, 169, 194, 216, 224
Ivask, Ivar 5, 103, 106, 107, 109, 110, 121, 132, 224
Iwamoto, Yoshio 73, 110, 224

Jacobs, Andrew 54, 143, 186, 224
James, Henry 113, 114
Jedrzejewski, Jan 205
Jelinek, Elfriede 120, 169, 175, 177, 188, 216
Jensen, Johannes V. 17, 41, 42, 63, 79, 83, 97, 162, 215
Jiménez, Juan Ramón 48, 82, 108, 152, 162, 173, 174, 194, 215
Johnson, Eyvind 2, 17, 53, 97, 98, 117, 141, 145, 167, 182, 202, 215
Jonson, Ben 5
Jonsson, Stefan 69, 224
Joshi, Umashankar 110
Jotuni, Maria 92
Joyce, James 5, 109, 114, 116

Kadir, Djelal 227, 238
Kafka, Franz 109, 116, 133, 160
Kagawa, Toyohiko 93
Kakutani, Michiko 54, 224
Kalmthout, Ton Van 219
Kämpchen, Martin 106, 224
Karaganis, Joe 104, 224
Karlfeldt, Erik Axel 4, 17, 39, 96, 97, 98, 115, 121, 161, 174, 178, 215
Kawabata, Yasunari 56, 72, 73, 85, 94, 96, 100, 110, 126, 127, 128, 165, 194, 206, 215, 229
Kemény, Franz 12, 60, 224

Kertész, Imre 119, 151, 170, 186, 190, 208, 216, 224
Key, Ellen 22
Khalkhali, Basilj 93
Khan, Mohammad Hosein 92
Khomeini, Ruhollah (Ayatollah Khomeini) 183, 202
Khoury-Gatha, Vénus 54, 224
Khrushchew, Nikita 140
Kincaid, Jamaica 108
Kipling, Rudyard 25, 26, 29, 48, 55, 56, 62, 65, 77, 107, 114, 121, 131, 134, 152, 156, 157, 158, 178, 215, 220, 224, 229, 236
Koni, Anatoly 150
Krajewski, Markus 60, 86, 225
Kreuder, Ernst 225
Kullberg, Christina 16, 193, 225
Kummerle, Josef 225

Lacontre, Robert 53, 225
Lagerlöf, Selma 17, 22, 26, 28, 32, 77, 87, 90, 96, 97, 98, 105, 114, 115, 120, 123, 145, 152, 157, 158, 196, 215, 221, 233
Lagerkvist, Johan 225
Lagerkvist, Pär 17, 46, 54, 97, 149, 162, 174, 215, 235
Lamont, William F. 5, 44, 98, 104, 105, 111, 113, 114, 115, 119, 120, 121, 140, 149, 150, 151, 175, 225
Lane, Richard J. 237
Lanfranchi, Anna 123, 225
Lang, Renée 5, 105, 112, 116, 121, 175, 225
Laretta, Enrique 92
Larsson, Carl 22
Lawrence, D.H. 115
Laxness, Kiljan Halldór 17, 48, 51, 97, 119, 215
Laye, Camara 111
Lead Belly (Huddie William Ledbetter) 194
Leandoer, Kristian 77
Le Clec'h, Guy 54, 225
Le Clerc Phillips, R. 31, 225
Le Clézio, Jean-Marie Gustave 96, 113, 128, 136, 151, 167, 168, 195, 216, 225

Lee, Mabel 238
Lemarchand, Jacques 50, 225
Lemos Horta, Paolo 100, 232
Lenormand, Henri-René 5, 176, 225
Lerou, Émilie 90
Lessing, Doris 96, 117, 118, 123, 169, 182, 189, 195, 216, 226
Leudet, Maurice 27, 68, 226
Levertin, Oscar 60, 61, 64
Lewis, Sinclair 34, 35, 36, 37, 38, 40, 43, 51, 56, 65, 66, 75, 87, 95, 99, 114, 115, 125, 131, 132, 144, 159, 160, 161, 176, 193, 206, 215, 218, 220, 221, 222, 226, 228, 229, 233, 234, 235, 238
Leypoldt, Günther 161, 164, 226
Leyris, Raphaëlle 186, 226
Liljefors, Bruno 22
Liljegren, Eva 83
Lindfors, Bernth 84, 86, 87, 111, 136, 176, 226
Lindqvist, Yvonne 126, 221, 226
Lloyd-Jones, Antonia 236
London, Jack 144
Lovell, Julia 54, 85, 132, 227
Lukács, György 53, 140, 227
Lundegård, Axel 86, 227
Lundkvist, Artur 74, 75, 116, 202, 210, 227
Lyall, Sarah 54, 186, 212, 224, 227

Määttä, Jerry 227
Machado, Antonio 194
Macpherson, Robin Fulton 77
Macron, Emmanuel 143, 222
Maeterlinck, Maurice 26, 27, 87, 95, 157, 215, 218, 227, 229, 230
Mahfouz, Naguib 18, 53, 54, 72, 76, 96, 110, 127, 128, 166, 185, 194, 216, 225, 227
Maia, R.B. 126, 227
Majumdar, Bensadhar 92
Malm, Mats 213
Malmström, Carl Gustaf 10, 62
Malraux, André 113, 118
Maltz, Albert 144
Mani, B. Venkat 101, 195, 227
Mann, Heinrich 112

Mann, Thomas 33, 35, 36, 51, 63, 83, 87,
  91, 93, 105, 107, 108, 117, 119, 135,
  145, 159, 161, 176, 215, 222, 224, 227,
  232, 236
Marcus, Greil 55, 227
Marcuse, Ludwig 112, 120, 122, 227
Martin du Gard, Roger 36, 37, 38, 43, 51,
  56, 75, 87, 120, 121, 124, 129, 159, 180,
  204, 206, 215, 225, 226
Martinson, Harry 2, 17, 53, 97, 98, 126,
  127, 128, 139, 141, 153, 174, 182, 198,
  202, 215
Márquez, Gabriel García 96, 104, 112, 117,
  119, 129, 145, 184, 190, 194, 216, 224
Marx, Karl 10, 130, 227
Maulnier, Thierry 52, 227
Mauriac, François 45, 46, 50, 66, 95, 106,
  113, 117, 141, 162, 163, 180, 215, 219,
  220, 222, 225, 227, 231
Mayer, René 47, 49
McDonald, Mark 54, 227
Melegari, Dora 91
Melin, Alfred 97
Melville, Herman 76, 195
Mestre, Laura 92
Meysenbug, Malwida von 90
Michaux, Henri 113
Mikhalkov, Sergey 140
Milosevic, Slobodan 186, 202
Milosz, Czeslaw 73, 76, 106, 107, 108, 117,
  132, 142, 145, 164, 175, 184, 187, 196,
  216, 227
Mishima, Yukio 73, 94, 100, 110
Mistral, Frédéric 2, 23, 24, 27, 65, 82, 83,
  120, 121, 150, 153, 156, 157, 174, 215,
  227, 231
Mistral, Gabriela 41, 42, 51, 56, 69, 70, 79,
  82, 83, 92, 93, 95, 99, 109, 116, 129,
  132, 162, 165, 174, 210, 215, 225
Mitchell, Margaret 75, 77, 92
Mizener, Arthur 228
Moberg, Vilhelm 140
Mommsen, Theodor 23, 105, 119, 120,
  150, 156, 215, 231
Monod, Gabriel 90
Montale, Eugenio 63, 83, 121, 174, 189,
  215, 228

Moore, T. Sturge 68
Morand, Paul 38, 228
Moretti, Franco 76, 81, 195, 197, 228
Morgan, Charles 31, 228
Morrison, Toni 54, 76, 96, 104, 108, 118,
  123, 167, 185, 191, 206, 216, 223, 228,
  231, 235
Mossu, René 42, 228
Mo Yan 54, 96, 117, 143, 151, 186, 188,
  190, 199, 216, 227, 238
Mphahlele, Ezekiel 111
Muhidine, Timour 205
Muir, Edwin 44, 228
Müller, Herta 123, 128, 136, 149, 151, 168,
  174, 186, 190, 216, 228
Munro, Alice 117, 118, 123, 188, 196, 216,
  228
Musil, Robert 70
Mussolini, Benito 209

Naipaul, V.S. 96, 108, 117, 118, 136, 151,
  168, 169, 185, 186, 194, 208, 216, 228
Najder, Zdzislaw 114, 228
Nathan, George Jean 228
Nazaroff, Alexander 39, 228
Negri, Ada 91
Nehru, Jawaharlal 140
Neidig, William J. 90
Neruda, Pablo 53, 68, 72, 96, 109, 117,
  129, 165, 175, 190, 206, 215, 228
Neuberger, Richard L. 38, 228
Neuhoff, Éric 55, 228
Neumeyer, Alfred 105, 112, 229
Neustadt Prize 4, 5, 9, 117, 137
Ngugi wa Thiong'o 108, 111
Nietzsche, Friedrich 90
Nimetz, Michael 221
Nirala, Suryakant Tripathi 110
Nishiwaki, Junzaburo 93, 100
Nobel, Alfred 1, 2, 4, 6, 7, 10, 11, 12, 19,
  20, 41, 45, 59, 60, 61, 64, 78, 80, 97, 99,
  100, 130, 133, 137, 147, 148, 149, 153,
  155, 157, 167, 174, 175, 177, 179, 180,
  183, 187, 189, 190, 198, 200, 208, 209,
  211, 217, 220, 235, 237
Nobel, Ludvig 1
Nordström, Vitalis 120

Nouilles, Mathieu de 91
Nuc, Olivier 55, 230
Nuridsany, Michel 53, 230
Nyblom, Carl Rupert 82, 83
Nykvist, Karin 186, 230

Öberg, Johan 143, 226
Öberg Lindsten, Kajsa 143, 226
Ocantos, Carlos María 92
Oe, Kenzaburo 76, 117, 166, 196, 212, 216, 230
Ogliastro, Jacques M.-J. 50, 230
Ohlsson, Per T. 235
Olsson, Anders 3, 77, 78, 94, 230
O'Neill, Eugene 38, 39, 51, 63, 83, 87, 95, 99, 105, 106, 108, 118, 125, 132, 149, 159, 201, 215, 221, 222, 225, 228, 229, 238
Orsini, Francesca 108, 230
Ortega y Gasset, José 112, 194
Orzeszkowa, Eliza 90
Oscar II 20, 24, 62
Osipova, Natalia V. 55, 230
Österling, Anders 3, 63, 66, 67, 71, 72, 73, 79, 82, 83, 84, 95, 111, 112, 114, 115, 177, 178, 179, 181, 210, 230, 237
Ovize 20, 230
Oyono, Ferdinand 111

Palamás, Kostís 82
Palme, Olof 13, 140, 173, 179
Pamuk, Orhan 85, 110, 117, 168, 186, 192, 193, 204, 216, 223, 231
Pareles, Jon 55, 230
Passy, Frédéric 21, 22, 222
Pasternak, Boris 45, 48, 49, 50, 51, 53, 56, 66, 84, 111, 139, 140, 145, 162, 174, 180, 181, 184, 186, 187, 201, 215, 219, 220, 229, 231
Paton, Alan 111
Patrício, Maria Magdalena de Martel 92, 93
Paz, Octavio 110, 117, 169, 174, 194, 216, 231
Pearson, Nicholas 189
Penney, Mary 220
Perruchot, Henri 105, 106, 112, 115, 131, 132, 231

Perse, Saint-John 66, 83, 95, 107, 108, 163, 174, 215
Peterson Berger, Wilhelm 22
Peyre, Henri 6, 67, 112, 115, 120, 123, 131, 176, 231
Pidal, Ramón Menéndez 88, 93, 100
Pinochet, Augusto 172, 184, 190, 210
Pinter, Harold 117, 168, 169, 190, 216, 231
Pinti, S.R. 227
Pinto, M.P. 227
Pirandello, Luigi 38, 39, 51, 64, 105, 108, 149, 160, 215, 226, 227, 231, 232, 237
Poblete, Egidio 92
Poe, Edgar Allan 76
Ponge, Francis 113
Pontoppidan, Henrik 2, 17, 29, 30, 65, 68, 90, 96, 138, 156, 178, 215
Poore, Charles 44, 231
Pound, Ezra 114, 180, 200, 210
Prasteau, Jean 45, 50, 96, 231
Pratt, William 6, 72, 73, 132, 136, 149, 176, 177, 185, 231
Pritam, Amrita 110
Prix Formentor 5, 9, 17, 117
Prix Goncourt 4, 5, 9, 57, 106, 109, 113, 118
Proust, Marcel 5, 109, 113, 116, 118, 133, 160
Prudhomme, Sully 2, 21, 22, 23, 27, 29, 62, 65, 77, 89, 120, 125, 134, 150, 156, 158, 169, 173, 175, 200, 205, 215, 222
Pulitzer, Joseph 4
Pulitzer Prize 4, 5, 9, 35, 57, 106, 118, 161, 176
Putin, Vladimir 143

Quasimodo, Salvatore 18, 66, 83, 107, 108, 112, 121, 163, 169, 174, 191, 192, 215, 232
Quinn, Susan 21, 232

Radhakrishnan, Sarvepalli 70, 92
Raffel, Burton 110, 232
Ragusa, Olga 121, 232
Rahnema, Z. 93
Raine, Kathleen 232
Ramras-Rauch, Gila 232
Ramsaran, John 110, 111, 232

Ramuz, Charles-Ferdinand 41, 112
Ratcliffe, Michael 112, 232
Raymond, George Lansing 90
Reagan, Ronald 172
Recouly, Raymond 32, 232
Reinhardt, Max 38, 232
Reis, Roberto 232
Remarque, Erich Maria 195
Rendirome, Renzo 31, 232
Rendón, Víctor Manuel 92
Réthelyi, Orsolya 219
Reuter, Gabriele 33, 232
Rexine, John E. 232
Reymont, Wladyslaw 31, 87, 121, 160, 166, 215
Richardson, Henry Handel (Ethel Florence Lindesay Richardson) 92
Richter, Elise 92
Richter, Max 12, 60, 232
Rilke, Rainer Maria 109, 112
Río, Angel del 121, 232
Ríos, Blanca de los 91
Robakidse, Grigol 92
Robbins, Bruce 100, 232
Robinson, Robert 42
Roditi, Édouard 112, 113, 114, 132, 175, 232
Rolland, Romain 29, 87, 120, 121, 124, 138, 158, 178, 180, 215
Romains, Jules 41
Roosevelt, Franklin D. 141, 235
Rosa, Guimarães 110
Rosch, Jonna 179, 232
Rosendahl Thomsen, Mads 104, 218, 219, 220, 221, 223, 227, 232, 234
Rostropovich, Mstislav 53, 140, 232
Rousseaux, André 36, 232
Ruger, F. White 28, 232
Rule, Sheila 54, 232
Rushdie, Salman 74, 110, 183, 202
Russell, Bertrand 13, 43, 44, 51, 95, 105, 117, 141, 151, 162, 163, 191, 215, 222, 226, 232
Rydén, Per 2, 4, 10, 20, 22, 59, 60, 61, 62, 64, 65, 66, 67, 68, 70, 71, 72, 79, 80, 81, 82, 83, 84, 85, 95, 97, 98, 109, 111, 112, 113, 114, 115, 120, 121, 130, 134, 175, 176, 178, 179, 180, 181, 182, 200, 201, 211, 232, 233

Sabatier, Paul 150
Sachs, Nelly 2, 17, 52, 97, 99, 165, 174, 185, 215
Said, Edward 185
Salinger, Herman 116, 175, 176, 233
Salminen, Sally 92
Sandburg, Carl 114
Sanders, Ivan 224
San Martín, Juan Zorrilla de 91
Santana-Acuña, Álvaro 129, 233
Sappho 123
Saramago, José 194, 216, 233
Sartre, Jean-Paul 13, 52, 53, 66, 72, 95, 106, 107, 117, 119, 141, 151, 167, 169, 181, 189, 215, 224, 225, 233
Schnitzler, Arthur 112
Schoolfield, George C. 233
Schück, Henrik 11, 60, 61, 62, 64, 69, 78, 230, 233
Schwartz, Cecilia 126, 221, 233
Seawell, Molly Elliot 90
Seferis, Giorgos 82, 83, 108, 125, 165, 174, 193, 215, 232, 233
Seidlin, Oskar 96, 111, 175, 180, 233
Seifert, Jaroslav 93, 104, 106, 121, 143, 145, 166, 167, 173, 174, 184, 187, 194, 216, 229, 233, 234
Selander, Sten 181
Semenov, Nicolay 139
Senghor, Léopold Sédar 67, 111, 113
Serao, Matilde 91
Shakespeare, William 5, 64
Shaw, George Bernard 18, 31, 32, 34, 87, 95, 105, 107, 115, 149, 159, 160, 173, 215, 217, 218, 228, 233
Shelley, Percy Bysshe 1, 11, 156
Shih, Hu 92
Shih, Shu-mei 16, 195, 233
Shklovsky, Viktor 171
Shneur, Zalman 93
Sholokhov, Mikhail 111, 117, 140, 145, 165, 181, 184, 186, 188, 201, 215, 233
Siems, Larry 54, 233
Sillanpää, Frans Eemil 17, 39, 40, 91, 93,

96, 100, 121, 138, 139, 145, 153, 160, 178, 201, 215
Sienkiewicz, Henryk 25, 65, 77, 84, 87, 138, 150, 215, 233
Silberschlag, Eisig 233
Simmel, Georg 112
Simon, Claude 14, 53, 54, 82, 104, 107, 113, 117, 127, 128, 166, 189, 216, 220, 230, 233
Simon, Sacha 53, 234
Sinclair, Upton 88, 144
Singer, Isaac Bashevis 73, 76, 132, 145, 165, 169, 190, 204, 216, 234
Sisario, Ben 175, 234
Siwertz, Sigfrid 72
Sjoestedt, Erick 21, 234
Slavejkov, Penco 90
Slochower, Harry 135, 234
Smejkalová, Jirina 143, 234
Smith, Patti 55
Snow, C.P. 8, 234
Soames, Mary 47
Söderberg, Hjalmar 22
Sohlman, Ragnar 19, 20, 61
Solzhenitsyn, Alexandr 53, 56, 140, 141, 145, 187, 191, 193, 201, 210, 215, 217, 219, 229, 234, 225
Sophocles 123
Sorel, Albert 150
Sorel, Albert-Émile 21, 234
Soyinka, Wole 18, 67, 72, 73, 75, 96, 111, 117, 127, 128, 143, 190, 216, 234
Spencer, Herbert 151
Spiller, Robert E. 106, 121, 124, 189, 210, 234
Spitteler, Carl 30, 57, 87, 90, 95, 107, 112, 119, 120, 138, 157, 178, 215
Spitzer, Gretel 142, 234
Staël, Germaine de 10
Stanton, Anthony 231
Steffens, Lincoln 144
Steinbeck, John 41, 76, 144, 164, 167, 179, 210, 215, 234, 237
Steiner, George 105, 107, 109, 117, 120, 126, 234
Stendhal (Marie-Henri Beyle) 63, 64
Stenhammar, Wilhelm 22

Stevic, Aleksandar 100, 234
St. Francis of Assisi 150
Stravinsky, Igor 142
Strich, Fritz 144, 211, 234
Strindberg, August 5, 22, 60, 98, 111, 112, 138, 200, 203, 208
Stromberg, Kjell 52, 235
Suttner, Bertha von 1, 10, 20, 235
Svegfors, Mats 10, 69, 235
Svensén, Bo 3, 12, 60, 63, 65, 66, 69, 70, 71, 79, 82, 86, 90, 111, 114, 115, 135, 147, 148, 149, 150, 152, 158, 159, 161, 177, 178, 179, 200, 201, 208, 210, 235
Sweven, Godfrey (John Macmillan Brown) 89, 90, 151
Swift, Jonathan 195
Swinburne, Algernon Charles 65, 114, 115, 120
Szymborska, Wislawa 123, 149, 174, 185, 192, 216, 235

Tagore, Rabindranath 17, 27, 28, 29, 51, 55, 56, 64, 68, 69, 70, 71, 85, 90, 95, 99, 106, 108, 131, 132, 145, 146, 156, 157, 158, 165, 173, 174, 197, 215, 220, 224, 225, 226, 232
Talvio, Maila 92
Tam'si, Tschicaya U 111
Tanizaki, Jun'ichiro 93, 100, 110
Tardos, Tibor 141
Tatlow, Didi Kirsten 54, 235
Tchernichowsky, Saul 92
Tegnér, Esaias 85
Tenngart, Paul 101, 221, 235
Thody, Philip 48, 236
Thomson, George P. 36, 37
Tiffin, Helen 185
Tiozzo, Paulus 179, 236
Tokarczuk, Olga 118, 128, 169, 184, 191, 192, 204, 205, 216, 236
Toksvig, Signe 41, 236
Tolkien, J.R.R. 88, 94
Tolstoy, Leo 5, 22, 111, 138, 177, 200
Tournier, Michel 113
Tranströmer, Tomas 17, 97, 104, 117, 149, 153, 169, 174, 216
Trevelyan, George Macauley 88

Tsang, Philip 100, 234
Tuong, Ho Huu 93
Twain, Mark 196

Unamuno, Miguel de 194, 201
Under, Marie 93
Undset, Sigrid 17, 32, 38, 51, 91, 96, 99, 105, 160, 161, 166, 215, 228

Valéry, Paul 70, 71, 79, 95, 109, 161, 180, 201
Vargas Llosa, Mario 18, 117, 168, 169, 186, 190, 204, 216, 237
Vazov, Ivan 90
Vermeulen, Pieter 128, 213, 237
Vesaas, Tarjei 52
Vilallonga, José Luis de 140
Vlach, Robert 121, 237
Vogüé, E.M. de 25, 62, 220
Vowles, Richard 180, 238

Wägner, Elin 70
Walcott, Derek 18, 54, 96, 108, 174, 185, 194, 206, 216, 232, 237
Waldinger, Ernst 175, 180, 237
Walesa, Lech 142
Walkowitz, Rebecca L. 132, 195, 237
Wallace, Irving 113, 237
Wallenberg, Raoul 13
Wallerstein, Immanuel 15
Warburg, Karl 8, 86, 237
Wästberg, Per 67, 75, 77, 125, 164, 203, 204, 212, 213, 238
Watson, David 16, 193, 225
Wedekind, Frank 112
Wells, H.G. 115
Wenzel, Jennifer 101, 208, 237
Westerström, Jenny 2, 10, 59, 60, 63, 64, 65, 66, 67, 68, 70, 71, 72, 79, 80, 81, 82, 83, 84, 85, 95, 98, 111, 112

Wharton, Edith 91, 92
White, Patrick 53, 68, 72, 96, 118, 126, 127, 128, 153, 165, 206, 215, 232
Whitman, Walt 28
Wickens, G.M. 110, 237
Wilhelm, Gertraude 94, 237
Willson, A. Leslie 237
Wilson, Woodrow 30, 33
Wing, Betsy 16, 222
Wirsén, Carl David af 2, 4, 20, 22, 23, 60, 61, 62, 64, 65, 68, 78, 79, 80, 82, 84, 86, 87, 97, 111, 113, 114, 115, 120, 130, 134, 156, 157, 177, 178, 132, 237
Wiskari, Werner 237
Woodbridge, Benjamin M. 238
Woolf, S.J. 34, 37, 238
Woolf, Virginia 116, 160
Wordsworth, William 63
Wormhoudt, Arthur 110, 238

Xiaobo, Liu 143

Yang, Jeffrey 54, 233
Ybarra, T.R. 30, 238
Yeats, William Butler 18, 31, 38, 66, 79, 85, 87, 105, 108, 115, 160, 166, 174, 193, 215, 217, 228, 229, 238
Yildiz, Hülyn 85, 238
Young, Robert J.C. 188, 238
Yourcenar, Marguerite 113
Yutang, Lin 92

Zadeh, Abolghassem Etessam 93
Zahn, Theodor 150
Zelk, Zoltan 141
Zeromski, Stefan 121
Ziolkowski, Theodore 106, 112, 119, 120, 121, 180, 238
Zola, Émile 32, 113, 138
Zorn, Anders 22

www.ingramcontent.com/pod-product-compliance
Lightning Source LLC
Chambersburg PA
CBHW070031010526
44117CB00011B/1776